DISCOURSE,

CONSCIOUSNESS,

AND TIME

DISCOURSE,

CONSCIOUSNESS,

AND TIME

The Flow and Displacement
of Conscious Experience
in Speaking and Writing

WALLACE CHAFE

The University of Chicago Press

Chicago & London

The University of Chicago Press, Chicago 60637
The University of Chicago Press, Ltd., London
© 1994 by The University of Chicago
All rights reserved. Published 1994
Printed in the United States of America
03 02 01 00 99   3 4 5
ISBN: 0-226-10053-7   (cloth)
        0-226-10054-5   (paper)

Library of Congress Cataloging-in-Publication Data

Chafe, Wallace L.
    Discourse, consciousness, and time : the flow and displacement of
conscious experience in speaking and writing / Wallace Chafe.
        p.   cm.
    Includes bibliographical references and index.
    1. Discourse analysis—Psychological aspects.   2. Consciousness.
I. Title.
P302.8.C46   1994
401'.41—dc20   93-50610
                                                                              CIP

For Marianne

Contents

Preface

Quite a few years ago I wrote a book whose purpose was to show how semantic considerations might form the basis for understanding grammar (Chafe 1970). It was a book that represented a certain culmination of my interests at the time, and subsequently I began to pay more attention to discourse—language beyond isolated sentences—but also to psychology. It had become clear to me that we can never really understand language without understanding the human mind, and vice versa. At that time I was especially interested in exploring the relevance to language of mental imagery, memory, and consciousness, and for a while I planned a book that would pull those topics together. Somewhat later, and for somewhat independent reasons, I also became interested in relations between spoken language and written language. The present book eventually materialized as an attempt to combine certain parts of these several interests into a single work.

People in the diverse fields and subfields of academia are trained to value certain ways of doing things. Each group has its own standards for responsible research that limit both the kinds of data it looks at and the kinds of theorizing it accepts as valid. Researchers are very different from one another in these respects. Reading what others have had to say about language and the mind, I have come to appreciate the extent to which varied training and experience predispose investigators toward diverse methods and findings. There are many linguists, for example, who believe that a particularly good way to advance our knowledge is to construct sequences of English words, some of which appear to fit the language better than others, and then to attempt to explain these "data" by manipulating abstract constituent structures. That kind of research is foreign to my own experience, and I will have almost nothing to say about it here. Psychologists, quite differently, spend most of their time conducting experiments. While I can understand the allure of that approach, its contribution to this work will be much smaller than some will find appropriate. There are still others who like to build computer models, an activity that is understandably seductive, but for me it lacks the special joy that comes from being in love with a constantly expanding body of natural observations.

My own approach owes much to Franz Boas, Edward Sapir, Floyd

Lounsbury, and others whose understandings of language (and ultimately the mind) were influenced by their contacts with the indigenous languages of the Americas. This tradition has emphasized the recording and analysis of natural language data. As a student I was taught how one could begin with tape recordings, transcribe them with all possible care, and—in collaboration with people who spoke these languages, having recourse also to one's own experience and insights—try to make sense of them in terms of grammatical structures, meanings, discourse processes, and the nature of the mind. This book grew out of an analogous procedure applied largely to my own language, with one chapter providing a brief foray into a language the reader will find less familiar.

I confess to a certain distaste for doing "normal science" in the sense of Thomas Kuhn (1970) and to finding more pleasure in exploring new ground. Working with little-known languages offers new discoveries at every turn, and that is one of the great appeals of such work, but probing the mysteries of language and the mind provides equally exciting challenges. For me these two activities have been inseparable parts of a single larger enterprise.

Whatever their background may be, readers of this book will find that it is not in the mainstream of anything. I think that it is all to the good, having always had a bias against mainstreams. Readers who have a problem with this attitude should perhaps reexamine their own commitments to whatever doctrine it is they believe in, for surely our quest for understanding cannot, in the long run, be profitably forced within the boundaries of any single true religion. Anyone who thinks we are close to final answers, or that we know how to find them, must surely be mistaken. This work suggests some things I hope will turn out to be of value as we grope, in our very different ways and by no means in a straight line, toward an understanding that may, if we are lucky, improve.

Acknowledgments

I owe many debts of gratitude, some of them to people I have never met. Here I mention only those individuals and institutions that have more or less directly affected the creation of this book. Prominent among them are the members of the "Pear Stories" gang that was active in Berkeley during the second half of the 1970s (Chafe 1980): Robert Bernardo, Patricia Clancy, Pamela Downing, John Du Bois, and Deborah Tannen, an unusually productive group of collaborators. I think we learned a lot together. That project was sponsored by Grant MH-25592 from the National Institute of Mental Health. Subsequently I benefited from collaboration with Jane Danielewicz in work aimed at comparing spoken and written language (e.g., Chafe and Danielewicz 1987). That project, sponsored by Grant G-80-0125 from what was then called the National Institute of Education, had a great deal to do with the genesis of this book. Pamela Downing and Knud Lambrecht provided valuable additional help, and additional financial support was received from the Sloan Foundation grant to the Berkeley Cognitive Science program. The establishment of the Center for the Study of Writing in Berkeley at the end of 1985 (now the National Center for the Study of Writing), under the sponsorship of the Office of Educational Research and Improvement of the U.S. Department of Education, provided crucial support for continued work on topics covered here. I am especially grateful to Sarah Freedman for her willingness to make that support available, and also to Loretta Kane, Adelfa Hain, Marie Iding, Danae Paolino, and Suzanne Wash for their assistance.

Conversations with Kristina Hooper played an important role in getting this book started and showed me that it is possible to survive an education in psychology without losing the ability to listen to one's own mind. In arriving at the final draft I benefited considerably from detailed comments provided by Patricia Clancy, Paul Hernadi, and Sandra Thompson, and from helpful discussions with John Du Bois and Carol Genetti. Other useful comments of various kinds came from Herbert Clark, Dorrit Cohn, Suzanne Fleischman, Monika Fludernik, Talmy Givón, Randy Allen Harris, Andrej Kibrik, Hyo Sang Lee, Ellen Prince, two anonymous reviewers, and a number of students at Berkeley, Albany, and Santa Barbara, to all of whom I am deeply grateful. I doubt that any of these people will completely approve of the final result, just as experience has taught me that I myself will soon wish I had said some things differently.

Alberta Austin has been an indispensable and highly valued collaborator in recent work on the Seneca language. Chapter 12 could not have been written without her guidance. Our combined efforts were supported by Grant BNS-9021263 from the National Science Foundation. Christopher Chafe and William Schottstaedt of the Center for Computer Research in Music and Acoustics at Stanford University elegantly reproduced the music used for illustrations in chapter 14. Marianne Mithun has been throughout my most valued source of ideas and encouragement.

Symbols Used in Transcriptions of Speech

′   primary accent (a pitch deviation accompanied by loudness or lengthening)

ˋ   secondary accent (a pitch deviation without loudness or lengthening)

..   a brief pause or break in timing

...   a typical pause (up to one second)

... (.36)   a measured pause

=   lengthening of the preceding vowel or consonant

,   a terminal contour which is not sentence-final

.   a sentence-final falling pitch

?   a yes-no question terminal contour

@   laughter

boldface   loudness (shown only in chapter 5)

[ ]   a segment of speech that overlaps with another segment

~   preposed to a constructed rather than observed example, but one judged likely to occur in real language

~~   preposed to a constructed example judged unlikely to occur in real language

PART ONE

Preliminaries

I

Introduction

As we take, in fact, a general view of the wonderful stream of our consciousness, what strikes us first is this different pace of its parts. Like a bird's life, it seems to be made of an alternation of flights and perchings. The rhythm of language expresses this, where every thought is expressed in a sentence, and every sentence closed by a period.

(William James 1890, 1:243)

Man is apparently almost unique in being able to talk about things that are remote in space or time (or both) from where the talking goes on.

(Charles Hockett 1960, p. 90)

The two quotes above, though written at different times in different styles for different purposes, nevertheless combine well to set the stage for a work that brings together the notions of consciousness and language. James was intrigued with the observation that consciousness is in constant motion, a motion which, he suggested, is reflected in language. Hockett was concerned with the "design-features" that differentiate human language from the communication systems of other animals, and he noticed that humans, more than other animals, often communicate about things that are displaced from the immediate situation of language use. I doubt that he would object to my extending his observation to include the human ability to be *conscious* of things that are absent from the immediate environment, whether language is involved or not.

If language and consciousness come together in both these ways, both ways are also related to time. In the first case the time is that in which language is produced: the constant flights and perchings of consciousness and their reflection in the rhythm of ongoing language. In the second case the scale of time is larger, separating the immediate situation of language users from the displaced time and space of the experiences they talk about. But since those experiences are also in the talker's consciousness at the time of talking, Hockett's insight adds depth to James's. The flights and perchings, in other words, need not be limited to awarenesses of what is present at the moment, but often have their bases in distal experiences that are sometimes remembered, sometimes imagined.

3

The two quotes have in common the fact that their insights have not been followed up. Thus there is room for a book of this kind. The twentieth century has focused its attention on matters quite remote from relationships between language, consciousness, and time. Yet there has always, of course, been an interest in the nature of language, and lately there is a reawakening interest in consciousness. If I am right, there will sooner or later be a broader recognition of the fact that neither language nor consciousness can be adequately understood until we succeed in combining them within a more comprehensive picture in which the nature of each will shed crucial light on the nature of the other. This book is an initial sketch of what such a picture might look like, or, at the very least, it is an attempt to demonstrate why constructing such a picture would be a good thing to do.

As long as I can remember, I have been fascinated by the way ideas come and go in my own consciousness. I have marveled at my ability, apparently shared with others of my species, to have thoughts that have nothing to do with what is going on around me, by the ability of language to capture and communicate those thoughts, and by the different ways both speaking and writing allow my consciousness to participate to some degree in the consciousnesses of others. This book is an attempt by one curious human being to understand these and related matters a little better. But also, because I am a professional linguist, I have a special interest in understanding how both the flow and the displacement of conscious experience affect the shape of language, and conversely how language can help us better understand these basic aspects of our mental lives.

It is impossible to pursue these concerns very far without recognizing their dependence on the various ways language is used. Conversing, for example, is in quite obvious ways different from writing, but writing itself has many different varieties. Of major interest here will be the fact that both the flow of consciousness through time and the displacement of consciousness in time and space have different natures and interact with language in different ways, depending on whether one is talking with one's friends or, for example, writing a book. We need, therefore, to take varieties of language use into account. I will focus here on conversational language and a few varieties of writing. I regret that space limitations have forced me to neglect the varied genres of so-called oral literature, whose important contributions to the total picture will have to be treated elsewhere.

In its major outline, the book is organized as follows. In chapter 2 I set forth certain beliefs with regard to what it means to "understand" the workings of language and the mind. Such a chapter is necessary because the world is at present full of conflicting views of "science," many of which are not receptive to the approach I follow here. I try to justify that approach. Chapter 3 confronts the vexing question of what consciousness is and points to certain properties, both constant and variable, that consciousness has. I also speculate on how much of our mental life lies outside of consciousness. Chapter 4 reviews some of the relevant characteristics of speaking and writing, and justifies the treatment of conversational language as the basic use from which all others are deviations. These four chapters of part 1 constitute a lengthy but necessary prelude to what follows.

Part 2 then explores the flow of consciousness and language in conversation. It is based on three major sources of data. In 1980 and 1981 Jane Danielewicz and I recorded twenty dinner-table conversations for the purpose of comparing the kind of language used in them with three other kinds of language—informal lectures, personal letters, and academic writings—produced by the same individuals. Our aim was to investigate differences between the two kinds of speaking and the two kinds of writing (e.g., Chafe and Danielewicz 1987). These data were analyzed to some extent on the basis of findings derived from the earlier Pear Stories study, in which speakers of a number of different languages saw a film and told what happened in it (Chafe 1980). Although the language in that earlier study was not conversational, it provided a first entry into some of the ideas developed here.

The dinner table conversations had two drawbacks that limited the generality of conclusions drawn from them: they involved a relatively homogeneous sample of speakers (professors and graduate students), and the portions of them that were intensively analyzed consisted largely of personal narratives. Thus, a more recent effort was made to deal with a more socially diverse group of speakers and to include more diverse interactions. This recent sample consisted of excerpts from five conversations among adult interlocutors of varied occupational and regional backgrounds: farmers, a factory worker and car salesman, missionaries, housewives, and students. The portion of each conversation that was analyzed both qualitatively and quantitatively in depth was approximately two thousand words, making a total of about ten thousand words on which certain quantitative statements are based. This corpus is a small one, but it is large enough for some of the purposes of this work. It is supplemented by findings and examples from the dinner table corpus of more than twenty thousand words as well as from the Pear Stories. Certainly this study is only a beginning, and I hope and expect that the future will see it extended to more varied and extensive materials.

To return to the organization of part 2, chapter 5 begins by identifying three states that information can have within the mind—*active, semiactive,* and *inactive.* It then focuses on a basic unit of verbalization, the *intonation unit,* interpreted as the expression of information in active consciousness. It ends by exploring the relation between intonation units and *clauses.* Chapter 6 uses the three states of activation to explain activation *cost,* often spoken of in terms of *given* and *new* information, to which is added a third category that I will call *accessible* information. Chapter 7 deals with the functional basis of grammatical subjects, interpreted as the expression of *starting points,* and introduces the *light subject constraint,* a limitation on what can occur as a subject in terms of activation cost and importance. Chapter 8 discusses *identifiability,* the functional basis for what is often called *definiteness,* with attention given to the relation between identifiability, activation cost, and starting points. Chapter 9 explores the hypothesis that intonation units are limited to the expression of one new idea at a time, reflecting a fundamental temporal constraint on the mind's processing of information.

Chapter 10 deals with discourse *topics* in the sense of coherent chunks of semiactive information, and two examples of topic development are discussed in detail. Chapter 11 explores the manner in which topics form a hierarchy, with basic-level topics occupying an intermediate position between *supertopics* and *subtopics.* This discussion provides a functional basis for understanding the elusive ontology of the *sentence.* Chapter 12 turns to a very different kind of language, the American Indian language Seneca, in a provisional attempt to explore which of the matters discussed earlier are universal, which language-specific. Chapter 13 compares the ideas developed in part 2 with a few of the best-known alternative approaches to similar matters: the Czech notion of functional sentence perspective, Michael Halliday's functional grammar, Herbert Clark and Susan Haviland's given-new contract, Ellen Prince's taxonomy of given-new information and related hierarchies, and Talmy Givón's view of grammar as mental processing instructions. Chapter 14 concludes part 2 with a brief divertimento in which I suggest that music both of Mozart and of Seneca religious observances exhibits a pattern of information flow analogous to that described in the preceding chapters. It is intended as a brief taste of a line of research that might, if pursued further, contribute importantly to our understanding of music and the mind.

Part 3 turns from the *flow* to the *displacement* of consciousness, investigating ways in which both immediate and displaced consciousness are represented, first in conversational speaking, then in several genres of writing. Chapter 15 explores the nature of conversational consciousness in the immediate and displaced modes, identifying qualitative differences between them. It ends with some remarks on the so-called historical present. Chapter 16 looks at the manner in which distal speech and thought are represented in conversational language, as viewed within the framework of immediacy and displacement.

The succeeding chapters explore consequences of the observation that it is common in writing for a representing consciousness to lose all functions except the creation of language. Chapter 17 discusses a type of first-person fiction in which qualities of immediacy are transferred to a distal represented consciousness. Chapter 18 extends that discussion to the representation of distal speech and thought in the same style. Chapter 19 extends the discussion further to a type of third-person fiction in which the distal consciousness belongs to a distal self. Chapters 20 and 21 look, respectively, at fiction and nonfiction in which a represented consciousness is at least partially absent. Chapter 22, which is in one sense the culmination of the book and in another sense nothing more than a starting point for further study, suggests ways of integrating the notion of displacement with that of flow. Chapter 23 briefly explores the relations between written paragraphs and discourse topics. The epilogue, chapter 24, rounds off what has been said, but a slightly more detailed overview of the book's contents can be gained from the summaries provided at the ends of all the chapters.

What has already been written on the topics covered in this book is vast and varied. To review it adequately would require several books the size of this one. Since my purpose is to articulate what I hope is a relatively coherent understanding of these matters, I am not able to devote much space to discussing alternative understandings. Many people's work impinges on, overlaps with, agrees with, or contradicts what I set forth here, and I regret not being able to discuss more than a small sample of it. Chapter 13, though the longest chapter in the book, succeeds only in sketching a few comparisons with certain alternative treatments of the subject matter of part 2. An analogous comparison for part 3, however desirable it might be, is restricted to a few remarks at the end of chapter 20 concerning the work of Franz Stanzel and Gérard Genette.

I believe the twentieth century will eventually be seen as a time in which the human sciences decided it was a good idea to ignore human experience. It can hardly be questioned that the century's greatest progress has been in technology, and it would be worth studying the extent to which attempts to understand humanity have been shaped by technologies from the adding machine to the computer—from behaviorism to cognitive science. If this book has a higher purpose, it is to provide a bit of evidence that sooner or later we will have to restore conscious experience to the central role it enjoyed in the human sciences a hundred years ago. Much, I believe, depends on such a reorientation.

2

Understanding Language and the Mind

We would do well to explore new models, to approach the domain of method with a new set of attitudes, and to experiment with new and different operational styles. Our strategies must relate both to the intellectual styles of the individual scholar and to the institutional structure of the enterprise. . . . The great disservice that results from the generic methodology associated with modernism lies in its stamping some procedures as scientific and the others as unscientific, some as legitimate and others not. (The narrowly conceived quarantine against introspection, in effect for so many years, is a useful example of what I have in mind here.) It would do us all good to loosen up and look around, not only to our closer relatives in the biological sciences and in the social sciences, but to the humanities as well.

(William Bevan, 1991, p. 479)

The sciences that deal with language and the mind are currently in something of an epistemological crisis. It should be obvious that there are many important things about language that can never be understood by constructing sequences of words that begin with *John* and end with a period, and asking oneself whether or not they are sentences of English. It should be equally obvious that there are many important things about the mind that can never be understood by measuring the amount of time it takes undergraduate students to press buttons. And it should be especially obvious that we cannot program machines to be like the mind without first learning what the mind is like. The machines themselves are not going to tell us that. As we approach the twenty-first century, it is a good time to think deeply about ways in which we can enrich what we know of both language and the mind by moving beyond the methods that have limited research on these topics during the century that will soon lie behind us.

Each of us constitutes a tiny part of a vast, complex reality—far too vast and far too complex for any of us, either singly or in collaboration, to understand very much of. The fact that language and the mind are so vast and so complex is well attested by the observation that, despite prolonged and intensive investigation by large numbers of intelligent people, we still understand them so poorly. To a linguist like myself it is quite remarkable that so many have tried for so long to fathom the nature of *language* with no consensus on basic issues in sight. I do not mean to belittle the many important things that have been discovered, but we remain very far from seeing anything like the whole picture. When it comes to the *mind,* Ulric Neisser had good reason to state some years ago, "If X is an interesting or socially significant aspect of memory, then psychologists have hardly ever studied X" (Neisser 1978, p. 4). The same could have been said of most other facets of the mind. Neisser has now found the situation changed: "Nowadays, if X is an ecologically common or socially significant domain of memory, somebody is probably studying it intensively" (Neisser 1991, p. 34). I'm not so sure, but in any case there is much that still eludes us. We are all blind, each of us touching his or her small part of an elephant that is very large, very complex indeed.

The Nature of Understanding

The human mind is an endowment that allows the human organism to deal with its surroundings in ways that are more complex and effective than anything available to other living creatures. It combines at least three remarkable achievements that enable it to surpass the accomplishments of other nervous systems, in degree at least, and perhaps in kind. One of them is language, whose contribution to humanness has long been recognized. Another is memory—the ability to store and recall a wide range of earlier experiences, even if not with verisimilitude. The third is imagination, which allows us to exceed the limitations of particular sense impressions, interpreting them as manifestations of more encompassing schemas that allow us to recognize, have expectations about, and act on our surroundings in flexible and complex ways.

In the most general terms, this description of imagination also describes the essence of human understanding: the ability to interpret particular experiences as manifestations of larger encompassing systems. Language plays a crucial role by categorizing and codifying the understandings, and organizing them in useful ways. Memory is obviously an essential part of this picture. But there is at bottom only one way to understand something, whether it is some everyday experience or the nature of the universe. Understanding is the ability to relate a particular, spatiotemporally limited observation to a more encompassing and more stable imagined schema, within which the observation has a natural place.

On a clear night the sky is full of thousands of points of light, forming patterns that move slowly across the sky as the night progresses. Among them are a few that wander independently among the more stable patterns. People in many times and places have observed these points of light and their movements, and have understood them in a variety of ways in accordance with diverse imagined schemas. The patterns in the sky have been imagined as beings of some kind who travel from one horizon to the other. They have been imagined as influencing the lives of persons who are born when they are in certain positions. The wanderers among them have been imagined to be heavenly bodies orbiting in cycles and epicycles around the earth.

Schemas like these are folk beliefs. All human societies have imagined numerous ways of understanding particular observations in terms of more encompassing systems. These understandings are acquired by individuals in part through their participation in a culture, in part through a lifetime of trying to deal effectively with experiences, and doubtless in part through patterns that have become wired into the human nervous system. Folk understandings have been articulated in rituals, folklore, laws, religions, and political systems, but all leave room for an unlimited variety of competing understandings. Despite that fact, each understanding assumes with stubborn conviction its own validity and denies any validity to the competition, which it prefers to annihilate. How different human history would be if the imaginative origins of folk understandings were generally recognized.

To a limited extent the conflicts engendered by competing folk understandings have been mitigated by the development of science: a more self-conscious, more systematic approach to the interpretation of particular experiences in terms of imagined schemas. Despite the popular belief that there is a unique "scientific method," science is really nothing more than a collection of diverse ways of improving the quality of folk understandings. Different sciences make their improvements in very different ways. What physicists do, what biologists do, what psychologists do, and what linguists of this school and that school do are all quite different things. But the general thrust of such efforts is illustrated well with the familiar example of the solar system—the schema that imagines our earth as being itself one of the wandering bodies, participating with them in elliptical orbits around the sun. The success of this schema in allowing us to understand better the wandering points of light derives in part from the more careful and systematic observations associated with Tycho Brahe, in part from the ability of men such as Copernicus, Galileo, and Kepler to imagine a larger frame of reference within which those observations have a natural place.

Understanding, then, of whatever kind is the ability, through imagination, to relate limited, particular, concrete observations to larger, more encompassing, more stable schemas within which the particular experiences fit. The observations are often called *data,* the schemas *theories.*

In general, folk understandings tend to emphasize certain qualities in the theory and are less concerned with the quality of the data or with the theory-data match. Folk theories are valued when they are aesthetically pleasing and interesting and have a potential relevance to daily life, regardless of whether they are supported by any substantial or careful observations. Thus, astrology has an aesthetic appeal and encompasses much that is important to people's lives, but its adherents are less concerned with systematically checking what they imagine to be the case against what actually is the case. The reader can easily multiply examples of folk theories that are strong on aesthetic appeal, interest, and everyday relevance but weak on what we like to call empirical validation.

Ideally, scientific understandings ought to pay equal attention to the quality of the data and the quality of the theory. In practice, it often happens that some aspect of one of these components is emphasized, while the other is treated in a manner that constitutes no improvement over folk understanding. For example, twentieth-century psychology has placed an extraordinarily high value on data that are publicly observable and replicable, while it has not distinguished itself for the quality of its theories. Much of contemporary linguistics has focused on the construction of elaborate theories invented for the understanding of minuscule and questionable observations. The human sciences thus suffer from various pathologies that block more complete understandings of language and the mind. There is some point, therefore, in examining a little more closely the nature of both observing and theorizing as they have been and might be applied to this elusive subject matter.

Observing

The quality of observations can be evaluated in various ways, but I will focus here on two dimensions that are especially relevant to understanding language and the mind. Each involves an opposition between two poles, and each of the poles has its good points and its bad points. It would thus be shortsighted to assert that any one way of observing is good or "scientific" and the other bad or "unscientific"; each pole of each dimension can contribute essentially to the total enterprise. With respect to both of these dimensions, progress in the twentieth century has been retarded by a commitment to one of the poles and a rejection of the other.

One of the dimensions is the opposition between public and private data—the question of whether the observations are accessible to anyone who wants to make them, or whether they are restricted to a single lone observer. The other is the opposition between manipulated and natural data—the question of whether the observations are set up by the observer, or whether they capture more directly what occurs in nature. My major point is that public and private, manipulated and natural data all provide important insights, and all have their limitations.

Public versus Private Observations

It is widely believed that some data are publicly observable in the sense that, given the right circumstances, different investigators can observe what are for their purposes the same data and can agree on what they have observed. When it comes to understanding the mind, publicly observable data usually take the form of *behavior*—publicly observable things that people *do,* including overt manifestations of language. The aspects of language that are publicly observable include especially the production of sounds and written symbols. There are other, certainly important aspects of language and the mind that are privately observable, accessible to each individual but not in any direct way to others. Meanings, mental imagery, emotions, and consciousness are in this category. Observing one's own mental states and processes is often called *introspecting.* Sometimes this distinction between public and private observing is characterized with the words *objective* and *subjective*: behavioral observations are objective, introspections subjective. It is unfortunate that the word *subjective* has connotations of vagueness and imprecision, since those qualities are no more intrinsic to private than to public observations. The only real distinction here is the matter of public accessibility.

It may seem obvious beyond question that scientific understandings must be based on publicly observable, objective data. Since one of the goals of science is to create understandings that can be shared by everyone, public verifiability seems essential. Without it, the argument goes, understanding degenerates into solipsism, a morass of private understandings that may have some significance for each individual but are clearly of no use to science because there is no way of publicly verifying them.

What, then, is wrong with continuing to base the scientific understanding of language and the mind on overt behavior alone? The trouble is that, at best, behavior can provide only indirect and incomplete clues to mental phenomena, while at worst it may distort or provide no evidence at all for what we most need to understand. Behaviorist psychology coped with this problem in an understandable, though highly peculiar way: by simply asserting that psychology was the science of behavior and not of the mind at all. Psychology should not seek to understand the mind or human experience, but only what people do. With respect to any broader understanding, a psychologist might, like Howard Kendler (quoted in Baars 1986:113), admit that "when I have such urges [such as knowing how one's phenomenological experiences compare with others'], I read novelists to whom I resonate. . . . They provide me with an intuitive grasp of the feelings of others and insight into the human condition."

Of course there is nothing wrong with studying behavior for its own sake, but if psychology lived up to its name it would not so easily abandon its historical interest in more inclusive aspects of human experience. There ought to be some science that studies the mind, and why shouldn't it be psychology? Ironically, even if understanding behavior were agreed to be psychology's only goal, ultimately it would be necessary to understand the mind that lies behind the behavior, for it is only through a major effort at self-delusion that one can avoid recognizing that people's actions are determined by what they think and feel.

The behaviorist bias has had a strong and lasting effect on linguistics too. Leonard Bloomfield's extraordinarily influential book *Language* (1933) was among other things a strong commitment to publicly observable data, to sounds and written symbols (though Bloomfield found the latter of secondary importance). The result was a reduction of language to the distribution of elements of linguistic form and a deliberate avoidance of what those elements meant or how they functioned. The much touted Chomsky "revolution" was hardly an advance beyond this tradition, its manifesto declaring "a language to be a set (finite or infinite) of sentences, each finite in length and constructed out of a finite set of elements. All natural languages in their spoken or written form are languages in this sense, since each natural language has a finite number of phonemes (or letters in its alphabet) and each sentence is representable as a finite sequence of these phonemes (or letters), though there are infinitely many sentences" (Chomsky 1957, p. 13). This tradition has continued to understand language as if it were observable only through its form, though in recent times it has also come to rely on an observational methodology far removed from anything acceptable to behaviorism.

It is interesting to note that the recently emergent cognitive psychology, billed as an alternative to behaviorism, has retained its predecessor's commitment to public verifiability at the same time that it has returned to an acknowledged interest in the mind. The result has consisted in part of efforts to understand the mind by observing how long it takes students to press buttons, a rewarding but obviously limited tie to the complexities of the mental universe. The other major thrust of cognitive science has been computer modeling, where there has been a tendency to treat observations of any kind in an offhand way, along with a conviction that what is good for computers must be good for the mind.

If observing overt behavior too severely limits our understanding of language and the mind, is there any chance that scientific understanding can be broadened to take systematic account of private observations? Is there any way to deal with the threat of solipsism, the conclusion that nothing beyond the individual self is knowable? A hundred years ago, introspection provided the chief basis for theories of the mind. As William James expressed it:

> *Introspective Observation is what we have to rely on first and fore-most and always.* The word introspection need hardly be defined—it means, of course, the looking into our own minds and reporting what we there discover. . . . since the rest of this volume will be little more than a collection of illustrations of the difficulty of discovering by direct introspection exactly what our feelings and their relations are, we need not anticipate our own future details, but just state our general conclusion that *introspection is difficult and fallible; and that the difficulty is simply that of all observation of whatever kind.* Something is before us; we do our best to tell what it is, but in spite of our good will we may go astray, and give a description more applicable to some other sort of thing. The only safeguard is in the final *consensus* of our farther knowledge about the thing in question, later views correcting earlier ones, until at last the harmony of a consistent system is reached. Such a system, gradually worked out, is the best guarantee the psychologist can give for the soundness of any particular psychologic observation which he may report. Such a system we ourselves must strive, as far as may be, to attain. (James 1890, 1:185, 191–92)

Once this insight was abandoned in the mainstream of psychology a few decades later, attention stopped being given to the possibility that introspections can be treated as data too. It was an unfortunate development, because it left much about the mind that could never be scientifically understood. The twentieth century gave behaviorism its chance, and only a limited understanding of the mind came out of it. A more balanced approach would recognize, not just the difficulty, but also the validity of private observations, joining the ghost of William James in seeing what can be done about incorporating them into systematic research.

There is an interesting irony in the fact that a great deal of modern linguistics is built on introspective data. Only in the subfield of phonetics and those areas of psycholinguistics dominated by the psychological tradition has an exclusive commitment to public data been maintained. Most of linguistics differs radically from psychology in this respect. To take a simple example, linguists are happy to talk about a past-tense morpheme, a plural morpheme, or the like. But pastness and plurality are based squarely on introspective evidence. Although Zellig Harris, for one, hoped that the necessity for introspection could be overcome by examining nothing more than the distributions of publicly observable sounds or letters in large corpora, no one has ever really done linguistics in that way (Harris

1951). Without an awareness of what one "has in mind" when one uses a past tense or plural form, semantics, for example, could hardly be practiced at all, and without semantics, linguistics would surely have diminished interest and significance. One goal of this book is to show how the study of discourse is equally dependent on introspective insights.

There are some things I will suggest in this book that will seem vulnerable to the charge of "circularity" if access to introspective data is denied. The charge will seem more serious to the extent that the introspection in question is more difficult. For example, I will suggest that weakly accented pronouns express *givenness,* a property of ideas that are judged by the speaker to be already active in the consciousness of the addressee. We cannot publicly observe the consciousness of either the speaker or the addressee, or publicly know what judgments the speaker is making. This characterization of givenness is based on introspection of a kind I believe is possible for all of us who are users of language. It may be that recognizing givenness is more complex and subtle than recognizing past tense or plurality, but the principle is the same.

The proper conclusion regarding public and private observation may be the following. Data that are *only* privately observable do not, by themselves, advance scientific understanding. That is not because they are worthless or invalid, but because they need to be substantiated through consensus as well as through some pairing with data that are publicly observable. When it comes to studying the mind, language provides the richest possible fund of publicly observable data of a relevant kind. Language can thus help to rescue us from the solipsism that results from pure introspection. Though difficult, introspection is an absolutely essential part of this picture. When careful and consensual introspective observations can be paired with public observations—and especially with overt evidence from language—the resulting combination may be the most powerful one we have for advancing understanding of the mind.

Manipulated versus Natural Observations

It is possible either to observe reality in its raw form, interfering with it as little as possible, or to manipulate it in such a way that the observations will test directly the match between a theory and the manipulated data. John Ohala has written of "a contrived observation":

> The contrivance may amount to being in the right place at the right time to make a crucial observation. An example is Eddington's test of Einstein's claim about the bending of the path of light near large masses; he traveled to the Gulf of Guinea when a solar eclipse would occur to see if a given star that should have been hidden behind the sun could actually be seen as its light curved around the sun.

More often the experimenter himself contrives the circumstances giving rise to the events that will be observed. An example is Pasteur's famous test of his anthrax vaccine by administering it to one group of sheep exposed to the disease and withholding it from another similar group. (Ohala 1987, pp. 1–2)

There is an important difference between those cases where the observer manipulates himself, as Eddington did, to be able to observe something that occurs naturally, and those cases where the observer manipulates reality, as Pasteur did. It is difficult to control the sun and stars or produce eclipses on demand, and thus Eddington was forced to move himself in order to take advantage of the opportunities reality offered him. Pasteur, on the other hand, modified reality by administering the vaccine and by deliberately separating the two groups of sheep. When I speak here of manipulated data I will be referring to observations of the Pasteur type.

The dominant twentieth-century view has been that manipulated observations are more useful than natural ones. The good thing about manipulating reality is that one can target one's observations on a particular question that has been isolated from the vastness of reality. One can deliberately construct the situation within which the observations take place, bypassing the need to wait for the relevant phenomena to occur in nature, if indeed they ever would occur. The value of controlling one's observations in this way has been an article of faith in both psychology and linguistics, as strongly held as psychology's commitment to public observability. But there is clearly a down side. There are important aspects of language and the mind that have more in common with the sun, stars, and eclipses—things that can only be understood by observing their occurrence in nature. No other way of observing them is possible. The importance of observing in this way is recognized in the traditional practice of ethnography as well as in more recent ethnographic approaches to language acquisition and sociolinguistics, and in the "ecological" approach to psychology. Mainstream psychology might have taken a different route if it had heeded Frederic Bartlett when he pointed out the limitations of the work of Hermann Ebbinghaus (see more recently Klatzky 1991): "The psychologist, whether he uses experimental methods or not, is dealing, not simply with reactions, but with human beings. Consequently the experimenter must consider the everyday behaviour of the ordinary individual, as well as render an account of the responses of his subjects within a laboratory" (Bartlett 1932, p. 12; see also Baddeley 1976, pp. 3–15).

The unnaturalness of the data on which so much of psychology and linguistics relies can be highly disturbing to anyone who is sensitive to what language is really like. To find examples one need only attend any psychology, linguistics, or computer science conference or open any journal from these fields. Opening a psycholinguistic journal at random, for example, I found the following used as an experimental stimulus:

(1) The royal guests danced in the palace to the music of an orchestra.

Opening a linguistics book I found an argument that was based on examples like

(2) He is the man to whom I wonder who knew which book to give.

"Data" like these follow an ancient tradition in which conclusions about language and the mind have been drawn from simpler, though still unnatural examples like

(3) The cat is on the mat.
(4) The farmer kills the duckling.
(5) The happy boy eats ice cream.

One purpose of this book is to explore understandings of language and the mind that explain why language like that in (1) through (5) does not occur in nature or, if it does occur, is restricted to very special circumstances. I will try to show how the very rarity or nonoccurrence of such language is itself an important observation, and how it is possible to learn crucial things about language and the mind by discovering the constraints that hinder its creation. It is a very peculiar thing that so much of contemporary linguistic research has been based on unnatural language. It is as if one tried to study birds by building airplanes that were rather like birds in certain ways, and then studied the airplanes, just because they were easier to control than the birds themselves. I suspect that ornithologists have come to understand birds more successfully by examining them as they really are. There is much to be gained from examining language as it really is too.

My point is not that manipulated or constructed data are worthless. I would not want to discard all the conclusions I have drawn from such data myself, and I continue to make modest use of constructed examples in this book. Certainly there are times when it is necessary to appeal to language that fails to emerge naturally. But the constructions are only useful to the extent that they mirror reality, and one can only judge their usefulness through immersion in reality itself.

Methodologies
The distinctions I have just made suggest a breakdown of observational possibilities into the four categories charted in figure 2.1, where I have included examples of methodologies appropriate to each category. The point I wish to emphasize is that there are both good things and bad things

	Public	Private
Manipulated	experimentation, elicitation	semantic judgments, judgments regarding constructed language
Natural	ethnography, corpus-based research	daydreaming, literature

Figure 2.1 Properties of Observations with Examples

about each of the four cells in this diagram. Each makes a contribution, but none has an exclusive claim on scientific validity. Psychology, in restricting itself to experiments, has stuck to the cell in the upper left—the intersection of publicly observable with manipulated data. The methods that have dominated linguistics have been those of the entire upper row, that is, linguists have focused on manipulated rather than naturally occurring data but, depending on the subfield, have been receptive to both public and private observations.

In the upper left cell I have included not only experimentation but also elicitation: a linguistic technique for investigating a language other than one's own in which the investigator produces, say, a constructed English sentence designed to shed light on some point of interest, and asks a speaker of the other language to translate it. The result is publicly observable in the sense that the consultant's reaction can be recorded and studied like any overt behavior. But people do not ordinarily use language to translate decontextualized sentences that were invented in a different language, and there is often little reason to think that the result is anything a speaker of the target language would ordinarily say. A variant on this procedure, also commonly employed, is for the investigator to make up a sentence in the target language, asking the consultant for acceptance or nonacceptance. Having asked the question "Could I say so and so?" many of us have encountered the response, "Sure, you could say that," and then, after a pause, "but *I* never would." In spite of these problems, elicitation, used with care, can be a useful way of investigating hypothetical patterns one thinks one may have uncovered through more natural means.

In the upper right cell of figure 2.1 I have listed "semantic judgments" and "judgments regarding constructed language" as typical ways of exploiting the intersection of manipulated with introspective data. I have already mentioned semantic data. Here we must also recognize the special use of introspection that has become the preferred method of working with one's own language. Investigators imagine a piece of language, nearly always an isolated phrase or sentence, which they then judge for its grammaticality. To achieve some degree of verifiability, they frequently ask acquaintances or students whether they "get" or fail to "get" the sentence in question. The answer evidently depends in part on the respondents' abilities to imagine a context for the decontextualized language, in part on their desire to support or contradict the hypothesis for which the evidence is crucial. With this cynical characterization I do not mean to suggest that constructing language and evaluating it is a worthless activity. Used with caution, it is a method that can provide insights unobtainable in other ways. I emphasize again, however, the need for a sensitivity, not just to the grammaticality of what the investigator has constructed, but also to its naturalness.

Continuing in a clockwise direction through figure 2.1, we come in the lower right-hand corner to the introspective observation of naturally occurring data. This type of observation is certainly the most difficult to accomplish in practice. It includes whatever passes through our tacit conscious experience in a natural way. Here belongs what is often called daydreaming (e.g., Singer 1975), which evidently consists in part of inner speech, in part of other kinds of experience. Data of this kind suffer in obvious ways from both unverifiability and accidentalness. They are at the same time the most interesting and relevant data of all, if only we could find satisfactory ways of observing them. One is tempted to leave this area to novelists and poets, but I wonder whether humanistic studies could and should not sooner or later be brought to dovetail more closely with "scientific" studies of language and the mind.

The last area in our clockwise journey offers possibilities that are much exploited in this work. The observation of naturally occurring overt behavior includes activities that have been termed ethnography. The ethnographic tradition has had considerable influence on some areas of linguistics, and it is out of that tradition that this book has arisen. I will be combining observations of natural language with introspective data concerning the meanings and functions of phenomena observable in compilations of naturally occurring corpora. It emerges from this discussion that linguistic corpora have the following advantages and disadvantages (Chafe 1992b). Since they record overt behavior, they are available to anyone who wants to examine them, and thus they offer the benefits of verifiability. Although behavioral data in general suffer from indirectness of access to mental processes, language is not as problematic in this regard as button pressing, since it provides an incomparably more complex and subtle window to the mind. While it does not tell us everything, it tells us more than any other single kind of behavior. Furthermore, both spoken and written corpora have the decided advantage of providing data that are natural and not manipulated. The problem with them is their accidental nature, the fact that they fail to allow the targeting of particular theory-relevant phenomena. That drawback is to some extent mitigated by the fact that the occurrence or non-occurrence of some phenomenon is in itself an interesting fact for which a theory must account. The collection and analysis of corpora, and above all of *conversational* corpora, are absolutely essential to a fuller understanding of language and the mind. Certainly corpus-based observations must be supplemented with introspections, constructed sentences, and experiments, which can carry us beyond the accidental limits of a corpus and give us further insights and further verifiability. But introspections, constructions, and experiments without corpora are fatally limiting.

In this book I distinguish between linguistic examples that were actually observed and those that were constructed. Observed language, which constitutes the majority of the examples cited, is not marked, whereas constructed examples are marked with a single tilda at the beginning of the example if it is judged one that might occur in ordinary speech, or with a double tilda if it is judged something that would not occur. These judgments are necessarily subjective, but they are based on a fair amount of experience in observing real language. The following examples illustrate these conventions:

(6) I tàlked to Lárry last nìght,
(7) ˜I tàlked to a láwyer last nìght,
(8) ˜˜He is the man to whom I wonder who knew which book to give.

I believe it would not be detrimental to the progress of linguistics if this practice caught on.

Research has come to be "professionalized" in such a way that the kinds of observing summarized in figure 2.1 are usually practiced in isolation. People enter the various disciplines through a period of graduate training that consists of indoctrination in one or another of these possibilities to the vehement exclusion of the others. The graduate experience tends to be a brainwashing experience, where people learn to turn off their minds in order to pursue one or another paradigm. Psychology students learn to do experiments while shunning both introspections and anything that occurs naturally. (I exclude here "ecological" psychology; e.g., Neisser 1982 and Cohen 1989. For the orthodox reaction to this development, see Banaji and Crowder 1989.) The result has been a preoccupation with unnatural data and a disregard for even the most obvious properties of conscious experience. Linguistics students are trained to construct and judge isolated sentences and avoid language as it really is. (I exclude here much that takes place within sociolinguistics, anthropological linguistics, and some child-language research.) The result has been a blindness to all the crucial things that can be learned from real language. If their separate myopias were recognized and corrected, both psychology and linguistics would be better poised to advance toward more significant understandings of their respective and joint concerns.

Theorizing

Beyond careful observing, understanding depends on the ability to imagine systems within which the observations find a natural place—to create theories. Theories can be evaluated in a variety of ways—in terms of their coherence, consistency, and precision, for example—but of course they should above all provide a place for what has been observed. I would emphasize the value of providing a place, not just for a few questionable theory-selected items, but for a maximally comprehensive range of observations. The more a theory encompasses, the more it increases understanding.

Theories have lately gotten out of hand, above all because academic status has become tied to prowess in inventing them, or at least in manipulating theories invented by others. In a way, that is how it should be, since the ability to place observations within imagined larger systems is the only path we have to understanding. But the current situation is problematic in at least two respects. One problem is that theories quickly become more associated with egos and political agendas than with their contributions to the growth of understanding. Linguistics, for example, has become a competition between X's This Grammar and Y's That Grammar, instead of a common search for understanding. Theories of language are swimming in an alphabet soup whose ultimate contribution to the understanding of language is murky. The other problem—a more serious one because it is intrinsic to the enterprise itself—is that every theory tends by its very nature to exclude observations rather than to embrace ever more of them. This problem is particularly acute with so-called formalisms, notational devices designed to account for only those aspects of reality that fall within their purview, ignoring the remaining richness which also cries out for understanding.

This book assumes that to understand language and the mind more fully it is essential to recognize that all aspects of language and all aspects of the mind belong to a complex, integrated system embracing everything that makes us human. My special focus is on consciousness, but nothing I discuss will exclude memory, imagery, emotions, social interaction, or anything else that contributes to the totality of human experience. I will try to give at least some space to whatever factors appear relevant, as they are relevant, and I hope that by focusing on consciousness I will not seem to have isolated it from the rest. Quite the contrary, I am convinced that neither language nor consciousness can be understood except within the framework of human experience as an integrated whole.

The Interplay between Observing and Theorizing

Observing and theorizing are complementary endeavors, and neither can be practiced in isolation from the other. Because reality is so vast and complex, the ways in which we observe it must be limited by our notions of which aspects of it are worth observing. Conversely, our larger imaginings are dependent on what we observe, at least to the extent that they will have any lasting validity. These seemingly obvious truths mean that it is impossible to begin by making wholly unbiased observations, only later carrying them home to our armchairs where we invent theories to explain them, any more than we can successfully do the reverse, first spinning theories in a vacuum and only later making whatever observations we think will sustain or demolish them. Even if one or the other of these activities may dominate our field of vision at any one time, useful understanding is dependent on a repeated shuttling back and forth between them.

In chapters 7 and 9 of this work I develop two understandings that illustrate this shuttling back and forth especially well. I call them the light subject hypothesis and the one new idea hypothesis. In both cases the hypotheses as first conceived on the basis of "quick and dirty" observations were easily seen to be untenable as soon as further data were examined. In both cases, however, when the counterexamples were examined carefully, they revealed consistent properties that might not have been noticed if they had not been illuminated by the initial hypotheses. These properties then led to restatements of the hypotheses, followed by further observations. These reciprocal activities eventually led to more satisfying theory-data matches. The results as reported here may very well be premature, but only further shuttlings back and forth will improve them, or replace them ultimately with something better.

Toward an Improved Science of Language and the Mind

In the first issue of *Psychological Science,* the journal of the newly formed American Psychological Society, George Miller wrote:

> If I were a young man, trained in cognitive psychology and interested in language, what would I prepare myself to work on? My response to this question is clear and immediate: I would try to

learn everything I could about biology and about computers. A psychologist who masters either one of these fields will be uniquely prepared for the future; a psychologist who mastered them both, in addition to psychology, would be a scientific superman. (Miller 1990, p. 13)

My view of the situation is very different. I am convinced that the young man who followed Miller's advice would be capable of understanding language and the mind in only limited ways.

We can ask three kinds of questions. The first kind focuses on _what_ happens in the mind, the second on _why_ it happens, and the third on _how_ it happens. Like most in cognitive science, Miller sees the _how_ question as the most important. On the one hand, we would like to understand such things as how the nervous system functions to produce memory: "Neuroscientists are making extraordinary progress in unravelling the processes that go on inside neurons and at synapses between neurons; understanding the biochemical basis for memory—for some kinds of memory, at least—seems only a few years away" (Miller 1990, p. 13). Alternatively, or concomitantly, we can test our theories of how these things happen through computer modeling: "I believe that the best opportunity for constructing and testing theories adequate to the intricacy of the brain and the complexity of human mental life is through the construction of computer simulations" (p. 14).

Without denying that valuable things can be learned in these ways, I want here to emphasize the need to know much more about the _what_ and _why_. My pocket calculator contains hardware within which electronic impulses do certain things. Someone interested in understanding calculators would certainly learn something about them from studying the hardware and the movement of electric charges. If one did no more than that, however, one's understanding of my calculator would be narrow. The physical structure and the changes that take place within it are the way they are because they were designed to mediate in a complex way between the pressing of little keys and the display of numbers on a little screen. _What_ my calculator does is to relate those keys and those numbers in certain ways that are useful to me and others. _Why_ those particular relations are useful has been determined by their relevance to certain human tasks as well as by the history of calculating as it unfolded within the context of those tasks. If I were to undertake a career that was aimed at understanding language and the mind, I would be less inclined to focus my major effort on hardware, wetware, and simulations and more inclined to undertake a course of development that would focus on two essential kinds of expertise—expertise in observing and expertise in imagining.

I have emphasized in this chapter the extent to which understanding depends on immersion in an extensive fund of careful observations. A scientist in the true sense needs to be in love with a rich store of data. As one who sought to understand language and the mind, I would aim to find out all I could about as many languages as I could, not just by reading grammars and hearing what others said about languages, but especially by coming in contact with diverse languages themselves. I would also continue to observe more and more about my own language. I would want to pay particular attention to what people really do when they use language, my own or another, in order to sensitize myself to the distinction between natural and artificial data. I would carefully observe not just linguistic form, but also function. I would see all this as a deep lifetime commitment—to continue to learn more and more about what language and languages are really like and what they really do—not something on which I focused for just a few years. I would not shun the continuing advances in technology that are enabling us to observe the physical manifestations of language ever more closely and accurately. But at the same time I would cultivate my powers of introspection, noticing everything I could about how my own mind worked and how its workings were interwoven with my language, and inviting introspections on the part of diverse other language users.

The second thing I would cultivate would be my imagination. I would want to become good at inventing more encompassing schemas within which my beloved observations had a place, for without that ability I would remain only an observer, not an understander. I am not so sure how I would do that—perhaps through continual exposure to art as well as data. Cultivating the imagination is not a standard or a recognized part of scientific training, but we should not be glad of that fact. I would take special care never to downgrade the role of imagination in the pursuit of understanding, always appreciating its crucial role.

If I could become both a broad and deep observer and at the same time a creative imaginer, then I would approach my own vision of what a "scientific superman" should be. My own training and experience have not lived up to these goals, but I will do the best I can.

Summary

I began this chapter by characterizing understanding as the interpretation of particular, limited observations in terms of a more encompassing imagined system within which the observations have a natural place. I suggested that folk beliefs and scientific understandings are essentially the same. It is only that science has attempted to improve the quality of folk beliefs by making more careful and systematic observations and by matching theories with observations in more explicit ways.

When it comes to observations, it is useful to think, on the one hand, in terms of public versus private data, and on the other in terms of manipulated versus natural data. Science has tended to place the highest value on data that are public and manipulated, but understanding language and the mind requires that we recognize both the advantages and the disadvantages of each pole of each opposition. Public, behavioral data are verifiable, but as manifestations of the mind they are indirect and often misleading. Private, introspective data provide a more direct access to the mind but suffer from the absence of public verifiability. One of the advantages of approaching the mind through language is that language can provide a rich check on introspective observations. Manipulated data are useful in allowing the investigator to focus on certain questions without waiting for the relevant observations to offer themselves in nature, but they often deviate significantly from naturalness. Whereas natural data suffer from their accidental quality, they have the advantage of being, like introspections, closer to reality. Observations of both kinds are necessary, but more attention needs to be paid to manipulating data in ways that remain sensitive to what naturally occurs.

I summarized some specific ways in which observation of these several kinds are realized in practice, and I discussed the good and bad of specific methodologies. My intent was to show that all ways of understanding language and the mind have value, but that each by itself is inevitably limiting. Stressing the counterproductiveness of pinning all one's hopes on a single method, I noted that this book is biased toward natural linguistic data combined with introspective data whose validity is linguistically supported. I expressed some dismay concerning self-conscious "theorizing" that leaves out more in the way of observations than it includes, and I advocated a holistic approach to language and the mind that views all of human experience as ultimately essential to a fuller vision.

In the end I took issue with a vision of the training of a "scientific superman" that focused on hardware, wetware, and computer simulation. I emphasized the importance of a deep and prolonged immersion in linguistic and introspective observations, combined with the cultivation of a creative imagination adequate to understanding those observations in maximally insightful ways. Skills in both observing and imagining were seen as essential ingredients of progress toward our elusive goal.

3

The Nature of Consciousness

If you come to cognitive science, psychology, or the philosophy of mind with an innocent eye, the first thing that strikes you is how little serious attention is paid to consciousness. Few people in cognitive science think that the study of the mind is essentially or in large part a matter of studying conscious phenomena; consciousness is rather a "problem," a difficulty that functionalist or computationalist theories must somehow deal with. Now, how did we get into this mess? How can we have neglected the most important feature of the mind in those disciplines that are officially dedicated to its study? There are complicated historical reasons for this, but the basic reason is that since Descartes, we have, for the most part, thought that consciousness was not an appropriate subject for a serious science or scientific philosophy of mind. As recently as a few years ago, if one raised the subject of consciousness in cognitive science discussions, it was generally regarded as a form of bad taste, and graduate students, who are always attuned to the social mores of their disciplines, would roll their eyes at the ceiling and assume expressions of mild disgust.

(John Searle 1990, p. 585)

As I begin to write this chapter, I can see through my window that rain is starting to fall on the ground and rocks outside, and on a huge old oak tree that dominates my view. To the two of us, the oak tree and me, this rain means a great deal, because we are in the midst of a serious drought that has lasted for six years. It is possible that the rain will benefit us both. I believe, however, that something is happening inside me just now that is not happening inside the oak. I am conscious of the rain, and I believe that the oak is not. If I am wrong I owe the tree an apology, but in this chapter I explore what it might mean for me to be conscious of something and for the oak not to be.

Human consciousness has various properties on which it is possible to introspect. My plan is to outline some of those properties as they appear to my own introspection. As I do so I will allude briefly to observable features of language that can be understood in terms of each of the properties. Much of the rest of the book consists of a more detailed exploration of the relations between these introspectively observable properties of consciousness and the linguistic evidence for them. If the linguistic evidence were missing, the enterprise would be nothing more than a commentary on my own mental processes, which might or might not be of interest to anyone else. It is the combination of introspective with linguistic evidence that I hope will give the project a more general significance.

What Is Consciousness?

To put it mildly, consciousness is not an easy thing to characterize. It is of course not a "thing" at all. We cannot point at something, as we might point at a hand or even a segment of language and say, "This is what consciousness is." Consciousness is what we experience constantly while we are awake and often while we are asleep. It is at the very core of our existence, but its exact nature continues to elude us. The mystery that surrounds it has led many to regard it as a manifestation of a nonphysical soul. But it is not necessary to believe that consciousness emerges from something beyond our own neurophysiology, even though understanding its hardware or wetware alone will not in itself enable us to understand the properties of consciousness that are explored here. The elusiveness of consciousness stems above all from the fact that it is an internal phenomenon, directly observable only to the experiencer. But another problem has been raised—the question of how consciousness can observe itself. How is it possible for us to have a conscious experience and at the same time be conscious that we are having it? This problem has often puzzled those who have thought about it and has stimulated a variety of answers (Natsoulas 1988, 1989). I will return to it shortly.

Every human being possesses a complex internal model of reality. Call it a worldview, call it a knowledge structure, this model is essential to the human way of coping with the world. I believe my oak tree does not possess such a model. When the soil in which it is embedded contains insufficient moisture, physical processes within the tree cause its leaves to dry out, its roots to shrivel, and its growth to be reduced. It does not, however, possess an internal representation of the larger world in which it is situated, "knowing," for example, that it is located in a geographic area in which there has been little rain for six years, that resources for local irrigation have been drastically curtailed, that I—in some arrogant sense its "owner"—am concerned about its fate, and so on. If the present rain lasts long enough, its leaves, roots, and growth may benefit, but it has no internal representation of the provenience or extent of this rain, no anxiety or hope for the future. Within me there is a great deal of information about the larger context of the drought and the rain, along with feelings and desires, all of which I believe are missing from the tree. Furthermore, and importantly, my model of the world cannot avoid being centered around my *self.* It is necessarily a model from my *point of view,* relative to my own location in space and time, as well as my own physical and social needs and desires. It was constructed on the basis of my own contacts with and reactions to the world, and the ways in which I interpret that world are necessarily of a kind that serves my own interests. I believe the tree does not possess any self-awareness of this kind.

Here is where consciousness fits in. Although every human mind is devoted to modeling a larger reality within which it (or the organism it inhabits) occupies a central place, only one small piece of that model can be *active* at one time. At any given moment the mind can focus on no more than a small segment of everything it "knows." I will be using the word *consciousness* here to refer to this limited activation process. Consciousness is an active focusing on a small part of the conscious being's self-centered model of the surrounding world. If the oak has no model of its environment centered on its own place within it, it can have no consciousness either.[1]

The question may arise as to whether we can be conscious of something larger in scope. I ask myself, for example, whether I can activate topics as ramified and complex as "my years as an undergraduate" or "my father." Of course I can arouse these grand experiential totalities in my consciousness and, as totalities, assign them the labels I just did, but there is no way I can be conscious all at once of their internal composition. I can focus on a particular person, place, or event within my undergraduate years, or on a particular image or action of my father, but the considerable store of knowledge I possess about either of these topics can be activated only one small part at a time. Although Mozart claimed that he could be conscious of an entire composition at once (Humphrey 1951, p. 53), his report is certainly at variance with what I suggest is the normal relation between consciousness and time.

Constant Properties of Consciousness

As we examine some of the properties of consciousness, it is helpful to divide them into *constant* properties, those that belong to all conscious experience, and *variable* properties, dimensions along which particular instances of conscious experience may vary. We can take brief note of how each property is reflected in language, and we can also speculate on

---

1. See Natsoulas 1983 for a useful discussion of various ways in which the word *consciousness* has been used; my usage corresponds to what he labels "consciousness$_3$."

the advantages to the conscious organism that each of these properties brings.

Consciousness Has a Focus

To say that consciousness has a focus simply repeats the observation that consciousness is the activation of only a small part of the experiencer's model of the surrounding world, not the model in its totality. This limited capacity of consciousness is reflected linguistically in the brief spurts of language that will be discussed as *intonation units* in chapter 5. Each such unit verbalizes a small amount of information which, it is plausible to suppose, is that part of the speaker's model of reality on which his or her consciousness is focused at that moment. In a socially interactive situation it is the portion on which the speaker intends that the listener's consciousness be focused as a result of hearing the intonation unit. This limited activation allows a person to interact with the surrounding world in a maximally productive way, for it would hardly be useful to activate everything a person knew at once. Aside from the burden such a process might place on neural resources, most of that vast store of information would be irrelevant to one's interests at any particular time. Since a particular situation always impinges on one's interests in a particular, limited way, it is advantageous, even essential, to restrict the activated information to whatever is relevant at the moment.

The Focus Is Embedded in a Surrounding Area
of Peripheral Consciousness

The active focus is surrounded by a periphery of *semiactive* information that provides a context for it. Recognition that the mind contains information in this semiactive state is crucial to this work. There are various important aspects of language that would be mysterious if the presence of semiactive as well as fully active information were not taken into account. One obvious way in which language gives overt expression to peripheral information is through the clustering of intonation units into larger segments that express larger coherences of information, thus providing contexts for the smaller segments. Later I will call these larger coherences *discourse topics*. It is obviously advantageous for the mind to have peripheral access to larger stores of knowledge within which the limited foci of fully active information have a place.

Consciousness Is Dynamic

The focus of consciousness is restless, moving constantly from one item of information to the next. In language this restlessness is reflected in the fact that, with a few exceptions, each intonation unit expresses something different from the intonation unit immediately preceding and following it. Since each focus is a discrete segment of information, the sequencing of foci resembles a series of snapshots more than a movie. Part 2 of this book deals with the dynamics of consciousness, tracing what happens in thought and language as one focus of active information is replaced by another, each finding coherence in the contexts provided by the surrounding semiactive information, with these clusters of semiactive information being replaced by other clusters at longer intervals. I characterize this process with the metaphor of *flow,* which is intended to capture the dynamic quality of the movement of information into and out of both focal (active) and peripheral (semiactive) consciousness.[2] Furthermore, this flow is experienced as continuous, a fact exploited by fiction writers in ways I explore in part 3.

Consciousness Has a Point of View
To repeat another observation made earlier in this chapter, one's model of the world is necessarily centered on a self. The location and needs of that self establish a point of view that is another constant ingredient of consciousness. I will expand on characteristics of a point of view at the end of chapter 10, where they can be related to a specific example. Point of view assumes a special importance in part 3, where its manipulation in written fiction will contribute to the discussion of displaced consciousness.

Consciousness Has a Need for Orientation
No self is an island, and it is necessary for peripheral consciousness, at least, to include information regarding the self's location in several domains, the most important of which appear to be space, time, society, and ongoing activity. Consciousness, it seems, cannot function properly without peripheral knowledge of spatial and temporal location, knowledge of the people with whom the self is currently interacting, and knowledge of what is currently going on. In chapter 10 we will see how so-called settings verbalize information of these kinds when it is not available otherwise.

Variable Properties of Consciousness

All conscious experiences have a focus and a periphery, all function as brief parts of a restless sequencing in which each focus is quickly replaced by another, and all have a point of view and an orientation. In addition to these constant properties there are other, variable properties that differentiate some conscious experiences from others.

2. This use of the term *flow* is obviously different from that popularized in Csikszentmihalyi 1990, although both uses are related to consciousness.

Conscious Experiences Arise from Different Sources

What kinds of things are we conscious of? In view of the fact that we spend not only all of our waking hours but even some of the time we are asleep experiencing a constant succession of focuses of consciousness, it is surprising that so little systematic effort has been devoted to identifying the kinds of things these experiences contain. As with other aspects of consciousness, the advantage of studying this question through language is that evidence from introspections can be supplemented with evidence from the kinds of things people talk about.

Philosophers often seem to assume that consciousness is made up of beliefs, intentions, and desires. It should take only a small amount of elementary introspecting, however, to realize that a large proportion of what we experience is *perceptual* (cf. W. Lyons 1986). Much of consciousness is taken up with perceptual-like events and states, along with the people and objects that participate in them. A short time ago, for example, I was conscious of rain outside my window. We are also conscious of our own *actions*: the things we do, the things we have done, and the things we might do. A brief moment ago, I was conscious that I was moving a piece of paper on my table. Consciousness is to a large extent made up of experiences of perceptions and actions. Concomitant with them, and usually if not always present at the same time, are the emotions, opinions, attitudes, desires, and decisions that they engender or, conversely, that engender them. I include here whatever aspects of conscious experience attach values to perceptions and actions. My perception of the rain, for example, was accompanied by a feeling of gladness and relief. As I moved the paper on my table I felt some curiosity about what lay beneath it. I will use the term *evaluations* to cover all aspects of conscious experience that involve emotions, opinions, attitudes, desires, and the like.

In addition to perceptions, actions, and evaluations, which evidently form the three basic ingredients of consciousness, there are sometimes also *introspections*—meta-awarenesses of what consciousness is doing. People may, for example, be conscious that they are remembering or that they are having trouble remembering. They may be conscious that they are undergoing perceptual experiences, that they are aware of their own actions, and that they are experiencing emotions or attitudes. I mentioned earlier the question of how the mind can be conscious of what it is conscious of, how consciousness can focus on itself at the same time that it focuses on something else. If we recognize peripheral as well as focal consciousness, the ability to observe one's own consciousness is no longer a problem. When one focus of active consciousness has been replaced by another, the first does not disappear from consciousness altogether, but remains for some time semiactive. During that time its earlier focal presence remains accessible to observation. Thus, one of the advantages of recognizing the existence of peripheral consciousness is that it removes the mystery from this ability of consciousness to observe itself.

Conscious Experiences May Be Immediate or Displaced

Sometimes the information in active and semiactive consciousness is directly related to immediate reality—the environment that surrounds the conscious being at that moment. One may be conscious of what is happening at the time and place of the experience itself. Such information is accessible in large part through the senses. My immediate consciousness of the rain comes in part from hearing its sound on the roof, in part from seeing streaks of rain against the dark background of distant trees and the spattering of drops on a rock that lies not far from the oak tree. All this I understand to be happening here and now, at the very time and place I am conscious of it, although intriguingly it has been suggested that what we experience as immediate perception actually reaches our consciousness a half second late (Libet 1981).

But not all of immediate experience comes from the external environment of the conscious organism; much arises from within. I refer here to the evaluative emotions, opinions, attitudes, and desires, some of which arise from established ways of evaluating externally induced experiences, some of which have sources that are wholly internal, as when positive or negative moods are induced by visceral chemistry. My feelings of happiness and relief on hearing and seeing the rain are an important ingredient of my focus on this immediate event. A total immediate experience combines perceptual and evaluative information into a single holistic interpretation of immediate reality.

Consciousness is by no means limited to immediate experience, however. We spend a great deal of our time being conscious of information that is *displaced*. I might, for example, shift my focus from the actual rain to remembering a weather report I heard earlier, or to imagining the future effect the rain might have on my parched garden. These two examples illustrate that such distal information can reach our proximal consciousness from either of two sources. One source is *remembering*—the construction of experiences that were immediate experiences at some earlier time but do not belong to the current environment. The other is *imagining*—experiences constructed by the conscious mind itself, though usually with some indirect relation to previous immediate experiences. The distinction between immediate and displaced consciousness affects language in ways that are discussed in part 3 of this book, where we will examine some important qualitative differences between the two kinds of experience. We can note here in passing that language provides evidence for the predominance of displaced experience in people's mental lives. And although language can give us public evidence for immediacy and displacement only when language is being used, one might suspect that,

if anything, silent thought devotes even more time to displaced experience.

Conscious Experiences May Be Factual or Fictional

It was just noted that displaced conscious experience comes in part from
remembering, in part from imagining. One might conclude that remembered and immediate experience together constitute *fact,* whereas imagined experience constitutes *fiction.* The distinction between fact and fiction can, however, be exaggerated. On the one hand, even immediate
experience is reconstructive rather than replicative. We do not record
objectively what is going on around us, but interpret it in accordance with
already familiar schemas. Even more so, information that has remained
inactive in the mind for some time and is now remembered will have
undergone additional processes of interpretation, being at the time of
remembering even less veridically replicative than at the time of first
acquisition. The remembering of once-immediate experience inevitably
entails a greater or lesser amount of invention (e.g., Loftus 1979). Conversely, imagined experiences—even those that are seemingly far removed from everyday reality—always have some basis in reality. Imagined
creatures and events bear a greater or lesser resemblance to creatures
and events that were once immediately perceived. If people have never
seen unicorns, they have at least seen horses and rhinoceroses. Combining
them is a process not wholly different in kind from remembering, as
Goethe appreciated when he titled his autobiographical work *Dichtung
und Wahrheit.*

Nevertheless, we cannot simply dismiss the factual-fictional opposition
as irrelevant, since it does have an effect on language and language sheds
light on its nature. What is factual or fictional in some objective sense is
distinct from what is *believed* factual or fictional by some human experiencer. The latter—the experiencer's judgment—has important echos in
language, which can express experiencers' assessments of ideas as being
or not being in accord with their conceptions of reality. The ·factual-
fictional distinction affects whole genres of language in ways that are
touched on in part 3. One thinks immediately of the classic distinction
between fiction and nonfiction in literature. It also affects more restricted
judgments reflected in linguistic distinctions of evidentiality and mood.
Assessments of what is real and not real permeate language in a variety
of ways.

Conscious Experiences Are More or Less Interesting

There is always a vast amount of information from which consciousness
might choose its current focus, including the myriad details of the current
environment, the much larger fund of possibilities available through remembering, and the limitless possibilities achievable through imagination.

Of all the items of information on which one might focus, why do certain of them enter consciousness and not others? The question is especially difficult to answer with respect to silent thought, where the reasons why consciousness scans the environment, remembers, and imagines in the ways it does are hardest to get at (but see Csikszentmihalyi 1975). But when consciousness is verbalized in overt language, we can at least examine the flow of things that are talked about and perhaps sharpen our understanding of why a speaker chose those things and not others.

In parts 2 and 3 of this book we will see that people tend to talk about things that are *interesting* to them and ideally about things they judge to be interesting to others. The question of what makes something interesting deserves much more attention than it will receive here, but interestingness seems above all to reside in conflict with mundane expectations. There is a general tendency to talk or write about the unexpected. On the other hand, interest can also be sustained when language confirms expectations already held. A satisfactory mental life depends on a balance between the expected and the unexpected, the stimulating and the comfortably reinforcing, kiwi sherbet and vanilla ice cream (cf. Meyer 1956 on the interplay of the expected and unexpected in music). Language suggests that the choice of what to focus on reflects these complementary criteria.

Conscious Experiences May Be Verbal or Nonverbal

Finally, is consciousness just a matter of talking to oneself, or are people conscious of more than language? The fact that consciousness consists *in part* of inner speech cannot be in doubt, but it is obvious at least from my own introspection that not all of what passes through my consciousness is language. Imagery, affect, and aesthetic experiences have natures of their own. Perhaps these are aspects of consciousness where significant individual differences exist, if I can believe what others tell me. My guess is that people differ in the proportions, but that some mixture of verbal and nonverbal experience is a general characteristic of everyone's consciousness.

It may seem paradoxical that language itself provides evidence that consciousness contains more than language, but in fact there are linguistic reasons to believe that the content of consciousness at any moment cannot be equated with any particular linguistic manifestation of it (Chafe 1977a). One kind of evidence is the presence of disfluencies. People often have trouble "putting thoughts into words" and may believe that they have not adequately stated what they "had in mind." If people were conscious of nothing more than words to begin with, the task of overt verbalizing should be effortless, simply a matter of vocalizing what was already present subvocally. But almost any observation of natural speech shows that talking is not that easy. Disfluencies are evidence for a nonconformity between what one is conscious of and what one says.

Other evidence is provided by repeated verbalizations of what is thought to be the same content. Much can be learned from observing the different ways a person relates the "same" content on different occasions (Chafe 1990a). The wordings are never in all ways the same, even with oral rituals that are repeated with great frequency. In all repeated verbalizations there is, to be sure, a greater or lesser overlap in wordings. There may, for example, be formulaic passages whose frozen wordings are constant, but even in rituals the less formulaic portions inevitably vary each time the ritual is performed. That is true to a much greater degree when the repeated subject matter is less ritualized—a narrative of a personal experience, for example, or something retold from another person's earlier account.

A third kind of evidence, beyond disfluencies and differences in repeated verbalizations, comes from experiments that are specifically designed to investigate this question. Experimental evidence also shows that people do not remember verbatim wordings very long, although they may remember particular salient words or phrases (e.g., Sachs 1967, Jarvella 1971, Hjelmquist and Gidlund 1985; see also Gernsbacher 1990, pp. 63–85).

One might conclude the following. Language suggests that we store and activate ideas of particular referents, events, states, and topics, and that we also store categories and schemas that allow us to "make sense of" those ideas by treating them as instances of things already familiar, thus relating them to each other and providing us with expectations regarding them, as well as with already known ways of behaving toward them. The referents, events, states, and topics, as well as the categories and schemas, are likely to be associated with both mental imagery and language, since they assume both forms in consciousness. Thus, my knowledge of a particular man is an abstract piece of knowledge that might appear in my consciousness as both a favorite image of that man and one of the various ways in which he can be named. The referent itself, my idea of that man, may be a stable and abstract mental constant, but his representations in consciousness can be quite diverse. Those representations are the only ways I can actively deal with my knowledge of him— recognize him, think about him, and act toward him—and thus they are crucial to the ways my mind and body are able to deal with my idea of him.

The Conscious and the Unconscious

This work is concerned above all with (a) the movement of ideas into and out of consciousness and (b) certain consequences of the observation that consciousness is often focused on ideas that are displaced from the current environment. Everything suggested here assumes that most of what is available to the mind at any given moment is *not* in a state of either active or semiactive consciousness. Thus, although this book focuses on the nature and relevance to language of conscious experiences, it assumes throughout that everyone possesses a vast amount of unconscious knowledge. The phenomena discussed involve no necessary commitment to any particular relation between the conscious and the unconscious, except for the assumption that consciousness has an important role to play in shaping both thought and language. Surprisingly (to me), that assumption is a controversial one.

The extent to which thought and behavior are influenced by the *unconscious* is, of course, an old question. There are, in fact, several questions here. One is the extent to which the unconscious affects the conscious. Even if consciousness is recognized as the locus of ongoing, constantly changing mental life, that life may be influenced to a greater or lesser degree by factors hidden from consciousness itself. The understandings developed in this book do not depend on that question being answered in any particular way. A different question is whether and how much the unconscious directly affects behavior without the involvement of consciousness at all. It seems obvious that people sometimes do things without being conscious they are doing them. Built-in behavior (blinking one's eyes) and acquired skills (driving a car) are evidently of this nature. How much of human behavior is like this? I would hardly want to deny that much of behavior is determined by processes that bypass consciousness or even that much of linguistic behavior is of that kind. For it is certain that people are generally unconscious of the vowels and consonants, the morphological and syntactic patterns that comprise linguistic form. Our interest here is in consciousness of the ideas that are expressed in linguistic form, not in consciousness of the form itself, but also and especially in ways in which consciousness of the ideas can (unconsciously) affect the nature of the form.

There is a currently popular view of language and the mind that questions whether consciousness plays any significant role at all or whether it is simply an "epiphenomenon," like the light on my computer showing me that a disk is active. Without that light my computer would function perfectly well. The light lets an observer know that something is happening, but it has nothing to do with *what* is happening. Might not consciousness play a similar role with respect to the functioning of the mind?

There appear at the moment to be three relatively clear positions on this matter. One is the position that characterizes the mainstream of cognitive science. It holds that most if not all of the important operations of the mind are inaccessible to consciousness. Generative linguistics, for example, has always posited structures and processes of a kind of which no language user could ever be conscious. And computers can certainly not be said to possess consciousness. While the effects of consciousness, as discussed in this book, could be mimicked by a computer, that would be quite a different enterprise from endowing the computer with consciousness itself. Mental processes are often, in fact, said to be computational processes, basic to the computational mind. An especially clear and forceful presentation of that view has been provided by Ray Jackendoff (1987), an important player in the development of generative linguistics, whose book is actually titled *Consciousness and the Computational Mind.* Jackendoff's view is built around what he calls the hypothesis of the nonefficacy of consciousness: "The awareness of an entity E cannot *in itself* have any effect on the computational mind. Only the computational states that cause/support/project E can have any such effect" (p. 25).

At the opposite extreme is the position taken by John Searle (1990, 1992), who suggests that the mind contains nothing but blind neurophysiological processes, on the one hand, and on the other hand processes that either are or *could be* accessible to consciousness. Searle's "moral is that the big mistake in cognitive science is not the overestimation of the computer metaphor (though that is indeed a mistake) but the neglect of consciousness" (1990, p. 585).

It is, of course, possible to take a position between these extremes. A well-thought-out and elaborated intermediate position is that represented by Bernard Baars (1988), whose theory of consciousness as a "global workspace" allows for complex interactions between conscious and unconscious processes: "The essential metaphor here is of a blackboard in front of an audience of human specialists who can only communicate with the group as a whole via the blackboard. Thus, solutions for novel or predictable problems, which cannot be solved by any single specialist, can be coordinated via the blackboard. Executive systems can also exercise control in this way" (Baars 1991, p. 440).

I believe everything discussed in this book is or could be made compatible with the positions of both Baars and Searle. But since the book's major thesis is that consciousness shapes language in important ways, there is a basic incompatibility with the hypothesis that consciousness is "nonefficacious." Indeed, I see consciousness as the obvious locus of humans' ongoing interaction with the environment as well as the site for inner thought and feeling. To deny that, to suppose that all the significant processes of the mind take place outside of consciousness, which is left with no more status than the blinking lights on my computer, is in my opinion a major act of self-deception, one that only demonstrates the extent to which "scientists" can go in ignoring their own experience.

As stressed above, it would be impossible to deny that there is much about a language that lies outside the consciousness of those who use it.

I find it helpful to think of linguistic form as if it were located in a pane of glass through which ideas are transmitted from speaker to listener. Under ordinary circumstances language users are not conscious of the glass itself, but only of the ideas that pass through it. The form of language is transparent, and it takes a special act of will to focus on the glass and not the ideas. Linguists undergo a training that teaches them how to focus on the glass, but fluent users of a language focus their consciousness only on what they are saying. People use language to organize and communicate ideas without being at all conscious of how their language does it. It is undoubtedly this transparency of language that makes it so difficult for most people to understand why language should have a science devoted to it. Still, there are many aspects of language a person can *learn* to be conscious of. Linguists do that professionally, and the experience of becoming conscious of previously unconscious phenomena is one of the principal joys of linguistic work.

Are there important and valid theoretical constructs which, though they are essential in explaining language and the mind, are different *in nature* from anything that could ever be accessible to consciousness? The cognitive science enterprise has a stake in a particular kind of theorizing that places the highest value on constructs that are maximally abstract, maximally removed from anything that can be observed. It is a matter of faith that theorizing of this kind has a superior status, but it is a belief at odds with the view of understanding presented in chapter 2, where a theory was seen as valuable in proportion to the depth and breadth of its ties to the observable. When it comes to choosing between competing understandings, there is no reason why abstractness should be regarded as an advantage. On the contrary, that understanding is to be preferred whose ties to observables are closer and more extensive. Such a criterion leads to skepticism with regard to mental representations which, although they may explain certain things, enjoy no deeper or broader ties to the vast richness of data that language presents to us. We need not necessarily take the position that everything present in the mind must be the kind of thing that could be brought into consciousness, if, indeed, it were possible to decide just what kind of thing that is. But at the very least the efficacy of consciousness—its crucial role in shaping and being shaped by language—is worth taking seriously. That should be enough to justify this book.

Consciousness, then, is regarded in this work as the crucial interface between the conscious organism and its environment, the place where information from the environment is dealt with as a basis for thought and action as well as the place where internally generated experience becomes effective—the locus of remembering, imagining, and feeling. It might not be too much to say that the purpose of both behavior and thought is to satisfy the interests of the organism as they are represented in that organism's consciousness. It is impossible to imagine how a human being could function as a human being without being conscious, lacking active awareness of anything, unable to focus on anything real or imagined, operating only in terms of blind physiology like the oak outside my window. There is a reason why those unlucky individuals who have fallen into a permanently unconscious state are referred to as vegetables. Trees, perhaps some "lower" animals, and computers all function in that way, but consciousness sets the rest of us apart.

Summary

So that we can commence this work with some idea of what consciousness is and what it does, this chapter suggested certain ways of understanding its overall nature, its constant properties, and dimensions on which it may vary. In so doing, it relied in part on introspection, in part on kinds of linguistic evidence that are developed in later chapters.

So far as the overall nature of consciousness is concerned, I suggested that it involves the activation of small portions of the experiencer's self-centered model of the surrounding world. Among its constant properties are its exhibition of both a focus and a periphery, its restless movement from one focus to the next, and its possession of a point of view, as well as an orientation in space, time, society, and ongoing activity. I then discussed five variable properties. The first had to do with the source of the experience—whether it was perceptual, actional, evaluative, and/or introspective. The second had to do with whether the experience was related to the immediate environment of the experiencer or whether it was displaced, arising from remembering or imagining. The third had to do with whether the experiencer regarded the experience as fact or fiction. The fourth involved the question of whether the experience was excitingly interesting or comfortably reinforcing. Finally, the fifth had to do with the verbality or nonverbality of the experience—whether it consisted of inner language or of other kinds of experience such as imagery and affect.

The picture to be developed in this book involves no necessary commitment to a particular role for the unconscious, which may influence what is present in consciousness and may be responsible for more or less of what people do. There is, however, a timely issue regarding the significance or nonsignificance of the role of consciousness itself. At one extreme it is possible that consciousness is no more than an epiphenomenon. At the other, mental processes may dichotomize exhaustively into those that are conscious or potentially conscious and those that are blindly physiological. One can easily imagine a position between these extremes. This book assumes at least that consciousness plays a crucial role in thought, language, and behavior. It does not preclude a role for more abstract mental representations, although it views those that have been invented so far with skepticism. It proceeds from the assumption that consciousness is the crucial interface between the conscious being and his or her environment, the locus of remembering, imagining, evaluating, and speaking, and thus central to the functioning of the mind.

4

Speaking and Writing

The relation between language and consciousness changes as language is used in different ways. In this book I assume that there is one particular use of language—ordinary conversation—whose special status justifies treating it as a baseline from which all other uses are deviations. Conversational *consciousness* shares this baseline status, and other ways of using language may involve special, derived modes of consciousness.

From a purely physical point of view, language is produced and received under three very different conditions. In one, the *speaking* mode, people do things with their lungs, throats, and mouths to make noises that pass through the air and strike the ears of others, typically in the immediate vicinity. In the *writing* mode people manipulate pens, pencils, brushes, or keyboards to make marks that are likely to be seen by others at times and places quite distinct from when and where the marks were made. In the third mode, verbal *thinking*, there are neither overt noises nor marks, and the only direct consumer of the language is the person who produces it.

All three of these uses bring a form to conscious experience that provides a handle on what would otherwise be less graspable images and feelings. All three shape unique, flowing experience into already established patterns that language provides. This process brings both gains and losses. Although the uniqueness of the unverbalized experience is sacrificed, there are advantages to converting something new and wholly particular into something familiar and handleable. Verbalized experience is easier to deal with because it fits within established expectations. But of course that is not all. When language is made overt, as in speaking and writing, it is able to provide a link between what would otherwise be independent nervous systems, acting as an imperfect substitute for the synapses that fail to bridge the gap between one mind and another. In short, language serves two basic functions. However it is used, it converts unique experience into something familiar and manageable, and overt language—speaking and writing—offers a way to narrow the chasm between independent minds.

I wish I could say more about the role of language in silent thinking, but this is a book about speaking and writing, whose advantage to us as investigators is the fact that each has an overt physical manifestation—

either audible sounds or visible marks. With a passing bow, therefore, in the direction of covert thinking, and a promise not to forget the importance of language and consciousness that never reach the sound or light of day, we can direct our attention to language we can hear or see, and the varieties of consciousness associated with them.

Differences between the Activities of Speaking and Writing

Although there has been dispute as to whether speaking and writing consistently produce different kinds of language (e.g., Akinnaso 1982, Tannen 1982, Biber 1988), there can be no question that the acts of speaking and writing themselves are very different. The dependence of the first on sound, the second on sight, has a variety of consequences, among which are the following (cf. Ong 1982; Ehlich 1983, 1989).

Evanescence versus Permanence and Transportability
Although sound remains in the mind for a brief period that has sometimes been called echoic memory, its evanescent quality compared to sight is obvious. This is the quality identified by Hockett (1960) as *rapid fading*. In the typical speaking situation, moreover, sound is limited spatially to a small radius from where it is produced. The relative permanence and transportability of visible marks make written language quite different in these respects. We can still read language that was produced several thousand years ago in places far away. To be sure, we now have technologies for storing and reproducing sound as well, but they are too recent to have affected the nature of either language or consciousness in fundamental ways. I have always found it ironic that the first step taken by a linguist who works with tape-recorded speech is to "reduce" it to written form. Written language, including transcriptions of spoken language, is not only preservable through time and space but can be dissected, analyzed, and otherwise manipulated at the leisurely pace essential to scientific investigation as we know it.

Differences in Tempo
On a different scale of time, speaking takes place at a speed that varies somewhat with speakers and circumstances, but remains within a relatively narrow range. Significant deviations from this range turn speech into gibberish as it accelerates and into a source of frustration as it decelerates. For purely mechanical reasons, writing is produced at a significantly slower rate than speaking, whereas reading, quite the opposite, has the potential to proceed at a faster pace. In other words, if the tempo of conversational speaking is taken as a baseline, writing is produced more

slowly and reading can be (though it need not be) somewhat faster. These differences cannot help but interfere with the tempo of conscious experience in both writing and reading, as compared with speaking, modifying written consciousness in fundamental ways.

Spontaneity versus Deliberate Working Over

In conversations, ideas tend to be activated "off the top of one's head" as a conversation proceeds. There is little time for elaborate preplanning when one is "throwing ideas around" and new ideas and topics must be activated quickly. Of course people sometimes plan what they want to say in conversations, but in the typical casual situation the flow of ideas and topics owes more to spontaneity than to any program laid out in advance. In writing, this spontaneity is replaced with quite a different process for which English provides no satisfactory term, but which might be called the property of being *worked over*. Writers have the opportunity to read and revise what they have produced, perhaps many times (at least a dozen for this chapter), before it is ever presented to an audience. Creating a piece of written language is, or can be, like creating a piece of sculpture, revising and reshaping a visual creation until its creator finds it adequate to display. It would be easy to conclude that writing, because it can be reworked in this way, produces a superior kind of language, but that is not necessarily the case. An obvious trade-off occurs between reworking and spontaneity. Ordinary speaking has an unfettered quality that writing can easily destroy.

Richness of Prosody

Speaking allows maximum exploitation of prosody—the pitches, prominences, pauses, and changes in tempo and voice quality that greatly enrich spoken expression. Prosody is an absolutely essential part of speaking, and one of the ways observations of language have often fallen short has been in not knowing what to do with it. Writing systems have never developed ways of representing anything that even approaches the range of spoken prosodic phenomena, and in that sense written language is seriously impoverished. In chapter 22 I will allude to the finding that written language does have a prosody that is experienced by both writers and readers through auditory imagery (Chafe 1988b). But writing itself shows only a pale reflection of the prosodic richness of speech.

Naturalness

Speaking is natural to the human organism in ways that writing can never be. It is plausible to suppose that humans are "wired up" to speak and listen, that the evolution of spoken language was inextricably interwoven with the physical evolution of our species. Obviously that cannot be true of writing. Only for a brief moment in the scale of evolution has writing been with us at all, and widespread literacy, extending beyond a few scribes or a small elite, is more recent still. Since we can hardly have evolved to write, it is intriguing to speculate on how we are able to do it as well as we do. Writing takes clever advantage of certain abilities that evolved for other reasons, among them an excellent sense of vision as well as great skill at making fine movements with the hands. It could not have developed without those abilities, both of which must have evolved to facilitate more essential interactions with the environment such as becoming aware of and grasping food. Further evidence for the greater naturalness of speaking comes from the fact that we learn to speak long before we learn to write, with no special instruction. Writing has to be taught, and the average person never really learns to do it very well. The acquisition of writing ability is more difficult by an order of magnitude than the acquisition of the ability to speak.

Situatedness versus Desituatedness

Use of the vocal-auditory channel has, during most of human history, been associated with a use of language in which the participants share the same space and time. The telephone has, of course, complicated the situation by making it possible for people to hold conversations even when they are physically apart, but the properties of spoken language must have reached their present stage long before the telephone was ever thought of. In writing, the language producer and receiver usually do not share the same space or time. It is in fact one of its major benefits that writing allows language to be carried from one place to another and to be preserved over long intervals of time. Nothing is without its costs, and writing sacrifices the benefits of copresence—above all, direct and immediate involvement with another mind. Copresence makes it possible for interlocutors to interact, alternating in their roles as speakers and listeners.[1] The speaker at one moment may be the listener at the next. The fact that the contributions of the several participants in a conversation constantly influence each other is emphasized in sociologically oriented studies of conversation. Writing, in contrast, usually lacks this kind of immediate interchange.

Copresence and interaction together define a property that can be called *situatedness*—the closeness language has to the immediate physical and social situation in which it is produced and received. The nature of

---

1. Since this work is concerned with recipients of language whose attention is focused on the ideas being presented to them, I will speak of *listeners* and *readers* rather than, for example, *hearers* or *addressees*.

conversational language and conversational consciousness is dependent on their situatedness. Written language is usually *desituated,* the environment and circumstances of its production and reception having minimal influence on the language and consciousness itself. In part 3 of this book we will examine some effects that desituatedness can have on the ways in which written language may represent consciousness.

Attitudes toward Speaking and Writing

People have reacted to the presence of both spoken and written language in different ways (see the bibliographic review in Chafe and Tannen 1987). Ancient tradition gave priority to writing. Speaking, if it was noticed at all, was seen as corrupt. While that view may have been the most common one in established literate societies, the opposite view—that speaking is the real thing and writing nothing more than an imperfect way of representing speech on paper—arose with modern linguistics in the late nineteenth and early twentieth centuries. The third option, of course, would be to regard speaking and writing as each having its own validity, each being an effective adaptation to the situations in which it is used. This more balanced view has never had wide currency, either with the general public or within the scholarly community, until very recently.

The idea that written language is primary goes back at least to the ancient Greek scholars who were among the first to look at language in a systematic way: "From the beginning Greek linguistic scholarship had been concerned primarily with the written language. . . . In so far as the difference between the spoken and the written language was perceived at all, the tendency was always to consider the former as dependent on, and derived from, the latter" (J. Lyons 1968, p. 9).

But the most influential linguists of the early twentieth century took the opposite tack, emphasizing the primary status of speech and treating written language as derived and secondary. The influential Swiss linguist Ferdinand de Saussure, for example, was explicit in his opinion that written language exists only to serve the spoken: "Language and writing are two distinct systems of signs; the second exists for the sole purpose of representing the first. The linguistic object is not both the written and the spoken forms of words; the spoken forms alone constitute the object" (Saussure 1916/1959, pp. 23–24). The equally influential American linguist Edward Sapir, if we can take him at his word, seems to have regarded written language as entirely isomorphic with spoken, but again as secondary to it: "Written language is thus a point-to-point equivalence, to borrow a mathematical phrase, to its spoken counterpart. The written forms are secondary symbols of the spoken ones" (Sapir 1921, p. 20). But it was Leonard Bloomfield, for a time the preeminent American linguist, who most clearly justified this point of view: "Writing is not language, but merely a way of recording language by means of visible marks.... A language is the same no matter what system of writing may be used to record it, just as a person is the same no matter how you take his picture" (Bloomfield 1933, p. 21).

This shift of focus from writing to speaking coincided with a shift of interest from languages that existed in written form to languages that did not. The realization that the world was full of unwritten languages of marvelous subtlety and complexity had consequences that took some time to sink in, but by the end of the nineteenth century it was clear that language by no means required writing for its full-fledged existence. It was then natural to conclude that an understanding of how language works would have to depend first and foremost on an understanding of how *spoken* language works.

To subscribe to that belief was not to act on it effectively. For some time the collection of information on spoken language was at the mercy of constraints associated with writing. Our hands being slower than our tongues, early attempts to record speech had to be kept to a snail's pace. During the heyday of linguistic text collection in the style of the late nineteenth and early twentieth centuries, an investigator sat with an oral performer and painstakingly transcribed words dictated by someone who must often have wished he could break into his normal way of talking. Some linguists of that period were remarkably skilled at capturing fine phonetic detail on paper. But, as we realize now with better technology, it was by no means the whole story so far as speaking was concerned.

Sophisticated sound-recording devices eventually revolutionized our ability to understand the nature of spoken language. The early wax cylinders made it possible for the first time to record language as sound, but quality was poor and it was impossible to manipulate the cylinder for accurate transcription and analysis. The phonograph discs that followed were sturdier and better in sound quality, but it was still awkward to make one, and it remained difficult to replay a segment of a disc for detailed study. Tape recorders finally provided a way to record with ease whatever one wanted to record, to copy and splice it, and replay brief segments in order to transcribe them in rich detail. They became widely available only during the 1950s, so it has not been very long that scholars interested in spoken language have had the opportunity to capture and work with it satisfactorily. In the meantime, other devices have made it possible to plot frequencies, amplitudes, and time intervals. Electronic technology has made it possible for the first time in human history to study spoken language as it really is.

As Michael Halliday has lamented, "the linguist's professional commitment to the primacy of speech did not ... arise from or carry with it an awareness of the properties of spoken discourse" (Halliday 1987, p. 56). Perhaps it was because neither of them ever used a tape recorder that both Sapir and Bloomfield, ironically, failed to recognize the special qualities of speech. Sapir apparently thought *the farmer kills the duckling* was a normal English sentence. It now seems curious that Bloomfield, while deploring the equation of language with writing, at the same time believed that writing is nothing more than "a way of recording language by means of visible marks." Per Linell (1982) has suggested various ways in which linguistics, even since the tape recorder became available, has maintained a written language bias.

There are various reasons why we still lack "an awareness of the properties of spoken discourse," but a strong one is the fact that, by an unfortunate coincidence, the tape recorder became available just as the properties of spoken language became irrelevant within the mainstream of linguistic theorizing: "Linguistic theory is concerned primarily with an ideal speaker-listener, in a completely homogeneous speech-community, who knows its language perfectly and is unaffected by such grammatically irrelevant conditions as memory limitations, distractions, shifts of attention and interest, and errors (random or characteristic) in applying his knowledge of the language in actual performance" (Chomsky 1965, p. 3). Real spoken language remained in this view corrupt: "A record of natural speech will show numerous false starts, deviations from rules, changes of plan in mid-course, and so on" (p. 4), an attitude that precluded any interest in exploiting such data to arrive at an understanding of what the mind is doing when people speak. Or even when they write. Linguists were led to devote all their energies to studying the grammaticality (or lack of it) of isolated pseudosentences:

(1) The fact that there is a picture of himself hanging in the post office is believed by Mary to be disturbing Tom.

The examples of this kind that came to pass for linguistic data were neither transcribed from tape recordings nor copied from writing. They were neither things people would say nor things people would write, but bizarre and contextless "strings" of words. Whatever grammaticality may have meant, it had nothing to do with *either* speaking *or* writing.

Against this background it is not surprising that opportunities to investigate language as it is actually spoken have been exploited more in sociolinguistics, where the limitations of theorizing from constructed data could be more easily ignored and attention could be focused on conversational interaction. "Conversation analysis" (e.g., Goodwin and Heritage 1990) and "interactional sociolinguistics" (e.g., Gumperz 1982) have gone their own ways in examining spoken language as it is. This book is concerned with other aspects of this rich domain.

Adaptation

Simply to divide the uses of language into speaking and writing is not enough, for each of these major uses comes in many varieties. Speaking appears in conversations, storytelling, joke telling, interviews, discussions, lectures, sermons, prayers, political oratory, and many other forms. Writing has, if anything, even more varied manifestations: personal letters, grocery lists, advertisements, novels, recipes, short stories, signs, children's books, dictionaries, encyclopedias, travel guides, academic articles, legal documents, and so on and on. The daily newspaper alone exhibits diverse varieties of writing in its news reports, editorials, letters to the editor, columns, comics, and classifieds. Douglas Biber (1988) studied a number of linguistic dimensions along which various kinds of language may differ, and in fact he found that nothing consistently differentiates all varieties of speaking from all varieties of writing.

The best way to conceptualize this situation is undoubtedly to view language as adapting itself to the ways it is used (Pawley and Syder 1983a). To borrow a maxim from what was once called modern architecture: form follows function. If "grammars code best what speakers do most" (Du Bois 1987, p. 851), it is also the case that each mode of language use produces a kind of language that codes best what the consumers of that kind of language find most adaptive. Front-page news reports use participles and prepositional phrases to pack a maximum amount of information into a minimum space:

(2) The Santa Barbara City Council overruled the advice of the city attorney Tuesday, ordering developers to reduce the height of a hotly contested parking garage in another round of a seven-year boxing match over Railway Plaza.

Advertisers attack us with short, snappy bursts:

(3) Merit declares extra dividend. Enriched flavor, low tar. A solution with Merit.

Researchers exceed the newspaper's employment of participles and prepositional phrases to deliver generalizations and reifications which achieve their expression in multiple nominalizations:

(4) It is generally accepted that the internal representation of a text includes inferences that arise out of the interaction between the information presented in the text and the reader's existing world knowledge.

There are many such ways in which written language adapts to the circumstances of its use, but different uses of spoken language show such adaptations too. Both speaking and writing have evolved in many directions to fit the many circumstances in which people speak and write.

To forestall possible misunderstandings, I should mention the easy tendency to attach values to particular ways of using language. Whenever people notice differences, there is a natural inclination to believe that one variety is superior to the others—in this case that there is something better about one of the many varieties of language. As we have seen, it is particularly common in literate societies for writing to be viewed as superior to speaking. In its most virulent form this prejudice surfaces in the notion that "written languages" are intrinsically superior to "unwritten languages." Any linguist who has worked with an unwritten language knows how wrong such a judgment is. In Sapir's famous words, "When it comes to linguistic form, Plato walks with the Macedonian swineherd, Confucius with the head-hunting savage of Assam" (Sapir 1921, p. 219). But it would be equally wrong to jump to the conclusion that there are no differences between the language of conversations, oral traditions, or the many kinds of writing. Each offers its own possibilities and imposes its own constraints. In observing ways in which language adapts to its use, there is no reason to conclude that to converse or declaim or write is "better" than to use language in some other way. Although, for reasons already set forth, I assume in this work that conversing is in certain respects the most natural use of language, there is no implication that other uses are inferior. They are just different. That is the spirit in which I hope this book will be understood.

A related question is whether all the seeds of literary language are present in conversational language. It may or may not be true that the things writers do with language are already available to those who converse, and that the peculiar environment of writing simply fosters the development or exaggeration of certain usages. To state it differently, the question is whether writing produces forms of language that are entirely new or whether it simply occurs in an environment which encourages usages that are at least incipiently present when people converse. It is at least possible that the differences amount to simply a redistribution, though often a radical redistribution, of the frequencies with which various linguistic devices are employed (cf. Tannen 1989).

Summary

One way of categorizing the uses of language is to divide them into three physically distinct types: language in thinking, speaking, and writing. Concentrating on the two uses for which there is publicly observable evidence, I listed several properties that distinguish speaking and writing: the evanescence of speaking versus the permanence of writing; the rapidity of speaking versus the slowness of written production and, on the other hand, the potentially even greater rapidity of reading; the irrevocability of speaking versus the worked over, edited quality of writing; the rich prosody of speaking versus the impoverished representation of prosody in writing; the naturalness of speaking versus the unnaturalness of writing; and finally the situatedness of speaking versus the desituatedness of writing. Since conversational speaking appears to have a special status as the most natural use of language, this book treats it as a baseline for discussing other uses that diverge from it.

Over time, various attitudes have been taken toward the study of speaking and writing: usually one or the other is regarded as primary and the other as secondary or of no interest. Technology has put us now, for the first time in human history, in a position to understand what spoken language is really like, though for various reasons we have not yet taken full advantage of this potential. The study of language and the mind can profit from a willingness and ability to exploit the insights now available to us through the careful observation and analysis of ordinary speaking.

There are many varieties of both speaking and writing, and each variety represents an adaptation to the circumstances of its use. I warned against the value judgments that are too easy to make when people notice differences. Clearly the best approach is to think of each kind of language as adapted to its own circumstances. In part 2 the focus will be on the flow of information into and out of the consciousness of people engaged in ordinary conversation. What we find will provide a baseline for interpreting the varieties of language and consciousness that emerge when language is used in other ways.

PART TWO

Flow

5

Intonation Units

Consciousness is like vision. The similarities are probably not accidental, since the eye is anatomically an extension of the brain, and since for most of us vision is so fundamental a part of conscious experience. One way in which consciousness and vision are alike is in the very limited amount of information each can focus on at one time. There is foveal vision and focal consciousness. Surrounding this small area of maximum acuity lies, on the one hand, peripheral vision and, on the other hand, peripheral consciousness, both of which not only provide a context for the current focus but also suggest opportunities for its next moves. Beyond peripheral consciousness lies a vast treasury of information, some of which will at some time be brought into focal or peripheral consciousness, but all of which lies unattended at the moment. Consciousness and vision are alike in one other way as well. Both are in constant motion, the eye with its brief fixations, the mind with its continual shifting from one focus to the next. Both vision and consciousness exist in a state of constant restlessness.

Activation States

According to whether some idea is in the focal, peripheral, or unconscious state, we can speak of it as active, semiactive, or inactive. Thought and language involve continual changes in these activation states. Our concern in part 2 is with the effects such changes have on language, and on what language can tell us about the nature of the changes.

It might not be too misleading to associate active and inactive information with short-term and long-term memory respectively. I do not use those terms here, partly because of their possible implication that memory is a place. In the long run it may be less fruitful to speak of something being *in* memory or retrieving something *from* memory than to view these phenomena in terms of activation. Western psychology may have been misled by the fact that in European languages the process of remembering is reified in *memory* as a noun. One of the endearing qualities of Frederic Bartlett (1932) is the fact that his book was titled not *Memory,* but *Remembering.*

However that may be, although psychology has exploited the notions of short-term and long-term memory, it has not so obviously allowed for a semiactive state. Such a state has been recognized indirectly in the notion of *context,* as when items in short-term memory are thought to be influenced by their surroundings. It seems to have been recognized more directly in James's use of words like *"psychic overtone, suffusion,* or *fringe,* to designate the influence of a faint brain-process upon our thought, as it makes it aware of relations and objects but dimly perceived" (James 1890, 1: 258). Bruce Mangan has recently stimulated renewed interest in James's distinction, and has drawn an analogy to the menu-bar on some computer screens that "functions to indicate the existence of ... information that can be *potentially* called to the screen in detail—just as the fringe radically summarizes information that can be called into focal attention" (Mangan 1993, p. 98). I believe, however, that a more apt analogy is to vision, as when Bernard Baars observes that "we would be missing something important if we only dealt with focal consciousness, just as we would miss something vital in human vision if we studied only foveal sight. Some of the most remarkable capacities of the visual system reside in the periphery ... and the same may be true of conscious experience in general" (Baars 1993, p. 135). The same analogy to vision was drawn seven hundred years ago by the theologian-philosopher Duns Scotus, who asserted that

> for every single perfect and distinct intellection existing in the intellect, there can be many indistinct and imperfect intellections existing there. This is evident from the example of vision, the field of which extends as a conical pyramid at the lower base of which one point is seen distinctly, and yet within that same base many things are seen imperfectly and indistinctly; but of these several visions, only one is perfect, namely, that upon which the axis of the pyramid falls. If this is possible in one of the senses, all the more so is it possible in the intellect. (Wolter 1986, p. 173; cf. Brett 1965, p. 295, and Mangan 1993, p. 89)

It is interesting too that James related "fringe" consciousness to (discourse) topics in a manner that will occupy us in chapter 10.

Speakers realize, of course, that one or more other minds are involved in the communicative use of language. As they speak, they not only take account of the changing activation states of information in their own minds, but also attempt to appreciate parallel changes that are taking place in the minds of their listeners. Language is very much dependent on a speaker's beliefs about activation states in other minds. Such beliefs themselves constitute an important part of a speaker's ongoing, changing knowledge, and language is adjusted to accord with them. Beliefs about other minds have various sources. To a considerable extent they are based on previous linguistic interaction—on things said within the same discourse, but also things remembered from previous talk. Others are derived from nonlinguistic interaction, from shared experiences, and from shared cultures. Whatever the sources may be, conversation could not function as it does unless speakers took account of activation states in minds beyond their own.

Before we look more closely at the interplay between the three activation states and language, it is worth noting that the number three is probably too small. Although it is convenient in this work to deal only with the distinction between active, semiactive, and inactive information, a fuller understanding must almost certainly allow for further divisions of this continuum.

At one end of the continuum may be located what has been called *echoic* memory, the ability to shift one's consciousness of sound from the semiactive to the active state during the first few seconds after it has ceased to be present in the air (e.g., Neisser 1967, Glucksberg and Cowan 1970). Sound remains briefly available to active consciousness even if it failed to enter that state while it was physically present. This ability is clearly observable through introspection, as when we are able to retrieve something that was said to us, even though we may have been reading a newspaper when it was actually said and failed to focus active consciousness on it then. It is an ability that has a clear relevance to language, for it allows us to process sound sequences as wholes, not just "from left to right" as the sound enters our ears. It means that there is no real difference in the way we process *the gray house* and *la maison grise,* because in both cases the phrase is available to consciousness in its entirety. This ability compensates, in a small but important way, for the evanescence of sound, making it briefly scannable as a whole in the way a visual scene can be scanned. In this chapter we will meet a unit of mental and linguistic processing—the intonation unit—that seems to be of exactly the right size to be processed in its entirety with the help of echoic memory, a fact suggesting that this ability functions crucially as a support for language. Indeed, it would not be far-fetched to speculate that echoic memory evolved as a necessary component of the evolution of language.

In a different part of the continuum, it is likely that the semiactive-inactive distinction includes more than just that simple dichotomy. In this book any information that is neither fully active nor demonstrably semiactive will be called inactive. But there are reasons, even linguistic ones, to suspect that inactive information may be stored at either a shallower or a deeper level, the passage from the former to the latter being influenced by sleep, time, and the relative salience of the information. As one manifestation of this shallow-deep distinction, the ability to recall the temporal sequencing of events—the knowledge that one event happened before another—may be retained at the shallower level but lost at the deeper one. This shallow-deep distinction and the manner in which it may influence the use of temporal adverbs and other linguistic features were explored in Chafe (1973). Although that work relied on constructed examples, it may nevertheless be suggestive of reasons for dividing the inactive category into at least a shallow and deep component.

Finally, we need to allow for the possibility that the three or more activation states are less categorical than they are depicted here—that they have fuzzy boundaries. However that may be, the effect of these states on language *is* categorical, and it is their linguistic effects that will concern us. Most of this chapter is devoted to the movement of ideas into and out of the fully active state. In later chapters, and especially chapters 7, 9, and 10, we will come to appreciate the relevance of semiactive information as well.

The Study of Prosody

The term *prosody* as used here embraces a variety of perceptual and physical properties of sound, including pitch, loudness, timing, voice quality, and the presence or absence of vocalization itself. In spite of ever-increasing research, the significant features and functions of prosody are still wide open to further exploration. Until roughly the second half of this century it was necessary to rely on the perceptual abilities of skilled investigators for prosodic observations. After World War II the sound spectrograph made it possible to observe the physical nature of pitch, loudness, and timing with considerable accuracy, but the labor involved in pitch measurements was arduous and time-consuming. More recently it has become much easier to make visual displays that open new worlds of observational possibilities. One way of dealing with this bonanza has been to approach prosody from the perspective of a phonetician, using displays of frequency, intensity, and duration as the primary data for understanding what language does with these aspects of sound. A well-known line of current research, for example, focuses on fundamental frequency for its primary data (e.g., Pierrehumbert 1980, Pierrehumbert and Beckman 1988), subsequently attempting to understand the semantic and discourse phenomena with which this one aspect of prosody is associated (e.g., Pierrehumbert and Hirschberg 1990).

The approach followed in this book developed out of a different tradition, in which the sounds of languages are transcribed in terms of perceived phenomena judged to express significant aspects of function and meaning. For this approach the breakthrough provided by current technology has been the ability to relate perceptual and physical observations. We perceive sounds in ways that do not fully correspond to their acoustic properties, but access to the latter can provide helpful insights into and correctives to our perceptual observations. As we try now to develop a better understanding of the flow of consciousness and language, prosody will be found to contribute in ways that cannot be ignored for spoken language or even, perhaps surprisingly, for written.

Intonation Units and Their Delimitation

Anyone who listens objectively to speech will quickly notice that it is not produced in a continuous, uninterrupted flow but in spurts. This quality of language is, among other things, a biological necessity. Because speech sounds are produced by expelling air from the lungs, the air must be periodically replaced if the speaker is to remain alive. It is remarkable that language and this obvious physiological requirement have evolved together in such a way that we are able to speak for long periods of time without getting out of breath. Eric Lenneberg once called attention to the fact that "breathing undergoes peculiar changes during speech. What is astonishing about this is that man can tolerate these modifications for an apparently unlimited period of time without experiencing respiratory distress.... I believe it is fair to say that we are endowed with special physiological adaptations which enable us to sustain speech driven by expired air" (Lenneberg 1967, pp. 80–81; see also Goldman Eisler 1968 on the relation between speech pauses and breathing). The need to breathe would alone produce the spurtlike quality of speech, but if one examines the linguistic and psychological nature of the spurts, it becomes clear that more is involved. Breathing would require nothing more than an interruption of vocalization at regular intervals. One finds, in fact, that this physiological requirement operates in happy synchrony with some basic functional segmentations of discourse.

These functionally relevant segments are not delimited by pauses alone, since pauses may occur within them, and although they are often separated by pauses, that is not always the case. From now on I will refer to these segments of language as *intonation units.* Various other names have been used for units of a similar, though not in all ways identical kind: *tone unit,* for example, by various British linguists, or *intonation group* (Cruttenden 1986), or *intonation(al) phrase* (Bing 1985; Pierrehumbert and Beckman 1988, where evidently it is the *intermediate phrase* that corresponds to the intonation unit here). There is also a correspondence between the intonation unit and what Dell Hymes (1981) calls a *line* (as in a line of poetry). Because these various other terms do not always delimit a unit that coincides consistently with the intonation unit as it is understood here, the use of a distinctive term is justified. Intonation units,

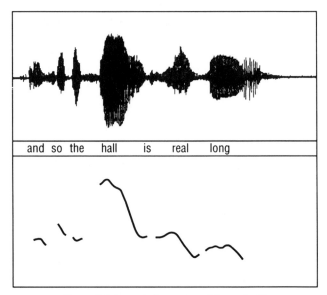

Figure 5.1 Acoustic Properties of Example (1)

for example, need not be limited to only one primary accent, as is arbitrarily required of such units in the British tradition (but cf. Ladd 1986).

Researchers are always pleased when the phenomena they are studying allow them to identify units. Units can be counted and their distributions analyzed, and they can provide handles on things that would otherwise be obscure. Unless all of us have been deceiving ourselves badly, language does make use of units of various kinds—vowels, consonants, and syllables, for example, or words and sentences, and now intonation units. It would be convenient if linguistic units could be identified unambiguously from phonetic properties: if, for example, phonemes could be recognized from spectrograms, or intonation units from tracings of pitch. For good or bad, however, the physical manifestations of psychologically relevant units are always going to be messy and inconsistent. If one breaks eggs into a frying pan, it may or may not be easy to tell where one egg leaves off and another begins. It may be similarly easy or difficult to read off the boundaries of intonation units directly from displays of acoustic data.

The features that characterize intonation units may involve any or all of the following: changes in fundamental frequency (perceived as pitch), changes in duration (perceived as the shortening or lengthening of syllables or words), changes in intensity (perceived as loudness), alternations of vocalization with silence (perceived as pausing), changes in voice quality of various kinds, and sometimes changes of turn. Figure 5.1 shows (above) the wave form and (below) the fundamental frequency of a well-defined intonation unit whose boundaries are confirmed in various of these ways. The relatively narrow transcription in (1) below attempts to capture certain acoustic properties that are relevant in the discussion that follows. Later, for practical reasons, I will fall back on a broader transcription system that will represent only those features that bear most directly on the topics discussed.

(1) .. and so the **háll** is rèal ló = ng%.
     ... (.36) [next intonation unit]

Preceding the vocalization is a very brief pause of about .07 second. Pauses of .10 second or less are transcribed simply with two dots. Following the vocalization and before the next intonation unit is a longer pause of .36 second, transcribed with three dots followed in parentheses by a measurement of the pause length (an accuracy to hundredths of a second is more than adequate). By convention, boundary pauses are shown at the beginning of each intonation unit. Among other things, then, (1) is set off by pauses.

One of the major cues to intonation unit boundaries is change in duration, captured in part by the notion of "anacrusis" (Cruttenden 1986, pp. 24, 39). Example (1) begins with a sequence of three rapid syllables (*and so the*) occupying roughly .10 second each, shown with smaller type. The transcription system employed in the rest of this work does not mark accelerated syllables in this way, but they will nevertheless play a role in the determination of intonation unit boundaries. After the first three words there are two words (*hall* and *real,* separated by a rapid *is*) whose duration lies in the range from about .20 to .30 second, a normal length for one-syllable words. The intonation unit ends with a word of extended length (*long*) occupying .43 second, the lengthening shown with an equals sign after the vowel. This pattern of acceleration-deceleration, proceeding from reduced-length syllables up to about .15 second, through normal-length syllables from about .15 second to about .35 second, to extended-length syllables longer than .35 second, is characteristic of many intonation units and may in some instances be the primary evidence for their delimitation. (Obviously these figures need to be adjusted for slower and faster speaking rates.)

When it comes to pitch, it happens that (1) coincides with a "declination unit" (Schuetze-Coburn, Shapley, and Weber 1991). There are three words with noticeably high pitch (*hall, real,* and *long*), each lower than the preceding (maxima of 299 hertz, 211 hertz, and 192 hertz respectively). As Schuetze-Coburn et al. show, such declination units often extend over several intonation units, but at least their beginnings and endings provide evidence for many intonation unit boundaries.

A more consistently present indicator is a terminal pitch contour of some kind at the end of each intonation unit. A variety of contours are observable in natural speech, where further study of their properties and functions is much needed. Example (1) ends with the familiar falling pitch contour associated with the end of a declarative sentence or a question-word question, transcribed here with a period. The terminal contours that are distinguished in transcriptions in this work include this falling pitch, a high rising pitch of the type associated with a yes-no question (transcribed with a question mark), and any other, nonterminal pitch contour (transcribed with a comma). These distinctions are adequate for our immediate purposes, but a better transcription system would replace the comma with markings of various more specific contours.

A particularly common change in voice quality is creaky voice (laryngealization or "fry"). It is conspicuous here at the end of the lengthened word *long,* where it is indicated with the percent sign. Intonation units often end and sometimes begin with creaky voice, which thus provides still another clue to their delimitation. Creaky voice may obscure acoustic displays of falling pitch contours, as is the case at the end of figure 5.1.

In summary, the identification of (1) as a coherent intonation unit is supported by a convergence of (a) the pauses preceding and following it, (b) the pattern of acceleration-deceleration, (c) the overall decline in pitch level, (d) the falling pitch contour at the end, and (e) the creaky voice at the end. These and other features are discussed and exemplified in more detail in Chafe (1992c).

Prominences

Besides perceiving speech as segmented into intonation units, we perceive certain elements within an intonation unit as more prominent than others. The acoustic correlates of prominence are also complex and variable. There are degrees of prominence, and there are several ways in which prominence may be realized. Here I arbitrarily use the term *accent* for prominences that are realized as pitch deviations from a mid or neutral baseline, usually a higher pitch but occasionally a lower one. I represent such pitch deviations with accent marks, regardless of whether they rise above or fall below the baseline. When one of these accented elements is also either loud or lengthened or both, I say that it has a *primary* accent and show it with an acute accent mark. A pitch deviation alone, without accompanying loudness or lengthening, is said to characterize a *secondary* accent, shown with a grave accent mark. Of course an element may be either loud or lengthened without a pitch deviation; in such cases I say only that it is loud or lengthened, but not that it is accented.

As an illustration of prominences, we can look again at the intonation unit cited in (1), repeated here (see again fig. 5.1).

(2) .. and so the **háll** is rèal ló = ng%.

Three of these words—*hall, real,* and *long*—are accented, all showing heightened pitch (with downstep). However, not only is *hall* higher pitched than the other two, it is also significantly louder, as indicated with boldface type. To anticipate the discussion in chapter 6, the exaggerated prominence of this word expresses its contrastiveness. The idea of this hall was introduced eight intonation units earlier, but in (2) the hall is contrasted with' the living room, the bedroom, and the bathroom, all introduced in the meantime. It is not unusual for contrastive elements to show exaggerated pitch deviation as well as exaggerated volume.

In the predicate of (2) the heaviest load is carried by the word *long,* which is both high pitched (before the fall) and lengthened. The intensifier *real* is high pitched but neither loud nor lengthened, and thus is said to carry a secondary accent. We find, then, three different manifestations of prominence in this intonation unit: the high-pitched and loud *hall,* the high-pitched and lengthened *long,* and the word *real* with high pitch only.

In this work, the prosodic features that are marked consistently in transcriptions include (a) pauses (marked by sequences of dots and sometimes, when relevant, by measured pause times); (b) terminal contours (marked with periods, question marks, and commas); and (c) accents (marked with acute and grave accent marks). Noted only occasionally, when relevant to the discussion, are changes in overall pitch level, accelerations and decelerations, and voice quality. All these features, however, enter into the segmentation of discourse into intonation units, indicated throughout by the placement of each such unit in a separate line.

Intonation Unit Sequences

The following conversational excerpt illustrates a few of the complications typical of intonation unit sequences. The notations (A), (B), and (C) identify different speakers. The preceding talk had been about a fatal accident that involved an elephant.

(3) a(A)   ... (0.4) Have the .. ánimals,
    b(A)   ... (0.1) ever attacked anyone ín a car?
    c(B)   ... (1.2) Well I
    d(B)   well Í hèard of an élephant,
    e(B)   .. that sát dówn on a V̀Ẃ one time.
    f(B)   ... (0.9) There's a gìr

g(B)   .. Did you éver hear thát?
h(C)   ... (0.1) No,
i(B)   ... (0.3) Some élephants and these
j(B)   ... (0.1) they
k(B)   ... (0.7) there
l(B)   these gáls were in a Vólkswagen,
m(B)   ... (0.4) and uh,
n(B)   ... (0.3) they uh kept hónkin' the hórn,
o(B)   ... (0.2) hóotin' the hóoter,
p(B)   ... (0.6) and uh,
q(B)   ... (0.4) and the .. élephant was in frónt of em,
r(B)   so= he jùst procèeded to sìt dòwn on the V̀Ẁ.
s(B)   ... (0.3) But thèy .. had .. mànaged to get óut first.

Noteworthy is the fact that (3)c, f, i, j, and k were truncated intonation units that never arrived at their terminal contours. One can also note that there was no pause separating the truncation in (3)c from the beginning of (3)d, or the truncation in (3)k from the beginning of (3)l. There was also no break between (3)q and (3)r, a segmentation dictated by a terminal pitch contour at the end of (3)q, a resetting of the pitch baseline at the beginning of (3)r, and a durational phenomenon the reverse of that observed in (2): the last five words of (3)q were accelerated, whereas the first word of (3)r was lengthened.

Segmenting speech into intonation units and identifying primary and secondary accents are skills that can only be learned with instruction and practice. (Useful guides are Cruttenden 1986, pp. 35–45 and Du Bois et al. 1992; see also Du Bois et al. 1993.) But nothing can substitute for hands-on practice with recordings of real language under the guidance of an experienced transcriber. Unfortunately these abilities, like the ability to record phonetic dictation of any kind, cannot be learned from a book. In a better world they would be as important a part of the training of a linguist as the ability to transcribe vowels and consonants.

The Function of Intonation Units

In spite of problematic cases, intonation units emerge from the stream of speech with a high degree of satisfying consistency, not just in English, but in all languages I have been able to observe and in fact in all styles of speaking, whether conversation, storytelling, oration, the performance of rituals, or even (or especially) reading aloud. That fact suggests that they play an important functional role in the production and comprehension of language. As we consider what that role might be, we can return to the notion of activation states. It is intuitively satisfying to suppose that each intonation unit verbalizes the information active in the speaker's mind at its onset. Let us hypothesize that an intonation unit verbalizes the speaker's focus of consciousness at that moment.

At the onset of an intonation unit, according to this view, often but not always following a pause, a certain small amount of information is active in the mind of the speaker. Typically, some of that information will have become active during the pause, though other parts of it are likely to have been activated previously. In chapter 9, we will meet a strong constraint on how much information can be newly activated at one time. It may be that all of the *information* to be verbalized in the upcoming intonation unit is active for the speaker at this onset point, but disfluencies show that people sometimes revise their choice of *wording* while an intonation unit is already in progress, as illustrated in (4):

(4) ... Her she has an enlàrged héart.

Evidently the speaker began to say *her heart,* but, for reasons considered in chapter 7, she quickly shifted to a different wording.

During these successive activations the minds of the speaker and the listener are necessarily out of phase. At the completion of an intonation unit the speaker must intend that a reasonable facsimile of his or her focus of consciousness will have become active in one or more other minds. It is through this dynamic process of successive activations, first for the speaker and then, through the utterance of an intonation unit, for the listener, that language is able to provide an imperfect bridge between one mind and another.

Types of Intonation Units

Viewed a little more closely, intonation units fall into several types. While many ways of categorizing them can be imagined, the following breakdown into three major types is useful because certain aspects of an analysis can be directed at one of these types to the exclusion of the others. We have already noticed that some intonation units are truncated or *fragmentary.* The successful units can be subcategorized into those that convey *substantive* ideas of events, states, or referents and those that have *regulatory* functions in the sense of regulating interaction or information flow. The distinction between substantive, regulatory, and fragmentary intonation units is illustrated in (5), which provided the context for (4):

(5) a(A) ... Well,   (regulatory)
    b(A) ísn't she hèalthy?   (substantive)

c(B)	.. Mhm,	(regulatory)
d(A)	... I mean she	(fragmentary)
e(A)	I knów she has	(fragmentary)
f(C)	More or léss.	(substantive)
g(A)	.. She has [something with her] gállbladder,	(substantive)
h(B)	[gállbladder and,]	(substantive)
i(B)	... héart tròuble and,	(substantive)
j(B)	[báck pròblems.]	(substantive)
k(A)	[She has héart] tròuble,	(substantive)
l(C)	... Her she has an enlàrged héart.	(substantive)

In a finer analysis, regulatory units can be subdivided further. Some regulate the development of the discourse, as when (5)a prepares for the contextually relevant question in (5)b. Others have to do with interaction between the participants, as when (5)c responds to the question in (5)b. Still others express the speaker's mental processes (as in expressions like *oh* or *let me see*), or judgment of the validity of the information being conveyed (like *maybe* or *I think*). Thus, regulatory units serve at least the following functions, whose boundaries are less categorical than this listing suggests:

textual   (e.g., *and then, well*)
interactional (e.g., *mhm, you know*)
cognitive   (e.g., *let me see, oh*)
validational   (e.g., *maybe, I think*)

Regulatory intonation units coincide to a large extent with the devices that have been discussed under the label *discourse markers* (Schiffrin 1987), which often constitute intonation units in themselves, though they may also be expressed as parts of larger units.

The Size of Intonation Units

A certain insight into consciousness and linguistic processing can be gained just from examining the size of intonation units. The simplest and most obvious measure is the number of words an intonation unit contains. Regulatory and substantive units differ significantly in this respect and for that reason are best measured separately. Fragmentary units can be ignored, since one can only guess how long such a unit would have been if it had been completed. To begin with *regulatory* intonation units, their mean length in the measured sample is 1.36 words, with a modal length of one. Thus the regulation of discourse flow, whether it functions textually, interactionally, cognitively, or validationally, is accomplished in very short segments of speech:

(6) So,
   Yeah.
   Hm.
   Sort of,

The mean length of *substantive* intonation units in the measured sample is 4.84, with a modal length of four. Apparently a focus of consciousness is typically expressed with four words of English.[1] It is important to realize that this figure is valid for English only; languages that pack more information into a word show fewer words per intonation unit, as discussed in chapter 12.

The word, it should be noted, is not a wholly satisfactory measure of information. Aside from the fact that different languages include different amounts of information in their words, both words and the morphemes of which they are composed express a variety of different types of information. In (7), for example, there is a sense in which the words *gal* and *Volkswagen* are more informative than the other words:

(7) these gáls were in a Vólkswagen,

Furthermore, there are many instances in which unitary ideas are expressed by sequences of words. In (8), for example, the two-word sequence *heart trouble* conveys one idea:

(8) She has héart tròuble,

It would thus be a mistake to assume that each word counts equally, or that the number of separate ideas verbalized in an intonation unit bears any simple relation to the number of words. Despite these reservations, it is a striking fact that the number of words in an intonation unit remains within a narrow range for any one language, reflecting in a gross way a strong constraint on the capacity of active consciousness.

Intonation Units and Clauses

Many substantive intonation units have the grammatical form of single clauses. Many others are parts of clauses, but the mean proportion of single-clause substantive intonation units in the measured sample is about

---

1. In earlier discussions of this topic I identified a modal length of five words. The discrepancy can be traced primarily to a more careful identification of intonation unit boundaries in more recent work, where more subtle criteria have increased the number of boundaries and thus reduced the unit size.

60 percent. It appears that speakers aim at verbalizing a focus of consciousness in the format of a clause, although for reasons explored in chapters 7 and 9 they are often forced to spread the clause across several intonation units.

A clausal intonation unit may assert the idea of an event or state. For example, (9) and (10) verbalize ideas of events, (11) the idea of a state:

(9) ... and these gàls were tàking píctures.
(10) .. but then your back gets swáy bàck.
(11) .. She has something with her gállblàdder,

In general, a state involves a situation or property that exists for a certain period without significant change, whereas an event typically involves a change during a perceptible interval of time. It is helpful to think of an event as something that *happens*—either something someone does (an action), as in (9), or something that happens to someone or something (a change of state), as in (10). A state, on the other hand, rather than happening, simply exists for a greater or lesser period of time, as in (11).

If we think of a typical substantive intonation unit as having the form of a clause, and if we think of a clause as verbalizing the idea of an event or state, we can conclude that each such idea is active, or occupies a focus of consciousness, for only a brief time, each being replaced by another idea at roughly one- to two-second intervals. Event and state ideas, in other words, are highly *transient* in active consciousness. They are constantly being replaced by other event and state ideas.

It can also be observed that each event or state idea is, by and large, activated only once within a particular discourse. This is not to say that the same idea cannot be reactivated; we will shortly notice ways in which that can happen. But transient and nonrepeated activation is the rule. It seems that the mind does not usually dwell on an event or state idea for more than a second or two. Any sample of ordinary speech will show a constant progression from one such idea to the next, of the sort illustrated by the sequence in (12):

(12) a(A) ... Cause I had a ... a thíck pátch of bárley there,   (state)
     b(B) ... mhm,   (regulatory)
     c(A) .. about the sìze of the .. kìtchen and líving
           room,   (state)
     d(A) ... and I went òver ít,   (event)
     e(A) .. and then,   (regulatory)
     f(A) ... when I got dóne,   (event)
     g(A) I had a little bit léft,   (state)
     h(A) .. so I tùrned aróund,   (event)

| i(A) | and I wènt and spràyed ìt twíce. | (event) |
| j(A) | .. and ìt's just as yèllow as ... can bé. | (state) |

This movement reflects our mental experience: "Thought is in constant change" (James 1890, 1:229). To some extent the continual replacement of event and state ideas reflects the world we live in, which is usually itself in flux. Even when that is not the case, however, consciousness continues to move from one such idea to another, and it seems impossible to keep it still. This restlessness forces us to keep sampling in small chunks the information available to us.

But there is another kind of idea that is more persistent. Each of these event or state ideas contains within it other, included ideas that can be said to be *participants* in the events or states. These participants are typically the ideas of people, objects, or abstractions, for which the term *referents* is appropriate. The state idea in (12)a includes as participants a referent verbalized as *I* (the idea of the speaker) and another verbalized as *a thick patch of barley.* The event idea in (12)d includes as participants these same two referents, verbalized this time as *I* and *it,* as also in (12)i. With a few exceptions such as *raining* and *being cold* (of the weather), things do not happen and states do not exist without the inclusion of referents who perform them, are affected by them, or participate in them in other ways. In English, referents are typically factored out from the events and states, to be verbalized as nouns and pronouns.

From this point on, in order to avoid the awkward phrases *event idea* and *state idea* I will often say simply *event* and *state.* It is important to keep in mind, however, that in this usage events, states, and referents are all ideas that exist in the minds of speakers and listeners. Whether or not they have correlates in the "real world" is irrelevant. I can (and do) think of the feats of Scarlett O'Hara as naturally as those of Marilyn Monroe. That only one of these referents ever existed in "reality" makes no difference to my thought or speech, at least with respect to the phenomena being discussed.

It is not unusual for an intonation unit to verbalize little or nothing more than a referent, as in intonation units a, c, f, i, and j of (13), originally presented as (3) above:

(13) a(A) ... (0.4) Have the .. ánimals,
     b(A) ... (0.1) ever attacked anyone ín a car?
     c(B) ... (1.2) Well I
     d(B) well Í hèard of an élephant,
     e(B) .. that sát dówn on a V̀Ẃ one time.
     f(B) ... (0.9) There's a gìr
     g(B) .. Did you éver hear thát?
     h(C) ... (0.1) No,

i(B) ... (0.3) Some élephants and these
j(B) ... (0.1) they
k(B) ... (0.7) there
l(B) these gáls were in a Vólkswagen,
m(B) ... (0.4) and uh,
n(B) ... (0.3) they uh kept hónkin' the hórn,
o(B) ... (0.2) hóotin' the hóoter,
p(B) ... (0.6) and uh,
q(B) ... (0.4) and the .. élephant was in frónt of em,
r(B) so = he jùst procèeded to sìt dòwn on the V̇Ẇ.
s(B) ... (0.3) But thèy .. had .. mànaged to get óut first.

Typically such *isolated referents* (expressed as so-called free NPs) are subsequently included as participants in events and states. But intonation units like these show that it is quite possible for speakers to focus on a referent alone.

Whereas events and states are activated transiently, many *referents* remain active for longer periods than any of the events or states in which they participate. For example, the idea of the speaker himself must have been active well before the sequence in (12) began, and it must have remained active well after that sequence ended. The idea of the *thick patch of barley* was activated in (12)a and remained active at least through (12)j. This is not to say that referents cannot be as transient as the events or states in which they participate. *The kitchen and living room* in (12)c provides one example of such a transient referent. Conversely, some events and states may remain active beyond a single intonation unit or may subsequently be reactivated. There are at least two ways in which the activation of an event or state may be made less transient than would normally be expected. Both ways are illustrated in the sequence in (13). Most obviously, the event verbalized in (13)n was *reverbalized* in (13)o. The speaker dwelt on the same event over the space of two intonation units, expressing it with different language. It is more frequently the case that an event or state persists by being converted into a referent—by being reified or *nominalized.* The event verbalized in the sequence (13)d–e was nominalized with the word *that* in (13)g. People are able to conceptualize events and states as if they had temporal persistence. Once an event or state has been given this derived status as a referent, it may then, like other referents, participate in and persist through a series of other events or states.

Later we will see the importance of recognizing that activated ideas do not immediately recede into the inactive state but remain for a time semiactive. For the moment, however, our major interest is in the fact that events and states are highly transient in fully active consciousness, each remaining for no more than a brief interval, whereas some but not all referents persist longer in the fully active state.

Summary and Prospects

Information in the mind may be in any one of at least three activation states: active, semiactive, or inactive. There may well be more activation states than these, and the boundaries between them may be less categorical than this division suggests.

Spoken language lends itself to segmentation into intonation units. Such units are identifiable on the basis of a variety of criteria, among which are pauses or breaks in timing, acceleration and deceleration, changes in overall pitch level, terminal pitch contours, and changes in voice quality. Intonation units are hypothesized to be the linguistic expression of information that is, at first, active in the consciousness of the speaker and then, by the utterance of the intonation unit, in the consciousness of the listener, or at least that is the speaker's intent. Intonation units may be substantive, regulatory, or fragmentary. Regulatory units tend to be one word long, while substantive units are fairly strongly constrained to a modal length of four words in English, a fact that suggests a cognitive constraint on how much information can be fully active in the mind at one time. Regulatory units tend to be simple particles, fragmentary units have no determinate structure, but the majority of substantive intonation units have the form of single clauses, though many others are parts of clauses.

Each clause verbalizes the idea of an event or state, and usually each intonation unit verbalizes a different event or state from the preceding, which is to say that events and states tend to be highly transient in consciousness. Most events and states include within them one or more referents—ideas of people, objects, or abstractions that participate in them. Many referents persist, remaining active through a series of intonation units, although some are transient, remaining active only during the activation of a single event or state. Conversely, events and states are sometimes converted into referents, or nominalized, a process that allows them to persist and appear as participants in other events or states.

Looking toward the future I would note that the properties of intonation units, both acoustic and perceptual, need to be more definitively established as part of a larger effort to relate physical sound to the perception of prosody. This is an ideal area in which to combine observations of natural speech with relevant experimental manipulations. The measurement of intonation units in terms of time, number of words, and grammatical composition will obviously benefit from access to more extensive and varied samples of speaking. Their classification into substantive, regulatory, and fragmentary intonation units can be elaborated and the bases of such classifications made more precise. Varying transitions between intonation units will be touched on in later chapters in terms of sentence-internal, sentence-external, and topic boundaries at various levels, but much more can be done in the way of relating strengths of intonation unit boundaries to the flow of consciousness. Finally, the relation of intonation units to clauses needs further study, both within and across languages.

6

Activation Cost

There is an intuitive plausibility in the notion that some of the information expressed in an intonation unit or clause is "new" while other information is "old." Because of the misleading connotations of the word *old,* the term *given* has often been used instead, but a different term does not in itself answer the questions that arise as soon as one tries to give more precise content to these words.

There is, for example, the question of the *domain* of newness or givenness. If someone said in a relevant context

(1) ~... I tàlked to a láwyer last nìght,

it might be supposed that the entire intonation unit expressed the idea of an event that was in some sense new within this discourse. In that sense the whole of (1) could be said to have conveyed new information. On the other hand, the distinction between new and given information can be applied independently to the referents that participate in events and states. Thus, the referent expressed by *I* might be thought to be information that was already given, because of the obvious presence of the speaker in the conversation, whereas that expressed by *a lawyer* might be thought to be new. This more local view of givenness and newness is appealing because it helps to explain why the idea of the lawyer was expressed in a full noun phrase with a primary accent, whereas the idea of the speaker was expressed in a pronoun with a weak accent. Examples like these suggest that language gives more prominence to new ideas than to given ones, prominence being recognizable in terms of full nouns (more prominent) versus pronouns (less prominent), and strong accent (more prominent) versus weak accent (less prominent).

This way of viewing things, however, still does not answer the question of just what is meant by new and given. In what sense was the idea of the lawyer new and that of the speaker given? An initial hypothesis might be that a new idea is an idea the speaker thought was previously unknown to the listener. Its newness could then be identified with its status as a new entry into the listener's mind, or at least the speaker's judgment that it had such a status. A given idea would then be one that the speaker thought was already known to the listener. The example in (1) fits such an interpretation, since the listener in this case could be assumed not to have known of the lawyer before he heard this intonation unit, whereas certainly he did already know of the person who was talking to him, the referent of *I*.

It is unfortunate, and has frequently led to misunderstandings, that the term *new* suggests the interpretation just described. One need not look far to find conflicting examples like the following:

(2) ... I tàlked to Lárry last night,

In the context in which this intonation unit actually occurred, the referent of the accented noun *Larry* was already as well known to the listener as to the speaker. The idea of this person was in no sense an idea that was being newly introduced into the listener's mind by this intonation unit, so it did not qualify as new information in the sense described above. Yet it was verbalized with a full noun with a primary accent, in contrast to (3):

(3) ~... I tálked to him last nìght,

where the referent of *him* had the same given status as that of *I*. There must then have been something else about the referent of *Larry* in (2) that would justify regarding it as new information and that led the speaker to express it with an accented noun.

It is ultimately impossible to understand the distinction between given and new information without taking consciousness into account (Chafe 1974, 1976). Once the distinction is viewed within the framework of active and inactive information set forth in chapter 5, it is easy to see that what is significant about the referent of *Larry* in (2) is not that the listener had no previous knowledge of this person, but that the idea of him was previously inactive and was activated at this point in the conversation by the speaker's utterance of (2). A more accurate characterization of *new* is thus *newly activated at this point in the conversation*. Conversely, *given* can be characterized as *already active at this point in the conversation*. We can add a third possibility to the distinctions just made by labeling information that has been activated from a previously *semiactive* state as *accessible*. Thus, we can recognize a three-way breakdown into given, accessible, and new information in place of the simple binary distinction of given versus new. The value of recognizing this third, accessible category will become clearer in later chapters.

Still some questions remain. Does *active* mean active for the speaker or the listener, for example, or for which of them at what moment? To focus first on the temporal aspects of givenness, accessibility, and newness, they can be visualized as shown in figure 6.1. Suppose that at a certain time, t_1, a particular idea is active, semiactive, or inactive. Suppose that at

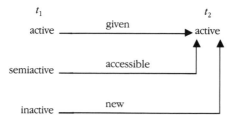

Figure 6.1 Activation States, Activation Costs, and Time

a later time, t_2, whatever its earlier state may have been, this idea is now active. If it was already active at t_1, we can say that at t_2 it is given information. If it was semiactive at t_1, it is accessible at t_2. If it was inactive at t_1, it is new at t_2. It is helpful to think of these three processes in terms of cognitive *cost*: given information is least costly in the transition from t_1 to t_2 because it was already active at t_1. Accessible information is somewhat more costly, and new information is the most costly of all, presumably because more mental effort is involved in converting an idea from the inactive to the active state. From now on, therefore, I will use the term *activation cost* to refer to the given-accessible-new distinction.

But there still remains the question of whether we are talking about processes in the mind of the speaker or in the mind of the listener, or both. Furthermore, just how do t_1 and t_2 relate to the timing of intonation units? I have tried to capture these additional considerations in figure 6.2, which relates the events in figure 6.1 to temporal and interactive factors involved in a typical intonation unit.

We can first think of these events from the point of view of the speaker. For that person, t_1 might coincide with pause onset time, and the events pictured in figure 6.2 might take place during the pause. At the end of the pause, all the ideas to be verbalized in the following intonation unit would be active for the speaker. From the speaker's point of view, then, an idea that was already active at the beginning of the pause would constitute given information; one that was semiactive, accessible information; and one that was inactive, new information. That is how these three activation costs might be characterized if we were concerned only with the speaker's own processes of activation.

But there are several problems with defining activation cost solely in these terms. For one thing, some intonation units are not preceded by pauses. If there is no pause, t_1 and t_2 are simultaneous. Perhaps an idea may change instantaneously from the inactive to the active state, but it is more satisfying to find at least a break in timing during which the change might have taken place. Furthermore, there is the very real possibility that a speaker might have activated an idea well before the pause onset, though

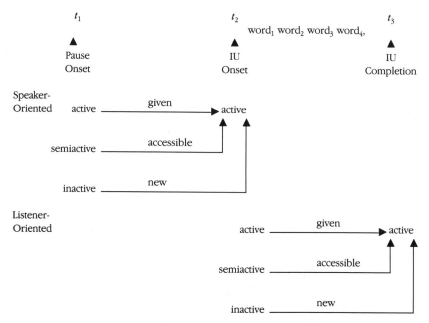

Figure 6.2 The Timing of Activation Costs with Relation to Speaker and Listener

he or she might nevertheless verbalize it as new information. We could not then say that it was an immediately preceding change from inactive to active in the speaker's mind that was responsible for newness.

At this point, therefore, it becomes more attractive to include the speaker's understanding of what is happening in the mind of the listener. This alternative timing is shown in the bottom right of figure 6.2. Here the speaker assumes that a particular idea is active, semiactive, or inactive in the listener's mind at t_2, the onset of the intonation unit. Activation cost is determined by what the speaker intends will take place in the listener's mind between t_2 and t_3, the completion of the intonation unit. The speaker assumes that hearing the intonation unit will either

(a) continue an idea that is already active for the listener, in which case the speaker will verbalize it as *given* information;
(b) activate an idea that was previously semiactive for the listener, in which case the speaker will verbalize it as *accessible* information; or
(c) activate an idea that was previously inactive for the listener, in which case the speaker will verbalize it as *new* information.

It would then have been the speaker's anticipation of the activation process in the listener's mind that determined the new status of *Larry* in example (2). And it would have been the assumed already-active status of the speaker referent in the listener's mind that determined the given status of the referent expressed as *I*.

I have just described two different perspectives on activation cost, the first dependent only on the speaker's consciousness and the second on the speaker's assessment of the listener's consciousness, but we may not need to choose categorically between them. Typically a speaker may assume that the processes in the listener's mind are in harmony with those in the speaker's own mind, allowing for the time lag occupied by the utterance of the intonation unit. In other words, the events pictured in the section of figure 6.2 labeled Speaker-Oriented are likely to be mirrored in the assumptions represented in the section labeled Listener-Oriented. In that case, so far as the speaker's production of language is concerned, there is no essential difference between, for example, a change from inactive to active in the speaker's mind during the pause and a predicted change from inactive to active in the listener's mind during the utterance of the intonation unit. Nevertheless, it must be the speaker's assessment of the listener's mental processing that takes priority if language is to perform its communicative function satisfactorily. We may all be familiar with cases in which someone said *he* or *she* under circumstances where we, as listeners, had no idea who the referent was, the speaker relying too much on his or her own mental processes and not enough on ours. Language works best when the expression of activation cost is listener-oriented.

The Expression of Activation Cost

With this understanding of the functional basis of activation cost, we can turn to the question of how givenness and newness are expressed. Accessible information tends to be expressed in more or less the same way as new, and discussion of its special characteristics is postponed to chapters 7 and 9. For the most part, both new and accessible information are expressed with accented full noun phrases, whereas given information is expressed in a more attenuated way. Often the attenuation takes the form of a weakly accented pronoun, as we saw in examples (1), (2), and (3). In some languages given information is likely to have no overt expression at all, as when the idea expressed in English as *I talked to Larry* might be expressed in Japanese as

(4) Lárry to   hanashita.
    Larry with talked

in a context where the role of the first-person referent was clear.

A given referent, however, is not *always* expressed with a weakly accented pronoun or ellipsis; sometimes it is expressed with a full, though still weakly accented noun:

(5) .. how did Jennifer reáct.

This question was asked in a context where the idea of Jennifer had been active during several preceding intonation units. Examples like this are easy to find in almost any extended conversation, and they more clearly raise the issue of why a speaker fails to use a pronoun—why this speaker failed to ask

(6) ~.. how did she reáct.

The context was one in which two women, Jennifer and Helen, were being discussed. The immediately preceding intonation units had dealt with the hospitalization of Helen, who was verbalized as *she* just prior to (5). Obviously, at the time of (5) there was competition for the pronoun *she*: two referents, both given, for whom it could be used. At this moment, however, *she* would have been more appropriate for Helen, since it had just been used for her. It is especially under such circumstances that a given referent is expressed with a full, though weakly accented noun.

While a new referent is usually expressed with a full noun or noun phrase, the more precise nature of the expression is determined by factors other than activation cost. For example, the difference between the "indefinite" phrase *a lawyer* in (1) above and the proper name *Larry* in (2) has to do with the nonidentifiability of the former and the identifiability of the latter, a matter to be discussed in chapter 8. Identifiable referents themselves may be expressed in different ways, depending on the listener's assumed familiarity with them (Prince 1981). Thus, the referent of *Larry* in (2) was assumed to be highly familiar to the listener, whereas that verbalized as *that Walter Simpson* in (11) below must have been less familiar. There has often been a tendency to confuse identifiability and familiarity with activation cost, a matter to which we will return in chapter 13.[1]

Contrastiveness

So far we have looked at examples in which given information was expressed with a weak accent, whether with a pronoun or a full noun, and one is tempted to conclude that it is the weak accent that is the most consistent manifestation of givenness. But there is one clear circumstance under which a given referent receives a primary accent and may even achieve a phonetic prominence exceeding that normally associated with

1. See Fox 1987 and Ariel 1988 for other ways of understanding these phenomena.

a primary accent. I refer to cases of *contrastiveness*. Take, for example, the following sequence excerpted from example (3) in chapter 5:

(7) a(A) ... Have the .. ánimals,
    b(A) .. ever attacked anyone ín a car?
    c(B) ... Well I
    d(B) well Í hèard of an élephant,
    e(B) .. that sát dówn on a V̂Ŵ one time.

Why did Speaker B assign a primary accent to the pronoun *I* in (7)d? The answer is clearly that the idea of the speaker himself was a contrastive one. The sequence (7)c–e began to answer the question posed by Speaker A in (7)a–b. There were two people present in this conversation who *might* have answered the question, and in (7)d Speaker B was contrasting himself with Speaker C, the other possible respondent. Even though the idea of himself was already active, and thus given, it received a primary accent because the speaker was selecting himself, rather than the other person, from the set of available candidates.

Contrastiveness is not at all uncommon in everyday language, and in fact it appears elsewhere in (7). The preposition *in* in (7)b received a primary accent because of a contrast with a tragic event discussed earlier in this conversation, an event in which someone had been trampled by an elephant *outside* a car. Here again there was a selection of one candidate rather than another from an available set. Prepositions, like personal pronouns, are typically weakly accented, but examples such as this show that words of any kind may be contrastively accented, as, indeed, may be parts of words: *I said morphéme, not morphíne.* Contrastiveness is often accompanied by affect, since a speaker who is expressing a contrast is likely to be emotionally involved in the assertion that it was X rather than Y. The result is that the heightened pitch and volume associated with a contrastive accent may be exaggerated beyond what would be normal for new information.

Contrastiveness is independent of activation cost. That is, a contrastive referent may be given, accessible, or new. The following sequence illustrates both contrastive-given and contrastive-new referents. Another speaker had just asked whether the person referred to as *she* had seen a doctor. The answer was

(8) a Well,
    b she wènt yésterday,
    c and the dóctor wasn't there,
    d but the physìcian's assístant ... lòoked at her.

The contrastive referent of *the doctor* was given, whereas the contrastive referent of *the physician's assistant* was new. In the sample examined, about 60 percent of the contrastive referents were given, about 30 percent accessible, and about 10 percent new.

I should perhaps mention at this point the term *focus,* which suffers from the same lack of precision that characterizes the term *topic* (see the end of chap. 8). There is certainly nothing wrong with saying that contrastive elements constitute a "focus of contrast." The interesting issue is whether the same term should also embrace answers to so-called WH questions, so that (9)b would also be said to constitute a focus:

(9) a .. Hòw mùch did the tágs còst you.
       b ... Fífty búcks.

The issue, of course, is whether contrastive elements and answers to WH questions have something significant in common. However that may be, the answer cannot lie in improbable constructed examples such as:

(10) ~~It was fífty búcks that they cost me.

For the time being I prefer to leave this question open, and to avoid any commitment to *focus* as a term.

The Establishment of Givenness

To return to activation cost, we have considered both its functional basis and its linguistic expression. We have not, however, considered all the ways in which the givenness of an idea may be established. In what may be regarded as the most typical case, an idea is first introduced into a discourse as new information and then remains given for a certain period of time, as in (11) with the referent that was introduced as *Walter Simpson* and then repeatedly verbalized as *he* (*Cats* refers to Caterpillar tractors):

(11) a Well,
       b then he talked to that ... Wàlter Símpson and,
       c ... he knóws Càts.
       d .. He used to hàve a Cát,
       e right now he works on ... Dètroit éngines.
       f .. As a spécialty,
       g but,
       h ... he stìll knows quite a lot about thése.
       i And,
       j ... he uh,
       k ... said,

This example illustrates a common scenario, but it is of course not necessary that ideas be activated solely through the use of language. In any normal context of language use there will be certain ideas that are active for nonlinguistic reasons. Most obvious is the usually active status of the ideas of the speaker and listener. Typically, during much of a conversation each of the participants is actively conscious of the other(s) as well as of himself or herself. References to first and second persons will thus typically be given, and verbalized with weakly accented pronouns like the *I* and *you* in (12):

(12) a(A) I òrdered a thóusand búsiness càrds.
     b(B) .. Yéah?
     c(B) .. You get em prìnted hére?

So far as third-person referents are concerned, the environment may contain people or objects in addition to the speaker and listener which for one reason or another have come to be in the active consciousness of the participants. Their salient presence will in one way or another have brought them into the focal consciousness of the interlocutors. For example, the person identified as Speaker A in the above example said,

(13) ... You sée that?

when he had just taken a business card out of his pocket and was showing it to the listener. He was able to assume that the referent of *that* was in the focus of the other's attention because he had just placed it before that person's eyes; hence he treated it as given information. Other origins of givenness were discussed in Chafe (1974, pp. 122–27).

There remains the question of how long a referent, once having acquired this given status, will retain it. No simple answer is possible, because it is up to the participants in a conversation to decide whether they will keep a referent active by repeatedly refreshing it throughout a sequence of intonation units, or whether, at the other extreme, they will let it recede from the active state after a single, glancing mention. What speakers do depends on the role of the referent in the topic under discussion. One thing that is clear, however, is that the number of different referents that can be active at the same time is very small, and that any referent, unless it is refreshed, will quickly leave the active state. Perhaps there is a stateable limit on the number of referents that can be fully active at one time, but it remains to be discovered.

I may have come close to implying that activation cost is a notion that applies only to referents: ideas of people, objects, and abstractions. That is clearly not true, but at the same time it is true that referents provide particularly good examples of activation cost. That is because such ideas are likely to persist in active consciousness through at least several intonation units, as discussed in chapter 5. Ideas of events and states, on the

other hand, are usually transient. Each such idea constitutes new information when it is introduced, but then, instead of being maintained in the
active state, recedes into the semiactive state as it is replaced in the next
intonation unit by the idea of another event or state. One or more referents usually remain active through such a sequence, but the events and
states in which they participate come and go in active consciousness in
quick succession.

The following, already familiar example illustrates the treatment of an
event as given information:

(14) a ... Have the .. ánimals,
     b .. ever attacked anyone ín a car?

The preceding talk had dealt with an attack by an elephant and the need
to remain inside one's car on a game preserve. From the fact that the
speaker uttered the word *attacked* with a weak accent in (14)b, it is
apparent that she judged that idea to be still active in the consciousness
of her listeners.

We have considered activation cost with respect to referents, events,
and states in verbalizing given, accessible, and new information. The use
of a strong or weak accent, as well as (usually) the choice between a noun
or a pronoun, was seen to hang on the given-new distinction. What then
of other parts of speech? We saw briefly that prepositions can, in the right
context, be contrastive, as can words of any kind. But can words of any
kind express ideas that can be given, accessible, or new? Apparently not.
Apparently it is only referents, events, and states that can function as domains of activation cost, as will be shown more clearly in chapter 9. I
therefore limit the term *idea,* as a technical term, to items of information
that have this property. Ideas, then, can be subcategorized into referents
(typically expressed in noun phrases and pronouns), and events and states
(typically expressed in verbs and adjectives). We will meet one other kind
of idea, the discourse topic, in chapter 10. Ideas are associated with what
have often been called *content words.* Non-idea information has such
functions as the specification of relations between ideas, as with conjunc-
tions or prepositions, or the inflectional or quantificational modification
of an idea, as with modals, negators, evidentials, intensifiers, articles, numerals, and so on. Words that express such non-idea information are often
called *function words.* This familiar distinction is useful here because, to
repeat, it is content words only that are associated with activation cost.

Summary and Prospects

We have seen that ideas of referents, events, and states, having previously
been active, semiactive, or inactive, may at a particular point in a discourse

either remain active or become active. This process underlies what is usually thought of as the distinction between given and new information, or what I am calling activation cost. I have added a third category of *accessible* information whose importance will be clarified in chapters to follow. Activation cost is determined primarily by the speaker's assessment of changing activation states in the mind of the listener. Given information is typically verbalized in English with a weakly accented pronoun, new and accessible information with an accented noun or noun phrase. There are various exceptions to this pattern, one of the most common of which is the occurrence of *contrastive* information, crosscutting the given-accessible-new dimension. Givenness may be established either linguistically or extralinguistically. It applies to referents but may also apply to events and states, although activation of the latter is usually more transient. Those elements that exact an activation cost will be called *ideas*. They are associated with so-called content words and pronouns. Other elements of language, especially those expressed by function words, remain outside the domain of activation and hence are irrelevant so far as activation cost is concerned.

The effect of activation cost on such linguistic phenomena as pronominalization versus the use of a full noun phrase needs further investigation within and across languages, and the same can be said for identifying the ways in which activation cost is established, both linguistically and extralinguistically. The most interesting questions here may involve the establishment and expression of accessible information, but that is a topic more easily elaborated in the next chapter.

7

Starting Points, Subjects, and the Light Subject Constraint

In chapter 5 we saw that ideas of events and states are typically expressed by means of clauses, which may occupy a single intonation unit or be spread out across several intonation units. In chapter 6 we saw that it is possible to distinguish the activation cost of the clause as a whole, which usually expresses new information, from the activation cost of its parts, which may express information that is either given, accessible, or new. We come now to another feature of the clause and its parts: the attribution of a uniquely special status to one of its referents by setting it apart from whatever other referents the clause may contain, the status of grammatical *subject*.

The English language, like some but by no means all other languages, has various manifestations of subjecthood. They are well known, and I will illustrate them only briefly with the following example, where the pronoun *I* is in the subject role:

(1) I'm thirsty.

For one thing, subjects appear in the nominative case. English marks cases only in a few pronouns, but in this example subject status is signaled by the use of *I* rather than *me*. Second, to a limited extent English verbs agree with the person and number of their subjects. The verb *be* shows this agreement more than other verbs, and in (1) we have a contraction of *am*, showing first-person singular agreement, rather than *are*, which would be appropriate with second-person or plural subjects, or *is*, which would be appropriate with third-person singular subjects. Third, in declarative sentences the subject usually appears before the verb. There are other, less immediately obvious kinds of evidence for subjecthood, all of which converge on what appears to be a highly distinctive constituent of an English clause (see, for example, Keenan 1976; Cole et al. 1980; Comrie 1989, pp. 104–23).

Subjects as the Expression of Starting Points

One might expect that a grammatical role as distinctive as subject would have an important functional role. Why would a language set certain referents apart in this way unless they did some important work? When Otto Jespersen asked this question in *The Philosophy of Grammar* (Jespersen 1924, p. 246), he quoted an answer that had been offered by the psychologist G. F. Stout, whose somewhat scattered statement Jespersen found to be useless. Nevertheless, Stout came up with one suggestion that was, I believe, correct: "The subject," he said, "is that product of previous thinking which forms the immediate basis and starting-point of further development." It is this notion that a subject expresses a *starting point* that I will amplify here. Clauses do not express a random collection of independent events or states, floating in the air like so many disconnected bubbles. Rather, each has a point of departure, a referent from which it moves on to provide its own new contribution. It is this starting point referent that appears grammatically as the clause's subject. In Chafe (1976, pp. 43–45) I used the metaphor of a *hitching post,* characterizing the subject referent as the one to which a new contribution is *attached.* Both metaphors have some value, but the more dynamic image suggested by a starting point is especially compatible with the metaphor of flow (cf. Sapir 1921, p. 93).

Sometimes we are helped in understanding a functional role when we encounter an example in which it appears to have been violated. I recently noticed the following sentence in a theater program:

(2) David Merrick was the producer of the original Broadway Production.

The sentence struck me at first as odd, because *David Merrick* seemed not to be a proper starting point. The idea of this person functioned, rather, as the heart of the new information the sentence provided. The fact that there existed a *producer of the original Broadway Production* might have been inferred from what one already knew about this play, and might thus have provided a more appropriate point of departure:

(3) ~The producer of the original Broadway Production was David Merrick.

David Merrick as the starting point in (2) seemed infelicitous because it ignored the role that subjects are tacitly understood to play. Lest the writer be judged unfairly, I should add that the context provided a motivation for this usage. The sentence in (2) appeared on the program under the heading *Thank You,* below which appeared *A very special thank you to Tim Blasby,* with other names following. *David Merrick* then functioned as another name in this list, one more person to be thanked. In that context his use as a starting point was not inappropriate, illustrating the fact that the starting point role can be manipulated for special effects, some of which are more easily achieved in writing than in speaking. (The same usage can be observed in the acknowledgments of this book.)

Sources of Confusion

Understanding the starting point role of subjects can be hampered by the quality of relevant data. If this role is determined by the flow of discourse, constructed sentences are no help. Nevertheless, subjects are frequently discussed in terms of constructed sentences that would be produced only under the most bizarre circumstances, if one could imagine them being produced at all:

(4) ~~The farmer kills the duckling.
(5) ~~A girl saw John.

The occurrence in conversational language of a full noun phrase subject like *the farmer* or *a girl,* especially when it expresses new information, is rare, as we will see. The unnaturalness of so much of the data that have been used in discussing subjects and related matters makes the discussions difficult to follow if one has observed subjects in natural discourse. Unnatural data predominate in psychological experiments as well. A useful summary of the latter was provided by Brian MacWhinney (1977), who preferred to associate starting points, not with subjects, but with "the first element in the English sentence" (see the discussion of Halliday's *themes* in chap. 13). While experiments may very well throw additional light on the nature of starting points, they too need a background of natural discourse for their interpretation.

Another problem has been the tendency to obscure the role of subjects by comparing them with the notions of "topic" or "what a sentence is about" (e.g., Gundel 1988, Reinhart 1982; see again chap. 13). The term *topic* (as distinct from *discourse topic*; see chap. 10) can be perhaps most usefully applied to a different phenomenon that is characteristic of Asian languages, but its contribution to an understanding of English has been far from clear. A spurious argument might be constructed as follows. In the following sentence, *bagels* is the topic:

(6) ~Bágels I líke.

Since the subject *I* is not the topic, subjecthood must not be an expression of topichood, but must rather be a purely syntactic phenomenon. If, however, such a sentence could be imagined in actual use, in all likelihood the first-person referent would be seen to function as a contextually relevant starting point, with the *bagels* "preposed" to heighten their contrastiveness, presumably with other foods that I don't like (but see Ward 1988 for a more inclusive discussion of this phenomenon).

Finally, when any functional role has been grammaticized, as the starting point role has been grammaticized in subjecthood, one can always expect to find cases where its function has been obscured. It is in the nature of grammaticization to extend functional instances to nonfunctional ones, and indeed that development can itself be seen as functional, since prepackaged constructions may simplify the act of speaking (Mithun 1989). Before we focus our attention in the rest of this chapter on functional subjects, therefore, we need at least to recognize the existence of subjects that are nonfunctional, if only to be able to ignore them in what follows. As an example, because English uses subjects so pervasively, it forces the presence of a subject even when a state or event has no referents that function as participants at all. Included here are the *ambient* states and events that suffuse the entire environment. By definition they are not restricted to the participation of any referent (Chafe 1970, pp. 101–2). Examples are the well-known weather expressions:

(7) It's réally hót.
(8) It's ráining out.

The *it* is there because English finds it impossible to get along without a subject even when no starting point is available to fill that role. Leaving special cases like these aside, we can turn to subjects as starting points.

Subjects, Activation Cost, and a First Pass at the Light Subject Constraint

If subjects express starting points, we might expect their referents to be given. It makes sense that one would employ as a starting point a referent that is already active in the discourse. And indeed one of the most striking properties of subjects in conversational language is the fact that such a high proportion of them do express given information. In the sample examined, 81 percent of the subjects were of this type, as in:

(9) ... I tàlked to Lárry last nìght,
(10) she wènt yésterday,
(11) .. how did Jennifer reáct.

Ninety-eight percent of these given subjects were, in fact, pronouns. The strategy I will follow in the rest of this chapter will be to explore the hypothesis that subjects conform to what I call the *light subject constraint*.[1] An informal way of stating this constraint would be to say that subjects carry a light information load, as is appropriate for starting points. Precisely what is meant by the term *light* will emerge as we proceed. But suppose we try at first to equate lightness with givenness. As we have just

1. It would be more accurate to speak of the *light starting point* constraint, but the term chosen here may be more effective rhetorically.

seen, that equation is to a large extent valid, but has some exceptions. A minority of functional subjects, 19 percent of them in this sample, do *not* express given information. We need, then, to see whether there are motivated ways of broadening the definition of *light* to include this other 19 percent.

Accessible Subjects

The first step, and by far the most important one, is to broaden the definition of *light* to include information that is accessible. That is, we can say that starting points may constitute either given or accessible information, but not new information. While it remains true that 81 percent of the subjects in the sample that was examined expressed given information, we can now also accept the fact that 16 percent of them expressed accessible information. There is a strong preference for starting points that are given, but accessible starting points are not rare. It is time, then, to take a closer look at accessibility.

Accessible information is usually expressed in the same way as new information, that is, by accented nouns or noun phrases. Often such words show a secondary rather than a primary accent, but aside from the fact that discriminating primary and secondary accents is not always straightforward, an accent difference between accessible and new information cannot always be depended on. If there is no foolproof way to distinguish accessible from new information in terms of prosody, a discourse analyst needs other ways of deciding which of these two statuses a referent has. A useful procedure is to take account of the factors that establish accessibility and ask, in the case of a particular referent, whether one of those factors is operative. There appear to be three possible reasons why an activated referent may be in the semiactive rather than the inactive state and thus be accessible rather than new. It may be a referent that (a) was active at an earlier time in the discourse, (b) is directly associated with an idea that is or was active in the discourse, or (c) is associated with the nonlinguistic environment of the conversation and has for that reason been peripherally active but not directly focused on.

The first of these grounds for accessibility is by far the most common. It is illustrated by the subjects of the following clauses:

(12) and my párents are going to be próud of me,
(13) Jénnifer thinks she's got a kídney inféction.

The referents of *my parents* and *Jennifer* were active at earlier points in these conversations. When they stopped being active, they did not then become fully inactive but receded into the semiactive state. They were then reactivated from that state in (12) and (13), and it is in that sense that, within those intonation units, they can be called accessible rather than new.

Less often, a referent may be accessible because it is directly associated with information that is or was fully active:

(14) but then your báck's .. gets swáy bàck.

The idea expressed by *your back* in (14) had not been specifically mentioned in the preceding discourse, but since the talk had been about backaches, backs were "in the air." The role of such associations in establishing accessibility needs more thorough investigation, and its limits need to be established, but it is clear that some instances of accessibility do arise in this way (Chafe 1993).

Finally, a referent may be accessible because it is the idea of something that is present in the environment, though it has not yet been directly focused on. Such a referent has been in semiactive consciousness for a nonlinguistic reason:

(15) Well the kìd's asléep,

This was said when *the kid,* a baby, had been lying in the speaker's arms during most of the conversation. Although the speaker had addressed a few passing remarks to her during the conversation, he had not previously referred to her. Obviously the idea of her was semiactive throughout the conversation and was thus easily employed as a starting point in (15).

It is interesting to observe that first-person referents, which might be thought active throughout a conversation and therefore always given, are sometimes judged by a speaker to have receded into the listener's semiactive state and are thus treated as accessible rather than given. Such cases are recognizable from the occurrence of accented *I* under circumstances where contrastiveness is ruled out. The following are examples:

(16) Í got to go have a tálk with em.
(17) Í'll tell Bíll.

In both these examples the speakers were evidently bringing the ideas of themselves back into the active consciousness of the listeners, following a period in which they judged that thought of them had become semiactive while active consciousness was focused on other matters.

We have now accounted for the activation cost of 97 percent of the subjects in this sample, characterizing their adherence to the light subject constraint in terms of ideas that were either given or accessible. If the figure were 100 percent, we could simply equate *light* with *not new*. Most subjects, we could say, express given referents, but a minority of them express accessible referents. This conclusion would be compatible with the hypothesis that subjects express starting points, for we might expect starting points not to be new. It is rewarding at this point to ask what characterizes the small number of exceptions to such a strong trend. As we turn to subjects that express new information, it is useful to digress for a moment in order to recognize another relevant property that referents can have.

Referential Importance

Independent of their activation cost, referents differ in their degree of what I will call *referential importance*—their importance to the subject matter being verbalized. I know of no better way to introduce the topic of referential importance than to summarize a story told in Indonesian.[2] It concerns a certain Malin Kundang, who was the son of a poor widow. Malin Kundang left home while he was still young, and eventually he became a successful merchant and married a beautiful princess. One day, while on a business trip, he and his wife landed their ship back at the island where his mother lived. His mother learned that he was there, came aboard the ship, and tried to get his attention. But Malin Kundang had told his wife that he came from a rich family. Pretending not to know this poor woman, he ordered a servant to give her some money and send her on her way. In the end, as punishment for his unacceptable behavior toward his mother, both he and his ship were turned to stone.

Intuitively, one can divide the characters in this story into three types. First there is the protagonist Malin Kundang, around whom the entire story is centered. Second there are his mother and his wife. Although subsidiary to Malin Kundang, they play important roles in the plot. Third there are incidental characters like the servant who is told to get rid of the mother. Such characters appear only briefly to perform a single, limited function. For reasons such as these we may speak of referents as having *primary* importance (Malin Kundang), *secondary* importance (the mother and the wife), and *trivial* importance (the servant).

There is interesting linguistic evidence in support of this three-way distinction (cf. Hopper 1986, pp. 319–20). The mother and her son are introduced at the beginning of the story as follows:

(18) a Pada jaman dahulu,
      at   time   in the past

   b di daerah Sumatra Barat,
     in region Sumatra West

---

2. The narrator was Catherine Wuritomo, the consultant in a linguistic field methods course at the State University of New York at Albany.

c hiduplah   seorang   janda,
  there lived   one person   widow

d dengan   seorang   anaknya   lakilaki.
  with   one person   her child   male

e Namanya   Malin   Kundang.
  His name   Malin   Kundang

Both Malin Kundang, the primary character, and his mother, a secondary character, are introduced with a classifier in the expression *seorang* 'one person.' Although they are linguistically alike in this respect, only the primary character is given a name, and he remains the only person throughout the story to have a name. The other secondary character, his wife, is introduced as follows:

(19) Kemudian   Malin   Kundang   menikah   dengan   seorang   putri,
     and then   Malin   Kundang   married   with   one person   princess

Like the mother, the princess is introduced with the classifier *seorang,* but she too fails to be given a name. The servant appears in the story as follows:

(20) a tetapi   Malin   Kundang   berkata   kepada   pembantunya,
       but   Malin   Kundang   said   to   his servant

   b berikan   kepadanya   uang,
     give   to her   money

Not only does he have no name, but he fails even to be introduced with a classifier. In short, the three levels of importance are verbalized in three distinct ways on the first introduction of a referent:

	Name	Classifier
Primary importance	+	+
Secondary importance	−	+
Trivial importance	−	−

Degrees of importance are not always as clearly represented as this, and the linguistic evidence for them may not be as systematic outside of a well-established narrative tradition. Probably the simplest indication of the importance of a referent during a segment of conversation is its frequency of mention. People seem to have a strong sense of ranking in this regard. Suzanne Wright and Talmy Givón (1987) found a high level of agreement among judges who were asked to rank-order referents in a discourse in terms of their importance.

Subjects That Express New but Trivial Information

With this understanding of degrees of referential importance, we can return to the question of subjects that express new information. An examination of such subjects shows that all of them, in addition to expressing new information, also express referents that are trivial. In other words, speakers do not use as starting points new referents that they expect will play any continuing role in the discourse to follow. Beyond their triviality, new subjects fall into several subclasses. I describe here those that have emerged from the sample examined. It is quite possible that further data will shed light on other circumstances under which new but trivial subjects can appear.

One clear use of new referents in the subject role is as sources of quoted information, typically as the subjects of verbs like *tell* and *say*:

(21) a But Dòctor Gílbert tòld me,

b that éverybody gets bàckaches.

(22) a ... Bìll Jóhnson said nó,

b .. just chèck your injéctor.

The referents verbalized as *Doctor Gilbert* and *Bill Johnson* constituted new information, but these were their only mentions and in each case it was the quoted information rather than its source that was important: the fact that everybody gets backaches or that the person addressed should check his injector. The phrases *Dr. Gilbert told me* and *Bill Johnson said* functioned only to mark the source of "hearsay" information. Thus, the term *light* can be extended to include referents that are sources of information, but trivial in the discourse.

In the following examples the new subjects occurred in parallel with a preceding referent with which they contrasted: *the physician's assistant* in (23)c contrasted with *the doctor,* and *only the educated* in (24)h contrasted with *a lot of people* back east.

(23) a Well,

b she wènt yésterday,

c and the dóctor wasn't there,

d but the physìcian's assístant ... lòoked at her.

(24) a it's not like a màjor indústrial town,

b back éast,

c .. where there are a lòt of people who are póor.

d .. Yeah,

e .. ríght.

f ... (4.1) No,

g ónly the é

h ónly the éducated are pòor in Seáttle.

Again, both of these new subject referents were of trivial importance; there was no more talk about the physician's assistant or the educated. Each, furthermore, was dropped by way of contrast into an already established frame. We can extend the term *light* to include such cases of parallel contrast as well.

There are a few cases in which a new subject is used to express surprise. In the following example the speaker had just voiced his suspicion that a certain woman, known to both him and the listener, had acquired a new boyfriend. At a time when he had been doing some work near the woman's house, he had observed an event that he related as follows:

(25) a ... Then one afternóon,

   b ... this ván pulls ìn thère,

The referent of the new subject *this van* was, like the others discussed above, trivial. Its use as a new subject conveyed iconically the surprise the speaker had felt when the van appeared. In effect, he expressed his surprise through the surprising placement of a new, though trivial referent in the subject role.

A Final Pass at the Light Subject Constraint

If we take into account both activation cost and importance, a particular referent at a particular time may be either given, accessible, or new with respect to activation cost, and it may also be of primary, secondary, or trivial importance. Combinations of activation cost values with importance values are limited by the fact that trivial referents cannot be either given or accessible, since they do not reappear in a discourse after their first and only mention. In other words, trivial referents are necessarily new. If we look at the distribution of these properties among subjects, it appears that the light subject constraint should be expressed in terms of two alternatives: a subject expresses a referent that is (a) given or accessible (i.e., not new), or (b) new but trivial. These two possibilities define *lightness*. A *heavy* referent is thus one that is new and of more than trivial importance. The light subject hypothesis says that heavy referents do not occur in conversational language as starting points; they are not verbalized as subjects.

We have dealt now with three dimensions on which referents may contextually vary. The dimension of *cost* (given, accessible, new) reflects the expenditure of mental energy as ideas are activated. The dimension of *referential importance* (primary, secondary, trivial) reflects the degree of participation of a referent within a stretch of discourse. The dimension of *weight* (light, heavy) is a product of both cost and importance. In conversational language subjects are usually but not always given, but they are always light. That fact accords well with their role as the expression of starting points.

Summary and Prospects

This chapter suggested that the function of a grammatical subject is to express a starting point to which other information is added. Several sources of confusion regarding subjects were noted: the use of questionable data, the confusion of subjects with topics (whatever they might be), and the existence of nonfunctional subjects such as those used in the expression of ambient events and states. Subjects are hypothesized to be governed by the light subject constraint. To understand this constraint it is necessary to understand lightness, first, in terms of either givenness or accessibility. Accessibility may be established either through prior activation in the discourse or through direct association with something activated in the discourse or with something present in the environment. It is also necessary to recognize a dimension of referential importance, including at least three degrees of importance that are relevant to the form that language takes. Ultimately the definition of *light* can be stated as either (a) not new, or (b) new and of trivial importance. We saw that in the few cases where subjects express new but trivial information they fall into one of several recognizable subtypes, including their use as information sources, as parallel contrasts, and as surprises. The fact that only light referents are expressed as subjects accords well with the view that subjects express starting points.

There is a need to work through extensive and varied corpora, characterizing subjects in terms of activation cost and importance, with the aim of specifying more precisely the nature of these properties and of the light subject constraint. Special attention needs to be paid to the conditions under which new but trivial referents may be employed as starting points. Not all languages have grammaticized the starting point role, as we will see in chapter 12, and it will be a large task of broad significance to sort out the discourse properties of those that do from the properties of those that don't.

8

Identifiability and "Definiteness"

Independent of both activation cost and starting points, but interacting with them in interesting ways, is another discourse property of referents that can be termed *identifiability*. To put it simply, an identifiable referent is one the speaker assumes the listener will be able to identify. If that statement seems straightforward enough, when identifiability is examined in detail it reveals some intriguing complexities. In the English language and some others, identifiability is often though by no means always associated with the use of the definite article. The literature on so-called definiteness is extensive. A small sampling might include Christophersen (1939), Karttunen (1968), Chafe (1972, 1976), Clark and Marshall (1981), Clark, Schreuder, and Buttrick (1983), Hawkins (1978), Du Bois (1980), Heim (1982), and Chesterman (1991), not to mention the philosophical literature on "definite descriptions." These authors and others have cataloged a variety of circumstances under which the English definite article is used and have explained its use in various ways. It remains here to integrate definiteness into a coherent picture of identifiability and the flow of conscious experience.

As an initial illustration of what has often seemed the most typical manifestation of identifiability and its effects, we can return once more to the passage cited in chapter 5:

(1) a(A)   ... Have the .. ánimals,
      b(A)   .. ever attacked anyone ín a car?
      c(B)   ... Well I
      d(B)   well Í hèard of an élephant,
      e(B)   .. that sát dówn on a V̇W̊ one time.
      f(B)   ... There's a gìr
      g(B)   .. Did you éver hear thát?
      h(C)   ... No,
      i(B)   ... Some élephants and these
      j(B)   ... they
      k(B)   ... there
      l(B)   these gáls were in a Vólkswagen,
      m(B)   ... and uh,
      n(B)   ... they uh kept hónkin' the hórn,

o(B) ... hóotin' the hóoter,

p(B) ... and uh,

q(B) ... and the .. élephant was in frónt of em,

r(B) so he jùst procèeded to sìt dòwn on the V̀Ẁ.

s(B) ... But thèy .. had .. mànaged to get óut first.

Two of the referents in this passage illustrate the typical pattern. One is the idea of the elephant introduced in (1)d, at that point *nonidentifiable* and expressed with the indefinite noun phrase *an elephant*. When the same referent then reappeared in (1)q, it was *identifiable* and expressed with a definite noun phrase. Parallel things can be said about the idea of the Volkswagen, first introduced as nonidentifiable with the phrase *a Volkswagen* in (1)l and then expressed as identifiable with the phrase *the VW* in (1)r.

Examined more closely, identifiability can be seen to have three components. An identifiable referent is one that is (a) assumed to be already shared, directly or indirectly, by the listener; (b) verbalized in a sufficiently identifying way; and (c) contextually salient. Initial discussion of these components can focus on the idea expressed as *the elephant* in (1)q.

First of all, the idea of this elephant was at this point shared by the speaker with his listeners, into whose knowledge it had been introduced by (1)d. Suppose that the *s*'s in figure 8.1a represent all the referents the speaker assumed were shared at this point in the conversation, and that this referent was one of them. The sharing alone was obviously not enough to make it identifiable. Second, then, this referent was verbalized with the word *elephant* to locate it as an instance of a category. The smaller box in figure 8.1b encloses shared referents that are instances of the category verbalized with the word *elephant,* as I have suggested by replacing the *s*'s with *e*'s. But being an instance of that category was still not enough to make the referent identifiable, since the interlocutors in fact shared knowledge of several elephants. Finally, therefore, it was necessary that the idea of this particular elephant was contextually the most salient instance for these interlocutors at this time. In this case it had been activated six substantive intonation units earlier and was a salient element in the topic being discussed. The capital *E* in figure 8.1c is meant to suggest the contextual salience of this particular instance of the elephant category as compared with others. We can now look at each of these components of identifiability in more detail.

Sharedness

In chapter 6 we saw that a *new* idea should not be defined as one that is being introduced into the listener's knowledge for the first time, that it

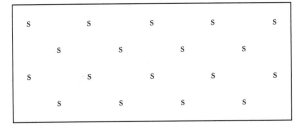

(a) Shared Referents

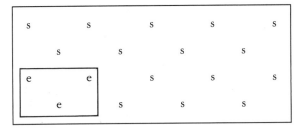

(b) Categorized Referents

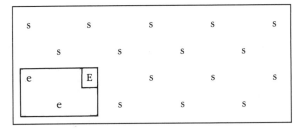

(c) A Contextually Salient Referent

Figure 8.1 Components of Identifiability

need not be *brand-new* to the listener. To repeat here the first two examples in that chapter:

(2) ~... I tàlked to a láwyer last nìght,

(3) ... I tàlked to Lárry last nìght,

We saw that each of these examples introduced a referent that could be regarded as new, although the referent of *a lawyer* was previously unknown to the listener and the referent of *Larry* was already shared. What was crucial so far as newness was concerned was the fact that neither referent had been previously activated in the current discourse. But although the question of whether a referent is known or unknown to the listener is irrelevant to activation cost, it is crucial to identifiability. The idea of *a lawyer* in (2) was assumed by the speaker to be unshared, whereas the idea of *Larry* in (3) was assumed to be shared. These are the properties Prince (1981b) labeled brand-new and unused, respectively. As Prince pointed out, only new ideas can be unshared. Given and accessible ideas are necessarily shared, since by definition the speaker believes them to be already active or semiactive in the listener's mind.

Does sharing of a referent mean that the referent itself must be in the knowledge of both the speaker and the listener? The examples of the elephant and the Volkswagen fit that pattern, as do other examples cited earlier:

(4) ... I tàlked to Lárry last nìght,
(5) ... Wèll the kìd's asléep,

The referents verbalized as *I, Larry,* and *the kid* in these examples were all assumed by the speaker to be, not just part of his own knowledge, but also already part of the listener's knowledge. The referent of *I* was of course the speaker himself, who was obviously known to the listener. *Larry* was a person known to both of them. And *the kid* was lying in the speaker's lap. Cases like these illustrate direct sharing.

Other examples, however, suggest that identifiability is not necessarily dependent on shared knowledge of the referent itself, but that it can be derived from association with knowledge already shared. One such example is provided in (1)n above:

(6) ... they uh kept hónkin' the hórn,

There was no reason for the speaker to believe that the idea of this particular horn was already part of his listeners' knowledge. The listeners would, however, have been expected to know that a Volkswagen has a horn, and it is in that sense that we can regard this referent as associated with already shared knowledge. Indirect sharing has been discussed by Paul Christophersen (1939, pp. 29–30), John Hawkins (1978, pp. 123–30), and others. It is interesting to note in passing that it is apparently easier to infer that something is indirectly shared (for purposes of assessing identifiability) than it is to infer that something is already semiactive in the listener's consciousness (with relation, for example, to the light subject constraint). Evidently accessibility through association requires a link that is more direct or essential than does identifiability. For example, in a discussion of a used-car purchase the friend of the purchaser said:

(7) .. and thèn you got to get *the tágs* on it.
   Rìght?

The association of buying a car with acquiring tags, or license plates, was enough to make the idea of the tags identifiable, but at the same time that idea seems to have been treated in (7) as new, not accessible. The speaker could not assume that it was already semiactive for the listener just because the car-buying scenario had been activated (Chafe 1993).

Sufficiently Identifying Language

If language is to function effectively, a speaker is obliged to categorize a shared referent in a way that allows the listener to identify it (fig. 8.1b). What qualifies as sufficiently identifying can vary over a wide range and is highly dependent on the context. We can look first at circumstances where the least verbalization is necessary and proceed gradually to circumstances that call for more substantial wording. The range is from personal pronouns through demonstrative pronouns, proper names, common nouns with the definite article or a demonstrative article, to more complex noun phrases that include some type of modification.

Short of omitting any overt verbalization at all, the minimum verbal specification that can be supplied for a referent is that which is captured in personal pronouns. The typical function of such pronouns is to verbalize given referents, but such referents are necessarily shared, and in the contexts where personal pronouns are used they usually suffice for identifiability, as with the *he* in (8):

(8) .. so he jùst procèeded to sìt dòwn on the V̂Ŵ.

Demonstrative pronouns like *this, that, these,* and *those* supplement the minimalism of personal pronouns with indications of proximity or distality, a pointing-like function that may be spatial, temporal, or discursal. In using the word *this,* the following speaker was referring to some partially eaten food that lay on the table before her listeners:

(9) I thìnk I should take this awáy.

A personal pronoun might not have been sufficiently identifying:

(10) ~I thìnk I should take it awáy.

The demonstrative function need not involve the immediate environment, but may be directed at something in a discourse-created scene:

(11) This is my jób you know,

Here the speaker used *this* to locate an idea that was being discussed but was not an object available to immediate perception.

Proper names are especially adapted to the expression of identifiable referents. They are, up to a point, unique labels for unique referents:

(12) ... I tàlked to Lárry last nìght,

Of course, names are not unique labels in any absolute sense, but only in a context where a particular holder of a name is salient. When I said to my wife recently,

(13) ... Bób called.

I depended on her knowing which of our various shared referents that could be verbalized as *Bob* was the one I had in mind. In the default case it was her brother. Of course longer labels are available when ambiguity might be a problem: *your brother Bob* or *John Johnson.*

One of the most frequent ways of verbalizing an identifiable referent is with a common noun that establishes a category to which the referent belongs, thus limiting the number of shared referents to the instances embraced by that category. Example (1) illustrated the familiar pattern in which a referent is first introduced into a discourse with a common noun in an indefinite noun phrase (*an elephant, a Volkwagen*), is subsequently allowed to become semiactive, and is then reactivated with a definite noun phrase containing the same or a similar noun. In these contexts, the phrases *the elephant* and *the VW* were sufficiently identifying, whereas neither the pronouns *he* or *it* nor the demonstratives *this* or *that* would have served identifiability as well. The definite article functions as a signal that the noun phrase does express an identifiable referent, one that fulfills the three criteria of sharedness, an adequate categorization, and contextual salience. Closely related to the definite article are the demonstrative articles. They are homophonous with the demonstrative pronouns, as with *this* in the following examples:

(14) .. They sèll Dódge on this lòt?
(15) Hòw many péople were .. ín this pàrty.

The difference between the demonstrative and definite articles is parallel to the difference between demonstrative and personal pronouns: the demonstratives add a pointing-like meaning that may have reference to the physical environment as in (14), or to the discourse as in (15).

As is well known, the proximal demonstratives *this* and *these* have also come to be used in modern spoken English to initiate indefinite phrases, thus signaling *nonidentifiability* (e.g., Prince 1981a; Wald 1983; Wright and Givón 1987, pp. 15–27). This usage retains the demonstrative function in the sense that the nonidentifiable referent is "pointed to" in a way that would be lacking if only the indefinite article were used:

(16) .. and this .. élephant came,
(17) .. these gáls were in a Vólkswagen,

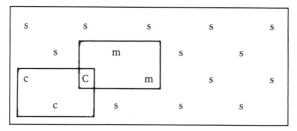

Figure 8.2 Identifiability through Modification

In the rare cases where nonidentifiable referents occur as subjects, as they do in (16) and (17), they are most often introduced with one of these indefinite demonstratives. Neither *an elephant* nor (*some*) *gals* with only the indefinite article would be likely to appear here. Because they may introduce both identifiable and nonidentifiable referents, the words *this* and *these* are of course ambiguous in isolation. In context, however, there is not likely to be any doubt whether identifiability or nonidentifiability is being signaled. Not long after (17) another speaker asked:

(18) What did these .. gìrls dó then.

The girls were now identifiable. *These* functioned as an indefinite demonstrative in (17), as a definite one in (18).

In cases where a common noun is not sufficient to identify a shared and salient referent, the noun may be modified in a way that produces identifiability. Modification creates an ad hoc, narrower category within which the referent becomes unique, when it would not have been unique within the category expressed by the noun alone. Figure 8.2 suggests this process, where the categorized referents in the lower lefthand box have been narrowed by the modifying box to its upper right in order to single out the unique referent shown as C. The intersection of the two boxes yields a sufficiently identifying ad hoc category. There are various types of modification that have this effect, including possessors, attributive adjectives, prepositional phrases, and relative clauses.

Identifiability may be created through a possessive pronoun or noun:

(19) ... And I had my náme put òn em,
(20) ... Did you sèe Sálly's bíke?

In these cases, *the name* or *the bike* would not have been sufficiently identifying, but the addition of the possessors made them so. An attributive adjective may serve a similar function:

(21) ... the Dútch pèople did the sàme thíng.

To have said just *the people* would not have been sufficient. Although one might expect the usage illustrated in (21) to reflect the typical use of attributive adjectives, it is interesting that actual examples are rather hard to find. When they do occur they are usually contrastive, as was *Dutch* in (21). It is more common for attributive adjectives to be used to create ad hoc categories that verbalize new and *nonidentifiable* referents (Thompson 1988):

(22) ... I use a Berlìtz-stỳle óral mèthod,

Berlitz-style and *oral* created an ad hoc category that provided adequate information about a new and previously unshared referent, rather than creating identifiability for a referent already shared.

A prepositional phrase may serve to create identifiability as well:

(23) .. the ròad into Múrrays,

In the context of this intonation unit, to have said simply *the road* would not have been sufficiently identifying. Finally, a relative clause, modifying a noun category with an event or state within which the referent is a participant, is another way of creating an ad hoc category that is sufficiently identifying:

(24) a .. and he shówed us,
     b the vèry pláce,
     c .. that it háppened.

Again, to have said only *the place* would not have been sufficient.

Contextual Salience

Contextual salience has to do with the degree to which a referent "stands out" from other referents that might be categorized in the same way (fig. 8.1c). It may be established by the discourse, by the environment within which a conversation takes place, by the social group to which the participants in a conversation belong, or by commonness of human experience.

The salience of the referent verbalized as *the elephant* in (1)q above was created by the discourse. The idea of this elephant had been introduced shortly before and was crucial to the story being told. Many identifiable referents achieve salience through their activation within the current conversation. On the other hand, a referent may have a salient presence in the external environment. Although the students who heard (25) were familiar with many blackboards, the referent here was the blackboard in the classroom where they were sitting:

(25) ... Whò wants to wrìte it on the bláckboard.

Typically, referents that are present in the immediate environment are more salient than more distant referents. Within every social group there are certain referents that are salient for the members of that group, though they would not be for the members of a different group. For the speaker of (26) there was a particular park that stood out in both his own experience and that of his listener:

(26) ... Are you hànging òut at the párk?

For the participants in the conversation in which one of the speakers said,

(27) ... I tàlked to Lárry last nìght,

there must have' been one person named Larry who was more salient than any others possibly known to them by that name. Some referents are salient for people everywhere, as with astronomical objects such as the sun and moon:

(28) ... Cóme sèe the móon.

Although there may be other referents verbalizable as *moons,* certainly one instance is preeminent in the experience of everyone on earth. Similarly with

(29) ... Look ùp in the ský.

Common experience removes any doubt as to what sky the speaker had in mind.

Further Considerations

Two referents in the following sequence illustrate another aspect of identifiability:

(30) a .. I have the opportúnity,
     b to tálk to pèople,
     c .. to get the phóne bòok,
     d ... you knów,
     e to get léads,
     f .. and talk
     g .. commùnicate with pèople on the phóne.

Neither *the phone book* nor *the phone* were in any literal sense shared referents, nor were they in any obvious way associated with other shared information. Rather, they illustrate referents whose particular identity was of no interest. One phone or one phone book is, for ordinary purposes, identical to any other. It is as if the various categorized referents pictured above in figure 8.1b were all equivalent, so that verbalizing the category alone was sufficient to create identifiability. Phrases like *the drugstore* and *the post office* are well known as belonging to this class.

There are also, as might be expected, idiomatic usages where the functional basis of identifiability has been obscured. In *put the cart before the horse* there is no point in talking about shared knowledge of or the salience of a particular cart or horse (cf. Chafe 1968). In other lexicalized expressions there is an appearance of *nonidentifiability*:

(31) a(B) ... I went òut for a stróll,
      b(B) on my first tìme on Chéstnut Street.
      c(B) ... and just
      d(B) ... just ... was astóunded,
      e(B) at how pléasant things wère.
      f(B) And às I was òut for a stróll,

If lexicalization were not a factor here, it might seem that what was called *a stroll* in (31)a was identifiable in (31)f and should have been verbalized as *the stroll,* but of course that would have destroyed the integrity of the lexicalized phrase.

Noun Phrases for Which Identifiability Is Irrelevant

Not all noun phrases participate in the identifiable-nonidentifiable distinction; for some it is irrelevant. There appear to be two distinct classes of noun phrases of this sort: those that have a *generic* referent, and those that have no referent at all, being *nonreferential.*

Generic Referents
It is possible to refer, not to the idea of a particular object or set of objects, but to a typical instance of a category:

(32) a An èlephant will either stámp on you,
      b ... if they wànt to kíll you,
      c .. or pìck you up in their trúnk,
      d ... and smàsh you against a trée.
      e .. This one dídn't.

The referent verbalized as *an elephant* in (32)a and retained through the next three intonation units was *generic* rather than particular. What was described here was the typical behavior of a typical elephant. English allows several possibilities for the expression of generic referents, among them the use of the indefinite article, as in (32)a, or a plural noun and no article:

(33) ˜Elephants will either stámp on you,

It is interesting to observe that the speaker of (32) inadvertently switched from the indefinite article in (32)a to the use of plural pronouns in the two intonation units that followed. She might have said:

(34) a ˜An èlephant will either stámp on you,
 b ... if it wànts to kíll you,
 c .. or pìck you up in its trúnk,

Although there is undoubtedly a subtle difference between the indefinite and plural expressions, it is evidently easy to slip from one into the other. A third way of expressing genericness in English is with a definite noun phrase:

(35) ˜The èlephant will either stámp on you,

This alternative is apparently more at home with narrowly delimited categories. Thus, the following might be more felicitous:

(36) ˜The Áfrican èlephant will either stámp on you,

 This brief discussion of genericness has been necessary because generic referents may appear to participate in the identifiable-nonidentifiable distinction, being verbalized sometimes with the indefinite, sometimes with the definite article. But sharing knowledge of generic referents is different from sharing knowledge of particular referents. Knowing a category, like the category that allows something to be called an elephant, entails knowing something about a *typical* instance of that category, whereas the sharedness involved in identifiability depends on knowing a *particular* instance.

Nonreferential Noun Phrases
Often noun phrases or pronouns are used when there is no referent at all, either particular or generic. There are various possibilities here. They do not form a coherent set, but constitute a miscellaneous collection of circumstances under which noun phrases or pronouns fail to refer. I will mention nonreferential uses of *it*, negatives and universals, question words, event-modifying nouns, nonspecific nouns, and predicate nouns.
 The nonreferential use of the pronoun *it* was listed among the several types of nonfunctional subjects in chapter 7:

(37) ... It's ráining out.

Other nonreferential examples belong to lexicalized phrases:

(38) a .. There were vèry fèw péople.
     b ... Màde it through.

In neither (37) nor (38) is there any point in looking for a shared referent for *it*. Negative pronouns like *no one* provide another example of nonreferentiality. The fact that they have no referent is intrinsic to their meaning:

(39) a .. Nò one ever wènt to Seáttle,
     b on their wáy to somewhere élse.

Similarly, universal pronouns also lack a referent:

(40) Èverybody had a víew.

as do pronouns like *whatever* and *whoever,* whose function is to communicate a lack of knowledge of the identity of a referent:

(41) .. whatèver the case may bé.

Also nonreferential are the question words that provide a lexical gap the interlocutor is requested to fill by supplying some referent or some other kind of information (Chafe 1970, pp. 325–33):

(42) ... ~Whò told you thát.
(43) ... ~Whàt's óut there.

The *who* and *what* do not verbalize referents. They are requests for referents.

At least three types of nonreferentiality involve the use of full nouns rather than pronouns. In one such type a nominal idea is used to specify more fully the nature of an event, as in

(44) ..~he was tèlling jókes.

Here a unified idea is verbalized with a conventionalized collocation of verb and noun. Other languages might express such an idea with a compound or with noun incorporation (cf. English *joke-telling*; Mithun 1984, p. 849). Referentiality is also absent from nouns in an irrealis context, where the event is not presented as factual but as hypothesized, predicted, denied, or the like:

(45) ~I thìnk I'll bùy a néwspaper.

Here the word *newspaper* need not have a referent. There is thus a relation between a lack of factuality and a lack of referentiality (Chafe, in press). The term *nonspecific* provides one way of labeling usages of this type. Finally, predicate nouns as in (46) are also nonreferential:

(46) ... maybe she's a hypochóndriac.

The function of *a hypochondriac* is to assign the referent of *she* to the hypochondriac category, not to verbalize a referent. These nonreferential noun phrases also fail to participate in the identifiable-nonidentifiable distinction, which depends on the existence of a shared referent. If there is no referent, there is nothing to be shared.

Identifiability and Activation Cost

Identifiability, as discussed in this chapter, and activation cost, as discussed in chapter 6, are independent properties, at least in the sense that an identifiable referent may be given, accessible, or new. We have already seen examples of all three possibilities. Example (1) at the beginning of this chapter illustrated the interplay of identifiable referents that are given and accessible. The idea of the elephant was first introduced in (1)d as *nonidentifiable* and new:

(47) well Í hèard of an élephant,

It subsequently receded into the semiactive state as other referents became active, and was then reactivated in (1)q as identifiable and *accessible*:

(48) ... and the .. élephant was in frónt of em,

It was then repeated in (1)r as identifiable and *given*:

(49) so he jùst procèeded to sìt dòwn on the V̂Ŵ.

But it is by no means unusual for an identifiable referent to be new as well (cf. Fraurud 1990, where numerous examples from written Swedish are discussed). We noted the newness of *Larry* in

(50) ... I tàlked to Lárry last nìght,

A common noun may also suffice to verbalize an identifiable new referent, as when someone asked his friend (repeated from (26) above),

(51) ... Are you hànging òut at the párk?

Although identifiable referents can thus be given, accessible, or new, *nonidentifiable* referents are nearly always new. It is at least unusual to pretend that a referent that is given or accessible cannot be identified.

Identifiability and Subjects

The fact that subjects adhere to the light subject constraint was used in chapter 7 as support for the notion that subjects express starting points, since we might expect starting points to constitute light information. The starting point notion is further supported by the finding that subjects are nearly always identifiable. In the sample examined, 99 percent of the subjects had that property. Both lightness and identifiability are properties we would expect starting points to have, and they do. The following are examples of identifiable subjects expressed with a pronoun, a common noun with the definite article, and a proper noun:

(52) .. She spent twèlve years of her lífe with me,

(53) Well the kìd's asléep,

(54) .. how did Jennifer reáct.

Most of the subjects that appear superficially to express nonidentifiable referents actually express generic ideas or are nonreferential, and thus fall outside the domain of identifiability. To repeat some examples of this kind:

(55) ... An èlephant will either stámp on you,

(56) ... Èverybody had a víew.

(57) ... ˜Whàt's óut there.

So far as the few nonidentifiable subjects are concerned, most of the potential instances share properties that may, on further examination, actually exclude them from the subject category. The following example is typical:

(58) a ... And this gúy,

b he wént,

c .. and he knèw Lássie,

At issue is the referent introduced in (58)a. It was introduced with the indefinite demonstrative *this,* as in (16) above. It was not new, but accessible, since slightly earlier the same speaker had said:

(59) a .. I think Sàlly has her a bóyfrìend.

b ... There's a gùy that còmes óut.

c .. A gùy that wòrks wíth her,

But most importantly *this guy* in (58)a expressed an *isolated referent,* as described in chapter 5. It constituted an entire intonation unit, and its referent was picked up again in (58)b with a resumptive pronoun. There is in fact no compelling reason to regard *this guy* in (58)a as a subject. Its referent only became a true starting point in (58)b, where it was integrated into a clause for the first time. Among the various uses of the term *topic,* that illustrated in 58(a) may bear a functional resemblance to the phenomenon that has been grammaticized in Asian languages (Li and Thompson 1976, Lee 1987), in view of the fact that the *guy* was introduced here to become the dominant referent in the portion of conversation to follow.

Summary and Prospects

I began this chapter by characterizing identifiability in terms of three properties a referent must have in order to be identifiable: it must be shared, it must be verbalized in a sufficiently identifying way, and it must be contextually salient. The sharing may be direct, as when the referent itself is already known to both speaker and listener, or indirect, as when the referent is associated with other shared knowledge. What constitutes a sufficiently identifying verbalization can vary over a wide range, depending on the context. With relatively uninformative personal pronouns at one extreme, sufficiently identifying language may require the use of a demonstrative pronoun, a proper name, a common noun with a definite or demonstrative article, or the addition of a modifier such as a possessor, an attributive adjective, a prepositional phrase, or a relative clause. The contextual salience of a referent may be relative to a discourse, to the environment, to a social group, or to people in general.

There are several types of noun phrases for which identifiability is irrelevant. Among them are those that express generic referents and those that are nonreferential. Generic referents may be expressed in the same way as both nonidentifiable and identifiable singular referents, or as nonidentifiable plural referents. Nonreferential noun phrases include nonreferential *it,* negative and universal pronouns, question words, event-modifying nouns, nonspecific referents in an irrealis context, and predicate nouns.

Identifiability and activation cost are independent, in the sense that identifiable referents may be either given, accessible, or new. Nonidentifiable referents, however, are nearly always new. Subjects are nearly always identifiable, a fact that accords well with the hypothesis that they function as starting points.

Among the aspects of identifiability that call for further study, the precise conditions of indirect sharing need to be investigated over a wide range of natural data. What exactly does it mean for knowledge of a referent to be associated with other shared knowledge, and just how does this kind of association differ from that involved in the establishment of accessibility? When it comes to sufficiently identifying language, it will be helpful to be able to relate what is meant by *sufficient* to specific contextual factors. It will also be valuable to establish more precisely the types of noun phrases for which identifiability is irrelevant, refining the breakdown into generic and nonreferential noun phrases, and the various subtypes of the latter.

9

The One New Idea Constraint

Sentences of the following type, popular as linguistic examples, are seldom if ever encountered in real life:

(1) ~~The man hit the colorful ball.

We have already seen that a noun phrase subject like *the man* is unusual, being likely to occur only if its referent is accessible information. But there is another reason why such a sentence is unrealistic.

A substantive intonation unit usually (though not always) conveys some new information. What we have seen so far is that the new information is not likely to reside in the subject of a clause. To the extent that an intonation unit adheres to the clause format, then, the locus of new information is usually the predicate. If the predicate consists of a simple intransitive verb, predicate adjective, or predicate noun, that is the whole story; the most likely pattern will be a given subject with a new predicate:

(2) It hélps.
    It's proféssional.
    I'm a proféssional.

The light subject constraint also permits a new predicate with a subject that is accessible rather than given:

(3) Jénnifer was rèally háppy.

where the idea of Jennifer had been activated earlier. What we do *not* find are intonation units in which both the subject and predicate express new information. It seems that an intonation unit like (3) would not occur in a context where the idea of Jennifer and the idea of being happy were both new.

So far we have explained such nonoccurrence on the basis of a constraint against subjects that express referents that are heavy, that is, new and nontrivial. In this chapter I explore a different constraint—one that keeps an intonation unit from containing more than one new idea, wherever it might be located. I will begin by focusing on predicates rather than subjects, and especially on predicates containing two or more content words with a primary accent. That may happen, for example, in the familiar verb-object construction:

(4) It bróke the chísel.

The question raised by such an example is whether it is possible for both the idea of an event and the idea of a referent participating in that event to be activated separately as new ideas. Could (4), for example, express the idea of breaking and the idea of the chisel as independent new ideas? In fact it appears that an activation cost structure of that kind is seldom if ever found in conversational language. Where a preliminary analysis might suggest such a configuration, the analysis can usually be rejected for one of several reasons. It happens that (4) was spoken in a context where both the idea of breaking and the idea of the chisel had been activated a short time before. The owner of the broken chisel had said,

(5) a Give me your chísel brò.
    b I bróke mine màn.

After some intervening talk during which the idea of breaking the chisel had become semiactive, (4) reactivated ideas that were accessible. In this case the number of new ideas was actually zero. The fact that in the end we are left with few if any cases in which there are two or more separately activated new ideas within the same intonation unit suggests the hypothesis that an intonation unit can express no more than one new idea. In other words thought, or at least language, proceeds in terms of one such activation at a time, and each activation applies to a single referent, event, or state, but not to more than one. If this is a limitation on what the speaker can do, it may also be a limitation assumed for the listener as well. It may be that neither the speaker nor the listener is able to handle more than one new idea at a time.

  Similar hypotheses have been proposed at various times, above all by Talmy Givón. Givón (1975, pp. 202–4) suggested that "there exists a strategy of information processing in language such that the amount of new information per a certain unit of *message-transaction* is restricted in a fashion—say 'one unit per proposition.'" In Givón (1984, pp. 258–63) he elaborated on what he called the "one chunk per clause principle," to the effect that "the majority of sentence/clauses in connected discourse will have only *one chunk*—be it a nominal, predicate (verb, adjective) or adverbial word/phrase—under the scope of asserted new information. All other elements in the clause will tend to be topical, background or presupposed old information." Du Bois (1987, p. 826) added evidence from the Sacapultec language for what he called the *one new argument constraint*: "Avoid more than one new argument per clause." There has thus been some convergence on the finding that an important segment of language, identified here as an intonation unit, is subject to a strong limitation on how much new information it can express.

We can now explore the ramifications of this hypothesis in more detail, focusing first on the way it applies to combinations of a verb with an object. After that we will look at several other constructions: a verb and a prepositional phrase, an adjective and a noun, and words or phrases that are conjoined. These are all constructions that bring together two or more content words, and thus they have the potential to provide situations in which each content word might separately express new information. We will see how the hypothesized constraint leads to the discovery of alternative analyses in most if not all such cases.

Verb Plus Object

Predicates that consist of a transitive verb plus an object noun might at first be thought to offer frequent counterexamples to the one new idea hypothesis: cases in which both the verb and its object, independently of each other, express new information. On the basis of our concerns here, it is possible to distinguish several varieties of this construction. In one, although the verb and object express independently activated ideas, only one of them, at most, expresses new information. In another, the verb is what I will call a *low-content* verb because it fails to carry a full load of activation cost. In a third, the verb-object combination is lexicalized and an activation cost is carried only by the combination as a whole.

Independently Activated Verb and Object
If the verb and its object are activated independently, the hypothesis says that no more than one of them will express a new idea. In the data examined, about a quarter of all the verb-object combinations contained a pronoun object that expressed a given referent. The verbs in such cases were about evenly split between those that expressed a new idea and those that expressed an accessible one. In (6) the idea verbalized as *relax* was new, while *it,* expressing the idea of someone's back, was given. (The sequence *needed to* was a modal-like inflection of *relax,* analogous to expressions like *had to* and *wanted to.*)

(6) and he just needed to reláx it.

In (7) the idea expressed by *killed* was accessible because there had been earlier talk about killing peas with a sprayer. The object *them* expressed the given idea of the peas. (The new information was carried by the lexicalized phrase *deader than a doornail.*) The fact that *killed* was spoken with a secondary accent appears related to its accessibility:

(7) and he kìlled them dèader than a dóornail.

In a smaller proportion of cases, about 5 percent of the total, both the verb and object expressed accessible information. An example was given in (4) above. Most of the examples with an independently activated verb and object belonged to one or the other of these two types: either the object expressed given information, or both the verb and the object expressed accessible information.

Low-Content Verbs
In many verb-object combinations there are reasons to think that the verb does not carry a full load of activation cost. Instead of expressing an independent idea of its own, the verb is subservient to the idea expressed by the object. There are two subtypes, the first of which is lèss problematic than the second. Based on their prosodic characteristics, I will refer to *unaccented* and *accented* low-content verbs.

The unaccented subtype involves a small inventory of unaccented verbs that occur very often, among them *have, get, give, do, make, take, use,* and *say*. Their frequency ranking on the (unadjusted) frequency list of Nelson Francis and Henry Kučera (1982, p. 465) lies between 9th (*have*) and 81st (*use*), which is to say that they are extremely frequent in written language, and presumably also in spoken. They are themselves classifiable into several functional varieties, which I will discuss in terms of possession, realization, use, presentation, perception, arrangement, and the attribution of quoted speech.

A low-content verb may convey the possession of the referent expressed by the object noun. The possession may be literal possession of property or a more figurative possession of, say, a disease or a problem. This was by far the most common variety of low-content verb in the data examined, constituting two-thirds of the instances. More than half of these instances used the verb *have*:

(8) have insúrance
    have a báckache

If verbs like *needed* in (6) are inflection-like, verbs of this other sort can be thought of as derivation-like. *Have,* for example, converts a *referent* like the idea of a backache into the *state* of having a backache. Like other derivational elements, such a verb also contributes a meaning of its own, in this case one of possession in a broad sense. But that meaning is more predictable, and thus less informative, then the meaning of verbs that contribute truly new information (as perhaps in *ignore his backache*).

Low-content verbs can also convert referents into *events*. The most common example is *get,* which expresses the coming into possession of something:

(9) get báckaches
     get some pílls

Not surprisingly, *give* may also function in this way:

(10) give it a hùndred tèn percént
      give me your chísel

Next in frequency to low-content verbs involving possession were those that expressed the performance or *realization* of an event expressed by the object. The verb *have* is used in this sense as well, as are *do, make,* and *take*:

(11) have a tálk
      do éxercises
      make a caréer chànge
      take a lòng lúnch

A low-content verb may also express the *use* of whatever is conveyed by the object noun. The most common verb of this kind is, in fact, *use*:

(12) use nùmber séven
      use nóse sprày

Such a verb may also express some sort of *arrangement* of items in a complex configuration:

(13) get you and him togéther

Finally, although its function is quite different from those illustrated above, being evidential rather than derivational, we can add to this list the attribution of a direct or indirect quote to its source. *Say* and its current colloquial equivalents *go* and *be like* can also be interpreted as failing to exact an activation cost of their own:

(14) She said thànks a lót.

(15) .. He tùrns to his móther and goes,
      ... I nèed to see Ròger's bíke.

(16) He's like wów.

We will return to quoted speech in chapter 16.

The low-content verbs discussed above are all distinguishable by their weak prosody and their high frequency in the language. There are other verbs that perform similar functions but are uttered with a secondary accent, are less frequent, and contribute more content of their own than the verbs just described. Some of them involve more specific changes of possession than *get* or *give*:

(17) bòrrow dàd's dísk
      pày sèven fífty

Other verbs of this sort express typical ways in which an object is used:

(18) drìve a Cát (a Caterpillar tractor)
      drìnk gállons of wáter

Still others serve to present or introduce whatever is expressed by the object:

(19) suggèst Lárry
      càll Bòb Jénkins

Closely related are verbs that specify how a referent was perceived:

(20) sèe Gáry
      lòok at Súe

Low-content verbs of this secondarily accented type are subsumed to varying degrees under what Benson, Benson, and Ilson (1986a) call *creation and/or activation* verbs; what Jan Firbas (1992) calls *appearance/existence* verbs; what Anna Granville Hatcher (1956) identified as verbs of existence-presence, absence, beginning, continuing-remaining, production, occurrence, appearing, and coming; and what Igor Mel'čuk (1982) calls *lexical functions*. It is to be hoped that further studies of natural speech will lead to a fuller understanding of these verbs and their special relation to activation cost.

Lexicalized Phrases
There are also many verb-object combinations that can be interpreted as *lexicalized phrases*—conventional collocations that are already established in the speaker's repertoire. They constitute a scale, extending from those that are most conventional to those that come closer to being free combinations, but their crucial property is that none of them are assembled by the speaker for the first time in the current utterance. The extreme of conventionality is represented by idioms, phrases that have taken on a semantic and syntactic life of their own (Chafe 1968). Idioms were quite rare in the data examined. They sometimes included an unaccented low-content verb, as in

(21) get on your cáse

meaning something like *bother* or *nag* you. In others the verb had more substance:

(22) thròw in their twó cénts worth

meaning something like *express their opinion*. The latter is a good example of an idiomatic *frame* that allows limited substitutions of semantically related items: *throw, toss, put in (one's) two cents worth*.

Much more common than idioms were word combinations that have become conventionalized through frequent use, but whose meanings are more predictable from the meanings of their parts. That is true, for example, of the phrase *wash dishes* in the following exchange:

(23) a(A) Because whò wants to wàsh díshes after,
     b(A) .. you know,
     c(B) .. [Ríght.]
     d(A) [after] a five-còurse méal.

Washing dishes is a familiar, unitary experience that is conventionally expressed with these words. Often such collocations acquire specialized uses, as with *enjoy the show* in the following example (to which we will return, for another reason, at the end of chap. 16). The speaker was talking about a friend who was constantly telling jokes:

(24) a ... Ì thought Géeze,
     b .. get yòu and hím together,
     c and Ì'd just sít there,
     d and enjòy the shów.

As with idioms, some collocations are tolerant of a range of substitutions. All of the following, for example, appear to be manifestations of a single *collocational frame*:

(25) lìft your shóulders up
     ˜lìft your híps up
     ˜ràise your féet up
     ˜pùt your féet down

The substitutions that are possible within such a frame require that there be semantic similarities among the substitutable parts; for example, in (25) the verb involves raising or lowering and the object is a body part. Andrew Pawley and Frances Syder (1983b; see also Pawley 1985) have stressed that one can never be a nativelike speaker of a language without learning the very large store of lexicalized phrases native speakers produce and recognize. It is quite possible that the word combinations most speakers produce most of the time are of this type.

The one new idea hypothesis depends crucially on acceptance of the notion that lexicalized phrases express ideas that are activated as integrated wholes—that lexicalized instances of the verb-object construction, for example, do not show verbs and objects that are activated independently. The hypothesis would be disconfirmed by clear cases in which both verb and object expressed independent new ideas. How, then, can we know whether a particular combination is lexicalized or not? The question has no single or easy answer, although perhaps the ultimate answer is that native speakers of a language simply *know* what is lexicalized. As a speaker of English I know that *wash dishes* is a familiar collocation.

A skeptic, however, may be either someone whose lexicalized repertoire is different from mine or who is bothered by the subjectivity of introspective evidence. What other kinds of evidence can there be? One might think of the familiar cloze procedure (Taylor 1953), a measure of redundancy in which people are asked to fill in blanks that have been inserted, say, for every fifth word in a text as a way of confirming the predictability of word combinations. In a modest attempt to apply this procedure, I found (to take an example that is perhaps too obvious) that subjects who were confronted with the following written sentence within a larger context unanimously filled the blank with the word *blown,* confirming the lexicalized nature of the phrase *blow the whistle on*:

(26) who were furious that we had "—— the whistle" on conditions in their cities

(For further discussion see Chafe 1992a.) Although the procedure is time-consuming and requires large numbers of subjects for small results, it does offer one way of confirming at least some judgments regarding lexicalized phrases. Another kind of confirmation can be offered by a very large corpus in which repetitions of a phrase may be discovered. Since, however, no corpus begins to approach the amount of language we hear and use in a lifetime, it may be a matter of luck whether the necessary evidence is available in a particular case. One can also consult a dictionary of collocations, of which the best current example for English is Benson, Benson, and Ilson (1986a; see also the discussion in 1986b), but any such dictionary can only sample the vast store of collocations a speaker knows. (The work just mentioned does include *wash dishes.*) Particularly important research of this kind is being conducted by Russian scholars on both Russian and French (Mel'čuk and Zholkovsky 1984; Mel'čuk et al. 1984/1988), but obviously each language must be investigated on its own terms. Evidence from other languages, however, may not be entirely irrelevant. It is at least suggestive that the idea of washing dishes is expressed in the Seneca language with a single word (see chap. 12) in which the noun root meaning 'dish' combines morphologically with the verb root meaning 'wash.' This *noun incorporation* is reserved for such familiar, lexicalized activities. One thing that is certain is that lexicalization and its broader implications are ripe for investigation both within and across languages.

To recapitulate, the one new idea hypothesis predicts that there are no constructions internal to an intonation unit with two items that independently express new information. The verb-object construction is one obvious place where such counterexamples might be found. We have seen that most if not all examples of this construction either (a) contain a verb or object that is given or accessible, or (b) exhibit an unaccented or secondarily accented low-content verb, and/or (c) constitute a lexicalized phrase—an idiom or a conventional collocation. If we can accept these explanations of potential counterexamples, the hypothesis stands up well. But any other construction that brings together two or more content words might also provide counterexamples, and it is thus appropriate to look at a few other commonly occurring constructions of that sort.

Verb Plus Prepositional Phrase

Another such construction is one in which a verb is followed by a prepositional phrase. Whereas a grammatical object typically expresses the semantic role of patient, prepositional phrases expand the ways in which a referent may participate in an event or state. There is a sense, then, in which the verb-plus-prepositional-phrase construction functions as an expansion of the possibilities offered by the verb-object construction, the preposition adding further semantic options. For example, whereas the verb-object construction in *I broke my knife* places the knife in a patient role in the event, *I fell on my knife* places it in a locative role, *I opened it with my knife* in an instrumental role.

In the data examined, the distribution of activation cost in this construction was like that found in the verb-object construction. Often a verb conveying new information was combined with a prepositional phrase conveying given information:

(27) everybody's próud of me

In other cases, the verb that preceded the prepositional phrase was an unaccented low-content verb. Most common was *be,* converting the prepositional phrase into a state that was predicated of the subject:

(28) she was in the hóspital

Less common were other low-content verbs, such as *have*:

(29) (cars) we have on the lót

Many examples containing low-content verbs are also lexicalized collocations; *be in the hospital* is an example. Example (30) illustrates a collocational *frame*:

(30) I'll gò in a tíe

One may also *go in a dark suit, tuxedo,* or whatever.

It is not unusual for a prepositional phrase to be separated from its verb by an intonation unit boundary. In such cases both the event or state expressed in the verb and the referent expressed in the prepositional phrase are likely to be new ideas. That is, it is not unusual for both the verb and the prepositional phrase to express new information, but when that happens each appears in its own intonation unit. Such cases, of course, support the one new idea hypothesis; since both the verb and the prepositional phrase express new information, the speaker is forced to focus on them separately:

(31) a you lìe flát,
     b with your knées up,

(32) a I'm going to stòp by the .. the fáctory,
     b ... màybe àfter work at níne,

Attributive Adjectives

In English and many other languages, adjectives provide one of the major ways of verbalizing ideas of states that are properties of referents (Dixon 1982, Thompson 1988). Adjectives are used in two distinct ways. We have already noted the use of *predicate* adjectives with a linking verb, used to *assert* that a referent has some property:

(33) It's proféssional.

Attributive adjectives, on the other hand, provide ways for a speaker to categorize a referent more adequately for some purpose than would be possible with a simple noun alone. When the following speaker said *asthmatic bronchitis* rather than just *bronchitis*:

(34) a She was in the hóspital,
     b thrée tímes,
     c with ... àsthmatic bronchítis.

she made use of a semantic category formed by the intersection of the *bronchitis* category and the *asthmatic* property. Since these attributive adjective constructions combine two content words, they provide another potential site for the independent expression of two separate new ideas.

The question arises, then, as to whether speakers actually do construct adjective-noun combinations in which both elements are independently new. It should already be evident that *asthmatic bronchitis* is a lexicalized phrase expressing the unitary idea of a particular malady. There is no question here of two separate ideas, one expressed by *asthmatic* and the other by *bronchitis,* that are activated independently. The following are some additional examples of this sort:

(35) ràpid prógress
      bèautiful wéather
      pèrsonal relátions
      a nèw jób
      a quìet wédding
      a rìgid schédule

In short, although combinations of adjectives with nouns might provide another site where the one new idea constraint could be violated, with the adjective and noun each separately expressing new information, such violations were absent from the data examined.

Conjoining

Another construction that offers a potential for combining separate new ideas within a single intonation unit is that in which two or more referents, events, or states are conjoined with *and, or,* or *but.* It is interesting to observe, therefore, that whenever the conjuncts do express separate new ideas, we find them in separate intonation units. In the following example the speaker was listing some medical problems:

(36) a Gállbladder and,
     b ... héart tròuble and,
     c ... báck pròblems.

That this speaker assigned a separate intonation unit to each of these new ideas confirms the validity of the constraint that would make it impossible to unite them within a single focus of consciousness:

(37) ~~Gállbladder and héart tròuble and báck pròblems.

There are, of course, numerous examples of conjoined expressions that do occur within a single intonation unit. Such cases have explanations similar to those described for the constructions discussed above, with lexicalized collocations such as

(38) kìtchen and díning room
    hànds and knées
    Jòhn and Máry (a known couple)
    grìnch and bìtch and móan

Summary and Prospects

Conversational language appears subject to a constraint that limits an intonation unit to the expression of no more than one new idea. We looked at four constructions with a potential for violating this constraint, each of them allowing two or more content words to come together in a single intonation unit. They included the verb-object construction, the use of a prepositional phrase after a verb, the use of an attributive adjective with a noun, and the conjoining of two or more content words. In some instances of these constructions, while one of the ideas might have been new, the other(s) expressed either given or accessible information. In other instances one of the constituents was a low-content word that did not exact a separate activation cost. In still others the combination was lexicalized in some way, exhibiting either an idiom or a conventional collocation. The data examined provided no clear examples in which two independent new ideas were contained within a single intonation unit.

Essential to the one new idea hypothesis is the exemption of a variety of linguistic elements from the domain of activation cost, among them quantifiers like *all,* numerals like *five,* and intensifiers like *very.* The full range of such exemptions needs to be established. One wonders also whether there is any limit on the total number of ideas, regardless of their activation cost, that can be included within an intonation unit—a question whose answer must depend in a complex fashion on various mixes of given, accessible, and new information in particular contexts. The fact that Japanese intonation units appear to be shorter and more fragmentary than those of English suggests that they may be subject to additional constraints of social interaction that add to their cognitive burden (Iwasaki, in press). The one new idea constraint sets an upper cognitive limit on the content of an intonation unit, but reasons why so many intonation units contain *less* than one new idea also need to be addressed.

In any case, the finding that people can activate only one new idea at a time, as well as the insight that finding gives us into what it means to constitute "one idea," may be at least as important as the finding that short-term memory is limited to seven items plus or minus two (Miller 1956). The magical number *one* appears to be fundamental to the way the mind handles the flow of information through consciousness and language.

10

Discourse Topics

In all our voluntary thinking there is some topic or subject about which all the members of the thought revolve. Half the time this topic is a problem, a gap we cannot yet fill with a definite picture, word, or phrase, but which ... influences us in an intensely active and determinate psychic way. Whatever may be the images and phrases that pass before us, we feel their relation to this aching gap. To fill it up is our thought's destiny. Some bring us nearer to that consummation. Some the gap negates as quite irrelevant. Each swims in a felt fringe of relations of which the aforesaid gap is the term.

(William James 1890, 1:259)

So far we have seen ways in which intonation units are affected by larger contexts, but we have not yet looked at the larger contexts themselves. Certainly speakers do not simply verbalize one focus of consciousness after another, with no concern for larger coherences. Producing language involves much more than adding new beads to a string. The larger coherences, of course, are crucial to the determination of activation cost, starting points, referential importance, identifiability, and similar features, but it is time to look more closely at the coherences themselves. In terms of consciousness, if *active* consciousness is incapable of focusing on more information than the event, state, or referent that is verbalized in a single intonation unit, what is the relation of consciousness to larger discourse elements? Especially relevant here is the notion of *semiactive* consciousness, whose capacity is greater than the very limited amount available to the fully active state.[1]

The suggestion so far has been that three kinds of ideas can be *fully* active: ideas of events, states, and the referents that participate in them. We need now a name for the larger amount of information that can be semiactive. I will use the term *topic* in this way, qualifying it when necessary as *discourse topic* to distinguish it from the other phenomena to which the term has been applied. The usage here is thus in accord with such expressions as *the topic of a paragraph, changing the topic,* and the like (cf. Keenan and Schieffelin 1976; Brown and Yule 1983, pp. 71–106).

1. Parts of this chapter are related to an earlier discussion in Chafe 1990b.

One of the things that seems intuitively true of conversations is that they focus on different topics, in this sense, at different times, moving from one topic to another. We can think of each such topic as an aggregate of coherently related events, states, and referents that are held together in some form in the speaker's semiactive consciousness. A topic is available for scanning by the focus of consciousness, which can play across the semiactive material, activating first one part and then another until the speaker decides that the topic has been adequately covered for whatever purpose the speaker may have in mind. It is interesting and instructive to compare the process of visually scanning a picture, as described by Guy Buswell (1935).

Certainly what I have just described is too simple. I know of at least three obvious ways in which it must be qualified. First, there is no reason to think that everything within a topic becomes semiactive as soon as the topic as a whole has entered that state. Some parts may be more immediately available than other parts, which may remain inactive until scanning of the topic is well advanced, if they even become semiactive at all. We need to allow for the variable availability of ideas within a topic. Second, the most typical kind of topic is probably best regarded as a *basic-level* unit. There may be *supertopics* that tie together a group of basic-level topics, which may in turn contain *subtopics* within them. We will return to this hierarchical organization of topics in chapter 11. Finally, it is important to realize that many of the ideas that become semiactive for the *speaker* will not be known to the *listener* until and unless the speaker verbalizes them. The speaker's principal intent may be to introduce those ideas to the listener for the first time. Thus, to the extent that the speaker assesses activation cost with relation to the listener's consciousness and not the speaker's own, such ideas will be treated as new and not as accessible, even when they have the latter status for the speaker.

The Quality of Being Interesting

Not everything that becomes semiactive during a conversation is verbalized. Topics may arise in the minds of interlocutors without ever being made overt in language. The most general thing to say in this regard is that people often verbalize a topic when they judge that it will be in some way *interesting* to their interlocutors. William Labov (1972, p. 366) suggested that the worst fate to befall conversational narrators is to have the audience ask "So what?" when they have finished. Labov also wrote of various "evaluation" devices that convey what I have called *involvement* (Chafe 1982, Tannen 1989). I mention here only one of several properties of topics that can make them interesting, but this one seems fundamental.

Our minds are full of expectations about how the world should be. So long as the events we experience accord with these expectations, we are able to deal with them smoothly. But it is obviously impossible to predict everything we encounter in daily life. Our minds, therefore, have evolved ways of coping with unexpected events, as we so often must. When we experience such events, we react with excitement, sometimes anger, and sometimes aggression. This arousal puts us in a state where we may be better able to deal with the unexpected, which constitutes a threat to our accustomed ways of dealing with our surroundings. Our primary reaction is to reject the unexpected by attempting to remove its source. Primitive feelings of excitement, anger, and aggression may make it easier to do this.

Since our minds are thus designed to cope with unexpected experiences, the absence of such experiences leaves us in a state of boredom. It may seem ironic that we are not content to be surrounded by a world that conforms to all our expectations, that we prefer to encounter enough of the unexpected to bring excitement to our lives, but this preference applies as much to conversations as it does to life in general. A narrative that fails to conflict with expectations is no narrative at all. The artificial intelligence literature has provided us with examples of nonnarratives like the following (Schank and Abelson 1977, p. 38):

(1) a John went to a restaurant.
    b He asked the waitress for coq au vin.
    c He paid the check and left.

Such examples illustrate the fact that our minds possess "schemas," "scripts," or "frames" that provide expectations with regard, for example, to what happens in restaurants. But simply to verbalize those expectations in a conversation would have no point (cf. Wilensky 1982). The topics worth verbalizing are those that have a point, which is usually to say that they conflict with expectations. To be an interesting and not a boring conversationalist, moreover, requires an ability to assess what will be interesting to one's interlocutors, not just to oneself. Here as elsewhere effective speakers are guided by assumptions about the minds of their listeners.

Once a topic has been semiactivated, and once a speaker has decided it is interesting enough to verbalize overtly, how does the verbalization proceed? If a topic contains a variety of ideas (events, states, referents), how does a speaker decide which to make overt and in what order? In the rest of this chapter I will explore two major patterns of topic development. One is development through *elicitation,* the other is through *narration.* We can focus first on elicitation.

Painting the House: Topic Development through Elicitation

An elicitation consists of a sequence of relatively brief utterances, or "turns," by two or more interlocutors. The forward movement through the topic and the direction the movement takes are created by these alternating contributions. Topic development is, in other words, driven by the interaction between the speakers. The roles of the speakers, however, are not balanced. One (the *eliciter*) introduces the topic, but it is the other (the *responder*) who possesses the bulk of the interesting information. The topic is, in other words, one about which the eliciter finds it interesting to gain more knowledge, and he or she accomplishes that goal partly by asking questions, partly in other ways.

The topic of the following excerpt can be labeled *Speaker B's painting of his house.* Speaker A, the eliciter, introduced this topic into the conversation and subsequently kept it alive through his questions and reactions. Evidently B, the responder, would not have continued it without A's prodding. A was motivated to continue by the repeated unexpectedness of B's responses. Although someone's painting of his house might not seem a likely topic for surprises, in fact each piece of information that B provided conflicted with some expectation held by A, who reacted with exclamations and explicit statements of what his expectations were.

The topic arose in A's consciousness during an unusually long pause. After about seven seconds of silence, A directed the following remark to the baby he was holding:

(2) (A) ... (7.1) Boy yóu're suppòsed to be gòing to slèep.

There are times during a conversation—one topic having been exhausted and a silence having followed—when the participants may search their minds for a new topic that will keep the conversation going. The search need not be conscious or deliberate; new topics may arise in mysterious ways. In this example A already shared with B, before this conversation took place, the knowledge that B was painting his house. Whatever the reason may have been, that knowledge became semiactive for A either during the seven seconds that preceded his remark to the baby in (2) or immediately after that remark. In any case, after about another second of silence, A introduced the topic by asking:

(3) (A) ... (1.1) Hòw're you dòin' with the hóuse.

B answered with some simple and straightforward information concerning the status of the job:

(4) a(B) ... Òh got it àll uh ... prímed just abòut,
    b(B) ... except twó sídes of it.

What were the possibilities at this point? A might have asked additional questions about the color of the paint or when B expected to finish, to which B might have responded in an equally straightforward manner. A conversational segment that proceeded in such a way would be an *interrogation*. It would leave the questioner with more information than when he started, but the total exchange would probably be considered dull by all concerned. Interrogations as such do not make for interesting conversations.

This exchange developed differently. B's implication in (4) that he was applying a primer coat turned out to be surprising to A, as evidenced by a standard exclamation of surprise, the word *oh*. What A then said was a little odd, but its function is clear:

(5) (A) Òh you shòot a prímer stùff.

Although it appears superficially to be a statement, (5) was actually a request for confirmation of what A had inferred from B's use of the word *primed*. At this point B could simply have answered *yes,* but in fact something different happened. B picked up on the word *shoot,* which suggested that A thought he was using a paint sprayer. He corrected A's assumption with:

(6) a(B) ... We're páintin' it with
    b(B) ... pàintin' by hánd.

This, as it turned out, was the most unexpected piece of information A received during the entire exchange. He now stated, under some confusion, exactly what his expectation had been:

(7) a(A) ... Óh = ?
    b(A) ... What's the
    c(A) ... oh I th
    d(A) .. I thought you were gonna spráy it.

Here was an invitation for B to explain just why he was painting by hand. Evidently he had tried a sprayer earlier:

(8) a(B) .. Òh = that gútless ... spráyer it
    b(B) ... The wínd blòws,
    c(B) .. and héck,
    d(B) .. it doesn't
    e(B) .. it just blòws it awáy.

To which A responded again with surprise:

(9) (A) Óh = ?

B then reinforced the information he had already given by converting into an assertion what he had first presented as an attribution in (8)a:

(10) (B) ... Thàt spràyer's gútless.

But this information too was surprising to A, whose expectation had been that B would have obtained a powerful rental sprayer:

(11) a(A) ... Dìdn't you
     b(A) .. dìdn't you .. rént one?

Again B provided the requested information, implying that he had rented one at an earlier time, but that the one he was talking about now came from a different source:

(12) a(B) .. Yéah =,
     b(B) .. we rénted one but,
     c(B) .. Géorge,
     d(B) .. bòught a ... a little tíny thìng,
     e(B) it hólds about a quárt,

Again A was surprised, but this time his falling pitch suggested more of an inclination to accept this information than he had shown in (9):

(13) (A) ... Óh =.

B now proceeded to elaborate on the contrast between rental sprayers and the one he had recently tried to use:

(14) a(B) ...(1.1) Nó,
     b(B) .. wè = rénted one,
     c(B) .. the ònes you rént,
     d(B) .. boy théy're hìgh
     e(B) ... théy're heavy dúty.
     f(B) .. Théy've got bá = lls to em.
     g(B) .. But thís thìng,

But A decided to find out why his expectation regarding a rental sprayer had not been fulfilled:

(15) a(A) You dìdn't tàlk Stève into réntin'?
     b(A) ... A líttle one,
     c(A) .. it còuldn't cóst much,
     d(A) .. do you thínk?

Again B responded to A's question in a way that was contrary to A's expectation, as signaled by A's *oh* in the middle of the following sequence:

(16) a(B) Ì'm
    b(B) .. Ì'm not súre.
    c(B) .. Ì think it's fifty dòllars a dáy.
    d(A) ... Ó = h.
    e(B) ... To rént one.

The situation now was the following. A was surprised that B was not using a sprayer, B had rejected the available sprayer as inadequate, and both now understood that renting one would be too expensive. B now tried to reassure A that painting by hand was satisfactory, despite what A had thought:

(17) a(B) ...(1.0) Óh it's ... gòing all rìght with the brúsh,
    b(B) .. it's nòt too bád,

A still found that hard to accept, though he tempered his incredulity with laughter. I will use the symbol @ to indicate a pulse of laughter, which in (18)g was congruent with the word *me*:

(18) a(A) .. You've got to pàint wíth it,
    b(A) .. èach and èvery shíngle though,
    c(B) .. Mhm,
    d(B) .. mhm,
    e(A) .. I'd thìnk that'd be gòin' pretty bád.
    f(A) .. @@
    g(A) for @mé,

B now repeated his assertion that his choice was adequate:

(19) a(B) Òh,
    b(B) .. it's
    c(B) .. it's góin' I guess.

We may notice that B's *oh* in (19)a was not A's *oh* of surprise, but the *oh* of resigned adherence to one's own position. B continued by introducing two mitigating factors, the size of the brushes and the presence of helpers:

(20) a(B) ... Ì got wìde brúshes,
    b(B) .. Hènry and Sálly are òver there,
    c(B) ... and Fréd,

A did not question the usefulness of the wide brushes but had some reservations about the helpers:

(21) (A) ... Are thèy much hélp?

But B reassured him again:

(22) a(B) .. Yéah.
     b(A) ... Hm,
     c(A) .. [so that]
     d(B) [Yea = h,]
     e(B) they pàinted quite a bít.

After a second of silence, A accepted B's statement, and in so doing provided closure for this topic. The several conflicts with expectations had
been resolved, and there was no point in continuing further:

(23) (A) ... (1.0) Góod.

The fact that the topic was closed was confirmed by more than two seconds of silence that followed (23) before A initiated an entirely new topic.
He did so again, after a preamble, with a question, maintaining his role
as eliciter:

(24) a(A) ... (2.3) Wè got back to the shóp last nìght,
     b(A) .. and sàw that your cár was still thère,
     c(A) .. and we remèmbered you dròve the Ḿ òver,
     d(A) .. we dìdn't knòw
     e(B) ... Hm,
     f(A) ... Hòw did
     g(A) how d'you get báck.

We need not follow this conversation further, but can review the lessons learned from the topic that was introduced in (3) and concluded in
(23). First, there were clear boundaries to the verbalization of this topic.
It was introduced with a question that was somehow activated in A's mind
during a long period of silence, and it was concluded with a simple
one-word evaluation and another silence. Second, the eliciter and responder played very different roles throughout the exchange, with B providing almost all of the new information and A eliciting it and reacting to
it. Third, the interest this exchange provided for the participants lay in
B's repeated introduction of information that was unexpected for A, with
the resulting expressions of surprise and attempts at resolution. A did
not simply acquire new information, but acquired new information that
conflicted with his earlier understanding of the way the world was.

The Two Women: Topic Development through Narration

The momentum that sustained the topic just illustrated was achieved
through alternating contributions by the eliciter and responder. Other

topics have their own internal momentum. Once initiated, they can be developed by a single speaker with a minimum of assistance. While there may be various forms such a development may take, the most common is that of a *narrative* (e.g., Johnstone 1990, Polanyi 1989). Like the dialogue discussed above, narratives contain something unexpected. The narrator, however, treats the unexpected event as the climax of a set of ideas leading up to and away from it. This schema sustains the verbalization without the need for prodding by an interlocutor.

Narratives tend to follow a typical pattern that determines the sequencing of activated ideas. Various ways of characterizing such a pattern have been suggested, but the basic organization of a conversational narrative was identified some time ago by William Labov and Joshua Waletzky (1967). It is no doubt relevant that their findings were based on naturally occurring spoken narratives, not written or constructed examples. I will suggest a similar but not identical schema, with a few changes in terminology, and will add some thoughts on the relation of this schema to the flow of consciousness. The pattern that emerges from conversational narratives tends to have the following major components, to which is sometimes added an initial summary, or "abstract": (a) orientation; (b) complication; (c) climax; (d) denouement; and (e) coda. The nature of these components and the manner of their realization can be illustrated with a typical conversational narrative, told in the course of a conversation among four participants. The narrative itself was told by Speaker A, with brief responses from Speakers B and C.

Orientation
The orientation of a narrative fills the crucial need of consciousness to be oriented with respect to several types of information (see Chafe 1980, pp. 40–47, for further discussion, as well as chap. 15 below). Language provides clear evidence that consciousness depends for its well-being on information regarding several aspects of the environment in which a person is located. Without such an orientation, consciousness simply cannot function coherently. A disoriented or, better, unoriented consciousness is unable to go about its normal duties of providing the mind with a coherent sequence of ideas. A topic, in the sense of the totality of information that is semiactive at one time, is never viable without an orientation.

There appears to be an especially important need for orientation in space and time—a solid basis, for example, for the folk belief that someone who has accidentally become unconscious says first, on regaining consciousness, "Where am I?" In such a situation the mind can accomplish nothing without first having information about its spatial location. But time may be equally essential, and we can easily imagine a person in the same situation continuing with "What time is it?" or "What day is it?" Just as important seems to be a knowledge of the social setting, the identities of people in whose midst one is located: "Who are you?" or "Who are these people?" Finally, consciousness needs an orientation in terms of what is happening, the ongoing events and states in the midst of which one finds oneself: "What's going on?" The fact that consciousness cannot function without being oriented in space, time, society, and ongoing background events explains the characteristic provision of what is usually called a *setting* as a narrative begins.

In the Two Women narrative, Speaker A began with the following setting:

(25) a(A) ... (1.4) The làst time Ì was thére,
　　　b(A) .. Ì was only there ónce,
　　　c(A) .. Tuo .. Tuólomne ónce.
　　　d(A) ... A = nd uh =
　　　e(A) ... a búnch of us were híking.

Spatial orientation was provided first by the repeated word *there* in (25)a–b, referring to the Tuolomne Meadows area of Yosemite National Park. That area had already been established as a spatial orientation in the preceding conversation, as A reminded the others in (25)c. Temporal orientation was provided by *the last time* and *once*. There is no need to specify times with any exactness; conversational topics are often initiated with expressions like *the other day* or *a couple months ago,* and something like *on July 12 at 10:34 a.m.* would be inappropriate. Intonation unit (25)e provided the background activity, *hiking,* a not unexpected kind of thing for the speaker to have been doing. Knowledge of the narrative schema, however, might already have suggested to the audience that during this hiking something unexpected would occur. The speaker would not have introduced this topic otherwise.

Complication

If the setting can be thought of as a baseline of normality from which the climax will provide an unexpected deviation, the complication introduces referents, events, and states that begin to move away from the normal toward that climax. Whereas the baseline is expressed in durative terms (*were hiking*), the complication shifts to a specific time, along with a specific location in space:

(26) a(A) ... And I guèss we'd hìked all dáy,
　　　b(A) .. Ì don't knòw,
　　　c(A) .. we were álmost to the tóp,
　　　d(A) .. to this láke,
　　　e(A) .. where we were gonna gó,

The above was spoken with a reduced pitch range as a singsong list of spatial goals. Intonation returned to normal with more specific foreshadowings of the climax:

(27) a(A) and it was
  b(A) ... áltitude was prètty
  c(A) .. I mean the áir was pretty thín.
  d(A) .. I mean you could féel it.

Often the complication also introduces other individuals who will participate in the events to follow. These others may be engaged in their own background activity, in this case parallel to that of the first protagonists:

(28) a(A) ... And there were these twó wómen,
  b(A) .. híking up ahéad of us.

Further events and states may lead closer to the climax, providing at the same time suspense as the audience waits for what it knows will conflict with its expectations, in this case expectations regarding a normal hike. Having mentioned the thinness of the air in (27), having introduced the two women in (28), and having thereby aroused an expectation that something involving both the rarefied atmosphere and the two women was about to happen, the narrator postponed the climax by inserting more talk about the terrain:

(29) a(A) ... (1.5) And you sòrt of gót,
  b(A) to a ríse,
  c(A) and then the láke,
  d(A) was kind of rìght thére,
  e(A) where we were gonna ... cámp.

Climax
Finally the unexpected event was revealed. In this case the revelation was spread over a sequence of intonation units, with (30)d the climax of the climax:

(30) a(A) ... And the twó of them,
  b(A) .. gót to the ríse,
  c(A) .. and the néxt mínute,
  d(A) ... (0.9) they just ... (0.6) f = éll óver.
  e(A) .. Tótally.
  f(A) .. I mean I guèss .. the s = tóp,
  g(A) .. was just too múch,
  h(A) .. and they .. bóth of them just tótally pássed óut.
  i(A) .. I mean

A climax is usually presented with bells and whistles. Here added suspense was created, not only by (29), but also by the hesitations preceding the words *fell over,* which were spoken with heightened amplitude and pitch, as well as a lengthening of the initial consonant of *fell.* The impact was reinforced with the word *totally* in (30)e. After an initial attempt at explanation in (30)f–g, there was further reinforcement through repetition with a different wording in (30)h.

Denouement

After a climax, what more is there to say? At this point the dynamic of a narrative involves moves that will return consciousness to a new state of normality in which expectations have been adjusted to include the new and unexpected knowledge. The readjustment can take several forms, and the denouement can have several parts.

It is typical for the climax to be followed by an interactive sequence during which one or more interlocutors express their surprise. These reactions can confirm the speaker's belief that the climactic event was indeed unexpected, and thus that the narrative was worth telling. She may even add her own comment on its unexpectedness, as in (31)c:

(31) a(B) You're kídding.
b(A) Nó.
c(A) It was amázing.

There followed an explicit statement of a return to normalcy:

(32) a(A) I mean wé didn't know what to dó with them.
b(A) I mean they bóth came to lífe.
c(A) .. You know,
d(A) .. very [quíckly] but,
e(B)   [yeah,]

and a more elaborate explanation of why the event may have occurred:

(33) a(A) ... I guéss,
b(A) .. the híke,
c(A) .. and then .. all of a sudden stópping,
d(A) and the óxygen thing,
e(A) must [have] réally confúsed them but.
f(B)   [Hm.]

The denouement ended with a final establishment of normalcy. First, in (34)a–b, there was mention of an event deliberately designed to return things to normal. There followed some gallows humor in (34)c–d, whose effect was to disable the seriousness attached to the affair (Chafe 1987b):

(34) a(A) ... So we hàd them òver for bréad,
    b(A)   @láter,
    c(A)   we .. figured we'll [a] .. còuld have lóst em,
    d(A)   [@@]
    e(A)   in the [mìddle] of the níght.
    f(B)   [Yéah.]
    g(C)   .. Gée.
    h(B)   ...(1.0) Hm.

Coda

A narrative may end with a coda that steps back from the narrated events to provide a metacomment on them. This speaker commented first on the strangeness of what she had told, essentially repeating her earlier postclimactic comment in (31)c. She then provided an additional perspective by comparing what had happened to the two women with her own experience, once more emphasizing the deviation of the climax from the norm:

(35) a(A) .. It was réally ódd.
    b(A)   ... Because .. Í felt kind of ... s = pácy,
    c(A)   .. but I didn't ... feel .. clóse to pàssing óut.

Her voice decreased noticeably in volume by the end of (35)c, signaling that the narrative was complete. After only a short pause, B began a wholly new narrative, with a new spatiotemporal orientation and new protagonists:

(36) a(B) ... (0.6) Wé went ... t uh
    b(B)   ... to the Óregon .. Cascàdes one time,

Topics and Point of View

One of the properties of consciousness listed in chapter 3 is the fact that consciousness is oriented from the point of view of an experiencing self. It is interesting now to observe that a conversational topic is usually, perhaps always, verbalized from some point of view. Terms like *perspective* (MacWhinney 1977), *viewpoint* (DeLancey 1981), and *empathy* (Kuno 1987) seem to be ways of capturing this phenomenon. Since people usually talk about events and states in which they themselves were participants, the point of view is usually that of the speaker. There are several kinds of evidence for a point of view, and they will acquire special importance when we look at written fiction in part 3. They are well illustrated by the Two Women story, which was told from the point of view of its narrator, the person I have called Speaker A.

A rough kind of evidence for a point of view is the sheer frequency with which a referent is activated. The Two Women story began with repeated references to Speaker A, verbalized as *I*:

(37) a(A) ... (1.4) The làst time Í was thére,
    b(A) .. Ì was only there ónce,

Quickly, however, she expanded this referent to include her fellow hikers:

(38) ... a búnch of us were híking.

From this point on, until the coda, the point of view was that of the referent verbalized as *we* or *us*. We learn nothing about the other members of the *bunch* introduced in (38), and there is nothing to distinguish the *we* from the *I*. In the coda the point of view returned to first-person singular:

(39) a(A) ... Because .. Í felt kind of ... s = pácy,
    b(A) .. but I didn't ... feel .. clóse to pàssing óut.

Thus, the story proper had a first-person-plural point of view that was framed within a first-person-singular point of view, but both represented what was essentially the point of view of the speaker. Aside from its frequency, this referent was also favored as a starting point. In all but one of its thirteen occurrences it was verbalized as a subject. There is thus an association of point of view, not only with frequency, but also with the starting point function. A third kind of evidence that the Two Women narrative was being told from A's point of view was provided by the several references to that person's emotions and evaluations. Two clear examples can be seen in (39). The following are some others:

(40) I mean you could féel it.
(41) It was amázing.
(42) .. It was réally ódd.

Information of this kind is directly available only to the consciousness from whose point of view something is being told. A fourth kind of evidence was the fact that the referent in question served as a center for spatial deixis:

(43) .. where we were gonna gó,
(44) .. híking up ahéad of us.

The ideas of *going* and being *ahead of* were relative to the spatial locations of A and her companions. To summarize, a point of view is evident from sheer frequency, from favored status as a starting point, from references to feelings and evaluations, and from status as a deictic center. In part 3 we will see how writers can manipulate such evidence to achieve the effect of a fictional displaced consciousness.

It is interesting to compare the Speaker A referent with the *two-women* referent, which also played a conspicuous role in this narrative but did not establish a point of view. Activated at least nine times, it rivaled the Speaker A referent in frequency. Its occurrences were more tightly clustered in the climax and the denouement, whereas the Speaker A referent was distributed more evenly from the beginning to the end of the story. In only four of its nine occurrences was the two-women referent verbalized as an overt subject, and three of those occurrences were in the climax. The feelings and evaluations of the two women themselves were never mentioned, and they never functioned as a deictic center. Except for its frequency of occurrence, then, the two-women referent lacked the properties that established this narrative as told from A's point of view.

It is also interesting to observe that the person from whose point of view something is told need not be the most important participant in the narrative, in the sense of referential importance discussed in chapter 7. The most important characters in this story may well have been the two women, since the story could justifiably be said to have been *about* them. It was their misadventure that constituted the climax, and it was at the climax that their occurrence as a starting point was centered. With no explicit awareness of these considerations, in fact, I chose to refer to this narrative as The Two Women story. Thus, point of view and importance can be independent (cf. Genette 1980, p. 245).

It is not only narratives that have a point of view. In the elicited topic of Painting the House discussed earlier in this chapter, the point of view was that of B, with or without his painting companions. That referent was verbalized by A as *you* (ambiguous as to singular or plural) and by B as *I* or *we*. For example:

(45) ... Hòw're you dòin' with the hóuse.
(46) .. we rénted one but,
(47) ... Ì got wìde brúshes,

It was a referent that was activated at least twelve times as the topic was developed. It was always verbalized as a subject. The feelings and evaluations of B were stated in several ways, for example:

(48) .. and héck,
(49) ... Thàt sprày er's gútless.
(50) .. Théy've got bá = lls to em.

Spatial deixis was also centered on Speaker B:

(51) .. Hènry and Sálly are òver there,

Being *over there* was relative to B's current location. The Painting the House topic, then, was elaborated from B's point of view, even though he did not produce it as a self-sustaining narrative.

While the point of view is usually that of a participant in the conversation, it need not be. In other words, it is possible for a topic to be developed from a third-person point of view. In the conversations examined, third-person points of view were of short duration and did not belong to topics that had the well-developed structures illustrated by Painting the House and The Two Women. In the following excerpt the speaker was talking briefly about an experience of her husband:

(52) a Because ... that ... one níght,
     b .. that he was so síck,
     c .. when he first got síck.
     d ... He was wálking stòoped óver,
     e .. his bàck .. hurt só bád.

The husband, narrowed to nothing more than *his back* in the last line, functioned throughout this sequence as a starting point. Although the durative event in (52)d could have been observed from either the speaker's or the husband's point of view, (52)e focused unambiguously on the husband's feeling. Third-person points of view in conversational language usually exhibit this fleeting quality. Typically it is a speaker's point of view that predominates.

Summary and Prospects

Discourse topics are aggregates of semiactive information that segment a conversation into larger chunks than intonation units. Topics are verbalized when they are judged interesting, which usually means that the speaker judges them to conflict in some way with normal expectations. Once a topic has become semiactive, it may be sustained through elicitation or narration. In elicitation, forward movement through the topic is driven by the interaction between two or more interlocutors, one functioning as an eliciter and another as a responder. Self-sustaining topics, those that do not require interaction for their development, typically take the form of narratives. Unless there is an initial summary, the narrative schema begins with an orientation that provides information essential to a well-ordered consciousness, including location in space and time, the identification of one or more protagonists, and specification of an ongoing normal activity. There follows a complication that leads away from that activity toward a climax in conflict with expectations. The denouement may begin with reactions by other parties to the unexpectedness, continuing with a series of events and states that return consciousness to a new normalcy. There may be a coda that includes comments from an external perspective.

Topics, whether elicited or narrated, include one referent from whose *point of view* the topic is developed. This status is manifested in several ways: through that referent's frequent occurrence, its favored use as a starting point, mention of its feelings and evaluations, and its use as a center for spatial deixis. Point of view is to be distinguished from importance. Using an analogy to the way we look at pictures, we can say that point of view has to do with the viewer, importance with what is viewed.

It will be valuable to examine many naturally occurring conversational topics in order to establish the ways in which they may be activated, to establish a better understanding of what it means for a topic to be interesting, and to see what types of topic development beyond elicitation and narration can be identified. The schema of orientation, complication, climax, denouement, and coda that drives the development of a narrative topic needs further study. To what extent does it hold up against a wide range of data, and what are its variants? What does it show about the way the mind interprets experience? How much of it is universal, how much culturally determined? Do some conversational narratives follow completely different schemas? Finally, how consistent are the kinds of evidence for a point of view that were identified in this chapter, and are there other kinds of evidence?

Topic Hierarchies and Sentences

Topics within a conversation show a hierarchical organization, with larger topics embracing smaller ones. The Two Women narrative discussed in chapter 10 was part of a larger topic that embraced a series of narratives concerned with the Tuolomne Meadows area of Yosemite National Park. A *supertopic* such as the idea of Tuolomne Meadows can persist through a sequence of narratives, and this conversation even exhibited a *supersupertopic,* the idea of adventures in the mountains. Broader in scope than the various things that happened at Tuolomne Meadows, this even more encompassing topic included other events in the Sierra Nevada as well as the Oregon Cascades. It was activated in this conversation well before the Tuolomne Meadows supertopic and continued well beyond it.

Basic-Level Topics

The presence of any hierarchical structure raises the question of whether there exists a certain level of the hierarchy that can be characterized as *basic.* When it comes to categories (e.g., Lakoff 1987), we know that a particular referent might be categorized as an animal, a dog, a spaniel, or a field spaniel, but there are various reasons for thinking that its categorization as a dog has a privileged status (e.g., Berlin, Breedlove, and Raven 1973; Rosch et al. 1976). That categorization is, for example, the default. All other things being equal, a passenger in a car may be more likely to say *Look out for that dog!* than either *Look out for that animal!* (at a higher level) or *Look out for that spaniel!* (at a lower one). The basic-level categorization is said to be the one learned earliest by children. It may also be the highest level at which it is possible to form a coherent mental image. While we can imagine a prototypical *dog,* the *animal* category does not lend itself to imaging in the same way. Below the basic level, words associated with the category are more likely to have a complex structure, like *field spaniel.*

Can narratives like the one discussed in chapter 10 be considered expressions of basic-level topics, in some ways analogous to basic-level categories? Perhaps, for example, such narratives represent the highest level at which one finds a coherent structure like the narrative schema. Supertopics achieve their coherence from the presence of some general orientation (the idea of Tuolomne Meadows or of adventures in the mountains), which extends through and supports a series of basic-level topics, but exhibit no unifying schema of their own. It is possible, too, that basic-level topics represent the largest amount of information that can be held in semiactive consciousness at once. In chapter 9 we explored a limitation on fully active consciousness, and it is intriguing to speculate on whether basic-level topics can provide evidence for limitations on semiactive consciousness. If semiactive consciousness is limited to the amount of information verbalized in a narrative schema, when more information is added it may have to be divided into a sequence of separate basic-level topics.

Narratives that are longer and more complex than the one discussed in chapter 10 may contain more than a single topic, since a longer narrative may overflow the bounds of semiactive consciousness. In such a case each basic-level topic within the larger narrative constitutes an included *episode* of which the longer narrative is constructed. Elsewhere (Chafe 1979; see also Chafe 1980, pp. 40–47) I discussed evidence from the Pear Stories that the boundaries between such episodes come in different strengths, depending on the degree of reorientation that is necessary. Judging from the degree of hesitating, the strongest boundary occurred at a point where a speaker shifted out of the story world into the "real" world of the pear film interview, a shift identified in part 3 of this book as a move from the displaced to the immediate mode. Nearly as strong a boundary was present when there was a total change of scene. There were lesser boundaries with lesser degrees of hesitating when a new character was introduced without a change of scene, or when there was some discontinuity in the sequence of events.

A written version of one of these pear stories, with no indication of paragraph boundaries or hesitations, was given to a hundred subjects who were asked to put a mark where they thought a paragraph boundary belonged. The resulting paragraph judgments showed a significant rank-order correlation with the lengths of hesitations in the spoken version. The longer the hesitation, the greater the tendency for readers of the doctored written version to insert a paragraph boundary on the basis of content alone. From such evidence I was able to suggest the following:

> Rather than think of an experience as being stored in memory in terms of distinct episodes, it seems preferable to think of a more complex storage in terms of coherent spaces, coherent temporal continuities, coherent configurations of characters, coherent event sequences, and coherent worlds. At points where all of these change

in a maximal way, an episode boundary is strongly present. But often one or another will change considerably while others will change less radically, and all kinds of varied interactions between these several factors are possible. (Chafe 1979, pp. 179–80)

If boundaries vary in strength in this way, basic-level topics of the type illustrated in chapter 10 can be seen as especially important determinants of discontinuity within a conversation, just because they are responsible for a convergence of most if not all of the factors listed.

Sentences

What about levels of organization below that of the basic-level topic? Are there identifiable conceptual units that are smaller than those expressed in basic-level topics but larger than intonation units? If so, how are such units related to the flow of consciousness (cf. Chafe 1987a)? It is helpful to consider the following sequence of two intonation units from the Two Women narrative:

(1) a ... And there were these twó wómen,
    b .. híking up ahéad of us.

The one new idea constraint explains why this information had to be distributed among two intonation units. A new referent, the idea of the two women, was activated in (1)a, and (1)b then focused on what they were doing and its location. The idea of *hiking* alone, since it was already accessible, would not have been enough to push (1)b into a separate focus of consciousness, but the new idea that the hiking was *ahead of us* did have that effect.

Despite the fact that the information in (1) was and indeed had to be expressed in two intonation units, there is an obvious unity to the sequence as a whole that is observable in several ways. First, the falling pitch at the end of (1)b, shown in the transcription with the period punctuation, as well as a decline in pitch and amplitude through the entire sequence, conveyed a clear impression that the speaker had come to the end of something. In contrast, the intonation contour at the end of (1)a, marked with a comma, conveyed incompleteness; there was more to come. The sense of completeness given by the overall prosody of (1) was reflected also in its syntactic structure. Although it might not be considered elegant if it occurred in writing, the grammar of this sequence is that of a complete sentence.

The fact that both prosody and syntax converge on the delimitation of a sentencelike unit suggests that it is a unit of some importance. The sentence has, in fact, seemed so important to so many that it has been the basic unit of grammatical study from ancient times to the present. There is today an entire industry that thrives on the study of sentences. But what exactly is a sentence? Why does language combine prosody and grammar to mark units of this kind? We have seen that *intonation units* verbalize the content of active consciousness, that basic-level *topics* verbalize the content of semiactive consciousness, but what do *sentences* verbalize?

I have speculated (Chafe 1980, pp. 20–40) that the evolution of the human mind has left us with abilities that are incomplete. Each focus of consciousness embraces just enough information to be effective in terms of the human organism's basic needs—to make it aware of food, danger, a mate, or whatever. Presumably foveal vision evolved with a similar adaptive limit on its capacity. We are thus physically designed to deal with only a very small amount of information at one time, the amount that can be comprehended in one focus of active consciousness. In the meantime, in concert with the remarkable growth of the human cortex, the capacity of our minds to store and manipulate ideas has greatly increased. Our powers of remembering and imagining have far outstripped those of other creatures. But this development has failed to include any increase in the capacity of active consciousness, which presumably remains as limited today as it was before the brain evolved to its present state. We are capable of thinking grand and complicated thoughts, but we can still focus our active consciousness on only very small parts of them at one time. The remainder can be present only semiactively.

We constantly try, nevertheless, to push the capacity of focal consciousness beyond the bounds of a single focus, attempting to embrace larger, more intellectually challenging conglomerates of information. I am not sure what to call these larger cognitive units, but earlier (Chafe 1980, p. 26) I called them *centers of interest,* following the lead of Buswell (1935), who used the term with relation to how people look at pictures. These centers of interest are not limited by our wired-in mental capacities, but represent attempts, with varying degrees of success, to push the mind beyond the constraints of active consciousness. In that sense they can be regarded as superfoci of consciousness, and they come to be expressed in language as super–intonation units. Too large to be embraced in a single focus, a superfocus can be dealt with only by allowing a series of more limited foci to play across it, fully activating first one part and then another. When speakers judge that the scanning of a center of interest has been completed, they express that judgment with a sentence-final intonation contour. With luck, the syntactic structure will show at that point the completeness associated with sentencehood. But people sometimes have trouble constructing sentences under the constraints of conversational speaking. Consistently successful sentence construction is possible only under the more leisurely circumstances associated with writing.

What kinds of information chunks, too big to be accommodated within single foci, make up these centers of interest? There is no single, straightforward answer to this question, since centers of interest derive, not from our neural makeup, as do foci of consciousness, but from a variety of "higher" intellectual considerations. There is no typical schema for a center of interest. Sometimes it may represent a component of a larger schema. It is common, for example, for the orientation component of the narrative schema to combine the introduction of a protagonist with the idea of an ongoing activity in which that protagonist is engaged. If both the protagonist and the activity are new information, they cannot both be activated simultaneously but require two separate activations expressed in two intonation units. Hence the situation illustrated in (1) above, where *protagonist engaged in background activity* defines the center of interest expressed in the sentence.

We can consider another example from a different part of the same conversation:

(2) a(A) .. I was on the bús todà = y,
    b(A) ... à = nd there was this wóman sàying,
    c(A) .. that her són,
    d(A) .. wòrks .. for the ránger sèrvice or whatever.
    e(A) ... And ... there was snó = w,
    f(A) ... chést hígh,
    g(A) at Tuòlomne Méadows.

Here there are two sentences: (2)a–d is separated from (2)e–g by convergent prosodic and syntactic criteria. What led the speaker to separate these two chunks of information, to deal with them as separate centers of interest? The answer seems clear. Intonation units (2)a–d verbalized information having to do with events on the bus, events that provided a source for the information that followed. Intonation units (2)e–g verbalized a state that existed in a totally different location, Tuolomne Meadows. This spatial difference was enough to establish these two segments as distinct centers of interest. Their separate functions, first as the source of some surprising news, then as the news itself, were congruent with that division.

More complexities emerge with the following example from the Two Women narrative:

(3) a(A) ...(1.0) And I guèss we'd hìked all dáy,
    b(A) .. Ì don't knòw,
    c(A) .. we were álmost to the tóp,
    d(A) .. to this láke,
    e(A) .. where we were gonna gó,
    f(A) and it was
    g(A) ... áltitude was prètty
    h(A) .. I mean the áir was pretty thín.
    i(A) .. I mean you could féel it.

Intonation units (3)a–h constituted one long prosodic sentence and (3)i a much shorter one. It is unclear how many syntactic sentences were included in (3)a–h; the grammar is not what one would produce in writing. The entire sequence, however, prepared the scene for the introduction of the two women and constituted a coherent center of interest in that respect. The prosody of (3)h suggests that the speaker believed she had concluded a center of interest at this point. She then added (3)i to provide evidence for what she had just said. It is common for speakers to complete the scanning of a center of interest, indicating completion with a falling pitch, and then supplement the information already conveyed with a brief additional focus of this kind. Such a supplement might be termed an *afterthought*. Functionally, and often syntactically, an afterthought belongs to the same center of interest as what precedes it. Intonational, syntactic, and functional boundaries do not always coincide.

There is nothing unusual about (3) as spoken language, but it seems to show more syntactic sentences than prosodic ones. Other examples, in contrast, show that one syntactic sentence can extend over several prosodic sentences:

(4) a ... And they stárted wálking.
    b ... Tòward these élephants.
    c ...(1.0) And these gàls were tàking píctures.
    d ... And àll of a sùdden òne of em tùrned aróund.
    e ...(1.0) And stàrted to còme tóward him.

Intonation units (4)a and (4)b are separate prosodically but belong together syntactically, as do (4)d and (4)e. In spite of such mismatches, which are common, spoken language in general gives the impression that speakers strive for sentences whose prosodic and syntactic boundaries coincide. When congruence is lacking, that fact usually goes unnoticed by either the speaker or the listener. Whatever drive there may be to produce sentences that are both prosodically and syntactically consistent, it is not a strongly compelling one, nor is it important to the effective use of speech.[1]

The period intonation, then, serves to express a speaker's judgment that he or she has completed the verbalization of some coherent unit of content, a unit I have called a center of interest, which is frequently more encompassing than an intonation unit. There exist a number of syntactic devices by which intonation units may be integrated into a coherent sequence. A speaker's use of these devices may range from simple adjoining of intonation units, to coordinating them with *and,* to employing more complex devices of embedding and subordination (for a discussion of these possibilities in conversational language, see Chafe 1988a). In speech, these last alternatives may require a greater commitment to the verbalization process than speakers can easily afford. Hence the one-clause-at-a-time constraint described by Pawley and Syder (1983a). Speakers tend to avoid elaborate syntactic complexities, and when they try to produce them they may find themselves "out on a syntactic limb." The trouble results from an overtaxing of the focus of consciousness, which, with its limited capacity and duration, cannot easily handle syntactic devices that commit too many of its resources to complex verbalizing.

It is interesting to find that a particular segment of experience does not necessarily dictate a particular division into sentences (prosodic, syntactic, or both). A speaker is likely to divide the same remembered or imagined experience into sentences in different ways at different times. This fact suggests that the material included in even a well-formed sentence does not necessarily represent a unit of perception, storage, or remembering, but results from an on-line, one-time decision that something has been completed. What that something is may range from a single focus of consciousness, to a component of a topic, to an entire topic. But the same speaker may decide to draw the boundaries differently in different verbalizations of the same information at different times.

To investigate thoroughly the hypothesis that the boundaries of sentences are assigned in the course of particular verbalizations and, unlike foci of consciousness, do not represent units of perception, storage, or remembering, it would be necessary to study many instances of retellings of the same subject matter by the same speaker. I have looked at a few such retellings and mention here only one example from two Pear Stories told by the same person six weeks apart. (Further discussion of this

---

1. It is interesting to note that in their twenty-minute sample of conversational speech, Ford and Thompson (in press) found that 98.8 percent of the "intonation completion points" (roughly, prosodic sentences) were also "grammatical completion points" (roughly, syntactic sentences), but that only 53.6 percent of the grammatical completion points were also intonation completion points.

example is available in Chafe 1979, pp. 173–76; see also Chafe 1977, pp. 241–45.)

(5) a ...(1.4) A = nd ...(1.0) we see it,
    b .. the gravel path,
    c from his point of view,
    d ...(.8) and the we see ..
      a girl riding a bike
    e coming the opposite direction.
    f ...(.9) And then .. the camera's
      backed up,
    g and you see them going like
      this.
    h .. And then you see it from his
      point of view again.
    i .. And .. his hat blows off,

    j ...(.55) when they cross,

    k .. and ...(.65) his bike hits into a
      rock.

(6) a And a camera follows him,

    b and um ...(2.95) tsk sudden
      there's a .. girl riding a bicycle,
    c coming the opposite direction,

    d ...(0.5) and as they cross each ..
      each other,
    e ...(1.25) the boy's cap .. flies off
      his head.
    f ...(.85) A = nd ...(0.5) he = .. hits
      something,

Two facts are worth noting. First, the content of intonation units is impressively robust, remaining virtually unchanged over a period of six weeks. Intonation unit (6)b can be equated with (5)d, (6)c contains exactly the same words as (5)e, (6)d matches (5)j and (6)e matches (5)i in a chiastic pattern, and (6)f verbalizes the same content as (5)k. To the extent that the same ideas are remembered, their content is close to identical in different tellings, even though they may be expressed with somewhat different words. Evidently intonation units do represent relatively stable units of remembering. Second, the organization of intonation units into sentences shows little of the same stability. Whereas this speaker concluded a sentence in (5)e after the introduction of the girl, in (6)c she just kept going. Intonation units (5)f–h had no counterpart in the second telling. But then in (5)i–k the hat, the crossing, and hitting the rock were combined into a single sentence, whereas (6)d–e combined the first two of these events (in the opposite order) within one sentence, relegating the hitting to a separate sentence in (6)f. Evidently *sentences* do *not* represent stable units in the mind. They are constructed creatively on the run, with varying degrees of functional, prosodic, and syntactic coherence.

Summary and Prospects

The kinds of topics illustrated and discussed in chapter 10 constitute a basic level of topichood at which pervasive schemas like the narrative schema determine the internal topic structure. Basic-level topics are often linked within more inclusive supertopics, the latter functioning as unifying ideas that persist in semiactive consciousness through longer stretches of conversation, triggering first one narrative and then another.

Below the basic level are coherences of a special sort, verbalized as sentences, which can be regarded as superfoci of consciousness. They bring together chunks of information too large to be accommodated within a single focus, often intermediate in comprehensiveness between a single focus and a basic-level topic. Sentences are recognizable in part in terms of sentence-final prosody, in part in terms of their syntactic completeness. While these two criteria often coincide, often they do not; sentences are not always easy for speakers to produce in such a way that they are both prosodically and syntactically well formed. The information brought together in a sentence seems not to represent any cognitively stable unit of perception, storage, or remembering. Rather, sentence boundaries appear when a speaker judges, during a particular telling, that a coherent center of interest has been verbalized at that point. There are a variety of grounds for judging such coherence, and those grounds are subject to variation in repeated verbalizations of the same subject matter.

It will be particularly interesting to study further the maintenance of topics during conversations. It seems likely that individuals differ with respect to the length of time a particular topic is held in the semiactive state. To what extent does such a difference create problems in interaction for interlocutors whose conversational styles are governed by shorter or longer topic maintenance times? If the difference between an intonation unit and a sentence reflects a difference between what humans are inherently able to process in one focus of consciousness and what they judge to constitute a "complete thought," many naturally occurring sentences need to be examined in order to establish the varied grounds for judging that a particular sequence of foci has achieved completeness. Finally, the cognitive stability of intonation units and the variability of sentences that was illustrated in (5) need to be investigated through the collection and analysis of multiple retellings of the "same" topics by the same tellers after varying intervals of time (Bartlett 1932, Chafe 1986). It is too bad that the favored paradigms of both linguistics and psychology have failed to take advantage of this most promising observational technique.

12

Another Language

No one should expect to learn everything there is to learn about language and consciousness (or, for that matter, anything else about language and the mind) from a single language. Some of the things discussed in the preceding chapters surely derive from the mental processes and abilities of all humans, no matter what language they speak, but other things must be specific to English. This is not the place for a wide-ranging exploration of what is universal and what particular, but a brief comparison with one very different kind of language can at least be suggestive. The language I will draw on is Seneca (e.g., Chafe 1967), spoken at present by fewer than two hundred people on the Allegany, Cattaraugus, and Tonawanda reservations in western New York State. It is a member of the Iroquoian language family, one of the major language families of the eastern United States and Canada. Its grammatical structure is unlike that of English in many ways, and for that reason it can be especially useful in separating what all languages have in common from the kinds of things that make them different.

The following excerpt from a Seneca conversation provides an initial insight into the nature of this language.[1] The speaker was telling two other people about a birthday celebration that had been held for him the previous evening in the Longhouse, the site for Seneca religious observances and other gatherings. Each of the five intonation units is presented in a three-line format: a transcription of the Seneca, a word-by-word translation, and a free translation of the entire intonation unit.[2]

(1) a ... Waęnǫdęnodǫ:nyǫ́:ʔ nǽ:h.
they sang plurally highlight
They sang songs.

---

1. The conversations excerpted here were recorded and transcribed by Alberta Austin of the Cattaraugus Reservation, who also collaborated in their analysis.

2. The vowels ę and ǫ are nasalized, æ is a low front vowel, ʔ is a glottal stop, the colon indicates vowel length, and the acute accent mark shows a vowel that is spoken with a higher pitch peak than other vowels. Seneca words may or may not contain one or more of these accented vowels, the location of which is for the most part phonologically determined. However, the accent on the last vowel of a word, as in (1)b–d, combined with the nonfalling pitch that is shown with the comma, is a signal that more is to come, that the end of a sentence (or center of interest) has not yet been reached.

b ... Waʔagwadékhǫ:níʔ,
       we ate
       We ate,

c ... saęnǫdęno:dę́ʔ kho áéʔ,
       they sang again and again
       and they sang again,

d ... gędzǫ oęnǫ́ʔ waęnǫdęno:dę́ʔ,
       fish   song   they sang
       they sang the Fish Dance,

e ęhséʔsáǫʔ   wa:ęniʔ.
   you will lead   they said
   "You will lead," they said.
   (i.e., "You will lead the dance.")

One of the most obvious properties of this language is the fact that many of its words contain more information than the words of English. In a rough way that fact is evident from a comparison of the Seneca words in (1) with their English translations. In (1)a, for example, the word *waęnǫdęnodǫ:nyǫ́:ʔ* is freely translated 'they sang songs.' One Seneca word is translated by three English words. But such a simple comparison does not come close to giving the whole picture. This Seneca word begins with a prefix *wa-*, which expresses the factuality of the event. Other prefixes would be used in this position if the event were anticipated or hypothesized. That prefix is followed by a so-called pronominal prefix *-ęn-* which indicates that the agents of the event were three or more individuals, at least one of whom was male. In the middle of the word is a stem *-ǫdęnod-* that categorizes the event as an instance of singing. Etymologically this stem is composed of three parts. It begins with a middle voice prefix, here with the shape *-ǫd-*, showing that the agents not only performed the action but were also in some sense affected by what they did. Then comes an incorporated noun root *-ęn-*, meaning 'song,' followed by a verb root *-od-*, which by itself means to 'stand something upright.' Thus, the complex stem meaning 'sing' is derived historically from a combination whose literal meaning is 'stand oneself a song upright' (compare English expressions that involve lifting one's voice in song). This stem is followed by a suffix *-ǫ:nyǫ-* indicating that more than one song sequence was sung. (The word at the end of (1)d, which referred to a single song sequence, differs from this word only in the absence of this suffix.) There is then a final punctual aspect suffix *-:ʔ*, expressing the fact that the singing of the song sequences was a particular event. In contrast to this complex word, the English word *sang* conveys nothing more than a categorization of the event as an instance of singing, plus the information that it was recalled from an earlier experience.

⌈Because Seneca words tend in this way to contain more information than English words, it is not surprising that Seneca intonation units tend to contain fewer words than English intonation units.⌋Example (1) provides a quick impression of the size of Seneca units, which range in this case from one to three words. The modal length is in fact two words, in contrast to four words in English. With respect to number of words, then, Seneca intonation units are half as long as English ones.

The Nature of Seneca Pronominal Prefixes

In comparing Seneca and English with respect to the flow of language and consciousness, pronominal prefixes are of particular interest. Illustrated by the element -*en*-, translated 'they,' in the word discussed above, they are a salient aspect of the morphology of all Iroquoian languages (Seneca has sixty-six of them). They have sometimes been seen as analogous to so-called agreement markers in more familiar languages. For example, corresponding to the agreement suffixes at the ends of German verbs

(2) ich   lieb-*e*   I love
    du   lieb-*st*   you love
    er, sie, es lieb-*t*   he, she, it loves

would be the prefixes at the *beginning* of Seneca words like

(3) *k*-nóǫhgwaʔ   I love
    s-nóǫhgwaʔ   you love
    ha-nóǫhgwaʔ   he loves
    ye-nóǫhgwaʔ   she loves
    ga-nóǫhgwaʔ   it loves

Others, however, have suggested the obvious alternative—that these pronominal prefixes are more like the English (or German) pronouns used to translate them than they are like the agreement markers (Mithun 1985; cf. Jelinek 1984). They verbalize referents directly and do not simply copy into the verb the person, number, and gender of external referents. But if the pronominal prefixes of Seneca are like the pronouns of English with respect to referentiality, they are different in other ways. We will find that (a) the use of these prefixes is not dependent on activation cost, and (b) they do not grammaticize starting points, that is, they do not mark the role of subject.

The Irrelevance of Activation Cost

We saw in chapter 6 that English pronouns express given (or, rarely, accessible) referents. The Seneca prefixes do not show the same relation to activation cost. Many do express given referents, as did -*ęn*- 'they' in (1)a. But a pronominal prefix often expresses a referent that is accessible. In the following example the referent that was verbalized in the second word of (4)a with the prefix *ho*- 'he,' and again in (4)b as *Hank Brown,* had been activated earlier in the conversation but could not have been in the listener's fully active consciousness at the onset of (4)a:

> (4) a ... nǫkho   *ho*-wę́gę̣:ǫ?   neh,
>   here   *he* was the former owner   that one
>   He was the former owner here,
>
>   b ... Hành Brówn.
>   Hank   Brown
>   Hank Brown.

But more divergent from English are usages in which a pronominal prefix expresses new information. In (5) a new referent was introduced by the prefix -*o*- 'he' (a variant of *ho*-) in the last word of (5)a, with a more explicit categorization provided in (5)b:

> (5) a ... Wa:e   gyǫ?ǫ́   shǫ: hé-ó-snye?ǫh,
>   then   hearsay   just   *he* uttered it there
>   He had allegedly just made a phone call,
>
>   b ... sǫ:gá:?   shagoye:nǫ́:s   i:gę:h.
>   someone   he catches them   who
>   someone who was a policeman.

In more natural English, perhaps 'I heard there was some policeman, who had just made a phone call.' The strategies in (4) and (5) are typical of Seneca discourse, and they suggest that the use of a pronominal prefix is independent of the activation cost of its referent. Instead of being used to express given information, the Seneca prefixes refer to the core participant(s) of events and states—referents that are obligatorily included in an event or state idea. When a Seneca speaker chooses to categorize an event or state in a particular way, that categorization dictates the presence of one, two, or occasionally three participants which are obligatorily expressed with a pronominal prefix. Their activation cost is irrelevant. Whereas English uses pronouns to verbalize given referents, Seneca uses pronominal prefixes to verbalize core participants. Aside from the fact that core participants are often given, the two functions are distinct.

The Irrelevance of Subjecthood

Some English pronouns occur in two forms, the difference determined in large part by whether or not they function as the subjects of their clauses—by whether or not they express starting points. The distinction between *I* and *me, she* and *her,* and so on, is of this nature. Seneca pronominal prefixes also show a division into two sets, and some examples suggest that the distinction is the same as in English, as exemplified by the prefixes *ye-* 'she' and *go-* 'her' in the following words:

(6) a *ye*-nóǫhgwaʔ
       she loves it

    b *go*-nóǫhgwaʔ
       it loves *her*

When a human participant is paired with a nonhuman one, as in both these words, the nonhuman participant ('it') fails to receive any overt representation in the Seneca verb. Thus, only the human participant ('she' or 'her') is represented by a prefix in either (6)a or (6)b. One might conclude that *ye-* in (6)a expresses a starting point, as does 'she' in the translation, and that *go-* in (6)b expresses something other than a starting point, as does 'her' in the translation ('it' being the English starting point). On that basis, Iroquoian pronominal prefixes have in fact sometimes been said to fall into a *subjective* and an *objective* set (e.g., Barbeau 1915, Lounsbury 1953, Chafe 1967).

But Iroquoian linguists have long realized that the distinction in these languages should not be equated with the subject-object distinction in English. The true nature of the distinction is illustrated in (7), where the pronominal element translated 'she,' everywhere an English subject, appears in (7)a as an agent (*-e-* being a variant of the *ye-* in (6)a), but in (7)b and (7)c as a patient (*-ago-* being a variant of the *go-* in (6)b and (7)b):

(7) a waʔ-*é*-khǫ:niʔ
       she cooked

    b *go*-dǫ́sweʔda:nih
       she's hungry

    c waʔ-*ágo*-hdaʔt
       she got full

In (7)a the agent performed the cooking. In (7)b and (7)c the patient either was in a state of being hungry or underwent a change of state to being full.

The functional basis of this agent-patient distinction has often been misunderstood for at least two reasons (Mithun 1991 provides an extended discussion of agent-patient marking languages). One reason is the fact that historical processes have sometimes frozen particular prefixes to particular verb roots whose meanings have changed. A cogent example is provided by the root meaning 'throw' in Seneca and related languages, where with seeming perversity the thrower is represented by a patient, not an agent prefix. There is evidence that at an earlier time this root meant 'lose' or 'be divested of,' with the divestee understandably expressed as a patient, a person to whom something happened. With the semantic change from 'be divested of' to 'throw,' the patient prefix was retained, yielding what now seems a semantic anomaly.

A second cause of misunderstanding has been the fact that the properties that define the agent and patient roles are not the same in all the languages that make this distinction and may not even be consistently distributed within a single language. In the Lakhota language a person who *hiccups* is verbalized as an agent, whereas in Seneca a hiccupper is a patient. Hiccupping is something a person does, and it is the role as the performer of the action that is chosen for the Lakhota prefix. But hiccupping is also outside a person's control, something that happens to a person, and it is the property of being involuntarily affected by the event that is verbalized in Seneca. Lakhota regularly verbalizes performers of actions as agents, regardless of whether they control the event or not. Iroquoian languages are less predictable, and with ambiguous events it is not always possible to guess what they will do. A person who *coughs,* unlike a hiccupper, is verbalized in Seneca as an agent, even when the event is not under the cougher's control.

One might expect that someone or something that is in a state would be expressed with a patient prefix. In Seneca that is true of states that are transitory and not inherent in the person or object concerned: states like being *happy* or *wet,* for example. But states that are inherent, like being *tall* or being a *white person,* are expressed with an agent prefix. Again there is room for variation. Being *old* in Seneca takes an agent prefix, as if the oldness were an intrinsic state, whereas in the closely related Onondaga language a patient prefix is used, as if oldness were something that happened to a person. Regardless of these differences in the distribution of agents and patients, it is clear that the function of a referent as a starting point does not determine the choice of a Seneca prefix.

It is interesting at this point to realize that, whereas English pronouns are determined by discourse factors (activation cost and the starting point role), Seneca pronominal prefixes are determined by factors internal to the event or state expressed by the verb to which they are attached. For a referent to be verbalized with a pronominal prefix depends on its being a core participant in the event or state expressed by the verb. Assignment to one or the other of the two major sets of prefixes depends on being an agent or patient of the event or state. While English pronouns are centrifugally oriented, looking outward toward the discourse context of the event or state, Seneca pronominal prefixes are centripetally oriented, looking inward to the event or state itself.

The One New Idea Constraint

We have seen that neither activation cost nor the starting point role is expressed by the Seneca pronominal prefixes. The starting point role seems, in fact, to be irrelevant to the language, but we are left with the question of whether activation cost has any effect outside the pronominal prefixes, and here the answer can be more positive. I hypothesized in chapter 9, on the basis of English alone, that speakers are incapable of verbalizing more than one independent new idea in each intonation unit, an idea being a person's mental representation of an event, state, or referent. Since Seneca speakers also produce language in the format of a sequence of intonation units, we might expect the same constraint to apply. Examples like (1) at the beginning of this chapter conform well to the one new idea constraint. The first three intonation units verbalized a singing event, an eating event, and another singing event, and in each case there was nothing to suggest the presence of more than one new idea:

(8) a ... Waęnǫdęnodǫ:nyǫ́:ʔ   nǽ:h.
        they sang plurally   highlight
        They sang songs.

    b ... Waʔagwadékhǫ:níʔ,
        we ate
        We ate,

    c ... saęnǫdęno:dę́ʔ   kho   áéʔ,
        they sang again   and   again
        and they sang again,

The next intonation unit began with a single lexicalized referent, the idea of the Fish Dance:[3]

(9) ... gędzǫ   oęnǫ́ʔ   waęnǫdęno:dę́ʔ,
      fish   song   they sang
      they sang the Fish Dance,

---

3. Although the Seneca phrase means literally 'fish song,' it refers to both a song sequence and an accompanying dance and is ordinarily translated into English as 'Fish Dance.'

The singing had already been introduced as new information in (8)c, and thus all that was new in (9) was the idea of the Fish Dance. The next intonation unit verbalized what might seem at first to be two new events:

(10) ęhsé?sáǫ?   wa:ęni?.
     you will lead   they said
     "You will lead," they said.

However, the second word functioned as the attribution of a quote, constituting a low-content verb in the sense of chapter 9. Example (10) did not focus on the fact that people said something but on what they said. Thus, nowhere in (1) was there a violation of the one new idea constraint. From the available evidence, that constraint applies as consistently in Seneca as it does in English. That is surely what we would expect, since the inability to verbalize more than one independent new idea per intonation unit must reflect a universal limitation on the flow of ideas through consciousness and language.

Identifiability

The pervasive concern for identifiability that is so evident in the English use of the definite article seems not to be universally shared. Many languages lack such an article, and speakers of other languages often experience difficulty learning how to use the English word *the* appropriately. Seneca, however, makes frequent use of a word *neh* whose function overlaps significantly with the function of *the*. (Its shape is *ne* when directly followed by another word, and it is sometimes reduced further to *n.*) *Neh,* like *the,* is used to mark identifiability:

(11) wadye:sę́   ne   gakhwa?
     it's cheap   the   food
     The food was cheap.

The referent of *gakhwa?* 'food' was shared and contextually salient, and thus identifiable, having been activated earlier in the conversation. Sufficiently identifying language may be provided in ways that are not unlike those found in English. In the following sequence the referent verbalized in (12)b might not have been sufficiently identified with the noun *gagáwihsa?* 'shovel' alone, but it was made identifiable by the addition of the modifying *ikha:?* 'I'm holding it,' whose function is comparable to that of an English relative clause:

(12) a ... hó:gwá: ǫga:di?,
                over there I threw it
                I threw it over there,

b ... ne   gagáwihsaʔ   ikha:ʔ.
   the   shovel   I'm holding it
   the shovel I was holding.

In spite of this considerable overlap between the uses of Seneca *neh* and English *the,* other uses show the extent to which languages can exploit similar resources in different ways.

The referents of proper names are inherently identifiable, and whereas English does not usually mark them as such with the definite article, many other languages do. Seneca often follows that course, saying, for example, *ne Clara,* literally 'the Clara,' just as German speakers might say *die Clara.* But whereas the definite article with proper names is familiar from European languages, its use with first- and second-person pronouns is not. Seneca uses such pronouns, in addition to its pronominal prefixes, when a first- or second-person referent is accessible, contrastive, or highlighted with the particle *nœ:(h).* Frequently such a pronoun is preceded by the article—literally, for example, 'the me,' as in (13)b:

(13) a ... Oʔwáʔswa?   gę:s,
      fire goes out   habitually
      The fire keeps going out;

    b ... nœ: n   í:ʔ   deʔgyęde:ih,
      highlight   the   me   I don't know how
      I myself don't know how

    c ... ne   ǫ:sagyędǫthoʔ.
      the   I would put wood in again
      to put more wood in.

The speaker was of course identifiable, but neither English nor other European languages would mark it as such. This usage is so common in Seneca that the combination *n i:ʔ* has been lexicalized and is generally regarded by speakers as a single word.

Of still greater interest is the fact that the Seneca definite article is used not only with nouns but also with verbs, as illustrated in (13)c. While *the me* is not said in English, its import can be understood, but a locution like *the (I would put more wood in)* may be more difficult to appreciate. Here the article functions to reify or nominalize the event, converting it from the transience normally associated with events to something with conceptual persistence. Intonation unit (13)c alone might be translated 'my putting more wood in.' In this case it functioned as the complement of *deʔgyęde:ih* 'I don't know how,' so that the translation as an English infinitive phrase, 'to put more wood in,' is appropriate. The reification of events with *neh* functions in a variety of contextually determined ways. In the following example it converted 'she had cooked' into 'what she had cooked,' creating a referent that functioned as the patient of the cooking. The use of *ne* with *Grandma* may also be noted:

(14) a ... Hó:k   o:nę   ga:nyóʔ   né:waʔ,
        so   now   when   this time
        So now when

    b ... wá:dikhwę:dáʔt,
        they finished eating
        they finished eating

    c ... ne   gokhǫ́ni:nǫ́ʔ   ne   Grandma,
        the   she had cooked the   Grandma
        what Grandma had cooked,

Reference may be to the agent as well as the patient of an event. The speaker of example (1) above went on to mention where some of the guests at his birthday celebration had come from. One of his interlocutors then asked,

(15) ... Né   wa:di:yǫʔʔ
      the   they came
      The ones who came?

referring to the agents of the coming.

How does this use of *neh* as a nominalizer relate to its use as a signal of identifiability? The answer is clearest in cases like (14)c, where the resulting referent was in fact the idea of an identifiable thing—the food that resulted from Grandma's cooking—and in (15), where it was the idea of identifiable people—the people who came. Less obvious is the relation between nominalization and identifiability in cases like (13)c, where reference was not to a *thing* as such, but to the *act* of putting the wood in the stove. Examples of this sort appear to be restricted to generic events. The speaker of (13) was not talking about a particular act of putting in wood, nor was the speaker of the following talking about a particular act of breathing:

(16) a ... sęhgé   shǫ:h,
        difficult   just
        it's just difficult

    b ... ne   gadǫ:dyeʔs.
        the   I'm breathing
        my breathing.

Apparently the identifiability in such cases derives from shared knowledge of an event *category*—the generic idea of putting wood in a stove, the generic idea of breathing. Generic events evidently have an intrinsic identifiability that makes appropriate their nominalization with *neh*.

I have described some of the ways in which Seneca *neh* differs from English *the*. These differences should not obscure the fact that both are used to mark identifiability, which has essentially the same function in both languages in spite of considerable differences in the places where it is marked and not marked. The fact that languages as different as these should both treat identifiability so prominently suggests that it has broad relevance to human thought and communication, even if other languages raise questions as to its universality.

Word Order

Seneca is one of those languages that have sometimes been said to have "free" or "pragmatically determined" word order. These are ways of saying that the order of words in a Seneca clause is more subject to discourse factors than it is in a relatively stable subject-verb-object language like English, or a subject-object-verb language like Lakhota or Japanese. I will focus here on the relative order of nouns and verbs.

We have seen that many Seneca words correspond to an English clause composed of several words. Although the English translations of the intonation units in example (1) contain various subjects, verbs, and objects, in all but one case the separately translated elements were fused within a single Seneca word. The one exception was

(17) ... gędzǫ oęnǫ́ʔ waęnǫdęno:dę́ʔ,
     fish   song   they sang
     they sang the Fish Dance,

The fact that the lexicalized phrase translated 'Fish Dance' occurs first here might suggest that Seneca conforms to an object-verb order. Other examples suggest the same:

(18) ... Ojí:yáʔ odi:gǫh.
     berry   they're eating
     They're eating berries.

But the situation is not that simple. For one thing, we have seen that Seneca pronominal prefixes do not mark referents as subjects and objects, but as agents and patients. We might, then, entertain the thought that (17) and (18) illustrate a consistent adherence, not to an object-verb order, but to a patient-verb order. That hypothesis is disturbed by the fact that sometimes the verb comes *before* the patient noun:

(19) ... oʔkhniyǫ:dǫ́:ʔ   gwisdę́ʔshǫʔǫh,
          I hung up plurally   some things
          I hung up some things,

(The speaker was talking about hanging out clothes to dry.) To what can the different orders illustrated in (18) and (19) be attributed?

It is helpful at this point to reconsider the internal structure of events and states. In chapter 6 we saw that activation cost may apply independently to the event or state itself and to one or more of its included participants. For example, a new event might include a given or accessible participant, or a given or accessible event might include a new participant. A good example of the latter is provided by (17), where the idea of the singing event was given, having been introduced in the previous intonation unit (see (1)c above), and it was the idea of the Fish Dance that was new. Such an example might suggest that Seneca orders its words so as to place new information before given.

Examples (18) and (19), however, raise doubts concerning that hypothesis. In both cases it was the entire event—eating berries, hanging up things—that was new, not the berries or the hanging alone. If activation cost was not responsible for the different word orders, what was? The answer seems to depend on recognizing another feature of discourse for which there is at present no established term. Marianne Mithun's notion of *newsworthiness* (Mithun 1992, pp. 39–46) and the Czech notion of *communicative dynamism* (Firbas 1992) may come closest to capturing what is involved here: the relative newsworthiness of a participant in an event—in (18) the berries, in (19) the things—as compared with the newsworthiness of the event itself. In (18) it was the berries that were the more newsworthy, but in (19) the speaker saw no need to verbalize, and perhaps did not even recall, the things she had been hanging up. It was the activity itself that was more newsworthy than the patient noun. (She was making the point that her physical condition made the activity difficult.) The lesser newsworthiness of the patient in (19) is of course confirmed by the speaker's failure to categorize it in anything beyond the most general terms.

There appears, then, to be an ordering principle in Seneca that can be stated as follows: a noun expressing a referent that is more newsworthy than the event or state in which it participates appears before its verb, while a noun expressing a less newsworthy referent appears after its verb. Other examples show that there is no reason to limit the referent in question to a patient noun. In (20) the agent of the coming appeared before the verb:

(20) ... Ye:nyǫ́ʔǫ   shǫ́:   yǫkdǫs   sedéhdziah.
   white woman just she comes in the morning
   A white woman just comes in the morning.

(The speaker was talking about someone who came to clean and cook for her.) The idea of the white woman was maximally newsworthy and for that reason placed before the verb. The opposite order appeared in (21):

(21) ... Da onę næ: ne:ʔ oʔthyę́:hda:thǫ́:ʔ   né   yada:thyo:ʔ,
   so now highlight it's they two ran around the man and wife
   So then the man and wife ran around,

The agent of this event was a composite of the man and wife. The man had already been introduced shortly before and was thus already accessible, and the addition of the wife added little to the newsworthiness of the composite referent. The running around was more newsworthy than the people who did it, and it was for that reason that the event was verbalized first. Mithun (in press) has suggested that this strategy takes advantage of the heightened pitch and amplitude associated with the beginning of an intonation unit, placing the more newsworthy idea in the prosodically more vigorous position. European languages follow a different course, setting the stage with a less newsworthy context and building toward that which is more newsworthy, a strategy emphasized in the study of "functional sentence perspective" as discussed in chapter 13. Both orderings are functionally motivated, but in wholly different ways.

The reader should note that in the course of this and earlier chapters I have introduced three similar terms in three distinct technical senses: *referential importance, contextual salience,* and now *newsworthiness.* The first of these, referential importance, has to do with the primary, secondary, or trivial role of a referent within a discourse, as with major or minor characters in a narrative. It tends to be a property that a referent retains over an extended stretch of discourse. Trivial importance is one of the ingredients of "light" subjects, as discussed in chapter 7. Second, a contextually salient referent is one that stands out in a particular local context for either linguistic or extralinguistic reasons. Salience in this sense was discussed in chapter 8 as one of the ingredients of identifiability. Finally, newsworthiness has to do with the relative prominence of participants in events and states as compared with that of the events and states themselves. It has been seen as determining the relative order of nouns and verbs in languages of the Seneca type. Though labeled in similar

ways, referential importance, contextual salience, and newsworthiness are
distinct properties of discourse.

Summary and Prospects

This chapter has compared a few aspects of the Seneca language with the
English phenomena discussed in earlier chapters as a way of suggesting
what may be universal and what particular. Many Seneca words contain
considerably more information than English words, and apparently as a
result the modal length of Seneca intonation units is half that of English
intonation units, measured in terms of words per intonation unit. Seneca
verbs contain pronominal prefixes that are in some ways similar to English
personal pronouns, especially in the fact that they *refer* to ideas of persons
and things, rather than simply *agreeing* with some external referent. They
differ from English pronouns, however, in two ways. First, their use is not
determined by activation cost—as, for example, English pronouns are
typically used to express given referents—but rather by their role as core
participants in events and states. Second, they are not marked, as English
pronouns are, for the distinction between subjects and nonsubjects, but
rather for the distinction between agents and patients. In general, Seneca
focuses more strongly than English on the internal composition of events
or states. There is no evidence that Seneca makes any use of the starting
point function, verbalized in English as subjecthood, but Seneca adheres
as consistently as English to the one new idea constraint. The ability to
activate only one new idea per focus of consciousness seems to depend
on limitations inherent in human mental processing, regardless of the
language one speaks.

Seneca makes use of a definite article that functions, like the English
article, to convey identifiability. The specific ways in which Seneca uses
the article, however, illustrate well the kind of variability that is characteristic across languages in this area. For example, Seneca frequently uses the
article not only with proper names but also with first- and second-person
pronouns. A more radical departure is the use of the article as a way of
nominalizing events and states. Two variants of this usage were identified.
In one there is reference to a participant in the event or state, in the other
the event itself is conceptualized as a persistent idea. Examples of the
latter sort are consistently generic rather than particular, and it would
seem that the identifiability derives from shared knowledge of the event
category rather than of a particular event.

Word order in a Seneca clause is determined by the newsworthiness
of a referent as compared with that of the event or state in which it is a
participant. A more newsworthy referent precedes the verb, a less news-

worthy follows. The specific nature of newsworthiness needs further investigation, and languages like Seneca are particularly adapted to its study.

The larger purpose of chapter 12 was to emphasize the need to extend investigations of the flow of language and consciousness to a wide variety of languages in order to sort out what is common to all humankind from the range of variation different languages allow. So far as the languages of North America are concerned, the task is one of extreme urgency.

13

Some Alternative Approaches to Information Flow

The work of numerous researchers overlaps significantly with what has been set forth in chapters 5–12. These other lines of research are rich and varied, and they illustrate well one of the points made in chapter 2—that language and the mind offer a vast territory for exploration, with no easy answers. It would be impossible to review all related work here, nor am I able to do justice even to the few examples I discuss. Nevertheless, I hope this chapter will provide some helpful comparisons with certain other major contributions to the relevant "literature." I have chosen several approaches that seem especially relevant to the present work, to the extent that the reader may be justified in wondering just what the similarities and differences are. Each has received considerable attention and has had significant influence. I hope there will be agreement that our mutual concerns involve dynamic changes in thought and language—in that sense a flow—and that these changes involve changes in the status of what may be called information, in the broad sense of negative entropy within the mind. Thus the term *information flow* in the title of this chapter seems appropriate as a way of embracing not only the consciousness-based approach of the preceding chapters, but also approaches in which consciousness has been left out of the picture.

Functional Sentence Perspective

The first scholarly tradition to bring information flow (in this broad sense) to the forefront of linguistic research, and to investigate it systematically and productively over many years, has been centered in Czechoslovakia. It has included, among other scholars, Vilém Mathesius, František Daneš, Josef Vachek, and Jan Firbas. Firbas has been and remains an especially active representative of this tradition, which has been labeled *functional sentence perspective,* a term derived from Mathesius's German term *Satzperspektive* (Mathesius 1929). An extended discussion of Firbas's approach has recently become available (Firbas 1992); there exists also a briefer and useful overview (Firbas 1986).

Functional sentence perspective has been driven by the insight that linguistic elements vary in their degree of *communicative dynamism,* characterized as "the relative extent to which a linguistic element contributes towards the further development of the communication" (Firbas 1992, p. 8). "It is an inherent quality of communication and manifests itself in constant development towards the attainment of a communicative goal; in other words, towards the fulfillment of a communicative purpose. Participating in this development, a linguistic element assumes some position in it and in accordance with this position displays a degree of communicative dynamism" (p. 7).

Communicative dynamism thus assumes, but does not explicitly develop, a theory of language use—one in which speakers, when they say something, have a communicative purpose, with the elements of their language contributing to that purpose to a greater or lesser degree. Discussions of functional sentence perspective rely on introspections regarding the goals of communicative acts, but they avoid any broader social or cognitive commitments: "I have not studied the relationship between degrees of CD and their counterparts in the mind of the language user, but I do not think that the language user is unaware of the development of the communication" (Firbas 1992, p. 107). We are left to guess what is meant by communicative purpose from constructed exchanges such as the following (Firbas 1986, p. 42):

(1) a What about Peter?
     b He has flown to Paris.

The purpose of the response in (1)b is said to be "to state the destination of Peter's flight." One can easily imagine other purposes this imaginary speaker might have had, but the lack of context leaves the question open. In any case, the word *he* is said to contribute the lowest degree of communicative dynamism, *has flown* an intermediate degree, and *to Paris* the highest degree, since it directly expresses Peter's destination. One of the findings of functional sentence perspective has been that, all other things being equal, the order of words in a sentence corresponds to an increase in communicative dynamism. To that extent, then, functional sentence perspective provides a functional explanation for word order.

But that is far from the whole story. Communicative dynamism is said to be "determined by" four factors identified as (a) linear modification, (b) the contextual factor, (c) the semantic factor, and (d) prosodic prominence (in spoken language only). Linear modification is a term taken from Dwight Bolinger (1952, p. 1125; also Bolinger 1965, p. 288): "gradation of position creates gradation of meaning when there are no interfering factors." Although Bolinger used this principle to explain a somewhat different phenomenon, Firbas has used it to capture the relation between word order and communicative dynamism, as illustrated in (1)b. The contextual factor involves "retrievability/irretrievability from the immediately relevant context" (Firbas 1992, p. 21), thereby creating the opposition *context-dependent* versus *context-independent*. It is evidently in part a matter of identifiability, but more a matter of activation cost. The semantic factor involves what are called *dynamic functions,* elements in a rather complex theory that attributes a semantic basis to parts of speech, grammatical relations, and other grammatical phenomena, an effort with which I am in principle much in sympathy. The well-known distinction between *theme* and *rheme* is included here. Finally, the study of prosodic prominence integrates functional sentence perspective with British intonation studies.

In terms of the present work, functional sentence perspective is a mixture of several things. If it were translated to accord with this work, it would say that there is a single dimension (communicative dynamism) that is "determined by" a complex interaction of word order (linear modification), activation cost and identifiability (the contextual factor), various semantic elements and relations that underlie grammar (the semantic factor), and prosody. Communicative dynamism probably corresponds most directly to a blend of what I have been calling referential importance (chap. 7) and newsworthiness (chap. 12). It is thus on the same plane as, but distinct from, activation cost and identifiability (chaps. 6 and 8). Word order and prosody, on the other hand, are aspects of linguistic expression. Semantics involves still other aspects of thought and language. Viewed in these terms, communicative dynamism is not a unified phenomenon.

Of particular interest to the present work is Firbas's recognition of the special status of (a subset of) what I have been calling low-content verbs—"verbs or verbal phrases that explicitly convey the meaning of appearance or existence on the scene" (Firbas 1992, p. 60). In constructed examples such as:

(2) A boy came into the room.

"the subject is context-independent and conveys the information towards which the communication is perspectived" (that is, it exhibits the highest degree of communicative dynamism). "The notional component of the verb introduces this information into the communication and in this respect recedes into the background" (p. 59). I would assign such verbs to the presentative subset of low-content verbs. It is interesting to see that quite different motivations led both avenues of research to assign a special place to verbs of this kind. Functional sentence perspective was motivated by the desire to assign a lower degree of communicative dynamism to verbs whose subjects carry a higher degree, as in (2). The recognition of low-content verbs in chapter 9 emerged from an examination of potential counterexamples to the one new idea hypothesis, some of which exhibit these verbs.

Viewed from the perspective of this work, then, functional sentence perspective unites several distinct discourse functions (activation cost, identifiability, referential importance, newsworthiness) within a single dimension of communicative dynamism. It stops short of understanding these matters within a larger socio-cognitive frame of reference and ignores the role of consciousness. More positively, it has pioneered in examining some of the basic questions in this area and has brought a variety of provocative issues to the forefront of research.

Functional Grammar

Michael Halliday, who has presented his carefully developed ways of understanding these aspects of language under the label *functional grammar,* has long been concerned with many of the aspects of language that are treated to this book. His work is highly ramified and covers far too many aspects of language to be summarized here. I will limit the discussion to just a few areas that are especially clearly presented in Halliday (1985b), on which most of the following remarks are based (see also Halliday 1985a). A recent sympathetic discussion of relevant aspects of his approach has appeared in Vande Kopple (1991).

Halliday has been one of the few linguists who have for some time been fully aware that conversational language and written language have different properties (e.g., Halliday 1987), and he has stressed that there is much to be gained from observing natural spoken language: "Perhaps the greatest single event in the history of linguistics was the invention of the tape recorder, which for the first time has captured natural conversation and made it accessible to systematic study," for "it is in spontaneous, operational speech that the grammatical system of a language is most fully exploited" (Halliday 1985b, pp. xxiii–xxiv).

Like the present work, Halliday has searched for correspondences between linguistic elements and their functions. One such element is the *tone group.* Importantly, "the tone group . . . is not only a phonological constituent; it also functions as the realization of something else, namely a quantum or unit of information in the discourse. Spoken discourse takes the form of a sequence of *information units.* . . . The information unit is what its name implies: a unit of information. Information, as this term is being used here, is a process of interaction between what is already known or predictable and what is new or unpredictable" (Halliday 1985b, pp. 274–75). The "already known or predictable" is what Halliday calls *given,* as opposed to the "unpredictable" or *new.* He amplifies these characterizations by explaining that "the significant variable is: information that is presented by the speaker as recoverable (Given) or not recoverable

(New) to the listener" (p. 277). Further, "the meaning [of given] is: this is not news." "The meaning [of new] is: attend to this; this is news."

The similarities and differences should be evident. Both the present work and Halliday's recognize the fundamental importance of what I have been calling intonation units, Halliday's tone groups. Both recognize that these units include some elements that are in some sense given and others that are in some sense new. But there are differences in what the terms *given* and *new* are taken to mean. The present work understands these terms with relation to the speaker's assessment of activation cost in the mind of the listener. Halliday also recognizes that "Given + New is listener-oriented" (1985b, p. 278), but he characterizes these properties in terms of recoverability. "What is treated as recoverable may be so because it has been mentioned before; but that is not the only possibility. It may be something that is in the situation, like *I* and *you*; or in the air, so to speak; or something that is not around at all but that the speaker wants to represent as Given for rhetorical purposes" (p. 277). Such a statement approaches but does not coincide with an explanation in terms of presence in active consciousness. Halliday does not recognize a degree of activation cost (or recoverability) that is intermediate between given and new, discussed here in terms of accessibility. He comes close to recognizing the one new idea constraint—"an information unit consists of an obligatory New element plus an optional Given" (p. 275), though it is not stated as such. The greatest divergence from the present work, however, appears in his treatment of subjects and themes.

To understand his use of these two terms, it is necessary to recognize the importance to all of Halliday's work of positing three "kinds of meaning," or "metafunctions," which he labels *ideational, interpersonal,* and *textual*: "Ideational meaning is the representation of experience: our experience of the world that lies about us, and also inside us, the world of our imagination. It is meaning in the sense of 'content.' . . . Interpersonal meaning is meaning as a form of action: the speaker or writer doing something to the listener or reader by means of language. . . . Textual meaning is relevance to the context: both the preceding (and following) text, and the context of situation" (Halliday 1985b, p. 53). Halliday sees a clause as functioning simultaneously as a *message* (the ideational function), an *exchange* (the interpersonal function), and a *representation* (the textual function). In a discussion of the following constructed sentence (p. 32),

(3) The duke gave my aunt this teapot.

the idea of the duke is said to function simultaneously as *theme, subject,* and *actor*. These three "functional concepts" are interpreted as corresponding to the three different modes of meaning:

(a) "The Theme is a function in the *clause as a message*. It is what the message is concerned with: the point of departure for what the speaker is going to say.

(b) "The Subject is a function in the *clause as an exchange*. It is the element that is held responsible: in which is vested the success of the clause in whatever is its particular speech function.

(c) "The Actor is a function in the *clause as a representation* (of a process). It is the active participant in the process: the one that does the deed." (P. 36–7)

It is by no means necessary that the same element (like *the duke* in (3)) be simultaneously theme, subject, and actor. In (4) *this teapot* is said to be the theme, *my aunt* the subject, and *the duke* the actor:

(4) This teapot my aunt was given by the duke.

There is no need to dwell on the *actor* function. It evidently corresponds to the agent role as discussed in chapter 12, one of various semantic roles a referent can have in an event. It may be a core role, as in (3), or it may be expressed by a prepositional phrase, as in (4). I am uncertain why the semantic role of actor should be associated with the textual function of language. However that may be, it is the subject and theme functions that contrast most noticeably with the interpretations set forth in this book.

A subject is said to be

something by reference to which the proposition can be affirmed or denied. For example, in *the duke has given away that teapot, hasn't he? . . .* the Subject *the duke* specifies the entity in respect of which the assertion is claimed to have validity. It is the duke, in other words, in whom is vested the success or failure of the proposition. He is the one that is, so to speak, being held responsible—responsible for the functioning of the clause as an interactive event. The speaker rests his case on *the duke + has,* and this is what the listener is called on to acknowledge. (P. 76)

In attributing subjecthood to "the clause as an exchange," Halliday sees it as "setting something up so that it can be caught, returned, smashed, lobbed back etc." (p. 76n.). For example, listeners might respond to (3) by saying *No he didn't,* thus showing that for them the proposition failed.

The tennis ball metaphor is related to Halliday's prescription for identifying a subject: "The Subject, in a declarative clause, is that element which is picked up by the pronoun in the tag" (p. 73). The fact that *he* in the tag at the end of (5) refers to the duke provides a simple way of identifying *the duke* as the subject of what precedes:

(5) The duke gave my aunt this teapot, didn't he.

The fact that *Yes he did* or *No he didn't* are so closely related to the tag is taken as evidence for the subject's role as the expression of "something by reference to which the proposition can be affirmed or denied." This view of the function of subjects is an interesting one, but I believe it can be seen as a consequence of their role as starting points. If that is correct, it would appear that Halliday has been prevented from acknowledging subjects as grammaticized starting points because that role has been pre-empted by what he calls themes.

What, then, is a theme? "In English, as in many other languages, the clause is organized as a message by having a special status assigned to one part of it. One element in the clause is enunciated as the theme; this then combines with the remainder so that the two parts together constitute a message" (p. 38). Particularly interesting is the statement, "The Theme is the element which serves as the point of departure of the message; it is that with which the clause is concerned." This might suggest that Halliday's theme is equivalent to what in this book is called a starting point, but that is not the case: "In speaking or writing English we signal that an item has thematic status by putting it first" (p. 38). Halliday says that in a sentence like (6),

(6) This teapot my aunt was given by the duke.

this teapot is the theme, while *my aunt* is the subject and thus in my terms the starting point. The theme need not be a referent at all. In the following examples the italicized initial phrases are all said to be themes (p. 39):

(7) *Once* I was a real turtle.
(8) *Very carefully* she put him back on his feet again.
(9) *On Friday night* I go backwards to bed.

Indeed, a sentence may have multiple themes, each of which may contribute either a textual, interpersonal, or ideational function. In the following example, *on the other hand* is said to be a textual theme, *maybe* an interpersonal theme, and *on a weekday* an ideational theme (p. 55):

(10) On the other hand maybe on a weekday it would be less crowded.

Halliday, then, interprets the first element in a clause as having a special functional status, labeled theme, though he allows for a sequence of themes of the type just illustrated. The function of a theme is to express what he has characterized as the starting point of a message. There is a clash of introspections here. Halliday sees starting points as expressed in the first element of a clause; I see them as expressed in subjects. Are both interpretations circular, since one says we know something to be a starting point because it occurs first and it occurs first because it is a starting point, while the other says we know something to be a starting point because it is a subject and it is a subject because it is a starting point? We know that introspections alone can lead to different conclusions, a fact well illustrated here, but that is no reason to discard them as having no validity. I suggested in chapter 2 that language is uniquely valuable for the study of the mind because it provides a wealth of complex phenomena that can be paired with introspections. The stronger the linguistic side of the pairing, the more validity can be attached to the introspection. There is something intuitively valid in the notion of starting point, but a full understanding of the nature and role of starting points depends on the richness and relevance of their linguistic correlates.

The question involves the extent to which the starting point function is convincingly paired with initial position versus the extent to which it is convincingly paired with subjecthood. I have tried to show not only that starting points are paired with subjecthood as a grammatical status, but that starting points also conform, in conversational language at least, to discourse properties one might expect of referents functioning in that way. With respect to activation cost, they exhibit the property discussed in chapter 7 as "lightness": most are given, some are accessible, and a small residue is new but of trivial importance. Almost all subjects show identifiability. Subjects tend to be the referents from whose point of view something is expressed. They also tend to exhibit the semantic property of humanness and to perform the semantic role of agent. All of these are properties we would expect starting points to have, and thus they provide multifaceted support for the introspection.

The property of being the first element in a clause is less coherent. Such an element may be, and often is, the subject, but it may alternatively be an orientation of some kind—spatial, temporal, epistemological, textual—or sometimes a referent that is being contrasted with some other referent. To say that *on the other hand maybe on a weekday* is the starting point in

(11) On the other hand maybe on a weekday it would be less crowded.

whereas *it* is the starting point in

(12) It would be less crowded.

misses, I believe, the function of *it* in both sentences, and confuses the starting point function with the orienting one. It may be that newsworthiness (chap. 12), contrastiveness (chap. 6), "topichood" in the sense mentioned at the end of chapter 8, and perhaps other factors lead to the placement of an element in initial position, but only the study of natural examples in context, with their prosody, can sort these matters out.

Halliday's work has covered much the same range of phenomena as the present work. One of its most useful features has been its recognition of the importance of prosody, and especially the importance of the tone group or intonation unit. I suggest that it has arrived at different conclusions partly because of the mixed quality of its data, partly because it has not recognized the role of consciousness, and partly because it has been committed to a unitary functional role for the diverse elements that may appear first in a clause.

The Given-New Contract

Well-known and influential work of a very different sort was reported by Herbert Clark and Susan Haviland in the 1970s (Haviland and Clark 1974, Clark and Haviland 1977, Clark 1977; see also Clark and Clark 1977, pp. 95–98) and has continued to influence research on the given-new distinction. Their underlying conception was that of a "given-new contract" agreed to by the speaker and listener, a contract that was seen as one aspect of the "cooperative principle" popularized by Paul Grice (1975). One of the attractive aspects of this view was the recognition that "the speaker tries, to the best of his ability, to make the structure of his utterance congruent with his knowledge of the listener's mental world" (Clark and Haviland 1977, p. 4).

Clark and Haviland were concerned not only with the speaker but also with the listener, from whose point of view "the given-new strategy is a three-step procedure for relating the current sentence to this knowledge base. At Step 1, the listener isolates the given and the new information in the current sentence. At Step 2, he searches memory for a direct antecedent, a structure containing propositions that match the given information precisely. Finally, at Step 3 the listener integrates the new information into the memory structure by attaching it to the antecedent found in Step 2" (p. 5). These three steps were illustrated with the following unusual constructed sequence (pp. 4–6):

(13) a Someone piqued the professor.

   b It was Percival who piqued the professor.

Having heard (13)a, the person who heard (13)b would begin processing it by dividing it into its given and new parts, the given being *X piqued the professor* and the new being *X = Percival.* (It was assumed that the nature of cleft sentences such as (13)b was to distribute given and new information in this way.) Second, the listener would search his or her memory for a unique antecedent that matched the given information, finding it in what had been acquired from the previously heard sentence (13)a. Third, the listener would integrate the new information in (13)b with this given information by replacing X with *Percival,* thus now knowing that *someone = Percival.*

Sometimes, however, the listener would not be able to find a direct match for the given information within knowledge already possessed, but would be forced to construct a *bridge* between what was known and what was treated as given:

(14) a Ed was given lots of things for his birthday.
     b The alligator was his favorite present.

The alligator in (14)b was said to express given information that had no direct representation in the listener's knowledge structure (Haviland and Clark 1974, p. 514): "With no direct Antecedent for the Given information in the target sentence [14b], the connection between the two sentences requires an extra inferential step, something like, 'Ah, one of those "things" must have been an alligator.'" Clark and Haviland hypothesized that this bridging operation would require a certain amount of extra time, over and above whatever time would have been involved in just searching memory for a direct match for the given information. Several experiments to measure reaction times were performed to see whether they would confirm this hypothesis.

In one experiment, subjects first saw on a tachistoscope a *context* sentence like (15)a:

(15) a We got some beer out of the trunk.
     b The beer was warm.

When they had read it, they pressed a black button, (15)a disappeared, and they saw a *target* sentence like (15)b. They were instructed to press a red button as soon as they understood what (15)b meant. It took them a mean time of 835 milliseconds to do that. Other subjects, instead of seeing a context sentence like the one in (15)a, saw a sequence like the following:

(16) a We checked the picnic supplies.
     b The beer was warm.

It took these subjects longer (1,016 milliseconds) to press the red button.

This observation was interpreted as support for the bridging hypothesis. Although the subjects *read* these sentences, Clark and Haviland (1977, p. 21) referred to them as "listeners." When subjects saw (16)a followed by (16)b, Clark and Haviland said, "there is no direct antecedent in the context sentence, and so the listener must build a bridge. He must draw the implicature that the picnic supplies contain a quantity of beer, and it is that quantity that is being referred to by the given information of the target sentence. Since drawing this implicature presumably takes time, the listener should take longer to comprehend the target sentence *The beer was warm*" in the *indirect antecedent* sequence—(16)a followed by (16)b—than in the *direct antecedent* sequence—(15)a followed by (15)b.

Experiments always leave room for alternative interpretations, and in this case Clark and Haviland noticed that context sentence (16)a did not contain the word *beer*, whereas context sentence (15)a did. "The direct antecedent sequences may have been easier simply because of the repetition of the word *beer*, perhaps making the second instance of *beer* easier to comprehend" (Clark and Haviland 1977, p. 22). To see whether it was just the repetition of the word that made the difference or whether it really was the process of bridging, sequences like the following were substituted for those in (16):

(17) a Andrew was especially fond of beer.
      b The beer was warm.

"Again as predicted, comprehension time for target sentences was faster for the Direct Antecedent pairs than for the Indirect Antecedent pairs, 1031 to 1168 msec. . . . These results, therefore argue that mere repetition of the critical noun is not enough to account for the results of Experiment I" (Haviland and Clark 1974, p. 516).

Viewed from the perspective of this book, Clark and Haviland's experiments raise some interesting questions. Let us at first assume that what is involved here is what I have called activation cost, although we will shortly see reason to doubt that assumption. The sequence in (15) then illustrates a straightforward case of givenness: the referent was activated in (15)a and retained its active status in (15)b. Of course, it would have been more natural in that case for (15)b to have contained a weakly accented pronoun:

(18) a We got some béer out of the trúnk.
      b It was wárm.

But we can accept the full noun phrase in (15)b as a not very disturbing manifestation of the psychologist's license to sacrifice naturalness for control. We might at least suppose that the subjects' auditory imagery of (15)b assigned a weak accent to the word *beer*:

(19) The beer was wárm.

In (16)b, on the other hand, the word *beer* would undoubtedly have been assigned a primary accent if it had been spoken, and must have been imaged auditorily as having such an accent when the subjects read it silently:

(20) a We chécked the pícnic supplìes.
      b The béer was wárm.

Thus, although they looked identical on the tachistoscope, (15)b and (16)b would have been perceived as prosodically different.

Why did it take the subjects longer to process (16)b? If the explanation is limited to activation cost, we can conclude that processing an already active referent takes less time than activating a referent that was previously in a less than completely active state. The question then arises as to whether the idea of the beer in (16)b, since it was not given, was new or accessible. A new referent would have violated the light subject constraint, so it is worth considering why the idea of the beer would have been semiactive at this point. Obviously its accessibility must have arisen through association with the idea of the picnic supplies. It is thus possible that the extra time taken to process (16)b was occupied in activating a referent that was previously semiactive and not fully active as in (15).

However, there is another and probably better way of explaining the longer reaction time. Not only was *the beer* in (16)b treated as accessible, it was also treated, through the use of the definite article, as identifiable. The contrast between (15)b and (16)b is precisely the contrast between indirect and direct sharedness as discussed in chapter 8. The idea of the beer in (15)b had already been established as a directly shared referent in (15)a. The idea of the beer in (16)b was identifiable because of the knowledge that picnic supplies are likely to include beer. The extra time it took to process (16)b would then have resulted from the reader's need to establish identifiability on the basis of indirect sharedness. In brief, Clark and Haviland's experiment might be interpreted as showing that an accessible referent takes longer to process than a given one. Alternatively, it could be interpreted as showing that an indirectly identifiable referent takes longer to process than a directly identifiable one. This second interpretation seems more likely to be correct, but it has nothing to do with the given-new distinction.

It is interesting also to give some thought to the second of Clark and Haviland's experiments, in which they found a longer processing time for (21)b as compared with (15)b. I have added accents that reflect the subjects' most likely auditory imagery:

(21) a Àndrew was espècially fònd of béer.
      b The beer was wárm.

Here the context sentence, (21)a, is generic and establishes only the generic idea of beer, not the idea of any particular beer. As noted in Chafe

(1974, pp. 125–27), a generic referent can establish *givenness* for any instance of the category in question. Hence, if (21)a had been followed by a sentence like

(22) He bròught some beer wíth him.

the phrase *some beer* would have had a given referent and would thus have been pronounced with a weak accent. For the same reason, the experimental sentence (21)b would have been most naturally pronounced with a weak accent on *the beer*. But (21)b would be an odd thing to say in the context of (21)a. What is odd is the fact that the idea of the beer was treated as identifiable. The context provided by (21)a did not establish the idea of any particular beer, but only of generic beer; hence there was no particular idea to be shared. It is, in fact, interesting to observe that indirect sharedness cannot be derived from a generic referent in the same way it is derived from a particular one like *the picnic supplies*. To repeat these two examples, (24) is peculiar in a way that (23) is not:

(23) a We chécked the pícnic supplìes.
     b The béer was wárm.

(24) a Àndrew was espècially fònd of béer.
     b The beer was wárm.

One could imagine (23) actually occurring. The natural occurrence of (24) is doubtful, unless the particular beer had been introduced earlier.

Judging from these examples, the findings concerning (23) and (24) might be reinterpreted as follows. Sentence (23)b required extra processing time because the identifiability of the beer had to be established on the basis of indirect sharedness. Sentence (24)b required extra processing time because of a more daunting problem with identifiability—the fact that there was no basis even for *inferring* a shared referent. The reaction times did not distinguish these two quite different processes, but there may have been a ceiling on how long subjects would take to push the red button no matter what they saw. Participants in an experiment learn not to be startled by unusual language. Experiments can be helpful, but they can leave basic questions unresolved so long as they are isolated from observations of natural language, and from crucial introspective evidence as well.

I should add that Clark's contributions to discourse understanding hardly ended with the research just described, which I have discussed at length because of its direct relevance to this book and the fact that it is still frequently cited. More recently, among other lines of research, he has added to our understanding of identifiability and has been especially concerned with the collaborative nature of mutual understanding (e.g.,

Clark and Wilkes-Gibbs 1986, Schober and Clark 1989, and other papers reprinted in Clark 1992).

Hierarchies of Assumed Familiarity, Accessibility, or Givenness

Ellen Prince's 1981 article on the given-new distinction provided a taxonomy of given and new information that has been used by a number of workers in this area. It should, therefore, be of special interest to compare her way of classifying these phenomena with the way they have been treated here. Prince's taxonomy brought together within a single category several discourse properties I have treated as distinct, uniting them under the heading *assumed familiarity*. Her exposition was based on an analogy to recipes, which may be verbalized in different ways depending on the writer's "assumptions about what the reader knows about ingredients, processes, and equipment, about what equipment the reader has available, and about what staples the reader keeps on the shelf" (Prince 1981b, pp. 234–35).

Accepting the cooking metaphor as a way of understanding assumed familiarity, we can consider first what is meant by *new*: "When a speaker first introduces an entity into the discourse, that is, tells the hearer to 'put it on the counter,' we may say that it is *new*" (Prince 1981b, p. 235). (Her *entity* is equivalent to what I have been calling a *referent*.) Ultimately, of course, it is necessary to get behind the cooking metaphor to arrive at an appreciation of the mental states and processes the metaphor is designed to help us understand. I believe there is no good way to understand what "putting a referent on the counter" means except as a way of visualizing what happens when someone places in active consciousness a referent that was previously inactive. In other words, Prince's explanation of new information need not conflict with an explanation in terms of consciousness, which it avoids by inviting us to compare mental processing with cooking.

Prince went on to distinguish two kinds of *new* referents: "In one case, the hearer may have had to *create* a new entity, akin to going out and buying a suckling pig, in which it is *brand-new*. In the other case, the hearer may be assumed to have a corresponding entity in his/her own model and simply has to place it in (or copy it into) the discourse-model, akin to taking some staple off the shelf when its presence is suddenly taken for granted in a recipe (e.g. salt). Call this type *unused*" (1981b, p. 235). This distinction is almost identical to that which I have labeled *unshared* versus *shared* (chap. 8). As I have presented it, however, sharedness is independent of activation cost, to which it is related solely through the logical necessity that only new ideas can be unshared.

Whether or not a referent is assumed to be newly activated in the listener's consciousness is a different question from whether or not it is assumed to be already part of the listener's knowledge. Activation cost is manifested linguistically in such phenomena as the use of a pronoun or a full noun phrase, as well as in weak or strong prosody. Sharedness, on the other hand, is one of the components of identifiability, which is manifested in various ways, but most conspicuously in the use of the definite article. There is nothing wrong, then, with saying that new referents may be either brand-new or unused (unshared or shared), so long as the latter distinction is understood to be on a different cognitive and linguistic plane from that which defines them as new. Since referents that are *not* new are necessarily shared, the term *unused* would seem to be an appropriate way of designating only those shared referents that are new, rather than all shared referents. As a term, therefore, *unused* has the disadvantage of conflating the separate domains of sharedness and activation cost.

Prince further distinguished brand-new entities that are *anchored* from those that are not. "Brand-new entities themselves seem to be of two types: *anchored* and *unanchored.* A discourse entity is Anchored if the NP representing it is *linked,* by means of another NP, or 'Anchor,' properly contained in it, to some other discourse entity" (1981b, p. 236). Although Prince's exposition made use of constructed sentences, she applied her taxonomy to a real conversational narrative taken from Nessa Wolfson (1982, pp. 94–95). This narrative contained several examples of anchored new entities, one of them at the very beginning:

(25) Well, I have a friend of mine called me:

The new referent expressed as *a friend of mine* was anchored because the idea of the friend was linked to the idea of the speaker with the phrase *of mine.* The anchor in such a case is usually, if not always, something other than brand-new: "In the data, all Anchored entities contain at least one Anchor that is not itself Brand-new" (Prince 1981b, p. 236).

Like sharedness, anchoring is distinct from activation cost as such. It does, however, raise some interesting questions and suggest the need for further research. It is instructive to look at the following sequence, which was part of the exchange discussed in chapter 10:

(26) a(A) ... Hòw're you dòin' with the hóuse.
    b(B) ... Òh got it àll uh ... prímed just abòut,
    c(B) ... except twó sídes of it.

The referents verbalized as *the house* in (26)a and *two sides of it* in (26)c are both new, and both can be interpreted as shared (unused). The first is unanchored, whereas the second is anchored with the phrase *of it.* We can see from this example that anchoring is not restricted to unshared (brand-new) referents. But there is a larger question here that involves the manner in which new referents—whether they are shared or unshared, anchored or unanchored—are introduced into a discourse.

Speakers tend not to introduce new ideas out of the blue, but fit them in some way into the ongoing interaction. To be sure, (26)a introduced a new topic into the conversation, but from Speaker B's response it is evident that knowledge of the painting of the house was already shared. Furthermore, although *the house* was, strictly speaking, unanchored, it was linked to its context with the word *you,* which made saying *your house* unnecessary. Thus, both *the house* and *two sides of it* were linked to shared knowledge, though in different ways. The former indicated that fact overtly only through the use of the definite article, whereas the latter included an overt anchor of the sort described by Prince. When Speaker B later introduced a new referent as

(27) (B) .. Òh = that gútless ... spráyer it

the idea of this particular sprayer may have been unshared. However, the immediately preceding intonation unit took the form of Speaker A's implied question:

(28) (A) .. I thought you were gonna spráy it.

In that context, mention of a new and unshared sprayer was quite natural. The point I am making is that anchoring must be one aspect of a larger strategy—the manner in which new ideas are related to their contexts. For *any* new idea we can ask how it is linked to the context in which it is introduced. Explicit anchoring, when it is present, provides an overt indication of what the link is, but there are other kinds of links that need to be investigated too.

Although Prince did not make a point of it, the concept of anchoring has a particular relevance to identifiability. In chapter 8 I discussed various types of what I called sufficiently identifying language—language sufficient to make shared referents identifiable. One type was the creation of identifiability through modification of a category: the use of possessors, attributive adjectives, prepositional phrases, and relative clauses. For example, in Prince's illustrative narrative the speaker said:

(29) Well, try the kitchen window,

in a context where presumably *the window* alone would not have been sufficient for identifiability. Prince's examples of anchoring, in contrast, involve *nonidentifiable* referents, like *a friend of mine* in (25). It appears, then, that anchoring performs two very different functions: relating a new idea to its context and creating identifiability.

As another category in her taxonomy, Prince used the term *evoked* as an equivalent for *given*. She explained the evoked status again with the culinary analogy: "Now, if some NP is uttered whose entity is already in the discourse-model, or 'on the counter,' it represents an *evoked* entity" (1981b, p. 236). She then distinguished *textually* evoked entities from those that are *situationally* evoked. The distinction is a matter of how givenness is established, and parallels the discussion in chapter 6 of activation through the discourse or through salient presence in the extralinguistic environment.

In addition to entities that are new and those that are evoked (or given), Prince recognized a third category: those that are *inferrable*. "A discourse entity is Inferrable if the speaker assumes the hearer can infer it, via logical—or, more commonly, plausible—reasoning, from discourse entities already Evoked or from other Inferrables" (p. 236). Her example was *the driver* in

(30) I got on a bus yesterday and the driver was drunk.

As she explained, "*the driver* is Inferrable from *a bus,* plus assumed knowledge about buses, that is, *Buses have drivers.*" This type of explanation might be more appropriate to explaining the *identifiability* rather than the givenness of a referent like *the driver,* as in the case of Clark and Haviland's *the beer*. In terms of the discussion in chapter 8, it would be said that the idea of the driver is indirectly shared as a result of association with the idea of the bus. However, it would appear that Prince regarded the referent of *the driver* as having a different status with respect to "assumed familiarity" and that she was not concerned with its identifiability. She provided no culinary analogy, and as a result the relation of inferability to the rest of her taxonomy remains uncertain.

Prince went on to suggest a "preferred hierarchy or scale for what type of entity is used" (1981b, p. 245). This scale was discussed with reference to the following constructed examples:

(31) a I bought a Toyota.
     b Ellen bought a Toyota.
     c One of the people that work at Penn bought a Toyota.
     d A person that works at Penn bought a Toyota.
     e A person bought a Toyota.

Prince continued: "It seems that, if a speaker is in a position to say one of these on basis of his/her hypothesis about what the hearer knows and chooses instead to say one lower on the scale (to refer to the same individual), s/he will be seen, if found out, to have been deviant in some way (e.g. evasive, childish, building suspense as in a mystery novel). Put differently, we may say that the use of an NP representing a certain point on the scale implicates that the speaker could not have felicitously referred to the same entity by another NP higher on the scale" (p. 245).

We can note that several disparate factors are at work in (31). For example, although the referents of *I* in (31)a and *Ellen* in (31)b might be given, the appropriateness of using one or the other would depend on who was speaking, Ellen or some third party. It is more relevant to the present discussion to leave (31)a out of account and try to imagine situations in which the subjects of the remaining sentences conveyed new information. Prince's point was that, for example, if the referent was shared (unused), (31)b would take precedence over the choices below it. That is certainly true, but it requires considerable imagination to think of situations where any of the others would be used at all. Beyond that, to say that if the referent is unshared (brand-new) but anchored, and thus (31)d would be used in preference to (31)e, is to say nothing at all, for it is precisely the presence of an anchor that differentiates (31)d from (31)e. The hierarchy as presented combines several distinct dimensions into one, but to point that out is not to deny the value of looking at how referents are most likely to be categorized, a process in which activation cost, sharedness, familiarity, context, and other factors play a role.

Finally, it is worth noting that Prince's examination of conversational language found that "nearly all of the subjects are Evoked"—that is, given (1981b, p. 242), and that in "informal conversational discourse" the tendency is "to reserve subject position for NPs at the higher end of the scale" in (31)—that is, identifiable (p. 246). These findings, of course, help support the validity of the light subject constraint. Prince also investigated the somewhat different patterns of information flow that are observable in written language, a topic to which we will return in Chapter 22.

More recently, two other hierarchies have been suggested, bearing some resemblance to that exemplified in (31), but each different in its own way. One is the "accessibility" hierarchy set forth by Mira Ariel (1988, 1990, 1991). In terms of the present work, this kind of accessibility involves what I discussed in chapter 8 as the use of sufficiently identifying language when a speaker is verbalizing a shared referent. Ariel lists the following types of linguistic expressions, ranging from those used when identifiability calls for a more informative verbalization—a situation she terms low accessibility—to those used when a minimum amount of verbal material is sufficient—a situation termed high accessibility (Ariel 1991, p. 449):

Full name + Modifier
Full name
Long definite description
Short definite description
Last name

First name
Distal demonstrative (+ Modifier)
Proximal demonstrative (+ Modifier)
Stressed pronouns + Gesture
Stressed pronouns
Unstressed pronouns
Zeros

This list can be compared with the discussion under the heading "Sufficiently Identifying Language" in chapter 8 above. The term *accessibility* is, of course, used in a way that is very different from its use in the present work. Although Ariel mentions different degrees of "memory availability" (e.g., 1991, p. 444), what is really involved here is the nature of the language necessary to make a shared referent identifiable in a given context. In that light, her discussion is a valuable extension of chapter 8 but could profit from an application to conversational examples.

The other recent way of viewing partially similar material is the "givenness" hierarchy described by Jeanette Gundel, Nancy Hedberg, and Ron Zacharski (1993). They list the following types of expressions, ranging from the least to the most "given." They include the generalized examples on the right which help to clarify labels that are less than optimally mnemonic:

Type identifiable	a N
Referential	this N
Uniquely identifiable	the N
Familiar	that N
Activated	that, this, this N
In focus	it

From the present perspective it appears that what is presented as a single dimension is actually a conflation of activation cost, identifiability, and the functioning of demonstratives. There is a recognition that identifiability is not the same as activation cost, but that problem is solved, not by separating the two dimensions, but instead by appealing to Paul Grice's maxim of quantity (Grice 1975). The validity of that appeal is something I would question, but in any case it would appear that Gundel, Hedberg, and Zacharski, along with Ariel, have forced into a single dimension several aspects of discourse that it would be more profitable to keep apart.

Grammar as Mental-Processing Instructions

Of all the work done in this area, that of Talmy Givón comes closest in spirit to what has been set forth in the present work. It is gratifying to find that his work has led to understandings that in many ways coincide with or complement those discussed here. We have been aiming at the same target, and if some of his shots seem from the present perspective to have been near misses, they illustrate well the diversity of interpretations that language allows. His recent thinking in the area of information flow was set forth in Givón (1990), where chapter 20 presents an especially useful summary for comparison.

Givón has forthrightly treated language and the mind as inseparably linked, each giving fundamental insights into the other. His perspective on their relationship views grammar (specifically, morphemes and syntactic constructions) as a set of "mental processing instructions ... designed to trigger specific mental operations in the mind of the speech receiver. . . . These mental operations," he suggests, "involve two well known cognitive domains: (a) attentional activation (b) search in memory storage." It is not obvious why it is necessary to separate activation from memory search, and in fact Givón mentions that "the two may seem coupled or even non-distinct" (Givón 1990, pp. 893–94). One thing he has in mind is the obvious fact that, *for the listener,* the activation of an idea that is new and unshared cannot involve the reactivation of an idea that is already present in the listener's memory. In such a case the listener's activation takes place without a memory search, although the listener still needs guidance from the speaker in placing the new idea with relation to other, already shared knowledge.

We have here one consequence of the fact that Givón's discussion "is formulated in terms of the speech receiver's ... perspective. This perspective is adopted for reasons of presentation, and does not prejudge the exact nature of the (at least in part isomorphic) mental processes that take place in the mind of the speech initiator" (p. 895). My own prejudice has been to describe information flow from the perspective of the language producer, who is by definition the person responsible for the form the language takes. I have tried to emphasize, however, how important it is to realize that the speaker's mind necessarily includes a dynamic model of what is happening in the mind of the listener.

Givón makes considerable use of the *file* metaphor, though he properly notes that such metaphors "tend to be more concrete than their intended mental referents" (p. 895). He says, for example, that "the grammar of referential coherence ... is about identifying and activating the locations ('files,' 'nodes') where verbally-coded text is stored in episodic memory. The nominal referents-topics serve as 'file labels,' they are used to access ('activate') the storage locations where incoming information is to be 'filed'" (p. 894). I take this to mean that when, for example, an idea that might be verbalized as *Larry* is activated through the use of that word, whatever might be said about Larry will then be assimilated in its proper mental location. It is worth noting that Givón uses the term *referent* for a piece of language (for example, the word *Larry*), and not (as in this book) for the *idea* that may be activated by such a word. What I am calling a referent (the *idea* of a person or object) is apparently equivalent to Givón's *storage location, file,* or *node.*

When Givón says that "verbally-coded text is stored in episodic memory," as in the quotation above, he is aware that it is not language itself that is stored. Elsewhere he points out that "grammatical clues in discourse processing decay rapidly after the message has been decoded, . . . and are thus *not* stored in episodic memory" (p. 940). Although he says that "something like a mental proposition, under whatever guise, is the basic unit of mental information storage" (p. 896), what he means is that "something analogous to the clause, minus its grammatical form, must be the basic unit of information processing in the mind" (pers. com.). In my terms this basic unit is what I have been calling an *idea,* most commonly an idea of an event or state, which, when it is verbalized, is likely to take the form of a clause. Given this recognition that information is not stored in verbal form, there remains a problem in understanding the nature of "text-based searches in episodic memory" (p. 941). Although Givón is apparently not suggesting that language comprehenders are literally searching through stored text as such, one wishes that the distinction between verbal and nonverbal storage were more clearly spelled out.

For Givón the notion of *grounding* has considerable importance. Grounding is based in part on the distinction between old and new information, which Givón characterizes as follows: "By 'old' one means 'assumed by the speaker to be accessible to the hearer,' and by 'new' 'assumed by the speaker to be inaccessible to the hearer'" (p. 897). Elsewhere he speaks of old information as predictable, redundant, or topical. Noting that "propositions (or clauses) in coherent discourse . . . tend to be informational hybrids, carrying both old and new information," (p. 898) he goes on to suggest that "the chunks of old, redundant ('topical') information in the clause serve to *ground* the new information to the already-stored old information. Cognitively, they furnish the *address* or *label* for the *storage locus* ('file') in the episodic memory" (p. 899). I hope to have shown, of course,. that the given-new distinction needs to be characterized in terms of consciousness. It should also be noted that Givón's view of grounding differs substantially from that made familiar by Paul Hopper (1979). Nevertheless, there is no arguing with the assertion that speakers include old (or given) information in their clauses as a background for whatever is presented as new.

More problematic, in my view, is Givón's notion of what he calls *topicality.* His development of this notion arose from an understandable dissatisfaction with the variety of ways in which the term *topic* had been used by different investigators (Givón 1983, p. 5). In an attempt to deal with the notion of a topic more effectively, and specifically in order to study the effect of topicality on the way a referent may be verbalized, he developed several ways of measuring the topicality of a particular referent in a particular context, or at least of finding measures he hoped would correlate with experimental findings on mental processing. These measures were ultimately viewed as ways of specifying two distinguishable components of topicality, which he calls *referential accessibility* and *thematic importance* (Givón 1990, pp. 907–8).

Referential accessibility (or continuity) was seen as measurable in terms of (a) *referential distance* (the number of clauses from the last occurrence of the same referent in the preceding discourse); (b) *switch reference* (whether the preceding clause does or does not have the same referent as an argument); and (c) *potential interference* (the number of semantically compatible referents within the preceding one or two clauses). Of these measures, referential distance became the one most often used in particular studies by Givón and others. Thematic importance was measured in terms of (a) *topic persistence* (the number of times the referent persists as argument in the subsequent ten (earlier three) clauses following the current clause); and (b) *overall frequency* (the total number of times the same referent appears as clausal argument in the discourse). Here it was topic persistence that was most often employed.

The reason for wanting to establish the topicality of a referent in a context was to discover the influence its degree of topicality might have on the way it was verbalized. According to the pattern discovered for English (Givón 1990, p. 913), referents verbalized with unstressed pronouns were found to have a mean referential distance measure of 1. That is, the same referent usually appeared in the immediately preceding clause. Referents verbalized with stressed pronouns were found to have a mean referential distance of 2.5. That is, the same referent appeared, on the average, two and a half clauses earlier. Referents verbalized with definite nouns were found to have a mean referential distance of 7, but deviation from this mean was so great that the figure could be regarded as meaningless. (For example, while 25 percent of the instances had a referential distance of 1, 40 percent of them had a referential distance of 20 or more.) Finally, so-called left-dislocated definite nouns were found to have a more reliable mean referential distance of 15. Left-dislocation included examples like the following, which must have consisted of two intonation units (Givón 1983, p. 349):

(32) my dad, all he ever did was farm and ranch

Thus, there appeared to be a kind of hierarchy which Givón (1990, p. 913) characterized in terms of (a) "continuing topics" being coded with "minimal-gap devices" such as unstressed pronouns; (b) "non-continuing topics with anaphoric antecedence within 2–3 clauses back" being coded with "small-gap devices" such as stressed pronouns; and (c) "non-continuing topics with relatively distant anaphoric antecedence" being coded with "long-gap devices" such as left-dislocated definite nouns. These various linguistic devices were seen as instructions to the listener concerning the manner in which the referent in question should be processed.

How would these measures be interpreted from the perspective of the present work? We can consider first the matter of referential distance—the number of clauses between a certain referent and an earlier occurrence of the same referent. This measure can be seen as a rough reflection of activation cost. A referent that was already present in the immediately preceding clause (better, intonation unit) would usually be *given* in the current one. Hence, its expression with an unstressed pronoun would be expected. Perhaps one could regard such a pronoun as an instruction to the listener to interpret the referent as given. It would be misleading, I believe, to interpret the pronoun as a signal of maximum topicality, since the latter term would not be an appropriate way of labeling givenness. What, then, of referents that have a mean referential distance of 2.5 and are verbalized with stressed pronouns? Stressed pronouns, we have seen, usually express contrastiveness, though occasionally they express accessible, noncontrastive referents. Each instance would have to be examined for such properties before one could arrive at any firm conclusions, but it would not be surprising to find that many contrastive referents, if that is what most of them were, were separated from their antecedents by two or three clauses. Referents that exhibit a large referential distance present a mixed bag from the point of view of activation cost, most of them being either accessible or new. The difference would depend on whether the referent was mentioned at all in the preceding discourse or whether it was being introduced into the discourse for the first time. Since Givón deliberately limited his "look-back" to twenty clauses, his data would not distinguish accessibility from newness in many cases. The fact that definite nouns show no consistent trend with relation to referential distance, being scattered fairly evenly across the range from 1 to 20 plus, reflects the fact that definiteness—or better, identifiability—is independent of activation cost.

In brief, the "topicality" that is measured roughly by referential distance is largely equatable with activation cost. Unstressed pronouns are usually unambiguous expressions of givenness, stressed pronouns may express either contrastive given referents or accessible referents, and the devotion of an entire intonation unit to an isolated referent (as in "left-dislocation") may be associated with either accessibility or newness. Identifiability, expressed by definite nouns, is another matter.

To turn to what Givón calls thematic importance, although it may be measured with either topic persistence or overall frequency it has been the topic persistence measure that has usually been applied—the number of times the referent persists as an argument in the subsequent ten (formerly three) clauses following the current clause. What is being measured here is evidently what I called referential importance in chapter 7, where I concurred with Givón's suggestion that one way of determining such importance operationally is to count the number of occurrences of the referent within the relevant stretch of discourse (cf. Wright and Givón 1987).

It is interesting to see how Givón relates topicality and subjecthood. "The quantified study of the topicality of grammatical subjects and objects in connected discourse" shows that "the subject is consistently more topical than the direct object, and the direct object more topical than the indirect object" (Givón 1990, p. 901). In terms of the present work, Givón's hierarchy would say that subjects are most often given and of primary importance, that direct objects rank somewhat lower on the scales of activation cost and importance, and that all other roles rank lower still. The strong correlation between givenness and subjecthood is beyond doubt, and it is true that most subjects are of either primary or secondary importance. These two properties are effects of the role of subjects as the grammaticized expression of starting points. Givón's model would be more congruent with the present one if topic were equated with starting point, referential accessibility with activation cost, and thematic importance with what I am calling referential importance. It would be necessary, however, to recognize the separate status of all three, being alert to the various ways in which they interact as well as the functional reasons for such interactions.

I believe it is not reading too much into Givón's work to suggest that he has, following a somewhat different path, recognized both the light subject constraint and the one new idea constraint. When, for example, he states as a "general principle" that "only one file is open at any given time" (1990, p. 939), I believe he could be translated as saying that each clause has a single starting point, which, as we have seen, is most likely to be "highly topical" or, in my terms, "light." And when he states that "a clause in connected discourse tends to contain *only one* chunk of new information" (p. 898), he is obviously talking about the one new idea constraint—as he puts it, "an expression of some *cognitive limit* on the processing rate of new information." Less clear is the question of whether he has created a place for what I have been calling accessible information, as might be the case when he says that "grammar-guided discourse processing seems to involve covert attention" (p. 939). Most important, however, is Givón's recognition that further understanding depends on a broader vision of our task, as when he writes of bringing together, "within a single coherent framework, facts from the hitherto disparate domains of grammar, discourse and cognitive psychology. All other things being equal, this is the type of increasing scope of coherence that one strives for in science" (p. 941).

Summary

From the perspective of this book, all the lines of research discussed in this chapter could profit from more clearly differentiating the roles of activation cost, contrastiveness, starting points, referential importance, identifiability, newsworthiness, and no doubt other discourse functions. Except for Halliday, these traditions have tended to lump together diverse functions under unitary labels such as "communicative dynamism," "givenness," "assumed familiarity," "accessibility," or "topicality." I believe, of course, that it is also essential to recognize the central role of consciousness, no longer characterizing given information, for example, as "known," "retrievable," "predictable," "recoverable," "familiar," "accessible," or the like. It would help to give a place to semiactive consciousness and its relevance to what I have called accessible information. Finally, although several of the researchers discussed in this chapter have explicitly recognized the importance of working with natural discourse, and especially conversations, all of them have in practice relied on mixtures of spoken and written, real and constructed data. Despite these differences, all of us have been groping toward much the same goal, and some convergence seems gradually to be emerging. A deeper and wider-ranging survey of the sort sketched in this chapter will undoubtedly shed useful light, not just on the subject matter itself, but also on the trajectories and discontinuities that have characterized the recent histories of linguistics and related disciplines.

14

The Flow of Consciousness in Music

Before we proceed to other aspects of consciousness and language, it may be of some interest to look for a moment at a rather different medium. Once one has become accustomed to observing intonation units, sentences, and paragraph-like units in speech, one finds oneself sometimes paying more attention to the segmentation of language than to what is being talked about. Beyond that, it becomes impossible not to hear analogous segments in music. Their presence there may be no accident. The convergence of language and music in this respect may very well show a human need to process information in relatively brief units in active consciousness, to combine such units within larger centers of interest, and every so often to shift from one cluster of semiactive information to another. In other words, music reflects foci of consciousness, superfoci, and topics. Both music and language, furthermore, associate such units with the pitch, amplitude, and tempo of sound. (For a different approach to the relation between language and music, see Lerdahl and Jackendoff 1983.)

Mozart

Not all music, of course, shows consistent analogies here. As a freely creative medium, music allows contemporary composers to do with it almost anything. But music that is faithful to the psychological constraints underlying language is bound to conform rather closely to what has been discussed so far. That is particularly true of the classical style that dominated European music at the end of the eighteenth century and the beginning of the nineteenth. Composers such as Haydn, Mozart, and Beethoven wrote "talky" music, in the sense that their compositions mirrored the kinds of organization of speech discussed in the preceding chapters. I will illustrate this point briefly with an excerpt from the first movement of Mozart's piano sonata in F major, Köchel 332, shown in figure 14.1. It illustrates straightforwardly the points I would like to make, without introducing distracting complexities. I hope the reader will be able to hear this music, either through auditory imagery, from a recording, or by

Figure 14.1 Mozart

playing it or having it played on a piano. Without some way of accessing its sound, the following remarks will be empty.

The first four measures contain a single intonation unit, followed by a pause. Language, consisting usually of one voice at a time, has nothing analogous to the Alberti base in the left hand, continuing through the pause, unless it can be thought of as background noise that corresponds harmonically and rhythmically with what is being said.

Measures 5 through 8 contain the second intonation unit, which ends this time not with a pause but with two sustained notes. The G in measure 8 suggests a conjunction linking this intonation unit to the next. This function is reinforced by an interpolated second treble voice, which leads to the F that harmonizes with the beginning of the third intonation unit in measure 9. The second and third intonation units are also linked by the overlapping repetition of intonation unit 2 in the bass. The bass speaker repeats what the treble speaker just said, continuing the overlap with an addition at the end, while the treble speaker begins the next intonation unit.

The third intonation unit lasts from measure 9 to the beginning of measure 12, where there is again a pause. It ends with a return to the tonic, clearly analogous to the sentence–final pitch contour that signals the end of a spoken sentence. Thus, the stretch from measure 1 to the beginning of measure 12 has much in common with a sequence of three spoken intonation units, the last of which is sentence-final, a typical pattern for speech. We have come here to the end of the first center of interest.

A new sentence, saying something quite different, begins at the end of measure 12. Its first intonation unit lasts from measure 12 into the first two beats of measure 16. The next intonation unit, which repeats much of the preceding one with embellishments and a different ending, lasts from the end of measure 16 to the beginning of measure 20. At this point there is another sentence ending, again signaled by a return to the tonic. This time, however, it is followed by two afterthoughts in measures 20–21 and 21–22, each of them reinforcing the finality of the conclusion by repeating the harmonic sequence of dominant seventh to tonic. By measure 22 we really know we are at the end of something.

Indeed, we find ourselves at the boundary between two major sections of the piece. The first beat of measure 22 turns out to be the end, not just of a sentence, but of a discourse topic. In terms of sonata-allegro form, it is the end of the principal theme. The new intonation unit that begins with the final beat of measure 22, while repeating the rhythmic pattern of the two preceding afterthoughts, moves us from the key of F to D minor, and an entirely new topic begins. This new topic turns out to be the bridge to the second theme that appears eighteen measures later in the expected dominant key of C major.

It is apparent that the various sections of a movement in sonata form function much like the discourse topics in speech, activating foci and superfoci (clauses and sentences) against a more extended background. The boundaries between these sections, where there is a significant change in semiactive consciousness, offer new ideas in new keys.

A great deal of music outside the classical style of Haydn and Mozart is also built of segments reminiscent of the intonation units of speech. Sentencelike and topiclike units are, however, often more difficult to find in contemporary music. I would hazard the guess that it is to a large extent the talkiness of the classical style, its closeness to the patterns that are so integral a part of language, that has brought such music its enduring

Figure 14.2 Seneca Music

popularity, with its unabating dominance of concert and radio program-
ming and record sales.

Seneca Music

It is particularly interesting to find music from a wholly different cultural
tradition adhering to the pattern exemplified in the Mozart example. Figure 14.2 shows the beginning of the Seneca song cycle known as the
gonéoɂ, in English the Drum Dance or Thanksgiving Dance (Chafe 1961),
an important component of several major Longhouse ceremonies. The
songs are performed by a lead singer and two other singers, one of them

simultaneously beating a water drum and the other shaking a horn rattle. For the most part these songs do not have meaningful words but are sung with vocables, or meaningless syllables.

In figure 14.2 I have placed each intonation unit in a separate measure, that is, bar lines indicate the boundaries of intonation units. After some initial drum beats, there is a whoop and the lead singer sings alone the first intonation unit (1). It ends with a sustained note of seven beats, with the drum silent on the last beat. Both the sustained note and the missed drum beat suggest the hesitating that typically appears between intonation units.

The same content is then repeated in 2 by the chorus, consisting of the two other singers. It ends with the same sustained note, but this time only five beats long, and the next intonation unit (3) follows directly without the drum skipping a beat. That intonation unit also ends with a five-beat note and no skipped beat, but the following intonation unit (4) ends with the same seven beats as 1, the drum once again skipping a beat. Thus, intonation units 2 through 4 form a unit analogous to a sentence, with greater hesitating preceding it and following it.

By the same criteria, the next intonation unit (5) forms a brief sentence in itself. There follows the sequence 6 through 8, again forming a sentence. At the end of 8 there is a more significant boundary than anything heard earlier. After the seven-beat note and the missed drum beat there are two emphatic syllables (9), the second of which trails off with a creaky voiced glissando. It is obvious that 9 serves as a highly marked conclusion to the first discourse topic, the first song of the cycle. The beginning of the second song in 10 shows a pattern analogous to the beginning of the first, but with melody and vocables completely new.

In summary, 1 through 8 are analogous to a conversational topic, which is emphatically concluded in 9. Within that topic are three sentencelike units, the first consisting of three intonation units (2–4), the second of one (5), and the third again of three (6–8). The second and third intonation units of the first and third of these sentences are almost identical. That is, although 6 is quite different from 2, 7 repeats 3, and 8 repeats 4. Intonation unit 1 at the beginning has a special status, allowing the lead singer to set the topic, as does 10 for the next topic. Each topic is thus initiated with something like a topic phrase, which is then repeated and elaborated by the other singers.

It is interesting also to observe the declination in pitch that is characteristic of a topic as a whole. Beginning in 1 on a D with a brief upward excursion to E, the first song finally ends on the G a fifth below—a decline reminiscent of spoken paragraphs. A decline is also observable within the first full sentence (2–4), and to some extent within the last sentence (6–8).

Summary and Prospects

Parallels to spoken intonation units, sentences, and discourse topics are discoverable not only in a composed eighteenth-century Austrian piano sonata but also, in a remarkably similar fashion, in a song cycle that forms part of an American Indian religious tradition. These far from isolated examples suggest that a wide range of music is fundamentally influenced by the same patterns that govern language, and that both language and music are shaped by properties basic to the flow of conscious experience.

It would be a useful undertaking to extend this line of investigation to other composers in the classical style, whose talkiness lends itself especially well to this approach, but it would also be rewarding to extend the study further to other Western music, and beyond that to music of quite different origins. Seneca music shows that cross-cultural studies along these lines would bear interesting fruit. The ultimate benefit would be a more inclusive understanding of human consciousness, independent of the particular medium in which its effects may be observed.

PART THREE

Displacement

The Immediate and Displaced Modes
in Conversational Language

... But bid life seize the present?
It lives less in the present
Than in the future always,
And less in both together
Than in the past. The present
Is too much for the senses,
Too crowding, too confusing—
Too present to imagine.

—Robert Frost, "Carpe Diem" (1938)

Among the variable properties of consciousness listed in chapter 3 was its ability to focus on displaced experience. An obvious but remarkable fact of human consciousness is that it need not be restricted to events and states that coincide with the time and place of the conscious experience itself. Much of it has its source in other times and places, even other selves, which enter it through processes of remembering, imagining, and that special kind of imagining we call empathy.

In part 3 of this book we will look more closely at the nature of this distinction between immediate and displaced consciousness, at linguistic evidence for it, and conversely at ways it can help us understand what we find in language. In the present chapter and the next we will look at immediacy and displacement in conversational language. In later chapters we will see how these two modes of consciousness can be manipulated in writing. What writers do with them has been actively investigated by many others, far too many to list here. Genette (1980, 1988), Stanzel (1984), and (especially relevant to this work) Cohn (1978) are some of the particularly wide-ranging discussions. As we proceed we will notice, as one part of this larger picture, a special use of language that has attracted a great deal of attention from both literary and linguistic scholars. It has been called a variety of names, among them *free indirect style, represented speech and thought,* and *erlebte Rede.* A selection of book-length treatments would have to include at least Weinrich (1964), Bronzwaer (1970), Hamburger (1973), Pascal (1977), Banfield (1982), Fleischman (1990), Ehrlich (1990), Fludernik (1993), and Lethcoe (1969). Leech and Short

195

(1981) give considerable space to it in their chapter 10, and it has been discussed in countless articles (McHale 1978 is a useful survey).

With so much already said about treatments of consciousness in literature, is there anything more to say here? I believe there is, and am hopeful that the approach developed here can add to our understanding in several ways. First, by starting with conversational language it will avoid the obvious one-sidedness of other work, which has dealt almost exclusively with written fiction. There is surely something to be gained from a perspective that takes ordinary speaking into account. Second, much of the earlier work has been preoccupied with representations of speech and thought—language conveying other language. Here our concern will not be with that topic for its own sake, but with a broader view of immediate and displaced consciousness. Third, I will suggest a more comprehensive understanding of immediate and displaced consciousness and their relation to language that I hope will be both coherent and intuitively satisfying. Literary devices can surely best be understood within a broader picture of consciousness as a whole. Literary scholars have for the most part limited their concerns to rather narrowly conceived "theories," avoiding more fundamental aspects of language and the mind. Fourth, I will offer various factual observations which, so far as I know, have not previously been made, much less accounted for. Finally, I will break sharply with tradition by failing to cite even one example from Virginia Woolf.

In this chapter we will explore certain aspects of immediacy and displacement in conversational language, but without taking account of language that represents other language, to which we will turn in chapter 16. Beginning with chapter 17, we will be concerned with some of the ways immediacy and displacement have been manipulated in writing.

The Immediate Mode

There are times in conversations when people verbalize experiences that are directly related to their immediate environments. For example, during a dinner party the following exchange took place between speakers A and B regarding some food that lay on the table in front of them:

(1) a(A) ... I thìnk I should tàke this awáy.
    b(B) .. Uh = ,
    c(A) are you gùys still éating it?
    d(B) .. I =
    e(B) .. I
    f(B) .. Just hóld it,
    g(B) .. for jùst a móment,

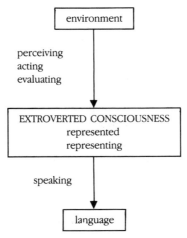

Figure 15.1 Speaking in the Immediate Mode

h(B) .. if you dòn't mínd,
i(B) .. and just slóp,
j(B) .. anòther lìttle bìt in hére.

During this exchange the consciousnesses of both A and B were focused on events which they perceived, acted on, and evaluated at the time and place of the conversation itself. I will say that they were speaking in the *immediate mode*.

The essential structure of the immediate mode is diagramed in figure 15.1. The box labeled *environment* at the top is meant to contain whatever elements immediately affect the content of consciousness. It includes perceived events and states in the "outside world" that surrounds the conscious self, but it also includes any actions performed by the individual that he or she is conscious of performing, as well as internally induced emotions and attitudes. The relation between the environment and consciousness can thus be summarized in terms of *perceiving, acting,* and *evaluating,* labels intended to cover any and all of the processes by which consciousness is immediately affected by whatever lies outside itself. A consciousness that is immediately affected by the environment can be called an *extroverted* consciousness.[1]

An extroverted consciousness may or may not be responsible for the

1. Extroversion, then, includes immediate internal evaluations, as opposed to evaluations remembered or imagined (see below). The reader should not attach too much importance to the direction of the arrows in figure 15.1 or any of the following figures. In this figure the top arrow suggests only that the environment may trigger extroverted experience; a reversed arrow could equally well be used to suggest that the experiencer functions as an interpreter of the environment.

production of overt language. Our primary interest here is in the cases where it is, as exemplified in (1) and as shown with the bottom box labeled *language* in figure 15.1. In later chapters it will become especially important to realize that consciousness enters into the production of language in two ways: it provides the ideas that are represented, but it is also responsible for representing them. On that basis we can speak of a *represented* consciousness and a *representing* consciousness. In most ordinary speaking these two functions are performed by one and the same consciousness, as shown in the central box. If the reader doubts at this point that there is any good reason to separate these two functions, those doubts will, I believe, dissipate by the time we come to chapter 17.

The Displaced Mode

A much larger proportion of the conversation from which (1) was excerpted showed displacement rather than immediacy. For example, the same speaker told the following brief anecdote to illustrate how pleasant it had been to move to a city with friendly inhabitants, in contrast to the city where he had lived before:

(2) a ... I went òut for a stróll,
    b on my first tìme on Chéstnut Strèet.
    c ... and just
    d ... just ... was astóunded,
    e at how pléasant things wère.
    f And às I was òut for a stróll,
    g ... a màn wàtering hi = s láwn,
    h .. túrned to mè,
    i .. as I wàlked pást,
    j .. and sáid,
    k ... góod èvening,

[handwritten marginalia: look — indicates what Mode is that this is coming]

His consciousness was focused now on experiences that were derived from another, earlier consciousness, not from his immediate environment. The essential nature of this *displaced mode* of speaking is diagrammed in figure 15.2. Crucial is the separation into two consciousnesses. There is a proximal consciousness which is no longer extroverted but *introverted*. It is that consciousness which is represented and which also performs the representing. Its input no longer comes from directly perceiving, acting on, or evaluating the immediate environment, but through the process of *remembering* what was present in a distal extroverted consciousness, or alternatively through the process of *imagining* what might be present in such a consciousness. Example (2) illustrated the remembering of an

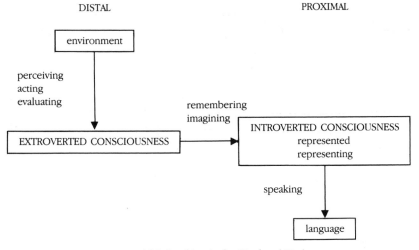

Figure 15.2 Speaking in the Displaced Mode

experience from the past. Example (3) illustrates the imagining of an experience anticipated for the future:

(3) a ... and uh = ,
     b .. now I'm going to .. sàve my móney,
     c and trỳ to get my ówn pad.
     d ... condomínium,
     e .. or whatever the càse may bé.
     f .. I'm going to be .. sàving a lot of móney,
     g working hére,
     h so = ,
     i if I'm màking decent móney,
     j I'll be áble to uh
     k to = gèt something on my ówn.

It is a striking fact that conversations tend to be dominated by the displaced mode. In the samples examined for this work, with only a few exceptions of the sort illustrated in (1), intonation units in the immediate mode were regulatory in nature, having to do either with the speaker's immediate mental processes:

(4) .. I don't remémber,
(5) .. Í get it,

or with immediate interaction:

(6) .. you knòw what I'm sáying?
(7) That's gréat.

We can speculate on reasons for this dominance of the displaced mode in conversations. At least four reasons suggest themselves. First, because the speaker and listener share an environment, the content of an extroverted consciousness is more or less equally available to both, whereas the content of an introverted consciousness usually begins as the property of the speaker alone. Of most interest to the listener are likely to be experiences of the speaker at other times and places, not what surrounds both of them just now. Second, speakers can choose to verbalize ideas from an introverted consciousness that are more interesting than the (typically) more mundane topics available from the immediate environment. Topics that conflict with ordinary expectations are more likely to arise in an introverted consciousness. Third, the repertoire that is available through remembering and imagining is incomparably larger than what is available from the environment. The scope of the latter is tiny when compared to the huge store of events, states, and topics available to an introverted consciousness. Finally, speakers will have had time to assimilate, reflect on, organize, and evaluate those remembered or imagined ideas: "these acts can be passed in review at will, appraised and compared—a thing quite impossible or only partially possible at the time when they are taking place" (Schlicher 1931, p. 49; cf. Fleischman 1990, p. 32). In general, then, what is available to an introverted consciousness tends to be less shared, more interesting, more extensive, and more fully processed than what is available to an extroverted consciousness, and for all these reasons more worth representing. This is not to say, of course, that there are no circumstances under which the greatest interest is to be found in the immediate environment. Obviously there are times when people have compelling reasons to talk about what they are doing, or what they are currently perceiving and evaluating. But the dominance of the displaced mode is a noteworthy property of most conversations.

When remembering and imagining are examined more closely, they can be seen to permit either or both of two major types of displacement. The type exemplified up to now has been *spatiotemporal* displacement—the ability to be conscious of events and states that are displaced in space and time. The other type is displacement of *self*—the ability to be conscious of events and states that originated in the consciousness of someone else. The ideas represented in (8) below did not have their origin in the extroverted consciousness of the proximal speaker, but in that of a third person. Presumably the present speaker learned of what was in another consciousness through other language produced by another person at another place and time:

(8) a ... And hé thought,
    b maybe the mótor was just wèaring òut,
    c it's got so màny hóurs on it,

As we proceed we will see various ways in which both spatiotemporal displacement and displacement of self affect consciousness and language. It is easiest to begin, however, by narrowing our sights in this chapter to displacement in space and time.

The Semiactive Presence of the Opposite Mode

Before we go any further, it is worth digressing for just a moment to recognize the role of semiactive consciousness in this picture. Consciousness alternates with the greatest ease between immediacy and displacement. People have no difficulty thinking or talking either about what is immediately present or what is remembered or imagined. It was easy for the same individual to shift from the immediate mode in (1) to the displaced mode illustrated in (2). These shifts, however, are perhaps never complete. Neither perceiving-acting-evaluating nor remembering-imagining dominates consciousness to the complete exclusion of the other. To say that consciousness alternates easily between the immediate and displaced modes is to say, more precisely, that *active* consciousness alternates in that way.

When consciousness is focused on something remembered or imagined, for example, experience of the immediate environment is usually, perhaps always, present to some degree. Among other things, that explains why first- and second-person referents are seldom if ever treated as new information. The ideas of the speaker and listener are assumed to be always present in the active or semiactive consciousnesses of both of them. Conversely, when the focus is on something immediate, there may usually if not always be a peripheral awareness of other, introverted experience. The fact that extroverted experiences are interpreted as instances of previously encountered categories and schemas argues that this is so. What happens now brings other things that happened before, as well as other things that might happen in the future, into the semiactive state. It is surely never possible to interpret experience of the immediate environment exclusively in its own terms.

Qualitative Differences between Extroversion and Introversion

It is of considerable interest, and it will become especially important in later chapters to note that extroverted and introverted experiences are qualitatively different. There is more to the alternation between the two modes shown in figures 15.1 and 15.2 than simply replacing an extroverted consciousness with an introverted one. The experiences themselves are of different kinds. Why they are different can be traced to the nature of the processes themselves: remembering and imagining are qualitatively different from perceiving, acting, and evaluating. We can focus first on differences in continuity and detail, with other differences emerging as we proceed.

Continuity

Extroverted consciousness has the quality of a continuous, uninterrupted flow. Any segment of it is experienced as part of a connected sequence, flowing out of what happened just before and into what will happen just after. The familiar metaphor of a *stream* of consciousness (James 1890, 1:224–90) captures this quality. In contrast, remembering and imagining yield isolated segments of experience whose antecedents and consequences are inaccessible. They produce experiential *islands,* disconnected from their surroundings, rising out of a dark sea of unawareness.

It is because of this islandlike quality of the displaced mode that when people begin to verbalize topics they remember or imagine, they typically provide an orientation or setting. Since consciousness is unable to function without such an orientation (chap. 10), it is typical for a speaker to begin representing a remembered topic with mention of space, time, and a contextualizing background activity:

(9) a   Í was wàtching him out here,
    b .. cúltivating,
    c ... làst níght,

In the displaced mode speakers know that they need to locate an experiential island in a way that will adequately orient the listener's consciousness. In the immediate mode the continuity associated with an extroverted consciousness makes such an orientation unnecessary.

Detail

An extroverted consciousness is not only continuous, it also has access to a wealth of detail, all of which is potentially available to focus on. If I look at the vase of irises on the table beside me, I believe I "see" everything that is there: the exact number of stems, leaves, and blossoms; their precise shapes and colors; the small unique markings on each. I need only turn my head away to discover that what my consciousness retains is only a sparse interpretation of that richness. Except perhaps for a brief span of iconic memory (e.g., Sperling 1960), I can remember only a general shape and texture, along with the few details on which I happened to focus while I was looking. As soon as I look back at the irises, the *availability* of the myriad details on which I *could* focus my attention creates an extroverted experience that is very unlike the experience available through remembering.

Conversation in the displaced mode exhibits the selectivity of introversion, not the fine-grained detail of extroversion. We can look again at the excerpt first given in (2):

(10) a ... I went òut for a stróll,
     b on my first tìme on Chéstnut Strèet.
     c ... and just
     d ... just ... was astóunded,
     e at how pléasant things wère.
     f And às I was òut for a stróll,
     g ... a màn wàtering hi = s láwn,
     h .. túrned to mè,
     i .. as I wàlked pást,
     j .. and sáid,
     k ... góod èvening,

There was an orienting background situation, a general feeling of surprise at people's pleasantness, and a brief illustration that climaxed with the neighbor's greeting. These were the newsworthy events and states, and no one would have expected this speaker to have talked about details like the number and variety of trees along the street, the appearance of the neighbor's house, or what the neighbor was wearing. It may be objected that conversational language in the displaced mode often does include more detail than I have just allowed for. Conversationalists do mention trivialities, like the name Chestnut Street in (10)b. Tannen (1989, pp. 140, 144) cites details like particular dates or house numbers that seem not to matter to the listener. But such isolated details are recalled by the speaker for isolated reasons, and it is important not to confuse them with the degree of fine-grained resolution that characterizes extroverted experience.

There is, however, one circumstance under which conversationalists remember events and states with a degree of detail which, though less than what is available to an extroverted consciousness, nevertheless goes beyond what is otherwise associated with the displaced mode. Some events and states are remembered generically. Experienced more than once, they are later recalled as types rather than tokens. When remembering is thus aided by rehearsal, events that are repeatedly refreshed can be more richly experienced. Furthermore, it is likely to have been the relative salience of such events that motivated their rehearsal in the first place, so that when they are remembered they are judged more worthy of telling.

The following example is taken from an account of the speaker's brush with death while he was diving off the coast of California. He was not only an expert diver but also an expert storyteller, and his account was a work of oral art. This segment of his story began with mention of his affective state:

(11) a ... and áfter the lòng swìm òut,
     b ... and my = wrèstling with the sèaweed,
     c Í was prètty tíred.

Having thus created an expectation of something interesting to follow, he interrupted the flow of particular events with a suspenseful description of the diving environment, before returning to the main sequence with the word *anyway*:

(12) a ... You dón't féel,
     b .. that being .. tíred down belów,
     c ... you're dówn thère,
     d .. you're tàking píctures,
     e ... thère're anémone dòwn thère that're,
     f ... Ì would say a fòot and a hàlf in diámeter like,
     g .. húge,
     h whíte,
     i flówers = .
     j .. With = ... with gréen,
     k .. thíck,
     l .. grèen,
     m stéms = .
     n .. They
     o ... Their stéms áren't really gréen.
     p .. When you tàke a pícture of them,
     q ... the uh .. stróbe líght,
     r ... shòws that they're a brìght réd.
     s ... Ányway,

Although it verbalized something remembered, this excerpt showed a degree of resolution greater than that which is typical of the displaced mode. But all of it was generic, as shown by the use of the generic *you* throughout, as well as the generic uses of the present tense—*you're down there*—and the progressive aspect—*you're taking pictures*. (Generic tense and aspect are discussed in Chafe 1970, pp. 168–78.) In conversational language, details like these are associated with generic remembering, but they still fall short of what is available to an extroverted consciousness.

In brief, we have seen that extroverted consciousness is continuous while introverted consciousness is islandlike, and that extroverted consciousness can be richly detailed while introverted consciousness is relatively impoverished. These qualitative differences will acquire special importance in later chapters when we turn our attention to manipulations of consciousness in written fiction.

The Deixis of Immediacy and Displacement

Language makes available various so-called deictic elements that locate an experience in space and time, and also with respect to a self (e.g., J. Lyons 1977, pp. 636–724; Rauh 1983). Viewed from the perspective of figures 15.1 and 15.2, deictic elements sort themselves into two types, in one of which the *represented* consciousness provides the deictic center, while in the other that role is played by the *representing* consciousness. The usefulness of this distinction will not become apparent until later chapters, but its basic nature can be introduced here.

Adverbs of space and time—words like *here, now,* and *today*—express the relation of an extroverted consciousness to a *represented* consciousness:

(13) a .. and just slóp,
     b .. anòther little bit in hére.

(14) a ... All ríght,
     b .. we're còoking nów.

The use of *here* in (13)b conveyed the fact that the place of the *slopping* coincided with the place of the consciousness being represented. Similarly, the use of *now* in (14)b conveyed the fact that the time of the *cooking* coincided with the time of the consciousness being represented. Words like *there* and *then* locate an event or state at a place or time that is *not* that of the consciousness being represented:

(15) a ... I was thère for abòut uh = síx
     b .. síx yèars.

(16) thèn I'll go my own wáy,

It makes no difference whether the event or state is remembered, as in (15), or imagined as in (16). *There* and *then* show that its place or time is different from that of the represented consciousness.

In chapter 17 we will see that linguistic elements associated with tense and person function differently from these adverbs of space and time. There is something to be gained from understanding tense as derived from consciousness, and not just from the abstract time relations in terms of which it is usually described. Tense is a way of linguistically marking the relation between the time of an extroverted consciousness and the time of a *representing* (not represented) consciousness. In the immediate mode there is no difference between the two, and the present tense expresses that fact. Figure 15.1, in other words, shows the situation that is typically expressed with the present tense. In the displaced mode the time of the extroverted consciousness and the time of the representing consciousness are different, as pictured in figure 15.2. In that case there can be more than one temporal relation between the two. Past tense means that the time of the extroverted consciousness preceded the time of the representing consciousness. Future tense means that the time of the extroverted consciousness is anticipated to follow the time of the representing consciousness.

I will return to person deixis later, but we can note here its parallelism to tense in the sense that it relates the *self* of the extroverted consciousness directly or indirectly to the self of the representing consciousness. First person expresses an equivalence between the two selves, second person equates the self of an extroverted consciousness with that of the listener, and third person expresses the fact that the self of the extroverted consciousness is neither the representing self nor the listener's self.

These deictic distinctions are difficult to justify convincingly in the present chapter, just because in conversational language the two types of deixis—that expressed by spatiotemporal adverbs (marking the relation between the extroverted consciousness and the *represented* consciousness) and that expressed by tense and person (marking the relation between the extroverted consciousness and the *representing* consciousness)—are almost always congruent. For example, when consciousness is in the immediate mode, *now* locates an event or state at the time of the represented consciousness, and the present tense locates it at the time of the representing consciousness. Since the represented and representing consciousnesses are the same, *now* is congruent with the present tense, as in (14). The same can be said for *then* and the past or future tenses, as in (16). *Then* locates an event or state at a time that is *not* the time of the represented consciousness, while the past or future tense locates it at a time that is prior to or follows the time of the representing consciousness. It is only in chapter 17 that we will come to see how these natural congruities between deixis centered on the represented consciousness and deixis centered on the representing consciousness may be disrupted when language is used in other ways.

The Relation of Immediacy and Displacement to Point of View

At the end of chapter 10 we saw that in conversational language ideas are represented from some point of view (typically that of the speaker), which may be manifested in several ways. Discussed in that chapter were the

frequency with which the holder of the point of view is mentioned, his
or her favored status as a starting point, references to his or her feelings
and evaluations, and his or her status as a deictic center. In chapters to
come we will see that a point of view is always associated with an extroverted consciousness. For the moment we can notice that in the immediate
mode, as in (1), the point of view can only be that of the single extroverted
consciousness, while in the displaced mode, as in (2) and (3), the point
of view is that of the distal extroverted consciousness and not that of the
proximal introverted consciousness. Thus in (2), repeated here still again,
the point of view was that of the speaker at the time of the original,
remembered event. It was at that time that he felt astounded, that the man
turned to him (as a deictic center), and that he walked past:

(17) a ... I went òut for a stróll,
     b on my first tìme on Chéstnut Strèet.
     c ... and just
     d ... just ... was astóunded,
     e at how pléasant things wère.
     f And às I was òut for a stróll,
     g ... a màn wàtering hi = s láwn,
     h .. túrned to mè,
     i .. as I wàlked pást,
     j .. and sáid,
     k ... góod èvening,

To repeat, it is always the extroverted (perceiving, acting, evaluating)
consciousness rather than the introverted (remembering, imagining) consciousness that provides the locus for a point of view.

The "Historical Present"

When one compares the qualities of extroverted and introverted consciousness in terms of continuity and detail, as discussed above, an introverted consciousness may seem to be impoverished, as suggested by both
its islandlike nature and its reduced detail. This impoverishment is not a
serious handicap when conversationalists verbalize remembered or imagined experiences, for there are compensations. By providing settings,
speakers compensate for the islandlike nature of remembering, and trivial
details are usually superfluous when it is important ideas that are of interest. But the major compensation is that the number and variety of experiences that are potentially available to a remembering or imagining con-

sciousness make the displaced mode incomparably richer so far as its repertoire is concerned.

Nevertheless, it is interesting to find speakers sometimes using devices whose purpose seems to be precisely to counteract in some way the usual quality of the displaced mode. Speakers in the displaced mode may pretend to be representing experiences that are closer to those of an extroverted consciousness in either or both of two ways. One device of this sort is the *historical present*; the other is *direct speech*. In the remainder of this chapter we will look at the historical present in this light. In the next chapter we will look at various ways of representing distal language, where we can interpret direct speech in a similar way.

The historical present is illustrated in intonation units (18)i–m:

(18) a   Like óne day I was just
     b   .. I was .. uh càrrying my gárbage,
     c   to the gárbage dùmp.
     d   ... And this gùy came bỳ on a mótorcycle.
     e   And thèn he went bàck in the óther dirèction,
     f   and wènt back in the óther dirèction,
     g   .. I was stìll càrrying my gárbage.
     h   And thén,
     i   .. I'm wálking = ,
     j   .. like bàck to my hóuse and,
     k   .. this ... mòtorcycle gets sló = wer and slówer and slówer,
     l   ... and lìke it's like .. ró = lling,
     m   and fínally this gùy is sàying,
     n   ... I lóve you.
     o   .. I lóve you.
     p   ... I lóve you.

In those five intonation units the present tense is used under circumstances where the past tense would ordinarily be called for, that is, in representing an event or state remembered from a temporally prior extroverted consciousness. The effect is to present the event or state as if its time coincided with that of the representing consciousness. Remembered information thereby acquires (but only with respect to tense) the deictic quality of immediacy suggested in figure 15.3. What in other respects conforms to figure 15.2 is, in this one respect, brought closer to 15.1. The historical present is a limited pretense that a remembered idea is an idea being perceived, acted on, and evaluated at the time of the representing.

Many commentators on the historical present have said something similar, relating its effect to immediacy. For example, Otto Jespersen characterized it as follows: "the speaker, as it were, forgets all about time and imagines, or remembers, what he is recounting, as vividly as if it were

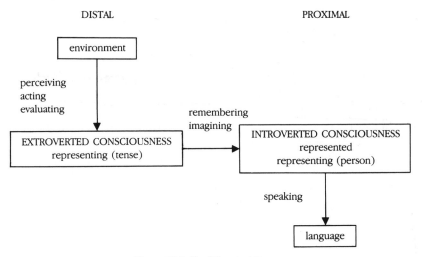

DISTAL   PROXIMAL

environment

perceiving
acting
evaluating
                        remembering
                        imagining

EXTROVERTED CONSCIOUSNESS   INTROVERTED CONSCIOUSNESS
representing (tense)   represented
                                      representing (person)

                                         speaking

                                          language

Figure 15.3 The Historical Present

now present before his eyes" (1931/1961, p. 19). Quirk, Greenbaum, Leech, and Svartvik (1985, p. 181) put it this way: "The historic present describes the past as if it is happening now: it conveys something of the dramatic immediacy of an eye-witness account." It is interesting to find that the immediacy conveyed by the historical present is occasionally reinforced through the use of *now,* which locates the event or state at the time of the *represented* consciousness as well as the representing. Wolfson (1982, pp. 39–40) cites several examples, among them:

(19) The door's closed and locked now and the guy in the next apartment
     bangs his door

As with other manipulations of consciousness we will meet later, it is important to distinguish between what the historical present *is* and what speakers *do* with it—between its *nature* and its *use.* To say that speakers sometimes make the displaced mode more like the immediate mode in this way is not to account for the circumstances under which they employ this option. Why, for example, did the speaker of (18) use the past tense in (18)a–g and switch to the present in (18)i–m? Deborah Schiffrin (1981, p. 60) reported that in one set of data there were "more occurrences of the [historical present] in the climax of a narrative (defined intuitively) and in the build-up to the climax (one-quarter of all preceding clauses) than in the clauses either preceding the build-up or following the climax." Example (18) illustrates that pattern. Evidently conversational narrators have a tendency to slip into the historical present at points in their talk where there is some reason for a remembered event or state to be expressed in a way that more closely resembles the immediate mode, a strategy likely to be most appropriate at, or shortly before, the climax of a narrative. This is not to say that climactic points are *always* signaled with the historical present, nor is it to rule out the possibility that this shift might be appropriate at other points as well. *prominent final*

One can also observe that the historical present is particularly common in attributions of direct speech, as exemplified in (18)m: *this guy is saying* (Schiffrin 1981, p. 58; Wolfson 1982, pp. 50–52). I will return in the next chapter to this special affinity between the historical present and direct speech. For now we can simply remember the historical present as one of several linguistic devices by which ordinary consciousness can be easily and naturally manipulated for special effect. This device, together with the use of direct speech discussed in chapter 16, as well as the use of generic remembering discussed above, are all options exploited by conversationalists to make the displaced mode more closely resemble the immediate mode in some way.

Summary

A fundamentally important property of human consciousness is its ability to focus, not just on the immediate environment, but also on remembered or imagined experience. This chapter looked at the nature and manifestations of immediate and displaced consciousness in conversational language. It was found that the displaced mode usually predominates over the immediate, and four reasons were suggested: introverted (remembered and imagined) ideas tend to be less shared, more interesting, more extensive, and more fully processed than what is available to an extroverted (perceiving, acting, and evaluating) consciousness. A distinction was made between spatiotemporal displacement—the ability to think and talk about experiences that were first present in an extroverted consciousness at a different space and/or time—and displacement of self—the ability to think and talk about experiences that were first present in the consciousness of someone other than the current thinker or speaker. This chapter was limited to spatiotemporal displacement.

Extroverted and introverted consciousness are qualitatively different. The differences can be attributed to differences between perceiving, acting, and evaluating on the one hand and remembering and imagining on the other. Extroverted experience has a continuous quality that contrasts with the islandlike nature of introverted experience. In representing introverted experience, speakers compensate by providing settings that locate an experiential island sufficiently to orient the listener's consciousness. Extroverted experience also has access to a wealth of detail, all of which is potentially available to focus on. In contrast, introverted experience is restricted to a coarseness of detail that is sometimes mitigated, though only partially, through recourse to generic experiences whose detail has been enhanced by rehearsal.

One can distinguish two types of deictic elements according to whether the deictic center is the represented or the representing consciousness. Spatiotemporal adverbs mark events and states as located at the space and time of the *represented* consciousness (*here, now*) or elsewhere (*there, then*). Tense and person, on the other hand, relate time and self to the *representing* consciousness. In conversational language these two types of deixis are congruent. In the immediate mode, for example, the use of *now* is congruent with the present tense, while in the displaced mode the use of *then* is congruent with either the past or future tense. These congruities may be disrupted when language is used in other ways, as we will see.

The chapter closed with a discussion of the historical present, which causes the displaced mode to resemble the immediate mode more closely by transferring to a remembered experience the tense that is ordinarily appropriate to an immediately perceived, acted on, or evaluated experience. A conversational narrator may switch to the historical present when there is some reason to express a remembered experience as more closely resembling an experience being directly perceived. This mitigation of displacement is especially appropriate at or just preceding climactic points in a narrative. It is also common in attributions of direct speech.

16

Representing Other Speech and Thought in Conversation

People often use language to repeat ideas that were, or might be, expressed in other language at another time and place. Sometimes the distal language was, or might be, produced by the proximal speaker, who now wishes to inform the proximal listener of what he or she said to another listener at an earlier time, or might say at a later time. But often the distal language was produced by someone else. Much of what people know was acquired through language that originated in and was first represented by a consciousness other than their own. During a subsequent conversation it may then become interesting to repeat what the other person said. The intention may be to pass on the information that was acquired in that way, or it may be to share with the current listener the fact that the earlier speaker was the kind of person who would have said that kind of thing. We can direct our attention first to overt language, language said aloud. In accordance with established usage, I will call such language *speech* in order to contrast it with *thought,* which is known only to the thinker. Later in this chapter I will turn to ways of representing the covert language of thought, or inner speech.

Representing Distal Speech

There appear to be four major ways in which language can be used to represent other language (cf. Leech and Short 1981, pp. 318–51). One of them is used predominantly in certain kinds of writing. Since in this chapter we are still concerned with conversational language, we can restrict our attention for the moment to three of the possibilities, turning to the fourth only briefly at the end of the chapter and postponing a fuller discussion of it to chapter 18. Of these three, one is what I will call *referred-to* speech. It corresponds to what Leech and Short call a "narrative report of a speech act," and to McHale's "diegetic summary" (McHale 1978, p. 258). A second is *indirect* speech (alternatively, indirect discourse or indirect quotation). The third is *direct* speech (direct discourse or direct quotation). Referred-to and indirect speech in conversational language conform to the structure of ordinary consciousness as it was described in chapter 15. Direct speech pretends more than ordinary consciousness is capable of, but as with the historical present it remains congenial to conversational language, where it is frequently used.

Referred-to Speech
Language often represents distal language simply by referring to it as a speech event, without attempting to represent the language itself. Sometimes there is a global reference to an entire conversation, most often one in which the current speaker was, plans to be, or could hypothetically be a participant. Behind such a reference often lies some intention the current speaker wished or wishes the reported conversation to accomplish:

(1) ... I was tàlking to ... a gàl at wórk,
(2) ... Ì gotta go have a tálk with em,
(3) .. Ì'll tell Bíll.

Sometimes the current speaker was the earlier listener:

(4) a well Í hèard of an élephant,
    b .. that sát dówn on a VẀ one time.
(5) .. Yóu're the one that tóld me all thìs,

But the earlier conversation need not be one in which the current speaker participated, or plans to participate, at all:

(6) Well thèn he tàlked to that ... Ròdney Smíth,
(7) a .. So hè was going to talk to ... Hènry,
    b .. and see what Hénry thought it was.

In (6) and (7) we understand that there was an intermediate conversation in which the current speaker learned about another conversation that was, or would be, twice removed from the current one.

References to speech events resemble references to events of other kinds. They show the same selective remembering, and are restricted to information that is or was of interest to the proximal speaker. They are useful to linguists in showing how people categorize speech events. Besides the unmarked references to *talking* and *telling* illustrated above, the following examples of referred-to speech suggest some of the variety found in less bland categorizations:

(8) ... I tòld ... Wàlter óff.
(9) a .. mòstly Jímmy,
    b .. got on his bándwagon,
    c about Mrs. Spéncer.
(10) .. he was tèlling jókes,
(11) People would gréet each òther.

(12) a .. You knòw it,

    b ... tòok him the first hàlf a dáy to,

    c ... grìnch and bìtch and móan about everything,

Indirect Speech

One way language about language may go beyond simply referring to a speech event is by rewording what was said, using indirect speech. This strategy does not pretend to replicate the actual words of the distal speech, but reconstitutes them in a way that acknowledges the inability of ordinary remembering to reproduce other language verbatim. The linguistic manifestations of indirect speech are well known (e.g., Leech and Short 1981, pp. 318–21; Li 1986). I will illustrate them with a brief example:

(13) .. and he sàid he didn't mínd it.

There is, first of all, a reference to the distal speech event and its agent, typically using the verb *say* (or *tell* if the distal listener is included). Phrases like *he said* or *he told me* constitute what may be called the *attribution* of the other language (e.g., Longacre 1983, pp. 129–33; oddly, they are sometimes also called "parentheticals"). The attribution is then accompanied by some approximation to the distal language, the indirect quote. Sometimes this quote is introduced with the word *that* (*he said that he didn't mind it*); more often it is not. Characteristic of indirect speech is the fact that the tense and person, not just of the attribution but also of the quote, treat the speech act as the distal event that it was. Most often it was an event that took place earlier, and thus it is expressed entirely in the past tense—in (13) with the past tense of *said* in the attribution and *didn't* in the quote. When the self of the distal speech act differs from the current representing self, it is expressed with a third-person pronoun, as in (13), or a second-person pronoun if the distal self is the current listener. If there is a spatiotemporal adverb, its deictic center is the consciousness of the proximal speaker. For example, if the distal speaker had said *I don't mind it now,* the indirect quote might express this idea as *he said he didn't mind it then.*

    An indirect quote is neither intended nor understood as a verbatim replication of the earlier language. One who hears (13) understands an open-ended set of possible speech events, only one of which is

(14) ˜I don't mínd it.

The earlier speaker might have said any number of other things that are easy to invent without limit:

(15) ˜It doesn't bóther me.

(16) ˜I'm wílling.

(17) ˜It àin't no skìn off mý àss màn.

Indirect speech, then, acknowledges that the quote is a reconstitution, not a replica. The proximal speaker intends it to convey the gist of the distal speech without replicating either its exact wording or evaluative features such as exclamations, colloquial language, repetitions, or prosody. Thus, one would not expect

(18) ˜˜He said that it wasn't no skin off his ass man.

Among other curious properties of (18), it would seem impossible to interpret the word *man* as anything other than a vocative addressed to the listener to the distal speech event, who of course is not present during the proximal speech event.

In terms of the structure of ordinary consciousness, indirect speech can be understood in the following way. First, there is a remembering (or imagining) of a distal speech event in which either the proximal self or some other self was (or might be) the speaker. When that other event actually occurred (or might occur), its verbatim wording and prosody remained briefly active in the listener's consciousness, but subsequently its gist was stored in a verbally uncommitted form. It is now recalled in that same form, under the constraints of ordinary remembering, into the proximal speaker's consciousness. With the decision to convey it to the proximal listener, it must be verbalized again. The tense (and, when relevant, person) of the indirect quote expresses the fact that the information comes from a distal consciousness. An indirect quote, then, acknowledges the proximal speaker's inability to remember (or imagine) distal language verbatim.

Direct Speech

Both referred-to and indirect speech thus recognize the constraints inherent in the ordinary remembering of an earlier experience or the imagining of an anticipated experience. The proximal speaker simply refers to the distal speech event or reconstitutes it. Direct speech, on the other hand, pretends to surmount the proximal speaker's inability to reproduce distal language verbatim. It includes an attribution that is no different from that in indirect speech (*he said, he told me,* and the like), but it differs from indirect speech in pretending to replicate the actual tense, person, and adverbial deixis as well as the verbatim wording, evaluative devices, and sometimes even prosody of the earlier language:

(19) ˜It àin't no skìn off mý àss màn he sàid.

Direct speech thus pretends to surmount the normal limitations of the displaced mode diagramed in figure 15.2 of the last chapter. How can that be done, if conversationalists remain subject to ordinary constraints on remembering? In cases where the verbatim language itself is newsworthy enough to have been rehearsed, or so formulaic that it can be accurately recalled, verbatim remembering is no problem. But what of the many cases in which neither the newsworthiness nor the conventionality of the language is sufficient to produce such a result? The answer, of course, lies in the proximal speaker's imagination.

Several linguists have recently taken pains to point out that direct speech is a creation of the proximal speaker (Tannen 1989, Mayes 1990). It is usually impossible to study directly whether that is true, because we do not usually have access to earlier speech events that we can compare with the current language. There is, however, convincing indirect evidence of several kinds. Sometimes speech acts are quoted that could not plausibly have occurred. Mayes (1990, pp. 333–34) mentions and exemplifies the following subtypes of evidence of this sort (cf. Tannen 1989, pp. 110–19). One subtype is the attribution of the same quote to several people:

(20) a ... All my friends said well,
     b ... you're not eating,
     c ... you're not doing anything,
     d ... what's wrong with you.

It would be hard to believe that all the friends said exactly this. Another subtype is a quote that is alleged to be said habitually:

(21) a ... I always say,
     b .. no more,
     c no more.

The literal interpretation is dubious here as well. Sometimes a quote contains a variable expression introduced by the proximal speaker:

(22) a .. And she said well,
     b .. so and so lives here,
     c and so and so lives there,

So and so are obviously the words of the proximal speaker, not the quoted one. Still another subtype involves language that was allegedly uttered in the absence of an interlocutor. The speaker of the following was known to have been at home alone:

(23) a ... and I said oh the heck with this,
     b I'll go to bed,
     c I was kind of tired.

More likely this person simply made a tacit decision to go to bed. Furthermore, as mentioned in chapter 3, it is clear from various kinds of evidence that completely verbatim language is, for the most part, remembered only within the span of active consciousness. If verbatim remembering is thus limited to the remembering of particularly newsworthy or rehearsed words or phrases, we can conclude that direct speech *must* rely to a considerable extent on imagination.

As we did with the historical present, we can turn our attention from function to use and ask what conversationalists *do* with direct speech. If both indirect and direct speech are in actuality reconstructions, why should language provide both options, one acknowledging that the language is reconstituted, the other pretending that it is replicated? A general answer can be that direct speech, like the historical present, is another way of bringing a quality of immediacy to a displaced experience. But what are the circumstances under which conversationalists would want to do that? The conversational data I have examined with this question in mind suggest two answers. By far the most common motivation for direct speech is to introduce evaluative information associated with an earlier speech event. The distal event is remembered as one that communicated affect through exclamations, repetitions, colloquial vocabulary, or prosody. The current speaker attempts to re-create the same evaluative quality by imitating those features. Direct speech can thus be seen as a way of expressing involvement (Chafe 1982, Tannen 1989). Most of the examples of direct speech in the examined conversational samples show this evaluative quality:

(24) .. I said well héll you'd be dóne with it nów,
(25) Ì said lóok,
(26) a .. He gòes,
     c just gìve it a hùndred tèn percént,
     d .. and and you'll dò góod.

But there is another usage that falls into a second category whose general nature is also clear. Direct speech may also be used when the verbatim language itself has some special relevance. There may, for example, be a repetition of some official wording, perhaps in a written document:

(27) a She pùt that,
     b I gàve this càr .. to Ròbert Ìngalls for a gíft,

(This example is also of interest in showing the complementizer *that* being used with direct speech.) Direct speech may also convey an instruction, advice, demonstration, or explanation—some authoritative speech act in which the language that was actually used has some importance because of its authoritativeness. Example (28) conveys advice given by a mechanic who had been asked about a problem with a motor; example (29) describes advice given by a physician:

(28) a ... Bìll Thórnhill said nó,
     b .. just chèck your injéctor.
(29) a .. She says nòw we're hàving them dò ... uh .. éxercises,
     b ... where you lìe flàt on your stómach,
     c ... and you lìft your shóulders ùp.

To summarize, whereas indirect speech suffices to convey adequately enough for many purposes the content of distal language, direct speech gives the speaker an opportunity to express involvement by reconstructing evaluative wordings and prosody. Sometimes, too, direct speech is used to convey the wording of an earlier speech event when that wording had some official or instructional significance.

As mentioned at the end of chapter 15, the attribution of direct speech is frequently given in the historical present:

(30) a I says Géorge?
     b ... I dón't wànt
     c ... àny more kíds.
(31) a .. He tùrns to his móther and goes,
     b ... I nèed to see Ròger's bíke.

The relation between direct speech and the historical present should now be clear. Both are artifices that bring qualities of extroverted experience to introverted experience. The first does so by pretending that there is no temporal difference between the distal extroverted consciousness and the proximal representing consciousness. The second does so by pretending that the proximal representing consciousness has direct access to distal verbatim language. Both devices convey a quality of immediacy that is lacking when introverted experience is represented in the ordinary way. It is thus not surprising that the historical present and direct speech are symbiotic. Both produce similar effects, and the two together can be more effective than either of them alone.

Some speakers use more direct speech than others. Some, in fact, seem to use it seldom if at all, though of course that is difficult to know from limited data. It is at least clear that the use of direct speech is a variable property of conversational style. Some speakers insert extended sequences of it at particularly involving points in their conversations:

(32) a .. a = nd .. he just .. said wéll,
     b thát thèory was .. debúnked.
     c ... I said Óh?
     d by whóm.
     e ... He said well by .. Péterson.
     f ... I said ... whó's Péterson.
     g .. He says you dòn't know Péterson?

h ... Óh my góodness.
i .. Why hè's one of our grèat ... lòcal .. geólogists.
j ... I said wéll,
k .. uh that's níce,
l but whỳ would hé be the òne to debúnk this.

With other speakers such language is rare, or perhaps absent altogether.

Representing Distal Thought

One might suppose that the covert language of thought is represented in a way that is wholly parallel to the representation of overt speech. The three options discussed above would then be convertible from overt to covert language merely by replacing the verb *say* with the verb *think,* yielding referred-to thought, indirect thought, and direct thought. The facts, when examined closely, are a little more complex. I will assume here that *thought* refers to the flow of information through a person's introverted consciousness. Since conscious experience can be either non-verbal or verbal, both possibilities need to be taken into account as we consider how a proximal consciousness can verbalize distal thought. Representations of speech always go back to distal *language,* but representations of thought are less committed in that respect.

Referred-to Thought
Just as conversationalists may refer to *speaking* without trying to reproduce it, they may also refer to *thinking* with no commitment to the verbal or nonverbal nature of the experience in question:

(33) .. It's nót a jòb that requìres a lot of thínking.
(34) .. You don't thínk about òther thìngs,
(35) ... and àll this tìme I'd be thìnking about Sálly.

In such cases one might suppose that the reported thinking involved a mixture of both verbal and nonverbal elements.

We noted above that referred-to speech can be useful in shedding light on the way speech events are categorized. The same is true of references to thought. The following are a few examples, analogous to (8) through (12) above, that illustrate the variety to be found in such categorizations:

(36) ... Nòbody had àny nègative thóughts,
(37) a .. You know I don't have to m wòrry about being fifteen mínutes,
      b or twénty mìnutes láte,
(38) your mìnd stàys ... stùck in that fáctory.
(39) .. which is a gòod .. gòod féeling to háve.

Each of these examples is typical in including an obvious evaluative component, sometimes negative and sometimes positive. Categorizing thoughts generally entails some evaluation of them. It may be that people seldom if ever remember thoughts without associating them with some kind of affect.

Pseudo–Indirect Thought: Beliefs, Opinions, or Decisions Rather Than Inner Speech

Superficially, examples like the following might seem parallel to indirect speech, as in (13) above:

(40) .. I thought you were gonna spráy it.
(41) .. I think it's fifty dòllars a dáy.
(42) ... I think I'll just mòve it back into the kitchen,

With a little reflection, however, it should be apparent that statements like these are not ways of paraphrasing inner language remembered from (or anticipated for) a distal consciousness. Example (40), for instance, does not report a distal experience which, if it had been reported directly, might have been stated as

(43) ~"He's going to spray it," I thought.

In (40) *I thought* does not mean 'I experienced the following inner language,' but rather something more like 'my belief up until now was that.' In (41) *I think* means something more like 'my opinion is.' When the following verb is in the future tense, as in (42), the meaning is something more like 'I'm deciding.' Why should that be? Why should what look like indirect quotations of inner language actually express beliefs, opinions, or decisions?

Indirect *speech*, as we have seen, recognizes the true nature of remembering, realistically acknowledging its limitations. It would now appear that language that once passed silently through a distal consciousness is not remembered in the form of language as such, but rather as a belief or opinion (in the case of prior experiences) or a decision (in the case of anticipated experiences). Although inner language flows through the mind as an immediate experience, at a later time we do not remember it as language, but as a belief or opinion. And we do not anticipate inner speech as such, but rather make decisions to do things. The result is the special meanings that have been acquired by the verb *think* in such contexts. The format of indirect thought remains true to constraints on remembering and imagining, and these constraints evidently substitute beliefs, opinions, and decisions for inner speech. I will use the term *pseudo–indirect thought* to refer to this special effect of what appears superficially to be indirect thought, parallel to indirect speech.

Example (41) calls for more discussion. Whereas it was possible to convert (40), by distorting its meaning, into a report of actual inner speech as in (43), the same is not possible for (41):

(44) ~"It's fifty dollars a day," I think (or I'm thinking).

What is noteworthy about (44) is that even in a format that mirrors *direct* speech, *think* in the present tense means to have an opinion. When one uses an attribution like *I think* or *I'm thinking* ostensibly to report a represented thought that is simultaneous with that attribution, interpretation as a direct quote is impossible. The reason may be that it would be tautologous to present what one is currently thinking as a quote, since (45) does the complete job:

(45) ~It's fifty dollars a day.

Example (45) is sufficient to verbalize what I am thinking, and there is no point in adding the information that I am covertly thinking it at the same time I am overtly expressing it. When the literal meaning of *think* is ruled out, it is the transferred meaning of having an opinion that takes over, as in both (41) and (44).

Direct Thought
Although speakers do not have natural access to distal covert language, they can *pretend* such access, just as they can pretend to remember overt speech. Conversations do contain examples of *direct* thought that are parallel to direct speech:

(46) a and I thought wèll,
     b .. wórse things could hàppen to the pòor gúy,
(47) a And Ì thought,
     b òh bóy.

The quoted portions pretend to replicate language that passed through the represented speaker's mind at an earlier time. But although such examples can be found, they are relatively infrequent compared to examples of either indirect or direct *speech*. They are also less frequent than the expression of beliefs, opinions, or decisions as pseudo–indirect thought. Examples like (46) and (47), furthermore, may be limited in conversational language to the remembering of the proximal speaker's own inner speech, as opposed to that of another person.

To turn from the nature of this device to its use, we can ask what speakers do with direct thought. Apparently they use it as they use direct speech, predominantly to convey involvement. Both (46) and (47) perform that function. So does the following:

(48) a ... Ì thought géeze,
    b .. get yòu and hím together,
    c and Ì'd just sít there,
    d and enjòy the shów.

But this last example has further implications, foreshadowing a kind of language to be discussed in chapter 18. Suppose that the covert language imagined by the speaker of (48) was something like the following:

(49) a ~Géeze,
    b get Jàck and Hárry together,
    c and Ì'll just sít there,
    d and enjòy the shów.

In (48) neither the person (*you*) nor the tense (*I'd*) were those of the pretended original in (49). The pronoun *you* referred to the listener of the proximal speech event, and the past tense of *I'd* expressed the difference in time between the distal consciousness and the proximal representing consciousness. In short, the person and tense of (48) were those of indirect speech.

  But (48) cannot be an example of indirect thought, which we have already seen to be preempted by beliefs, opinions, and decisions. Example (48) did not express a belief. In fact, I introduced it as the concluding example in a discussion of *direct* thought, and I did that because it preserved verbatim qualities of the pretended original. There was the exclamation *géeze,* the elliptical syntax of the first clause, and the colloquial phrase *enjoy the show,* all of which suggest verbatim language. The peculiarity of (48) is that it combines the person and tense associated with indirect speech or thought with the verbatim language associated with direct speech or direct thought. Language like (48) is rare in conversations. It is an example of so-called free indirect style, a kind of language sometimes said not to occur in conversational speaking. We have here a good example of how the seeds of a literary device may be found in conversations.

Summary

This chapter looked at representations of distal language as they appear in conversations. Concentrating first on representations of overt speech, as opposed to covert thought, we noted three devices in common use. *Referred-to* speech simply mentions an earlier or imagined speech event. It is of interest in showing the various ways in which people naturally categorize such events. *Indirect* speech acknowledges the inability of a representing consciousness to replicate distal language verbatim, and in that sense it reflects the true relation between the immediate and displaced modes of speaking. *Direct speech* pretends that the early language *is* replicated verbatim. It is used either to introduce evaluation and thus express involvement or to suggest verbatim wording when that wording has some legal or instructional significance. Direct speech often includes an attribution in the historical present, both devices bringing a quality of immediacy to displaced experience. Its use is characteristic of certain conversational styles.

Thought, or inner speech, is represented in ways that are partially but not wholly parallel to the representation of overt speech. It may be simply referred-to, providing insights into natural ways of categorizing thought events. Indirect thought, parallel to indirect speech, is replaced by remembered or anticipated beliefs, opinions, or decisions. Evidently inner speech as such is not reconstituted through remembering. I introduced the term *pseudo–indirect thought* for this phenomenon. However, the presence of *direct* thought in conversational language shows that it *is* possible to *pretend* access to verbatim language that is not directly available to the representing consciousness. Like direct speech, direct thought is used to express involvement.

I closed the chapter with an unusual example in which verbatim language, suggesting direct thought, was combined with the person and tense appropriate to indirect thought. The discovery of such a combination in conversational language leads fittingly into the subject matter of the next chapter, where we will encounter written language for the first time, although discussion of ways in which distal speech and thought are represented in written language will be postponed to chapter 18.

17

Displaced Immediacy in Written First-Person Fiction

There may be a special compatibility between writing and fiction. To make that suggestion is not to downgrade written nonfiction, which obviously accounts for a high percentage of all written material. Nor do I mean to suggest that fiction is unimportant in speaking. Aside from the occurrence of storytelling in conversations, the range and diversity of fictional genres in oral traditions are broad and deep. But the deliberate composition of carefully planned works of fiction by unique individuals is something for which writing provides an especially happy environment. The proliferation of individually authored novels, short stories, and dramas of all sorts and sizes is an obvious feature of literate societies.

Undoubtedly the desituatedness of writing has something to do with this. The writing situation is itself unreal in its detachment from the co-presence and interaction which are normal for conversational language. If all writing is, in that respect, intrinsically unreal, the further step to total fiction is not a big one. Writers, too, can enjoy the leisure that is conducive to imaginative creation, with ample time for contemplative imagining between and during the conversion of imagined experience into visible words. Beyond that, face-to-face interaction may tend to keep conversationalists in a more factual mode, whereas a faceless, unknown audience eliminates that barrier to imaginative license. Removed from eye contact, writers can be less concerned with the need to adhere to what they believe is true. It is not that writing encourages prevarication, though it may do that too, but that it is especially hospitable to the spinning of carefully thought out fantasies for both enjoyment and edification. Once it has begun, fiction snowballs. A writer's imagination acquires a momentum that leads from one imagined event to another. In brief, the intrinsic unreality of the writing situation, the availability of contemplative leisure, the absence of face-to-face interaction, and the snowballing effect all combine to support a result that can be captured in the saying "writing fosters fiction."

Writing with a Fictional Representing Consciousness

The logic of fiction demands a special status for the representing consciousness. A conversational storyteller or the author of written fiction exists in what we regard as the "real" world, but the events such a person tells or writes about exist in a different, imagined world. When someone tells a joke or relates some other type of acknowledged fiction during a conversation, we do not regard him or her as a liar, but are willing temporarily to dissociate the representing self from the real self that is embodied in our presence. Many languages employ a special device to signal this dissociation, as when Seneca speakers liberally insert the word gyǫʔǫh (roughly, 'it is said') into their stories to make it clear that what they are saying is not their own perception of reality.

In written fiction there are two ways to handle this dissociation. One option is for the author to assume a fictional self, so that the representing consciousness becomes a fictional consciousness that is at home in the fictional world. The language has, as we say, a fictional narrator who belongs to the world of the story. The other option is for the author to relinquish any self at all, in which case the representing consciousness can be said to be *unacknowledged*. In this chapter and the next we look at writing that has an acknowledged but fictional representing consciousness. In chapter 19 we will turn to writing with an unacknowledged representing consciousness, a consciousness that has been, so to speak, disembodied or, perhaps more accurately, *de-selfed*.

If fictional language is to acknowledge a fictional self who is its producer, that self usually belongs to a person who has access to fictional events because he or she took part in them. Hence the strategy of writing with a first-person narrator whose distal consciousness is the source of the experiences that are represented. This artifice bears some resemblance to the situation in which someone narrates a remembered personal experience in the midst of a conversation. But, aside from the fact that the narrator is fictional rather than real, what is actually represented can have a very different character from anything a conversationalist would produce.

Here is the first paragraph of *The Ox-Bow Incident*, a western novel by Walter Van Tilburg Clark (1940):

(1)   Gil and I crossed the eastern divide about two by the sun. We pulled up for a look at the little town in the big valley and the mountains on the other side, with the crest of the Sierra showing faintly beyond like the rim of a day moon. We didn't look as long as we do sometimes; after winter range, we were excited about getting back to town. When the horses had stopped trembling from the last climb, Gil took off his sombrero, pushed his sweaty hair back with the same hand, and returned the sombrero, the way he did when something was going to happen. We reined to the right and went slowly down the steep stage road. It was a switch-back road, gutted by the run-off of the winter storms, and with brush beginning to grow up in it again since the stage had stopped running. In the pockets under

the red earth banks, where the wind was cut off, the spring sun was hot as summer, and the air was full of a hot, melting pine smell. Rivulets of water trickled down shining on the sides of the cuts. The jays screeched in the trees and flashed through the sunlight in the clearings in swift, long dips. Squirrels and chipmunks chittered in the brush and along the tops of snow-sodden logs. On the outside turns, though, the wind got to us and dried the sweat under our shirts and brought up, instead of the hot resin, the smell of the marshy green valley. In the west the heads of a few clouds showed, the kind that come up with the early heat, but they were lying still, and over us the sky was clear and deep. (Pp. 5–6)

This language departs from that of a conversational narrative in several obvious ways. For one thing, it would be hard to imagine a conversation in which one of the participants succeeded in holding the floor long enough to produce language that would fill several hundred pages. For another thing, there is no specific, acknowledged audience. Like much that is written, the language is openly available to anyone who picks up the book, and it may be adjusted to the needs of generalized readers as discussed below in chapter 22, but it is addressed to no one in particular. Our major interest here, however, is in other properties of such language: special possibilities offered by the desituatedness of writing for the representation of consciousness.

Displaced Immediacy

As emphasized in chapter 15, ordinary conversational consciousness, whether it is in the immediate or the displaced mode, does not distinguish the representing from the represented consciousness. That is to say, one and the same consciousness is responsible for producing the language and is expressed by the language. It might at first be supposed that these two roles are inseparable—two sides of a single coin—and in the ordinary use of language that is so. Language like that illustrated in (1), however, shows that it is possible to dissociate the two. The representing consciousness in (1) is that of the fictional narrator at the time of narrating, but the represented consciousness is a different one. Although it belongs to the same self as the representing consciousness, it is separated in space and time. The separation is possible because the desituatedness of writing weakens, as it were, the hold of the representing consciousness. In conversations the language emerging from the mouth of the speaker expresses what is passing through the consciousness of that person then and there. A situated representing consciousness maintains a tight grip on the repre-

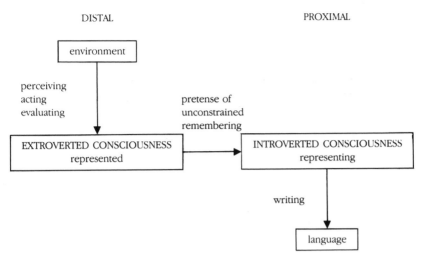

Figure 17.1 Writing in the Displaced Immediate Mode

sented consciousness. But when writing removes copresence and interaction, the hold is weakened and the represented consciousness is free to migrate to a different time and place. Figure 17.1 diagrams the result (compare figs. 15.1 and 15.2 in chap. 15). The language of (1), in ways to be discussed, verbalizes an extroverted consciousness that directly perceives, acts on, and evaluates its environment. It is appropriate to characterize this situation as one of *displaced immediacy*, since it combines an introverted representing consciousness (belonging to the proximal fictional narrator) with an extroverted represented consciousness (belonging to the same self at a distal time and place).

Like the historical present and direct speech, displaced immediacy is a departure from the ordinary structure of consciousness described in chapter 15. It is, however, more global and complex in its manifestations and effects than either of those other devices, and, unlike them, it is more at home in written language than in spoken. It is more global in the sense that it may extend through an entire short story or novel, instead of being limited to relatively short segments of language. It is more complex in the sense that its linguistic manifestations are not limited to a single easily described feature such as the use of the present tense in representing a remembered event, or the pretended remembering of verbatim language. Rather, it is manifested in a cluster of features that work together to signal its presence.

Before we examine what those features are, we can observe that a distal represented consciousness belonging to the same self as the representing consciousness suggests a narrator who is gifted with an unrealistic ability to remember distal experiences, an ability so powerful that he is able not just to remember, but actually to relive what happened in the past. Reliving implies fictional powers of *unconstrained remembering*, the ability to remember a distal consciousness as if it were a proximal consciousness. A cursory reading of (1) may suggest what I mean. We can now look more closely at what is involved: first at evidence for immediacy, then at evidence for displacement.

Evidence for Immediacy

What is the evidence in (1) for the immediacy of the represented consciousness? We can look at three features that were identified in chapter 15 as distinguishing extroverted from introverted experience: continuity, detail, and the deixis of immediacy.

Continuity
We saw in chapter 15 that the islandlike nature of remembering motivates conversationalists to provide an orientation for each new discourse topic through the provision of a setting. If (1) were translated into conversational language, perhaps the narrator would have begun by saying,

(2) a ~Last spring I was out riding with my friend Gil.
    b Did I ever tell you about him?

Instead, (1) begins in medias res. There is no introduction of Gil, no explanation of what the two companions were up to. The fact that they were crossing *the eastern divide* or that it was *about two by the sun* fails to provide the kind of orientation that would satisfy a conversational listener. The reader is given the impression of an experience that has flowed without interruption out of a preceding experience, and that now flows without interruption into whatever will follow. This impression of continuity is reinforced by the pretense of identifiability for *the* eastern divide, *the* little town, *the* big valley, and so on. The definiteness of these noun phrases expresses the conceit that their referents are already shared and identifiable. In actuality, of course, there is no recognized audience to do the sharing, and it is sufficient that these referents are identifiable to the fictional narrator in the midst of his ongoing, fictionally extroverted experience (cf. Backus 1965; Fillmore 1974, p. V17).

Continuity is also evident in the more or less uninterrupted flow of experience, which lacks the major temporal and spatial lacunae that surround the islands of ordinary remembering. This uninterrupted flow is evident in (1), but it continues through the chapter and even crosses chapter boundaries. Thus, chapter 1 ends with

(3) I pushed past him and went down onto the walk, Gil right behind me.

and chapter 2 begins with

(4) Farnley was climbing onto his horse.

with no apparent break in time or space between these two events.

Detail

Example (1) also exhibits an access to fine-grained detail that is uncharacteristic of ordinary remembering. A writer has the ability to supplement the coarse-grained detail of ordinary remembering with a wealth of trivial information (cf. Barthes 1982, which, however, does not come to grips with the broader cognitive significance of this device). The importance of such language lies in establishing the illusion that the consciousness it represents is a consciousness that has access to such details. Their presence is the most obvious property of (1), leaving no doubt that what is represented is an extroverted consciousness, even though it is at the same time a distal one.

We can speculate for a moment on the practical question of how a writer is able to provide such detail. How did an isolated writer like Clark, sitting alone at his desk, have access to it? It is intriguing to compare writers with painters in this regard. Painters typically gain access to fine-grained detail by positioning themselves next to the environment itself, painting from a model or scene that provides them with constant access to as much detail as they need. While it is quite possible for a writer to do that too, one doubts that Clark sat on a horse on the eastern divide, observing the rivulets of water trickling down on the sides of the cuts and the jays screeching in the trees as he wrote about them. In practice these details typically arise from a writer's remembering and imagining. But are not remembering and imagining limited by constraints on detail? Where does a writer's detail come from? With no final answer, I suspect that the detail authors are able to exploit in passages like (1) results from a blending of imagining with generic remembering. Having seen more than one rivulet of water, having heard more than one jay screeching in more than one tree, Clark was able to reconstitute a total experience of this kind.

Those with a quantitative bent might find an interest in measuring the degree of trivial detail in a language sample, thus obtaining some confirmation of the difference between a reliving and a remembering consciousness in this regard. The most straightforward measure that suggests itself is the proportion of trivial referents to total referents. If the importance of a referent can be measured by its frequency of occurrence (chap. 7), then trivial referents are characterized by their minimal frequency. In (1) about 65 percent of the concrete, tangible referents are represented only once (the *jays,* the *trees,* and so on), nor do they appear later on. By way of contrast, in the conversational Two Women story discussed in chapter 10, the only comparably trivial referent may have been the *bread* in the statement *So we had them over for bread.* The triviality index was no greater than 3 percent. In the Two Women story the represented consciousness was an introverted one.

The Deixis of Immediacy

The immediacy of the represented consciousness in *The Ox-Bow Incident* is further supported by the use of deictic adverbs. In chapter 15 it was asserted that adverbs like *now* and *today* are related to the deictic center of the represented consciousness. Language like this demonstrates that the constant property of these adverbs is indeed the fact that they locate an event or state at the time of the *represented,* not the *representing* consciousness. Since in conversation the represented consciousness normally coincides with the representing consciousness, we are apt, mistakenly, to associate *now* with the time of representing. But in *The Ox-Bow Incident,* with a distal represented consciousness, the meaning of words like *now* and *today* is fully compatible with the past tense that locates an event or state prior to the representing consciousness.

(5) [The bar] was clean and dry now, (P. 8)
(6) I didn't see how anybody could find anything to laugh at today. (P. 203)

In conversational language we see an incompatibility between immediacy and pastness, since we expect the represented and representing consciousness to be the same. When the two are separated, the incompatibility vanishes and uses like those illustrated in (5) and (6) are just what we should expect.

Evidence for Displacement

We have now seen three kinds of evidence for the immediate quality of the language in *The Ox-Bow Incident*: continuity, access to detail, and the deixis of immediacy. To show that this immediacy is *displaced*—that the represented extroverted consciousness is not the representing consciousness (as it was in the immediate mode diagramed in fig. 15.1 of chap. 15)—it is enough to observe that the novel is written in the past tense. The past tense shows that the represented extroverted consciousness is temporally prior to the representing consciousness which provides the deictic center for tense. Without this displacement the language would read, for example,

(7) ˜We don't look as long as we do sometimes; after winter range, we're excited about getting back to town. When the horses (have) stopped trembling from the last climb, Gil takes off his sombrero, pushes his sweaty hair back with the same hand, and returns the sombrero, the way he does when something is going to happen. We rein to the right and go slowly down the steep stage road.

In effect, the novel would be written in the historical present.

Why is the language of (7) less effective than that of (1), as I assume to be the case? Why is displaced immediacy more effective than a sustained use of the historical present? For one thing, as we saw in chapter 15, it is less common in ordinary speaking to talk about an immediate experience than about a displaced one. Conversational narratives report remembered or imagined experiences. Whereas the use of the past tense retains this natural property of conversations, (7) does not. To be sure, conversational narrators slip into the historical present from time to time, but they never use that tense exclusively; the present always alternates with the past. A consistent use of the historical present during an entire narrative would thus depart from conversational practice.

But since (1) deviates from conversational usage in other ways, the ordinary association of past tense with narration would seem not to be the only factor that favors (1) over (7). More important may be the fact that an event remembered from a distal consciousness necessarily belongs to a more complexly structured repertoire than an event that is currently being experienced. A distal event can be related to other distal events in more than just a temporal sequence. It can, for example, function as background for a foregrounded event. The language of displaced immediacy expresses such a background-foreground relation easily:

(8) When the horses had stopped trembling from the last climb, Gil took off his sombrero

The horses' cessation of their trembling provides a background for Gil's taking off his sombrero by being expressed in the past perfect and by being placed in a subordinate clause. It is easy to background an event in this way if one already knows the full set of events and their relationships. Example (8) does not translate well into the present tense:

(9) ˜When the horses (have) stopped trembling from the last climb, Gil takes off his sombrero

Because immediate events are experienced in sequence as they occur, the horses' trembling must be reported independently of Gil's taking off his sombrero, the next event. Simultaneous reporting would preclude the subordination so easily achieved in (8) but so awkwardly attempted in (9), yielding perhaps

(10) ˜The horses are trembling from the last climb. They stop trembling. Gil takes off his sombrero

But (10) is hardly an effective a way of relating these events. The backgrounding made possible by the more inclusive vision attainable through remembering is possible only within the broader perspective provided by a distal represented consciousness.

There is also a fundamental aesthetic reason why (1) is more effective than (7). The impact of (1) depends on this very separation of the represented consciousness from the representing one. If the separation is removed, that effect is dissipated. Art is created through whatever devices a medium may provide for "holding the mirror up to nature." In (1) the mirror is the representing consciousness and nature the represented. To remove that difference, to present only an undifferentiated representing-represented consciousness as in (7), is like replacing a statue with a living model, a portrait with its subject. To maintain a representing consciousness alongside a different consciousness which its language represents stimulates our powers of interpretation and appreciation, causing us to marvel at what language can achieve. In (7) the duality essential to art in all its forms has been destroyed.[1]

Evidence for a First-Person Point of View

The presence of a point of view in *The Ox-Bow Incident* sheds still further light on the nature of displaced immediacy. At the end of chapter 10 and again in chapter 15 we saw that conversational narratives reflect the point of view of a self whose presence is indicated in several ways: the frequency with which the self is mentioned, its favored status as a starting point, references to the self's feelings and evaluations, and its use as a deictic center. *The Ox-Bow Incident* is narrated consistently from the point of view of the fictional narrator. The function of first-person language is to express an equivalence of the self of the extroverted consciousness with the self of the representing consciousness: the perceiver-actor-evaluator is identical with the producer of the language. In this novel the self of the distal represented consciousness is consistently expressed with first-

---

1. Drama and film, which may seem to portray events more directly than is possible for written language alone, are still of course easily distinguishable from our perceptions of reality.

person pronouns. In fact, we learn the protagonist's name only because someone else asks it fairly late in the novel:

(11) a "Who ah you, suh?"
     b. "Art Croft," I told him. (P. 116)

First-person supplements past tense as further evidence for the presence and role of an unacknowledged representing consciousness. If past tense expresses a difference between the time of the extroverted consciousness and the time of the representing consciousness, first person expresses a coincidence of the extroverted self with the representing self.

There are several kinds of evidence that *The Ox-Bow Incident* is narrated from the point of view of this first-person self. For example, we find mentions of that self's perceptions, actions, evaluations, and introspections. Perceptions are illustrated in passages such as

(12) I heard him talking again. (P. 106)
(13) We came to a steeper pitch, where I could feel Blue Boy's shoulders pump under the saddle and hear his breath coming in jerks. (P. 112)

Actions performed by this self are ubiquitous:

(14) I ate some of the dry food and cheese. (P. 15)
(15) I looked at Gil's hand. (P. 20)

and so on. Evaluations are evident in, for example,

(16) I felt mean. (P. 106)
(17) Gil and I were quiet, because men had moved away from us, but I was excited too. (P. 35)

Introspections appear in passages like

(18) Previously, in my dozing, I'd been remembering a story I'd heard once about the Flying Dutchman, and wondering vaguely if that was the way we were getting. (P. 137)
(19) I'm slow with a new idea, and want to think it over alone, where I'm sure it's the idea and not the man that's getting me. (P. 50)

Such passages make it clear that the language represents Art Croft's point of view. They also help us identify the ingredients of consciousness itself, as discussed in chapter 3, by providing evidence that consciousness does indeed include perceptions, actions, evaluations, and introspections. There are also examples throughout the novel of spatial deixis that reflects the self's point of view in a quite literal sense:

(20) Except right in front of us and right behind us, we couldn't see the riders.
(P. 108)
(21) The man near me was coming closer. (P. 116)

Examples like these show that the extroverted represented consciousness
has a physical point of view that provides a reference point for the experienced events and states.

In summary, the use of first person confirms the presence of an extroverted consciousness belonging to the same self as the representing consciousness. The fact that a narrative is represented from the point of view
of that self is shown in part through expressions of the self's perceptions,
actions, evaluations, and introspections, in part through the use of spatial
deixis with the self as center.

Occasional Acknowledgment of the Representing Consciousness

Since language of this kind expresses the content of a distal represented
consciousness, the content of the representing consciousness itself is unacknowledged. Its presence is manifested in the use of past tense and first
person, but its own experience remains unexpressed. Although we may
understand that the language is being produced by a narrator who has an
unconstrained ability to relive experiences of his distal consciousness, the
narrator's consciousness as he produces the language is irrelevant. There
are, however, a few passages during which the represented consciousness
briefly snaps back into congruence with the representing consciousness,
reminding us explicitly that the latter does exist:

(22) Now I can see that he was perhaps still having a struggle with himself that
he was here at all, but then it just angered me that one of us failed to be
alert; (P. 143)
(23) It was a heavy wind with a damp, chill feel to it, like comes before snow,
and strong enough so it wuthered under the arcade and sometimes whis-
tled, the kind of wind that even now makes me think of Nevada quicker
than anything else I know. (P. 53)

These passages amount to brief excursions into the ordinary immediate
mode discussed in chapter 15. It is interesting to compare the immediacy
expressed by the word *now* in (22) and (23) with the immediacy expressed by the same word in (5) above. In (5) the use of *now* with the
past tense emphasizes the presence of a distal extroverted consciousness.
In (22) and (23) its use with the present tense shows momentarily the
presence of a consciousness in the ordinary immediate mode.

I close this chapter by mentioning the longstanding dispute over whether there can be language without a producer, language in which "no one speaks" and "the events seem to narrate themselves" (Benveniste 1971, p. 208). Ann Banfield (1982) has been a strong advocate of such a possibility, while others like Roland Barthes (1966), Tzvetan Todorov (1966), and Gérard Genette (1988) have just as strongly asserted the opposite: "Your narrative without a narrator may perhaps exist, but for the forty-seven years during which I have been reading narratives, I have never met one" (Genette 1988, p. 101). The distinction between a represented and representing consciousness offers a way to settle this disagreement without either side abandoning its position entirely. It would appear that all language has a representing consciousness which may or may not belong to an acknowledged self. Its presence is always manifested in the choice of tense and person, both of which depend on the representing consciousness as their deictic center. When there is either a separate represented consciousness, as in the present chapter, or no represented consciousness at all, as in chapters to come, the representing consciousness may be partially or wholly unacknowledged. Barthes, Todorov, and Genette have noticed the constant presence of a representing consciousness, acknowledged or not, while Benveniste and Banfield have noticed that language may separate off or even eliminate altogether a represented consciousness, while leaving the representing consciousness unacknowledged. In chapters to come we will see how these possibilities play themselves out in other kinds of writing.

Summary

I began this chapter by pointing out the special affinity between writing and fiction, attributing it in part to the fictionality that is inherent in the desituatedness of writing, in part to the writer's leisure that fosters imaginative creativity, in part to the absence of the face-to-face interaction that encourages factuality, and in part to the snowballing effect of fictionality, once begun.

The focus of the chapter was on writing in which there is a fictional self with access to fictional events because he or she took part in them, that is, a first-person narrator who was part of the action. My primary interest was in identifying differences between this kind of narration and the ordinary narration of a personal experience within a conversation. The desituatedness of writing (the lack of copresence and interaction) may lead, not just to fiction, but to a represented consciousness that is separated from the representing consciousness. This displaced immediacy conveys the impression of reliving past experiences as if they were immediate experiences, rather than remembering them in the ordinary way.

Evidence for the immediacy of such writing comes in part from the continuity that is established by beginning in medias res and proceeding without major temporal gaps, but especially from the provision of fine-grained detail. Adverbial deixis adds to the effect by juxtaposing words like *now* and *today* with the past tense, a juxtaposition that is motivated if one realizes that spatiotemporal adverbs depend on the *represented* consciousness for their deictic center, whereas tense depends on the *representing* consciousness. Evidence for displacement in such writing is provided by the past tense, which locates the extroverted represented consciousness as prior to the representing consciousness. This use of the past tense to establish displaced immediacy is more effective than an extended use of the historical present, above all because displaced immediacy creates the duality that is essential to art.

An extroverted consciousness is associated with a point of view. The presence of a first-person point of view in the writing discussed in this chapter is established partly through references to the self's perceptions, actions, evaluations, and introspections, partly through spatial deixis centered on that self. We also saw how a novel written in this style may give occasional recognition to the otherwise unacknowledged representing consciousness, reminding the reader that such a consciousness exists, and in this way reinforcing the effect of the displaced immediacy on which the rest of the novel is based.

It was noted in conclusion that the dispute over whether there can be language without a producer boils down to a recognition by one side that language always has a representing consciousness, acknowledged or not, and by the other side that the represented consciousness may be separated from the representing consciousness, which may even, as we will see, be entirely unacknowledged.

18

Representing Other Speech and Thought in First-Person Fiction with Displaced Immediacy

If an author wanted a fictional narrator like Art Croft to remain true to saying nothing more than he could remember from direct experience, the narrator's knowledge would have to be confined to situations in which he himself had been present. But in fact no one's knowledge is limited to events in which he or she participated directly. In ordinary life, much of what anyone knows was first in the consciousness of someone else and is later shared through language. Language makes it possible to transcend immediate perceptions, actions, and evaluations and allows a person to experience secondhand what others experienced firsthand. *The Ox-Bow Incident* is a good example of a novel that makes extensive use of other people's language to expand the narrator's range of information well beyond his own immediate experiences, using referred-to speech, direct speech, indirect speech, and a fourth type that I will call *verbatim indirect speech*.

Referred-to Speech

As in conversational language, there are references in this novel to entire conversations:

(1) He stood by Moore, talking to him for a while. (P. 15)
(2) I saw him talking hard and quickly to Joyce again, (P. 80)

More interesting are passages in which the internal content of a conversation is recapitulated by referring to the kinds of things that were said and the way they were said, and often referring to parts of conversations in the order in which they were uttered (what McHale 1978, p. 259, calls a less "purely" diegetic summary).The following is an example of this more elaborate variety of referred-to-speech:

(3) and Davies went out, keeping it casual, to talk to Bartlett. Bartlett wasn't so wild any more, just touchy, the way a man is who feels strongly about something, but is a muddy thinker. He answered a bit short, but didn't blow off. He kept looking at his watch, a big silver turnip, and then at the sky, and only paid a fretful half-attention to Davies. Davies knew better than to argue the soul of society with Bartlett, and even held out on his notion of the men not going at all, and just stuck to legal deputation and try-

ing to get a promise Bartlett wouldn't act without Risley. And he stayed friendly while he made his points, always seeming to be making just suggestions, and asking Bartlett's opinion, and Ma's, and even Winder's. The men let him talk because they had to wait, anyhow, though I noticed a few, close to him, seemed to be listening. Bartlett, though, wouldn't hear more than once about bringing prisoners in. Short justice was the kind he wanted. And Ma kept taking the point out of Davies' talk by making jokes. (P. 80)

Passages like these convey the essence of conversations, including the intentions of the various interlocutors, without pretending to capture actual language. The degree of detail in such cases may surpass what would be available through ordinary remembering, and so passages like (3) also reinforce the effect of displaced immediacy. We need thus to distinguish between references to nothing more than speech acts themselves, as in (1) and (2), and references to the content and/or manner of those speech acts, as in (3). On the one hand there is *simple referred-to-speech,* on the other *elaborated referred-to speech,* or in fact a continuum that ranges from the simplest examples to those that refer with increasing detail to what was said and how it was said.

Direct Speech

Chapter 16 discussed the fact that in conversational language direct speech is largely a reconstitution, and that it is usually associated with affect and involvement. Fiction writers may use direct speech, in addition, to provide access to a wider range of information, bringing in events and characters that were not experienced directly by the fictional narrator. A great deal of space in *The Ox-Bow Incident,* as in many novels, is taken up with the direct speech of conversations which provide a great deal of information that would not have been available to the narrator firsthand. The narrator and others may exploit this source by asking frequent questions. Two different interactive formats are employed, reflecting the distinction between *elicitation* and *narration* that was made in chapter 10.

Some questions initiate rapidly alternating exchanges, whose purpose is to elicit information the narrator could not have known directly:

(4)   "And the count came short this spring?"
      "Way short," Canby said. "Nearly six hundred head, counting calves."
      "Six hundred?" I said, only half believing it.
      "That's right," Canby said. "They tallied twice, and with everybody there."
      "God," Gil said.
      "So they're touchy," said Canby.
      "Did everybody lose?" I asked after a minute.

"Drew was heaviest, but everybody lost."

"But they would, wouldn't they, with that kind of a job," Gil said angrily.

"The way you say," Canby agreed.

We could see how it was, now, and we didn't feel too good being off our range. Not when they'd been thinking about it all year.

"What's Risley doing here? Have they got a lead?" Gil asked.

"You want to know a lot," said Canby. (Pp. 16–17)

In this way the author can dole out small pieces of secondhand information necessary to the development of the story. Sometimes, though, the narrator's questions elicit long narrative-like answers rather than quick exchanges, thus providing extended chunks of secondhand information in a single reply:

(5)   "Are they sure about this rustling?" I asked Canby when he came back.

"Sure enough," he said. "They thought they'd lost some last fall, but with this range shut in the way it is by the mountains, they'd been kind of careless in the tally, and couldn't be too sure. Only Bartlett was sure. He doesn't run so many anyway, and his count was over a hundred short. He started some talk that might have made trouble at home, but Drew got that straightened out, and had them take another tally, a close one. During the winter they even checked by the head on the cows that were expected to calve this spring. Then, it was about three weeks ago now, more than that, a month, I guess, Kinkaid, who was doing the snow riding for Drew, got suspicious. He thought one of the bunches that had wintered mostly at the south end was thinning out more than the thaw explained. He and Farnley kept an eye out. They even rode nights some. Just before roundup they found a small herd trail, and signs of shod horses, in the south draw. They lost them over in the Antelope, where there'd been a new fall of snow. But in the Antelope, in a ravine west of the draw, they found a kind of lean-to shelter, and the ashes of several fires that had been built under a ledge to keep the smoke down. They figured about thirty head, and four riders." (P. 16)

We can wonder how Canby himself knew all these things, but the natural inference is that he learned them from still other conversations. Displaced immediacy, then, provides a degree of access to verbatim language that goes well beyond what a conversationalist would enjoy, repeating large amounts of actual language in fine-grained detail.

Indirect Speech

The proportion of indirect speech in this novel is small, but there are occasional examples of it:

(6) At his salute the men all shouted. They told him loudly that they were with
    him too. (P. 36)

Conceivably one of the men might have said *We're with you too,* but the
indirect format leaves open exactly what their various words might have
been. Sometimes referred-to and indirect speech are mixed together, as
in the following:

(7) Tetley maintained that was all the more reason for pressing the chase.
    With their trail covered with snow, and a day or two start, time to switch
    brands, what would we have to go on? . . . Winder and Ma sided with Tet-
    ley. Winder was accusing Davies, and even Moore, of being so scared of
    the job they'd rather let a murderer slip than do it. Davies admitted he'd
    rather let ten murderers go than have it on his soul that he'd hung an hon-
    est man. Tetley said he wasn't going to hang an innocent man; he'd make
    sure enough of that to suit even Davies. To Farnley, even Tetley's manner
    smacked of delay. He told them he'd rather see a murderer hanged than
    shot, it was a dirtier death, but that he'd bush-whack all three of those
    men before he'd let one of them get out of the mountains free. (Pp.
    114–15)

The effect is similar to that of (3), but alongside the referred-to speech
(*Winder and Ma sided with Tetley*) there is an admixture of indirect
speech (*Tetley maintained that was all the more reason for pressing the
chase,Tetley said he wasn't going to hang an innocent man, He told them
he'd rather see a murderer hanged than shot*). It is worth noting that the
ordinary-speech attribution verbs *said* and *told,* the staples of conversational language, were supplemented with the more specific and literary
maintained and *admitted.*

Verbatim Indirect Speech
Some of the indirect speech in (7), however, has a quality that sets it apart
from indirect speech of the ordinary kind. We can focus on the second
sentence:

(8) With their trail covered with snow, and a day or two start, time to switch
    brands, what would we have to go on?

For one thing, there is no attribution immediately included in this sentence. We understand it to be the speech of Tetley because of the attribution in the previous sentence (*Tetley maintained . . .*). The effect of omitting the attribution is to strengthen the extroverted quality of the distal
consciousness. If the narrator is reliving the actual experience, there is
no need to identify who said things. Reducing the number of attributions
is thus still another means of conveying immediacy.

The omission of an attribution is a relatively trivial matter and is not a consistent feature of writing of this kind. Much more interesting is the fact that (8) seems to contain verbatim language. The succession of the three comma-separated phrases with which the sentence begins suggests an unplanned piling up of ideas, and the colloquial wording at the end of the sentence suggests that Tetley actually said *What will we have to go on?* Something similar can be observed in other instances of indirect speech in (7):

(9) he'd make sure enough of that to suit even Davies.

(10) he'd bush-whack all three of those men before he'd let one of them get out of the mountains free.

If there is any lingering doubt about the inclusion of verbatim language here, it dissipates completely when, a few pages later, we read the following:

(11) Now Winder was wanting to know what the hell the stage was doing on the pass at night anyway. (P. 126)

Verbatim language is unmistakably present, not only in the phrase *what the hell,* but also in the use of the word *anyway.* But in spite of this evidence of verbatim replication of what was actually said, (11) and the earlier examples are not direct speech. What Winder actually said, underlying (11), must have been something more like

(12) ~What the hell are you doing here at night anyway?

Although his question must have been in the present tense, (11) follows the pattern of indirect speech in using the past. Furthermore, the phrases *the stage* and *on the pass* in (11) categorize their referents more explicitly than would have been appropriate at the time of the event, given the shared knowledge of the speaker and his listeners. In that respect they suggest the vantage point of the representing, not the represented consciousness, and thus they reinforce the separation of the two.

Language like that in (11) has been called in English *free indirect style* (e.g., Dillon and Kirchhoff 1976), *free indirect speech* (Leech and Short 1981), *represented speech* (Jespersen 1924, Banfield 1982, Ehrlich 1990), and *narrated monologue* (Cohn 1978). (See too other references at the beginning of chap. 15.) Although it is not at all wise to proliferate terminology beyond necessity, I find it more than a little useful to refer to it as *verbatim indirect speech,* capturing thereby its seemingly conflicting properties. Its interest here lies in the fact that it represents other language in a manner that is especially compatible with displaced immediacy. While it is certainly not the only way of representing other language in this environment, and while it may occasionally occur even in conversations, as we saw at the end of chapter 16, displaced immediacy provides it with its most congenial home. In brief, verbatim indirect speech combines the verbatim quality of direct speech with the tense and person characteristic of indirect speech. There is also a tendency to omit the attribution, though that is not a consistent property. In terms of consciousness, verbatim indirect speech uses tense and person to signal the separation of the represented from the representing consciousness, but at the same time its use of verbatim language conveys the immediacy of an extroverted represented consciousness. It is this combination that makes it so compatible with the other manifestations of displaced immediacy discussed in chapter 17.

These are the linguistic and consciousness-related properties of verbatim indirect speech, but how is this device used? One finds that it is used in different ways in different works, and even within the same work. Its range of uses turns out to be far greater than anything I can describe here, but in this chapter and the next I point to a few things that have been done with it (cf. Leech and Short 1981, pp. 334–36: Kühn 1988).

The use of verbatim indirect speech in *The Ox-Bow Incident* is clear. Examples are clustered in a single part of the novel. Example (11) occurs just after the narrator has been shot by a stagecoach guard. Immediately after (11) he says:

(13) I felt far away, like watching a picture.

The indirectness of verbatim indirect speech—the explicit indication that the represented and representing consciousness are separated—is exploited as a means of conveying the split nature of the narrator's consciousness. The linguistic split functions as a mirror of the split between the narrator's inner self (the representing consciousness) and the external events he was imperfectly perceiving (the represented consciousness). This effect is strengthened by the use in (11) of the progressive *was wanting to know,* instead of *wanted to know.* Winder's statement would normally have been perceived as a punctual event, but it entered Croft's impaired consciousness as if he were tuning in on part of a speech event that was diffuse and out of focus (cf. Fleischman, in press). A few pages later there is a major cluster of examples of verbatim indirect speech, all within the same long paragraph (pp. 130–31). Just before that paragraph the narrator lost consciousness while his wound was being cauterized with a red hot pistol barrel. When he regained consciousness he said:

(14) I felt shaky and empty . . . I felt weak, all washed out . . . the voices talking were like those of people in another room, heard through the wall. They didn't concern me. (P. 130)

His split consciousness is nicely represented in the language that follows:

(15) But when Davies told me that "the fools still meant to go on," but there
was room for me in the coach, and I'd better go back and rest at Canby's
and get some hot food and get out of the wind, I told him hell no, there
was nothing the matter with me. (Pp. 130–31)

Davies's speech is a noteworthy example of verbatim indirect speech,
since part of it is even presented in quotation marks in spite of the word
that which is normally associated with ordinary indirect speech. The
phrase *the fools* clearly replicates what Davies said. On the other hand,
Davies would have used the present tense ("The fools still mean to go
on"), so that the past tense again shows the representing-represented
split. The narrator's own contribution at the end of this excerpt is treated
in a similar way, with its verbatim *hell no,* but again with the past tense.
Later in the same paragraph come the following additional examples:

(16) Then Winder came and told me not to be a damned fool, to get in the
coach and go on home, where I wouldn't be in the way. Gil told Winder
to mind his own business, that he'd look after me himself if I needed any
looking after. . . . Rose broke it up this time by letting go of my arm and
telling Winder to let the idiot, meaning me, go ahead and act like an idiot
if he wanted to, it was none of their funeral.

Among the evidences of verbatim language here are the phrases *be a
damned fool, go on home, mind his own business,* the repeated word
idiot, and *it was none of their funeral.* The last phrase illustrates how
verbatim indirect speech, like other indirect speech, can shift person as
well as tense. Rose must have said *It's none of our funeral.*

Representing Thought

We saw in chapter 16 that when conversational language represents
thought it limits itself to referred-to and direct thought, with what I called
pseudo–indirect thought conveying a belief, opinion, or decision. These
limitations are mirrored in writing, but there are other options too. We
can begin by looking at varieties of thought found in *The Ox-Bow Incident.*

As an example of *referred-to thought,* in (17) a moment of thinking
directly precedes some overt speech:

(17) I thought. "No," I said, "I guess not." (P. 209).

In (18) there was a conversational lull during which the narrator pondered
what had just been talked about. Since neither party spoke, the narrator
infers that his companion was pondering the same thing:

(18) We both thought about it for a minute. (P. 215)

Examples like these convey the idea that thinking of some kind was going on without providing any specific information as to its nature.

There are a few examples of *direct thought*. All of them are the inner speech of the narrator himself, who would have had access to another consciousness only as reported through another person's overt language. In direct thought, as in direct speech, the words that passed through the narrator's mind are supposedly reproduced verbatim:

(19) I thought, by God, if he's killed me, what a fool way to die; what a damn fool way to die! (P. 124)
(20) Shut up, you brainless bastards, I thought. (P. 204)

As in conversational language, what appears superficially to be *indirect thought* is actually *pseudo–indirect thought,* reporting a belief or opinion:

(21) I thought Gil was off the track, but he wasn't. (P. 111)
(22) He thought maybe it had nicked a rib, but nothing much more. (P. 130)

In (21), for example, the narrator does not mean that he experienced inner language like *Gil is off the track,* but that he had a certain belief about Gil. In chapter 16 I speculated that ordinary, constrained remembering has access to earlier mental acts like the forming of beliefs and opinions and the making of decisions, but not to earlier inner speech. It is interesting to see this restriction carried over into written language. Writers, it appears, do not have the freedom to change the meaning of the word *think* in such a context in order to associate it with inner speech.

The Ox-Bow Incident seems not to contain examples of verbatim indirect thought that would be parallel to the examples of verbatim indirect speech quoted above in (11), (15), and (16). It is instructive, therefore, to look at another work in which "free indirect style" has been said to represent the first-person protagonist's thoughts: Iris Murdoch's *The Italian Girl* (1967), whose relevant properties were discussed at length by W. J. M. Bronzwaer (1970). Like *The Ox-Bow Incident,* this novel makes pervasive use of displaced immediacy, exhibiting all the properties reviewed in chapter 17. It begins in medias res:

(23) I pressed the door gently.

It has access to fine-grained detail:

(24) He moved across the lawn to the shadow of the house and I followed him. The moonlight fell in streaks through the overgrown lattice of the porch, weighed down with honeysuckle, and revealed the fumbling hand and the key. Then the door gave softly to show the thick waiting blackness of the house, and I followed the boy out of the honeysuckle fragrance into the

old stuffy foxy darkness of the hall. The door closed and he turned on a light and we look at each other. (P. 13)

Temporal adverbs have their center in a distal represented consciousness, as illustrated not only by the word *now* but also by the word *ago* in the following:

(25) I recalled now that my sister-in-law Isabel, the news-giver of the family, had written to me some time ago about a new apprentice. (P. 13)

So far as language about language is concerned, there is no need to sample the many representations of overt language, most of which take the form of direct speech. What is striking is the extent to which this novel represents the distal *thoughts* of the narrator.

There is very little in the way of *direct* thought of the kind that appears exceptionally in the last sentence of the following:

(26) "Well, and how much has our Inspector found out?" asked Isabel, poking the fire vigorously. . . . "Everything, I should think," I said gloomily. And more than I shall tell you, poor Isabel, I thought. (P. 80)

Most of the narrator's thoughts are expressed in a manner of which the following is typical:

(27) The thought that I might go away and leave them all there asleep made me pause with a sort of elation. There was an air of vengeance about it. That would be to leave them forever, since if I went away now I was sure I would never return. Indeed, whatever happened I would probably never, after this one time, return. My mother's existence here had been the reason for my not coming. Now her non-existence would provide an even stronger reason. (P. 12)

This and many similar passages convey displaced immediacy, not only through the deictic *now* but especially through the ability of the narrator to remember the flow of ideas through his distal consciousness. The question is whether those ideas were verbal or nonverbal. In fact, there is nothing in (27) or most of the similar passages in this novel to suggest distal *language*. There is no reason, for example, to suppose that the following words passed through his distal consciousness:

(28) ~My mother's existence here was the reason for my not coming. Now her non-existence will provide an even stronger reason.

Passages like (27) are the proximal narrator's verbalization of distal experiences whose status as verbal or nonverbal (or as a combination of both) is left open.

We learn from such examples that, because thought may be at first wholly or partially nonverbal and only later captured in verbal form, it can be represented in a way that is not relevant to the representation of speech. Example (27) corresponds neither to ordinary indirect speech nor to verbatim indirect speech, both of which purport to be derived from distal language. Rather, it is an example of what Paul Hernadi (1972) calls *substitutionary narration* and Dorrit Cohn (1978) *psycho-narration,* a reconstruction by the representing consciousness of distal experiences whose status as verbal or nonverbal is left indeterminate. I will call it *verbally uncommitted thought.* To the extent that its language is constructed by the representing consciousness and is not verbatim, it bears some resemblance to ordinary indirect speech. It differs from indirect speech, however, in its lack of derivation from distal language as well as in its employment of the distal represented consciousness as the deictic center for spatiotemporal adverbs. It also lacks an attribution. Since, as we have seen, an attribution with the verb *think* would automatically transform such a thought into a belief, opinion, or desire, it is obvious why that verb cannot be used here:

(29) ~I thought that my mother's existence here was the reason for my not
      coming.

Example (29) has quite a different meaning from the corresponding sentence in (27). The fact that (27) begins with the words *the thought that* provides an effective substitute for the misleading attribution in (29).

Although this device of verbally uncommitted thought is pervasive in *The Italian Girl,* there are a few places where inner language is unambiguously represented, most explicitly in the following:

(30) Yet, ardently as I desired to go, and even as I advised myself to return to
      my simple world before something worse should happen to me, I knew I
      could not. It was my duty to stay: that harsh word riveted me to the spot.
      (P. 72)

Up to the colon this passage is like the many others in which earlier thoughts may have been nonverbal. The final clause comes as something of a surprise. The protagonist must literally have thought the word *duty* in order for it to have riveted him to the spot. But the very unexpectedness of this example helps confirm the observation that the rest of the novel does not involve verbatim indirect thought. Most of the remembered thinking in *The Italian Girl* consists of distal experiences that are first clothed in language by the narrator's later representing consciousness. Whether there are first-person novels in which verbatim indirect thought (as opposed to verbatim indirect speech) plays a clearer role remains an open question, but the fact that a novel like Murdoch's, in which it *might* have been used extensively, shows so little of it suggests that it may be at best an uncommon strategy with a first-person narrative.

It should be helpful at this point to review the several ways of representing speech and thought that have been identified and labeled in chapter 16 and the present chapter, using constructed examples for easy comparison. The various options have been rearranged in order of increasing approximation to verbatim language, whether it is overtly spoken or covertly thought:

Simple referred-to speech:	I talked to him.
Elaborated referred-to speech:	I bored him with my schedule for the next day.
Indirect speech:	I said I'd go the next day.
Verbatim indirect speech:	OK, I'd go tomorrow (I said).
Direct speech:	"OK," I said, "I'll go tomorrow."
Simple referred-to thought:	I thought.
Elaborated referred-to thought:	I thought about my schedule for the next day.
Pseudo–indirect thought:	I thought I'd go the next day.
Verbally uncommitted thought:	The thought that I'd go tomorrow . . .
Verbatim indirect thought:	OK, I'd go tomorrow (I thought).
Direct thought:	"OK," I thought, "I'll go tomorrow."

The term *free indirect style* has been used in ways that include three of these types: verbatim indirect speech, verbatim indirect thought, and verbally uncommitted thought. Certainly it is helpful to recognize the differences between these three, and it is not clear that a single cover term is desirable. At the very least a clear distinction should be made between the two types that involve verbatim language (whether spoken or thought) and the third, verbally uncommitted type of thought.

Summary

The Ox-Bow Incident represents other language extensively, thereby greatly extending the range of information available to the fictional narrator, since he need not be limited to events in which he himself participated. Referred-to speech is used repeatedly, often in an elaborated form, recapitulating whole conversations with a degree of detail that is possible only with displaced immediacy. Direct speech is also exploited throughout, especially as a means of introducing secondhand information and not only, as in conversational language, as a way of conveying involvement. The quoted speech may be elicited by a questioner or it may take the form of an extended narration. Indirect speech of the ordinary kind is less common, but is sometimes mixed with referred-to speech in recapitulating a conversation.

The most interesting representation of other language in this novel takes the form of what I call *verbatim indirect speech*. In such usage, foreshadowed at the end of chapter 16, verbatim language conveys the immediacy of the represented consciousness, while the past tense and changed pronouns (where appropriate) signal the separation of the distal represented consciousness from the proximal representing consciousness. Thus, verbatim indirect speech is especially compatible with displaced immediacy. This device is used by different authors in different ways, but it is interesting to see how Clark uses it to express the separation of the wounded protagonist's consciousness from the events surrounding him.

Turning to the representation of thought, we noted examples of referred-to and direct thought, and the same use of pseudo–indirect thought to express beliefs and opinions that was observed in conversational language. Verbatim indirect thought seems not to occur in *The Ox-Bow Incident,* and so we looked to Murdoch's *The Italian Girl,* where examples of it might have been expected. The search illuminated instead still another way of representing distal thought—what I called *verbally uncommitted thought*. The chapter ended with a review of the various types of speech and thought representation that were identified here and in chapter 16.

19

Displaced Immediacy in Written Third-Person Fiction

When displacement was first discussed in chapter 15, I noted briefly that there may be displacement not only in space and time, but also of self. Displacement of self was set aside while chapters 15–18 concentrated on spatiotemporal displacement. It is time now to turn our attention to the ability of consciousness to focus, not only on distal experiences of the representing self, but also on experiences of a different represented self. Under ordinary circumstances, information regarding another self is available through perception of another's actions and states, together with the ability to empathize—to imagine what it is like to possess another person's mind. One might, for example, imagine what it would be like to be the person who was doing some particular thing or who looked a particular way. When ordinary language is used to represent the experiences of a distal self, it still passes through the consciousness of the proximal self. Knowledge of another consciousness is filtered through whatever constraints there may be on the power to empathize. In written fiction, on the other hand, one effect of the desituatedness of writing can be a total displacement of the represented consciousness to another self. There is no longer a proximal self who relives his or her own distal experiences, as in chapters 17 and 18; there are only the distal experiences of the other.

Figure 19.1 suggests the structuring of consciousness that is achieved in this way. It differs from figure 17.1 of chapter 17 in three respects. First, the represented consciousness belongs to a different distal self, not the self of the proximal representing consciousness. Second, the representing consciousness is unacknowledged; there is no recognized narrating self. Finally, access to the distal self is achieved through a pretense of unconstrained *empathizing* with another's consciousness, not through unconstrained *remembering* of the representing self's own distal consciousness. The separation manifests itself in this case not only in the use of past tense (showing temporal displacement) but also in the use of third person (showing displacement of self).

A good example of this kind of writing is provided by Ernest Hemingway's short story "Big Two-Hearted River" (1987, pp. 163–80), which deals with a fishing trip in northern Michigan by a lone fisherman. The whole reason for this piece of writing seems to be its attempt to put the

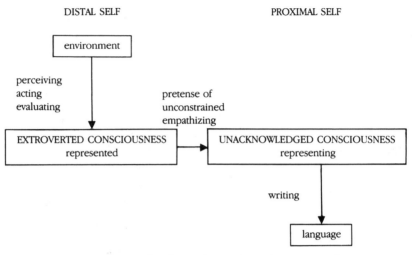

DISTAL SELF   PROXIMAL SELF

environment

perceiving
acting   pretense of
evaluating   unconstrained
                                empathizing

EXTROVERTED CONSCIOUSNESS   →   UNACKNOWLEDGED CONSCIOUSNESS
represented   representing

writing

language

Figure 19.1 Displaced Immediacy with Displacement of Self

reader inside the protagonist's mind to experience what he was experiencing. It begins as follows:

(1) The train went on up the track out of sight, around one of the hills of burnt timber. Nick sat down on the bundle of canvas and bedding the baggage man had pitched out of the door of the baggage car. There was no town, nothing but the rails and the burned-over country. The thirteen saloons that had lined the one street of Seney had not left a trace. The foundations of the Mansion House hotel stuck up above the ground. The stone was chipped and split by the fire. It was all that was left of the town of Seney. Even the surface had been burned off the ground. (P. 163)

There are several kinds of evidence for a represented consciousness that belongs to a distal self, the person called *Nick.*

Evidence for Immediacy

Example (1) obviously begins in medias res. Certain events and referents were in Nick's consciousness as the story opens. He was already perceiving the movement of a train away from a known location. As we read on, the baggage man pitching the bundle out of the baggage car must have been an accessible event, perceived just a short time before. The language thus reflects what was already active or semiactive in Nick's mind from the very beginning. All that is left to verbalize are his new experiences as the story unfolds. The language also reflects Nick's background knowledge, as shown by the references to *the* train, *the* hills of burnt timber, *the* baggage man, *the* town of Seney, *the* Mansion House hotel. The definiteness of these noun phrases pretends that their referents are identifiable. It is not that knowledge of them is shared with a listener, as would be the case with identifiable referents in a conversation. Nick shares this knowledge with himself. We will return to implications of this kind of identifiability in chapter 22.

The effect of reliving Nick's immediate experiences derives above all from the inclusion of fine-grained detail, as is well illustrated in the following passage:

(2)   He started a fire with some chunks of pine he got with the ax from a stump. Over the fire he stuck a wire grill, pushing the four legs down into the ground with his boot. Nick put the frying pan on the grill over the flames. He was hungrier. The beans and spaghetti warmed. Nick stirred them and mixed them together. They began to bubble, making little bubbles that rose with difficulty to the surface. There was a good smell. Nick got out a bottle of tomato catchup and cut four slices of bread. The little bubbles were coming faster now. Nick sat down beside the fire and lifted the frying pan off. He poured about half the contents out into the tin plate. It spread slowly on the plate. Nick knew it was too hot. He poured on some tomato catchup. He knew the beans and spaghetti were still too hot. He looked at the fire, then at the tent, he was not going to spoil it all by burning his tongue. (Pp. 167–68)

It might be possible for a person to remember the way bubbles rise to the surface as food is cooked over an open fire, but such remembering would ordinarily be generic, not the remembering of a particular event as here. Even less, of course, would it involve the experience of another person. The detail of (2) reflects perception rather than remembering or hearsay. What is represented is an extroverted consciousness. Temporal adverbs like *now* and *today* give further evidence of immediacy:

(3) Now as he looked down the river, the insects must be settling on the surface, for the trout were feeding steadily all down the stream. (P. 166)
(4) Nick did not want to go in there now. . . . He did not want to go down the stream any further today. (P. 180)

These adverbs show the temporal coincidence of the represented consciousness with the distal extroverted consciousness.

Evidence for Displacement

Displaced immediacy requires evidence not only for immediacy but also for displacement. In first-person fiction, where displacement is restricted to space and time, the past tense is sufficient to show that the extroverted represented consciousness is separated from the representing consciousness. With displacement of self, separation from the representing consciousness is signaled in addition by the use of third person.

We can again ask what is to be gained from such displacement. Although the language represents Nick's extroverted consciousness, its use of tense and person keeps that consciousness at a distance from the unacknowledged representing consciousness. If the separation were not maintained, the passage in (2) would have been written with present tense substituted for past, and first person for third:

(5) ~~I put the frying pan on the grill over the flames. I am hungrier. The beans and spaghetti get warm. I stir them and mix them together. They begin to bubble, making little bubbles that rise with difficulty to the surface. There is a good smell. I get out a bottle of tomato catchup and cut four slices of bread. The little bubbles are coming faster now. I sit down beside the fire and lift the frying pan off. I pour about half the contents out into the tin plate. It spreads slowly on the plate. I know it is too hot. I pour on some tomato catchup. I know the beans and spaghetti are still too hot. I look at the fire, then at the tent, I am not going to spoil it all by burning my tongue.

Chapter 17 suggested that a preference for narrating in the past tense may be inherited from conversational language, but also that the use of displaced information allows ideas to be interpreted in a broader perspective than is possible with immediate experience. Although those two factors may favor the use of past tense, they do not explain why a first-person account in the past tense would be any less effective than the actual third-person account:

(6) ~I put the frying pan on the grill over the flames. I was hungrier. The beans and spaghetti got warm. I stirred them and mixed them together. They began to bubble, making little bubbles that rose with difficulty to the surface. There was a good smell. I got out a bottle of tomato catchup and cut four slices of bread. The little bubbles were coming faster now. I sat down beside the fire and lifted the frying pan off. I poured about half the contents out into the tin plate. It spread slowly on the plate. I knew it was too hot. I poured on some tomato catchup. I knew the beans and spaghetti were still too hot. I looked at the fire, then at the tent, I was not going to spoil it all by burning my tongue.

Indeed, (6) may be a more effective piece of writing than (5). I will not attempt to weigh the relative merits of first- and third-person writing (see the fascinating discussion in Cohn 1968), but only point out that (2), by increasing still further the distance between the represented and representing consciousnesses, strengthens the aesthetic duality mentioned in chapter 17. The distance between the artistic mirror (the representing consciousness) and the nature it reflects (the represented consciousness) is increased here beyond what is established by the past tense alone. With respect to this duality, displaced immediacy in the third person (displacement in space, time, and self) may enjoy some advantage over displaced immediacy in the first person (displacement in space and time alone).

Evidence for a Third-Person Point of View

In chapter 17 we saw that the equation of the self of the represented consciousness with the self of the representing consciousness was reinforced by evidence for a first-person point of view. The displacement of self in the Hemingway story is analogously reinforced by evidence for a *third*-person point of view, confirming a separation of the represented from the representing self. Relevant here are reference, experiencing, and deixis that are all centered on a third person.

Third-Person Reference

If a first-person point of view is established, among other ways, by first-person pronouns, we might expect that when the experiencing consciousness belongs to a different self it will be expressed with third-person pronouns. To a large extent that is true here; the majority of references to the distal self are expressed with *he*. Nevertheless, a surprisingly large number of references also use the name *Nick,* as can be seen in examples above. In (1) the represented self is first identified as *Nick* before he is called *he*, in accordance with the ordinary pattern for introduction of a third person. This first introduction might be seen as stemming from a realization by the representing consciousness that the represented self needs to be given more of an identity than would be provided by *he* alone, a motivation to which we will return in chapter 22. However, the frequent subsequent use of *Nick* goes far beyond what would be found in conversational language and appears to be an affectation of Hemingway's style. It tends, nevertheless, to be a systematic use: we find the name used when some other referent has intervened in the role of subject. In other words, *he* functions as a "same-subject" marker, whereas *Nick* is used when the immediately preceding subject is different. *Nick* is thus an indicator of what linguists call "switch-reference" (Haiman and Munro 1983, Mithun 1993):

(7) The swamp was perfectly quiet. Nick stretched under the blanket comfortably. A mosquito hummed close to his ear. Nick sat up and lit a match.

The mosquito was on the canvas, over his head. Nick moved the match quickly up to it. The mosquito made a satisfactory hiss in the flame. The match went out. Nick lay down again under the blanket. He turned on his side and shut his eyes. He was sleepy. He felt sleep coming. He curled up under the blanket and went to sleep. (P. 169)

Hemingway was fond of using proper names in this way, as also with the *Robert Jordan* that appears so frequently in *For Whom the Bell Tolls* (Hemingway 1940):

(8) "Sit down," Robert Jordan said to Anselmo. The old man sat down at the table on one of the hide-covered stools and Robert Jordan reached under the table and brought up the pinch-bottle of whiskey that had been the gift of Sordo. It was about half-full. Robert Jordan reached down the table for a cup. (P. 329)

With one brief and interesting exception discussed below, references to the self in the "Big Two-Hearted River" vary between *Nick* and a third-person pronoun.

Third-Person Perceptions, Actions, Evaluations, and Introspections
"Big Two-Hearted River" contains many references to Nick's perceptual experiences, confirming the fact that his consciousness is an extroverted consciousness. The following visual experiences, for example, appear in the second and third paragraphs:

(9) Nick looked at the burned-over stretch of hillside. . . . Nick looked down into the clear, brown water . . . and watched the trout. . . . As he watched them they changed their positions. . . . Nick watched them a long time. He watched them holding themselves with their noses into the current. . . . At the bottom of the pool were the big trout. Nick did not see them at first. Then he saw them at the bottom of the pool. (P. 163)

There are frequent mentions of Nick's evaluations—his attitudes and feelings—which also contribute to marking the point of view:

(10) They were very satisfactory. (P. 163)
(11) Nick's heart tightened as the trout moved. He felt all the old feeling. . . . He was happy. (P. 164)

It is possible to distinguish events that can be known directly *only* by a represented consciousness from events that can also be known by an outside observer. In the first set—unambiguously internal events—belong evaluations like those in (10) and (11) as well as perceptual experiences like seeing and hearing. Only a seer can know directly what he is seeing. Internal events like these contribute to the effect of displaced immediacy. Other events are ambiguous as to internal versus external experience:

(12) Nick walked back up the ties to where his pack lay in the cinders beside the railway track. . . . He adjusted the pack harness around the bundle. . . . Nick leaned back against a stump and slipped out of the pack harness. . . . Nick sat down. (P. 164)

These are not perceptions or evaluations but actions, and as such they could be perceived by an external observing self. However, when they are placed in a context of displaced immediacy that has been established in other ways, Nick's overt actions are also interpreted as experienced by him. A sensitive reader may appreciate the fact that a statement like *Nick sat down* is ambiguous in terms of consciousness. Its ordinary interpretation may be one in which an outside observer remembered this event. But in the context of this story the same statement is understood as expressing Nick's own experiencing of what he did. The fact that the many externally observable actions in Hemingway's story consistently call forth this internal interpretation provides a subtle but compelling confirmation of its displaced immediacy (cf. Chatman 1975, p. 238, n. 26). Finally, although Nick did not introspect a great deal about his own mental processes, he did so occasionally:

(13) He could not remember which way he made coffee. He could remember an argument about it with Hopkins, but not which side he had taken. He decided to bring it to a boil. He remembered now that was Hopkins's way. (P. 168)

Such rememberings, attempts at remembering, and decisions add to the effect of an extroverted consciousness that belongs to Nick.

Third-Person Deixis

The initial paragraph of "Big Two-Hearted River," cited in (1), immediately establishes the spatial location of the distal self. To read *the train went on up the track out of sight* is to empathize with the consciousness of the person from whose location it *went on up* and from whose *sight* it disappeared. As a result, when *Nick* is introduced in the second sentence, there is already an understanding that the language represents the consciousness of the person so named. This Nick-centered spatial deixis is maintained throughout the story. The final three sentences read:

(14) He looked back. The river just showed through the trees. There were plenty of days coming when he could fish the swamp. (P. 180)

In the first two sentences there is Nick-centered spatial deixis, but the reference to *plenty of days coming* shows a temporal orientation: the coming days are anticipated with respect to Nick's current location in time.

Representing Speech

Hemingway's story contains little in the way of language about overt language, since its protagonist is the sole human being in the entire story. What speech there is is expressed in direct quotes, one of them addressed to a grasshopper:

(15) "Go on, hopper," Nick said, speaking out loud for the first time. "Fly away somewhere." (P. 165)

Another is a remark to himself, to justify preparing his supper:

(16) "I've got a right to eat this kind of stuff, if I'm willing to carry it," Nick said. His voice sounded strange in the darkening woods. He did not speak again. (P. 167)

But he did speak again, as soon as he had taken his first spoonful:

(17) "Chrise," Nick said, "Geezus Chrise," he said happily. (P. 168)

These speech events also convey Nick's own experiencing of what he did, and in that respect they are like *Nick sat down*. Just as he did many nonlinguistic things, he also did a few linguistic things. In all his actions the language conveys Nick's own experiencing of them, not some other person's observations of them.

Representing Thought

Most of the language in Hemingway's story represents Nick's perceptions, actions, evaluations, and introspections, and there is some verbally uncommitted thought as in the following excerpt, cited above as an example of introspection:

(18) He could not remember which way he made coffee. He could remember an argument about it with Hopkins, but not which side he had taken. He decided to bring it to a boil. He remembered now that was Hopkins's way. (P. 168)

There are a few examples of direct thought. As Nick fried a buckwheat cake in a skillet,

(19) I won't try and flop it, he thought.

The last two words of the following must also be a direct thought, but this time without an attribution:

(20) Across the river in the swamp, in the almost dark, he saw a mist rising. He looked at the tent once more. All right. (P. 168)

The following has to do with a trout that had been thrown back in the water:

(21) He's all right, Nick thought. He was only tired. (P. 176)

Although the first sentence in (21) conveys direct thought, the status of the second sentence is different. The past tense, contrasting with the present tense of the first sentence, suggests either a nonverbal or a verbatim indirect thought.

Verbatim indirect thought is in any case certainly present in the latter part of the following example:

(22) He thought of the trout somewhere on the bottom, holding himself steady over the gravel, far down below the light, under the logs, with the hook in his jaw. Nick knew the trout's teeth would cut through the snell of the hook. The hook would imbed itself in his jaw. He'd bet the trout was angry. Anything that size would be angry. That was a trout. He had been solidly hooked. Solid as a rock. He felt like a rock, too, before he started off. By God, he was a big one. By God, he was the biggest one I ever heard of. (P. 177)

The first three sentences express verbally uncommitted thought. The fourth sentence switches to verbatim indirect thought, a device we found rare in first-person writing. Verbatim language is evident in the wordings *He'd bet, that was a trout,* and the repeated exclamation *by God.* A further and more remarkable switch occurs in the last sentence, where the word *I,* in place of *Nick,* appears out of the blue. For one brief moment the third-person indicator of separation between the represented and representing consciousnesses is eliminated. In this one sentence even the representing consciousness, otherwise unacknowledged, belongs almost completely to Nick. I say "almost" because the past tense remains to preserve the distinction. If Hemingway had written *By God, he's the biggest one I ever heard of,* the momentary suppression of displacement would have been complete. The presence of verbatim indirect thought but even more the switch to first person suggest that (22) expresses some sort of climax in the story. It is a story without a clear plot, but the devices employed in (22)—moving from verbally uncommitted thought to verbatim indirect thought to (almost) direct thought—make it appear that Nick's encounter with this unusually large trout constituted the high point of his experience.

Summary

We have looked in this chapter at examples of a represented consciousness that is separated from the representing consciousness in two ways, belonging not only to a distal time and place but also to a distal self. Whereas a distal first-person consciousness is signaled only by past tense, a distal self is signaled by the use of third person as well. Hemingway's short story exhibits all the symptoms of immediacy: in medias res, fine-grained trivial detail, and the deixis of immediacy. It shows a distal point of view in its third-person reference, its expressions of the distal self's perceptions, actions, evaluations, and introspections, and in spatial deixis centered on the distal self. There is a small amount of direct speech in this story, and some verbally uncommitted thought and direct thought. Of particular interest is one brief passage that moves through several kinds of thought representation to a climactic momentary switch to first person. We will return to Hemingway's story in chapter 22.

20

Written Fiction That (Partially) Lacks
a Represented Consciousness

Since chapter 15 we have gradually diminished the role of the representing consciousness. In the immediate mode of speaking the represented and representing functions are fused within a single extroverted consciousness (fig. 15.1). In the ordinary, conversational displaced mode the represented and representing consciousnesses remain fused, but the extroverted consciousness occupies a different, remembered or imagined place and time (fig. 15.2). In the displaced immediate mode, fostered by the desituatedness of writing, the extroverted and represented consciousnesses are reunited, but both are separated from the now stranded representing consciousness (fig. 17.1). With the displacement of self, even the self of the representing consciousness becomes irrelevant (fig. 19.1). In this chapter we will see how even the *represented* consciousness may disappear, leaving nothing behind except an unacknowledged representing consciousness. We will be looking at examples of written fiction that lack, or at least sometimes lack, a represented consciousness. In chapter 21 we will look at something similar in nonfiction.

Stephen Crane

The following paragraph begins Stephen Crane's short piece of journalistic fiction titled "The Men in the Storm," first published in 1894 (Katz 1969, pp. 147–53):

(1)   At about three o'clock of the February afternoon, the blizzard began to swirl great clouds of snow along the streets, sweeping it down from the roofs and up from the pavements until the faces of pedestrians tingled and burned as from a thousand needleprickings. Those on the walks huddled their necks closely in the collars of their coats and went along stooping like a race of aged people. The drivers of vehicles hurried their horses furiously on their way. They were made more cruel by the exposure of their positions, aloft on high seats. The street cars, bound up-town, went slowly, the horses slipping and straining in the spongy brown mass that lay between the rails. The drivers, muffled to the eyes, stood erect and facing the wind, models of grim philosophy. Overhead the trains rumbled and

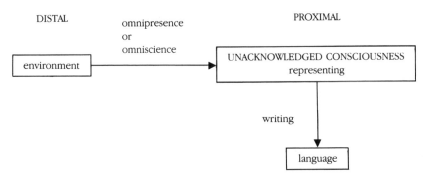

Figure 20.1 Language Without a Represented Consciousness

roared, and the dark structure of the elevated railroad, stretching over the avenue, dripped little streams and drops of water upon the mud and snow beneath it. (P. 147)

Like both *The Ox-Bow Incident* and "Big Two-Hearted River," this piece begins in medias res. Although some temporal setting is provided, the February afternoon and the blizzard are treated as already shared, identifiable referents. Especially noteworthy is the wealth of detail. This is a paragraph that clearly exhibits qualities of extroverted experience. We might thus have expected its details to have been perceived and evaluated by some represented consciousness, but what is interesting about the example is the fact that there is nothing to suggest a point of view, no evidence of an experiencer who either evaluates or functions as a deictic center for the events and states described. Instead, the writing leaves us with an unacknowledged representing consciousness that has direct access to a fine-grained environment, but no represented consciousness at all.

To our list of processes through which information can be accessed (immediacy, remembering, imagining, and empathizing) we can now add *omnipresence,* the ability of an unacknowledged representing consciousness to be anywhere. Later we will see how omnipresence may be upgraded to *omniscience,* but for now we need only recognize the pretense in (1) that the information is simply there—not acquired by way of any conscious experience or self, but available directly. This situation is diagramed in figure 20.1, where the content of the distal environment is accessed directly, through omnipresence, by the unacknowledged representing consciousness, bypassing any represented consciousness.

The representing consciousness continues to exert an effect on the language, even though it is unacknowledged. Not only does it provide, as always, the deictic center for tense and person, it may in some writing of this kind have its own spatiotemporal point of view. Hemingway's story "The Killers" (1987, pp. 215–22) is a good example. It consists largely of conversations observed by an unacknowledged representing consciousness that possesses not only a physical location but also a limited fund of knowledge. When we read at the outset

(2) The door of Henry's lunch-room opened and two men came in. (P. 215)

the deixis of the verb *came* establishes the representing consciousness as inside the lunchroom (Fillmore 1974, pp. V19–20), not outdoors or in the kitchen:

(3) Al's voice came from the kitchen. (P. 217)

The regular occupants of the lunchroom (George and Nick Adams) are already known to the representing consciousness by name, but the names of the two strangers (Al and Max) are known only after they have given them. One of the strangers is referred to with phrases like *the other man* and *his friend* until his companion says:

(4) "Ain't he a bright boy, Max?" (P. 216)

after which he is called *Max*. Omnipresence need not imply that the representing consciousness is everywhere at once, but only that it occupies whatever location is appropriate for the progress of the story. Later in the Hemingway story, for example, it follows Nick on his visit to Ole Andreson:

(5) Nick opened the door and went into the room. (P. 220)

where the deixis of *went* places the representing consciousness at first outside Andreson's room.

To return to Stephen Crane, his best-known work, the Civil War novel *The Red Badge of Courage* (1895), alternates between the absence of a represented consciousness and the presence of such a consciousness in the displaced immediate mode. The following paragraph from the first chapter of that work shows the same lack of a represented consciousness that was illustrated in (1). Henry Fleming, the protagonist, listened to some men discussing the likelihood of an upcoming battle. He then retired to his hut:

(6)   He lay down on a wide bunk that stretched across the end of the room. In the other end, cracker boxes were made to serve as furniture. They were grouped about the fireplace. A picture from an illustrated weekly was upon the log walls, and three rifles were paralleled on pegs. Equipments hung on handy projections, and some tin dishes lay upon a small pile of firewood. A folded tent was serving as a roof. The sunlight, without, beat-

ing upon it, made it glow a light yellow shade. A small window shot an oblique square of whiter light upon the cluttered floor. The smoke from the fire at times neglected the clay chimney and wreathed into the room, and this flimsy chimney of clay and sticks made endless threats to set ablaze the whole establishment. (P. 192)

The detail here is fine-grained, but there is no represented consciousness because there is no evidence for a represented point of view. The absence of such a consciousness is in fact explained by the frame surrounding this passage. The immediately preceding sentence is:

(7) He wished to be alone with some new thoughts that had lately come to him.

And immediately after (6) comes the statement:

(8) The youth was in a little trance of astonishment.

These two statements say explicitly that Henry's consciousness was not extroverted, as it would have to have been if it were the source of the information in (6). The reference to his trance is a way of saying that his consciousness was focused with special intensity on an introverted experience, not on what is described in (6). Instead, (6) conveys the immediate situation as known through an omnipresent, unacknowledged representing consciousness that is not Henry's.

But we do not have to look far to find a represented consciousness. The next paragraph reads:

(9)   The youth was in a little trance of astonishment. So they were at last going to fight. On the morrow, perhaps, there would be a battle, and he would be in it. For a time he was obliged to labor to make himself believe. He could not accept with assurance an omen that he was about to mingle in one of those great affairs of the earth. (P. 192)

These were events and states in Henry's consciousness. Whereas the earlier statement *he lay down on a wide bunk that stretched across the end of the room* reports an event that could be perceived by an external observer, (9) tells things that could be known only to Henry. Although the initial characterization of him as *the youth* might seem at first to have been imposed externally, we find that he is characterized as *the youth* throughout this novel, just as the protagonist of the Hemingway story is called *Nick*.

Although all of (9) exhibits a represented consciousness, there are interesting differences in *how* Henry's thoughts are represented, with the author utilizing three of the options discussed at the end of chapter 18.

The first sentence only *refers to* his mental state. The second and third sentences, in contrast, are examples of verbatim indirect thought. The words *so, on the morrow,* and *perhaps* leave no doubt as to the verbatim quality of this language, and the repeated *would* reflects the future tense that was present in his represented thoughts. The (now somewhat dated) language that actually passed through Henry's mind must have been:

(10) So we are at last going to fight. On the morrow, perhaps, there will be a battle, and I will be in it.

Finally, the fourth and fifth sentences show verbally uncommitted thought. Thus, the sequence in examples (6) and (9) together moves from no represented consciousness in describing Henry's environment, to referred-to thought in describing his mental state, to a climax in verbatim indirect thought that expresses his anticipation of the battle, with a reflective denouement expressed as verbally uncommitted thought. We can now examine another work in which the author manipulates the absence and presence of a represented consciousness with special skill in order to provide an increased understanding of characters and their motivations.

Eudora Welty

Eudora Welty's beautifully crafted short story "A Curtain of Green" (1983, pp. 107–12) deals with the protagonist's powerlessness before a fate that killed her husband a year earlier. She has occupied herself in the meantime by working in her garden, whose state mirrors the state of her mind. During the first part of the story, people, places and events are set forth without a represented consciousness, and we are thus given an external orientation on Mrs. Larkin and her activities:

(11)   Within its border of hedge, high like a wall, and visible only from the upstairs windows of the neighbors, this slanting, tangled garden, more and more over-abundant and confusing, must have become so familiar to Mrs. Larkin that quite possibly by now she was unable to conceive of any other place. Since the accident in which her husband was killed, she had never once been seen anywhere else. Every morning she might be observed walking slowly, almost timidly, out of the white house, wearing a pair of the untidy overalls, often with her hair streaming and tangled where she had neglected to comb it. (P. 107)

In the first sentence the words *must have* and *quite possibly* make it clear that Mrs. Larkin's mental processes are external inferences. Her habits, similarly, are presented from an external point of view: *she had never once been seen anywhere else,* and *she might be observed.* Access to this kind of information is achieved through omnipresence. After nine paragraphs without a represented consciousness, the story is printed with an extra space between the ninth and tenth paragraphs, and at that point Mrs. Larkin's consciousness takes over.

For example, she relives the circumstances of her husband's death:

(12)   But memory tightened about her easily, without any prelude of warning or even despair. She would see promptly, as if a curtain had been jerked quite unceremoniously away from a little scene, the front porch of the white house, the shady street in front, and the blue automobile in which her husband approached, driving home from work. It was a summer day, a day from the summer before. In the freedom of gaily turning her head, a motion she was now forced by memory to repeat as she hoed the ground, she could see again the tree that was going to fall. There had been no warning. But there was the enormous tree, the fragrant chinaberry tree, suddenly tilting, dark and slow like a cloud, leaning down to her husband. From her place on the front porch she had spoken in a soft voice to him, never so intimate as at that moment, "You can't be hurt." But the tree had fallen, had struck the car exactly so as to crush him to death. She had waited there on the porch for a time afterward, not moving at all—in a sort of recollection—as if to reach under and bring out from obliteration her protective words and to try them once again . . . so as to change the whole happening. It was accident that was incredible, when her love for her husband was keeping him safe. (P. 109)

These are perceptions and feelings that can only come from Mrs. Larkin's remembering consciousness, in this case focused on events twice removed from the unacknowledged representing consciousness. Most of them are expressed in verbally uncommitted thought. There is an obvious contrast with the earlier, external mention of *the accident in which her husband was killed* in (11). Details of her extroverted consciousness subsequently provide unmistakable evidence of displaced immediacy:

(13)   In the light from the rain, different from sunlight, everything appeared to gleam unreflecting from within itself in its quiet arcade of identity. The green of the small zinnia shoots was very pure, almost burning. One by one, as the rain reached them, all the individual little plants shone out, and then the branching vines. The pear tree gave a soft rushing noise, like the wings of a bird alighting. She could sense behind her, as if a lamp were lighted in the night, the signal-like whiteness of the house. (P. 111)

At the climax of the story, Mrs. Larkin is momentarily tempted to take control of fate by using her hoe to kill Jamey, the hired man, a feeling that subsides with the advent of the rain. At almost the end of the story, after she faints, we obtain brief access to Jamey's consciousness, made explicit by the repeated phrase *he remembered*:

(14) He remembered how something had filled him with stillness when he felt her standing there behind him looking down at him, and he would not have turned around at that moment for anything in the world. He remembered all the while the oblivious crash of the windows next door being shut when the rain started. (P. 112)

The story thus shifts at crucial moments from no represented consciousness at the beginning, to a complex representation of Mrs. Larkin's consciousness, and then briefly at the end to Jamey's consciousness. These shifts bring a rich understanding of powerful internal experiences beneath events that are on the surface of little consequence.

Nathaniel Hawthorne

The Crane and Welty examples show the alternating absence and presence of a represented consciousness. With Hemingway's "The Killers" we observe in addition that an unacknowledged representing consciousness, even though it is not a represented consciousness, may nevertheless have its own spatiotemporal point of view and even a limited fund of knowledge. Nathaniel Hawthorne's *The House of the Seven Gables* (1851/1961) illustrates the extent to which such a consciousness can intrude itself while still stopping short of acquiring the status of an acknowledged consciousness. It opens as follows:

(15)   Halfway down a bystreet of one of our New England towns stands a rusty wooden house, with seven acutely peaked gables, facing towards various points of the compass, and a huge clustered chimney in the midst. The street is Pyncheon Street; the house is the old Pyncheon House; and an elm tree, of wide circumference, rooted before the door, is familiar to every townborn child by the title of the Pyncheon Elm. On my occasional visits to the town aforesaid, I seldom failed to turn down Pyncheon Street, for the sake of passing through the shadow of these two antiquities—the great elm tree and the weather-beaten edifice.

The aspect of the venerable mansion has always affected me like a human countenance. (P. 11)

The narrator, whose self remains without explicit acknowledgment throughout the novel, is generically remembering his own past experiences. There are even occasional references that include the audience, although the desituatedness of the writing restricts such references to the third-person *reader*:

(16)   The reader may deem it singular that the head carpenter of the new edifice was no other than the son of the very man from whose dead gripe the property of the soil had been wrested. (P. 15)

This narrator is able to exercise discretion in what he observes, while using first-person plural pronouns to invite the audience to share in that discretion (cf. Longacre 1983, pp. 18–19):

(17)   It still lacked half an hour of sunrise, when Miss Hepzibah Pyncheon—we will not say awoke, it being doubtful whether the poor lady had so much as closed her eyes during the brief night of midsummer—but, at all events, arose from her solitary pillow, and began what it would be mockery to term the adornment of her person. Far from us be the indecorum of assisting, even in imagination, at a maiden lady's toilet! Our story must therefore await Miss Hepzibah at the threshold of her chamber; only presuming, meanwhile, to note some of the heavy sighs that labored from her bosom, with little restraint as to their lugubrious depth and volume of sound, inasmuch as they could be audible to nobody save a disembodied listener like ourself. (Pp. 32–33)

He even has it in his power to enter the world of the story by addressing one of its (deceased) characters directly:

(18) Pray, pray, Judge Pyncheon, look at your watch, now! (P. 237)
(19) Alas, this dinner! Have you really forgotten its true object? (P. 238)

The novel thus admits at various points a representing consciousness that belongs to an insubstantial being who stands in the wings as he relates his story, every so often popping out to look at something, or discreetly choosing not to, and even rhetorically questioning one of the characters, albeit a character who cannot respond. He remains, nevertheless, a deselfed, nameless phantom who never participates in the story's events. These and other examples suggest that an unacknowledged representing consciousness may intrude in represented events to varying degrees, ranging from the simple provision of a deictic center for tense and person, to overt commentary on characters and what they do, to limited participation in the events themselves.

There are places in *The House of the Seven Gables* where Hepzibah's consciousness is represented in the format of verbally uncommitted thought:

(20)   Holgrave took his departure, leaving her, for the moment, with spirits not quite so much depressed. Soon, however, they had subsided nearly to

their former dead level. With a beating heart, she listened to the footsteps of early passengers, which now began to be frequent along the street. Once or twice they seemed to linger; these strangers, or neighbors, as the case might be, were looking at the display of toys and petty commodities in Hepzibah's shopwindow. She was doubly tortured; in part, with a sense of overwhelming shame that strange and unloving eyes should have the privilege of gazing, and partly because the idea occurred to her, with ridiculous importunity, that the window was not arranged so skillfully, nor nearly to so much advantage, as it might have been. It seemed as if the whole fortune or failure of her shop might depend on the display of a different set of articles, or substituting a fairer apple for one which appeared to be specked. So she made the change, and straightway fancied that everything was spoiled by it; not recognizing that it was the nervousness of the juncture, and her own native squeamishness as an old maid, that wrought all the seeming mischief. (Pp. 46–47)

Hepzibah's point of view is evident in her perceptions, actions, and evaluations. She is the one to whom the footsteps seemed to linger, and to whom the fortune of the shop might depend on the display. We have access to her emotions, including her beating heart as she listens. But we are not left in this mode for long. After the presentation, at the beginning of the last sentence, of what Hepzibah *fancied,* there is a sudden shift to what she failed to recognize, something explicitly beyond her consciousness.

We are now in a good position to distinguish omnipresence and omniscience, the two means of access to the distal environment specified in figure 20.1. Examples like (1), (6), and (11) record events and states as they would be observed by any external observer, whereas (20) exhibits an access to information that would normally be hidden from anyone except the experiencer herself. The unacknowledged representing consciousness in (20) had access to Hepzibah's consciousness. The term omniscience is a useful way of characterizing access, not just to overt behavior, but to a consciousness. While omnipresence is limited to knowledge of events and states that ordinary human beings would be able to observe if only they were there, omniscience adds a godlike access to consciousness itself.

Cohn stresses the point that verbally uncommitted thought, or psycho-narration, can illuminate nonverbal consciousness in ways that are impossible for either direct thought or verbatim indirect thought, with their commitment to ideas that the distal consciousness itself has verbalized: "Not only can it order and explain a character's conscious thoughts better than the character himself, it can also effectively articulate a psychic life that remains unrepresented, penumbral, or obscure. Accordingly psycho-narration often renders, in a narrator's knowing words, what a character 'knows,' without knowing how to put it into words" (Cohn 1978, p. 46). The insight (20) gives us into Hepzibah's consciousness might have been diminished, even trivialized, if it had been presented in terms of inner *language*.

A Brief Comparison with Narratological Studies

Before we look at nonfiction in the next chapter, we need to turn our attention, however briefly, to narratology, an area of scholarship that relates more closely than any other to the topics of chapters 17–20. It would be appropriate to compare in detail the understandings developed in the present work with the broad range of narratological studies, which rightfully deserve at least as much space as was devoted in chapter 13 to other research on information flow. My position as an outsider to those studies makes me hesitate to undertake such a comparison, but I am hampered as well by lack of time and space. The few remarks that follow, fleshed out with examples, could easily be expanded into another book, a prospect that is not without its enticements.

The first and most important thing to say is that the motives of the present work and those of narratologists are not the same. This work is aimed at understanding the nature of the mind as determinable through consciousness and language, whereas narratologists have been concerned with categorizing or typologizing written fiction in terms of criteria that are applicable either to whole works or to their parts. Our different motives have led to somewhat different results, and I can only comment that a perspective on linguistic products that views them within a larger frame of reference, embracing mental life in its entirety, can only enrich our understanding of the devices by which authors illuminate the complexities of human experience.

Particularly interesting for comparison is the model developed over many years by Franz Stanzel, culminating in Stanzel (1984). He categorizes literary narratives in terms of three basic oppositions: *person* (first versus third), *perspective* (internal versus external), and *mode* (narrator versus reflector). *Person* is clear enough. In terms of the present work it is a question of whether or not the self of the (usually distal) extroverted consciousness is identical with the (usually unacknowledged) self of the representing consciousness. *Perspective* appears to be a matter of whether or not there *is* a represented consciousness. In other words, are events and states presented as if they were passing through a consciousness (internal perspective), as in (12) above, or not (external perspective), as in (11)? *Mode* is to me more problematic and makes coherent sense only when understood against the history of narratology, with origins in the Platonic distinction between diegesis and mimesis, later characterized as telling versus showing, narrating versus reflecting, and the like. If there is no represented consciousness (that is, if the perspective is an external one), the narrating mode would seem to be the only possibility. When there *is* a represented consciousness (the perspective is internal), the question is whether it belongs within the world of the story or lies outside it, as it does with the phantom narrator of *The House of the Seven Gables*. In these terms, the works discussed in chapters 17–19 are all in what Stanzel would call the reflector mode, whereas those discussed in the present chapter are *sometimes* in the narrator mode. Stanzel arranges his three oppositions in a continuous circle, whose somewhat forced nature has been effectively discussed by Cohn (1981) and Genette (1988, pp. 114–29).

Genette's own work exhibits similarities and differences that are also discussed in the two references just given. In general, Genette is less concerned with achieving an integrated typology and more with understanding just what writers are doing. It is easy to identify the *person* opposition with Genette's *voice,* where first person is hellenophilically labeled *homodiegetic,* third person *heterodiegetic.* Stanzel's *mode* has its correspondence in Genette's *distance* (*diegetic* or *mimetic*), which Genette seems to agree with me in finding problematic (Genette 1988, p. 116). Stanzel's *perspective* bears only a partial resemblance to Genette's *focalization,* which has less to do with consciousness than with who has access to what information. Genette (1980, pp. 188–90) makes a threeway division between *zero* focalization, or what in this chapter I called access through omniscience, *internal* focalization, or access through an acknowledged consciousness, and *external* focalization, or access through omnipresence: "the hero performs in front of us without our ever being allowed to know his thoughts or feelings" (as exemplified by the novels of Dashiell Hammett).

Typologies nearly always leave one in the end dissatisfied, in ways of which these scholars are fully aware. Stanzel, for example, begins his book (1984, p. 1) with a quotation from Goethe regarding the manner in which Goethe had been influenced by Linnaeus: "in the innermost recesses of my being I felt that that which Linné had attempted to forcibly keep asunder must be striving for union." The greatest ultimate benefit of typological studies may be the light they shed on the deeper recesses of their subject matter, whether it be consciousness, language, or the ways in which the writers of fiction perform their magic. Bringing all three together would seem a worthy goal.

Summary

In contrast to the works discussed in chapters 17 through 19, some written fiction is without a represented consciousness, or at least partially so. Such writing, though it may include evidence of immediacy in the inclusion of detail, lacks another crucial component of a represented consciousness: evidence for a point of view. The short story by Stephen Crane, excerpted in (1), is written consistently in such a style, and other works sampled in this chapter contain passages of this kind. There is only a stranded, unacknowledged representing consciousness, whose access to information comes, not from unconstrained remembering or imagining, not from unconstrained empathy, but from either omnipresence or omniscience. Omnipresence is limited to overtly observable events and states, whereas omniscience has access to consciousness as well. It is a common practice of some authors to alternate passages that lack a represented consciousness with other passages in which there is displaced immediacy. Alternating the absence and presence of a represented consciousness can enhance the understanding of the human condition which authors aim to provide, as exemplified in this chapter with excerpts from Crane, Welty, and Hawthorne. I ended this chapter by briefly comparing the findings of chapters 17–20 with some well-known narratological analyses.

21

Written Nonfiction

In this chapter we will look at a few of the options for the treatment of consciousness that are available to someone who writes nonfiction. As compared with a fiction writer, a writer of nonfiction is in one sense more like a participant in a conversation, in another sense less like one. A nonfiction writer deals with experiences viewed as real, rather than imagined, and that is what conversationalists also do most of the time. But desituatedness can weaken or destroy the represented point of view that is fundamental to conversational language, with the result that written nonfiction is congenial to the suppression of a represented consciousness. Without a represented consciousness, nonfiction may call on information from a variety of sources, and its worked-over quality can include access to research, which in turn can radically change its knowledge base. These are, however, only possibilities. Written nonfiction is so varied in its purposes and access to information that its ways of handling consciousness can and do vary over a wide range. We can begin by looking at a genre that is closer than most to conversational language.

Personal Letters

The personal letter can substitute for conversing when people are separated in space and time. Letters are one of the oldest and commonest uses of writing. For some people they constitute its major use, even if the telephone now provides an alternative that resembles situated conversation more closely, lacking only copresence. In letter writing the separation of the language producer from the receiver means, of course, that no *immediate* interaction is possible. But unlike many other written genres, personal letters are usually exchanged by people who know each other. More often than not they have had face-to-face conversations in the past, and further encounters may be anticipated for the future. Letter writing involves interaction at a distance in both space and time. Consciousness and language are handled in ways that depart somewhat from the norms of conversation, but less radically than with most other kinds of writing.

In chapter 10 we saw that the alternating contributions of two or more interlocutors can sustain a conversational topic. The absence of immediate

271

interaction in letter writing means that collaborative topic development of this kind is impossible. Writers must therefore rely to a greater extent on their own topic-sustaining resources. It helps to have narratives or other topics that keep the language moving forward. The following paragraph elaborates on the topic summarized in the first sentence as *getting sick a lot,* which triggered a rich sequence of ideas:

(1)   Another problem I've had has been getting sick a lot. It was strange to read your letter about all the ailments in California, since I've come to think of it as a faraway land of good health. I have a perpetual cold here, the mild continuous sore throat and runny nose I remember from winters in N.Y. Twice it turned into a really bad cold. The hard part is that here the apartments are built Calif-style with absolutely no insulation, yet the winters are like east-coast winters. There's no central heating, so I end up carrying my little heater around the room and into the kitchen. My electric blanket keeps me warm at night, but when I wake up in the morning and see the clouds of white steam my breath is creating, I'm afraid to get up! I'm really not sure why the Japanese haven't gotten around to installing reasonable heaters, at least in the new apts. and houses; it may have something to do with the institution of the kotatsu, which is a kind of coffee table with an electric heater attached and a futon covering which creates a nice hot space for your legs. It's very cozy but definitely not designed for people who can't sit cross-legged. (I've tried with no success to imitate the way Japanese women sit back on their legs, twisting their ankles at right angles so that their feet virtually disappear.) Right now I'm just recovering from my second truly violent reaction to food. The first time I assume was my own fault, since I got sick after a Christmas party with a lot of mixing of strange drinks. But the night before last, for absolutely no reason that I can think of, I got sicker than I can remember being in my whole adult life. All I had eaten was some rice and the same vegetables, stored in my refrigerator, that I had eaten the night before with no reaction whatsoever. I'm so glad that I've become good friends with the woman in the next apartment; after 7 hours of vomiting attacks (I was really beginning to worry) I heard her get up to go to work, and borrowed some pills that she had, which cured me in time to rush over to meet Prof. Tanaka as we had arranged. If I knew what I had done to cause it, I would certainly never do it again. It reminds me of the allergy you had on your hands; isn't it an insecure feeling not knowing what brought it on? I look round my kitchen suspiciously, but can't figure it out.

There is a resemblance here to speaking in the ordinary displaced mode, the format that prevails in conversational language. The presence of a point of view, essential to a represented consciousness, is shown by the frequent references to the experiencing self (*I, me, my*); the frequent references to that self's perceptions (*when I wake up in the morning and see the clouds of white steam, I heard her get up to go to work*), evaluations (*it was strange, I'm so glad*), and introspections (*I remember, it reminds me of*); and the self-centered deixis (*here, now,* the *faraway land*).

Compared with conversationalists, letter writers tend quite understandably to show more egocentricity. Conversations may encourage an interplay of egocentricity and empathy, fostered by both copresence and immediate interaction, but letters are produced in solitude. An earlier study found that first-person pronouns were used in letters considerably more often than in conversations, which themselves greatly exceeded lectures and academic papers in this regard (Chafe and Danielewicz 1987, pp. 106–7). The absence of face-to-face interaction focuses a letter writer's attention more completely on him- or herself, and readers of letters are placed in a world where they experience events and states more completely through the writer's mind. Example (1) is typical in that respect; the frequency of first-person references is obvious. We can note the recognition of the distant second person in the second sentence and the next to last, but the writer quickly returned to her own experience to round off the topic.

Autobiography

Many people write letters. The kinds of writing that will occupy us for the rest of this chapter are more likely to be produced by professional writers, or at least by those whose professional activities include a significant amount of writing. The special properties of these genres may thus call on more in the way of acquired skill in order to be used effectively. Letters are unusual among written genres in that they are addressed to specific, recognized individuals and that interaction is typically expected, even though it is delayed. In contrast, most writing is characterized by the absence of even delayed interaction, and by a situation in which the language producer does not know precisely who will read what is written, or when or where they will read it. The absence of an acknowledged reader is often coupled with the absence of an acknowledged writer as well, but it need not be. A genre in which the producer of the language remains very much in evidence is the autobiography. In some respects an autobiography resembles a personal narrative, a conversationalist's account of something that happened to him or her, but in this case an account that is divorced from an interacting audience. An autobiography also bears some resemblances to a first-person novel like the one discussed in chapters 17 and 18. There is, however, a major difference. Whereas *The Ox-Bow Incident* exhibited displaced immediacy, autobiographies may be recounted with a representing consciousness in the ordinary displaced mode, and access to information may be attained either through ordinary constrained remembering or through research.

An autobiography may now and then exhibit a consciousness in the immediate mode, as illustrated by the following passage from *The Autobiography of Bertrand Russell* (Russell 1967):

(2) My first vivid recollection is my arrival at Pembroke Lodge in February 1876. To be accurate, I do not remember the actual arrival at the house, though I remember the big glass roof of the London terminus, presumably Paddington, at which I arrived on my way, and which I thought inconceivably beautiful. (P. 7)

The passage is interesting, not just for its immediacy, but also because of its explicit recognition of constraints on ordinary remembering.

Some of the information in an autobiography is likely to be derived from written sources that were closer to the events themselves—diaries, letters, clippings—but much of it is reactivated from the memory of the writer and thus exhibits the coarse-grained detail typical of constrained remembering. Writing about his maternal grandmother, Russell recalled:

(3) Once when I was about twelve years old, she had me before a roomful of visitors, and asked me whether I had read a whole string of books on popular science which she enumerated. I had read none of them. At the end she sighed, and turning to the visitors, said: "I have no intelligent grandchildren." (P. 33)

This passage resembles conversational narratives in its restriction to only newsworthy detail. Russell did not describe the roomful of visitors, nor did he provide a list of the books his grandmother enumerated. He did report his grandmother's words in a direct quote, which might even have reflected verbatim remembering. For someone who regarded himself as intelligent, those words may have been disagreeable enough to have been rehearsed after the event. In any case, we can guess that what he wrote captures most of what he remembered of this incident.

It is instructive to compare (3), in the ordinary displaced mode, with the following passage from Eudora Welty's short story "A Memory" (1983, pp. 75–80), where displaced immediacy is evident from the mixing of detail with a point of view:

(4) One summer morning when I was a child I lay on the sand after swimming in the small lake in the park. The sun beat down—it was almost noon. The water shone like steel, motionless except for the feathery curl behind a distant swimmer. From my position I was looking at a rectangle brightly lit, ac-

tually glaring at me, with sun, sand, water, a little pavilion, a few solitary people in fixed attitudes, and around it all a border of dark rounded oak trees, like the engraved thunderclouds surrounding illustrations in the Bible. Ever since I had begun taking painting lessons, I had made small frames with my fingers, to look out at everything. (P. 75)

In (4) an experience is being relived in a manner that is absent from (3).

Expository Writing

Both letters and autobiographies retain from conversational language a represented consciousness that belongs to a recognized individual. They contrast with much other written nonfiction—many news reports, histories, academic articles, and so on—which lack any represented consciousness at all. In these genres the language is maximally desituated, with no acknowledged representing consciousness, no acknowledged reader, and no acknowledged time or place in which the language is either produced or received.

The following is part of a biographical sketch of a Santa Barbara architect named Harriet Moody (Andree and Young 1980):

(5)   Born in Santa Barbara on May 9, 1891, Harriet Moody attended college in Santa Barbara, but received most of her architectural training in the office of Serferly, a local architect. She began designing houses in 1912 for her father, a building contractor. After he retired in 1922 she joined the city engineer's office under George Morrison and served as assistant city engineer until 1925. After the earthquake she and Morrison formed an engineering partnership and did subdivisions in the Goleta and Isla Vista area for private, city, and county concerns. (P. 285)

There is nothing in (5) that represents either Harriet Moody's or the writer's consciousness. Language of this kind exhibits a high degree of "autonomy." However, no language can avoid the assumption of knowledge shared by its producer and receivers, even when their selves are unacknowledged. Example (5) assumes shared knowledge of the geography of the Santa Barbara area, including the adjoining communities of Goleta and Isla Vista. It also assumes shared knowledge of a local earthquake in 1925, referred to with a definite noun phrase. Assumptions like these are appropriate in a book on Santa Barbara architecture; the typical reader could be expected to know such things. The point is that even unacknowledged writers and readers are assumed to share knowledge, and often very specific knowledge. It is hard to imagine how language could function without such sharing; one need only read expository writing from an unfamiliar area to appreciate its importance.

An especially good example of a genre in which desituatedness coexists with major assumptions of shared knowledge is academic writing. One linguistic article *begins* as follows:

(6)   Generative morphologists have been much exercised by the problems posed by lexical expressions which seem to demand two distinct constituent structure assignments. (Spencer 1988, p. 663)

What in the world is a generative morphologist? What are lexical expressions? What is a constituent structure assignment? Why would the problems described here be the kinds of things that would "exercise" anyone? Certainly only a tiny segment of the population could answer these questions, but of course this writing is aimed at just those people. The degree of autonomy of desituated language without a represented consciousness (Olson 1977, Kay 1977) can be exaggerated.

Mitigations of the Lack of a Self

Writers often find ways of mitigating the lack of a self that is fostered by the desituatedness of expository writing. It is not uncommon, for example, even for this kind of language to make value judgments or have opinions. Later in the biographical sketch of Harriet Moody (Andree and Young 1980) quoted in (5) comes the following statement:

(7) Enhanced by delicately painted details, a Moody house is a quaint work of art, charming and light as a drawing from the English illustrators she loved. (P. 285)

If delicacy, quaintness, and charm are in the eye of the beholder, who is the beholder here? There is no acknowledged individual with whom one could argue that Moody's buildings are *not* quaint works of art, if one were so inclined, but evaluations like these give evidence of a representing consciousness (what might be called an "implied author"; e.g., Booth 1961, Hernadi 1976), even though that author's self remains unacknowledged.

Just as desituatedness need not eliminate evaluations by the writer, it also need not do away completely with what might be called "implied readers." In the present book, for example, a sharing of knowledge with unknown readers is pretended through frequent use of the inclusive *we,* as at the beginning of this chapter. Or through questions, as illustrated just below examples (6) and (7). Or through imperatives when the author issues commands:

(8) Consider more closely the relation of I to its complement VP.

Sometimes, of course, the first- and second-person references of ordinary language are replaced by third persons through expressions like *the writer* and *the reader*. One understands, after all, that there is a writer, and although it may be impossible to know any specific person as the reader, it can at least be assumed that some reader will be involved in each of the many unpredictable individual acts of reading.

Summary

Written nonfiction deals, however subjectively, with what are perceived to be "facts," and in that respect it resembles typical conversational language. At the same time it can be highly unnatural in its lack of a represented consciousness and its dependence on an unacknowledged representing consciousness. A genre of nonfiction that remains closer than most to conversational language is the personal letter, where there is likely to be much shared knowledge and the possibility of interaction, though with a considerable time delay. The absence of immediate interaction means that collaborative topic development is impossible, so that letter writers must fall back on self-sustaining topics.

Autobiographies may retain a single representing-represented consciousness, largely in the displaced mode. Access to information may be constrained by limitations on remembering, supplemented by whatever documentary sources are available to the writer. Thus, descriptions of events are likely to exhibit the same coarse-grained detail typical of conversations.

Unlike personal letters and autobiographies, expository writing typically shows no represented consciousness, and the representing consciousness is at least unacknowledged. This is the "autonomous" language sometimes viewed as the genre especially favored by writing. Such writing, however, nearly always assumes a significant amount of shared knowledge, even if it is shared by an unacknowledged writer with an unacknowledged audience. The effects of the lack of a self in expository writing are often mitigated, as with the expression of opinions or evaluations, and there may be any of various kinds of recognition of the audience. There is, of course, much more to say about the many varieties of written nonfiction, but this chapter has tried to sketch the major options such language provides for the handling of consciousness.

22

Displacement Integrated with Flow

With some understanding now of the nature of immediacy and displacement, we are finally in a position to begin to integrate that topic with aspects of the flow of consciousness and language that were discussed in part 2. Bringing flow and displacement together can enrich our understanding of each, while at the same time giving us a more complete picture of consciousness in its entirety. The task is a very large one, and this chapter can only suggest what future work may uncover. Ultimately, the relation between the flow and displacement of consciousness needs to be studied with reference to many genres and styles, both spoken and written, in many languages.

The most general finding may be that flow as described in part 2 constitutes a special case, albeit the most common and natural one. Other modes of immediacy and displacement, as discussed in chapters 17–21, can affect the flow of consciousness and language in special ways. The chief reason for these differences is the fact that these other modes distort the relation of the language producer to the language receiver. The discussion in part 2 depended on assessments by the speaker of what is happening in the mind of the listener. Activation cost, for example, involves assumptions about activation states in the listener's mind. Identifiability involves assumptions about the sharing of referents. The light subject constraint involves assumptions as to how the listener is able to process starting points. The one new idea constraint reflects a limitation on the speaker's own processing capacity, but it probably also reflects the speaker's awareness of a parallel limitation in the mind of the listener. In all these cases the shape of language emerges from an ongoing interaction of what is happening in the speaker's mind with the speaker's assessment of what is happening in the listener's mind.

Addition of the Listener to the Displaced Mode

It thus becomes necessary to pay more attention to the role of the listener (or, in the case of writing, the reader) in the modes of immediacy and displacement that were discussed in chapters 15–21. It is easiest to reverse the order of presentation in chapter 15, beginning with the ordinary dis-

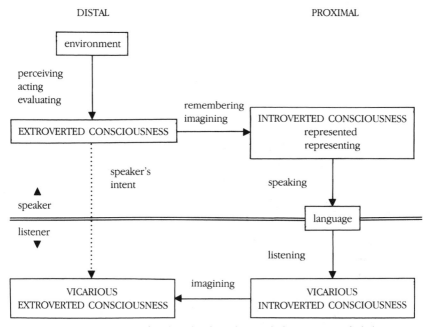

Figure 22.1 The Displaced Mode of Speaking with the Listener Included

placed mode first diagramed in figure 15.2, revised here in figure 22.1 to include the listener. The minds of the speaker and listener are separated by the double line in the middle, the speaker's mind above and the listener's below, with language providing a bridge between the two.

The speaker's represented consciousness receives its input from a distal consciousness that is remembered from some time in the past or imagined for some hypothetical time. The intent of the speaker is to influence the listener's consciousness in such a way that the listener imagines a distal experience resembling the speaker's own distal experience. I have indicated this intent with the dotted line connecting the two distal consciousnesses. The speaker's intent is realized (in the righthand portion of the diagram) by means of language designed to produce in the listener a vicarious introverted consciousness which, like the speaker's, is actively focused, not on the immediate environment of the conversation, but on the distal experience the speaker is remembering or imagining. This is not to say, of course, that the listener is unable to shift attention to the immediate environment of the conversation, but that is not what the speaker intends. The listener's mental processes recapitulate the speaker's in reverse, except, of course, that the listener is led to imagine, not remember, the distal experience. To the extent that the language bridging the two minds causes the contents of the two distal consciousnesses to be

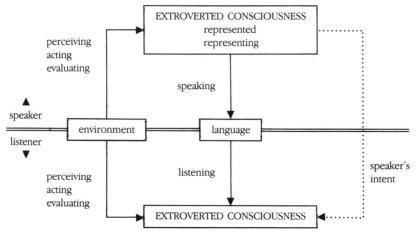

Figure 22.2 The Immediate Mode of Speaking with the Listener Included

similar, language will have fulfilled its communicative purpose. The resemblance, of course, can never be more than partial and imperfect; neither language nor anything else will ever bring two minds completely together.

Addition of the Listener to the Immediate Mode

If we similarly include the listener in the structure of the immediate mode that was first diagramed in figure 15.1, the result is as shown in figure 22.2. Again, the intent of the speaker is to make the content of the listener's consciousness resemble, so far as possible, the content of the speaker's own, as again indicated with the dotted line connecting the two consciousnesses. Aside from the absence of displacement, the noteworthy property of figure 22.2 is the fact that the separate consciousnesses of the speaker and listener are both exposed to the same nonlinguistic environment. The speaker is talking about something that is at the same time available to the listener. Although conversationalists in the *displaced* mode also share an environment, it is not what their consciousnesses are supposed to be focused on.

This sharing of the environment can be seen as one of the reasons why the immediate mode is less common in conversations than the displaced mode. If the environment is providing input to the speaker's and listener's consciousnesses simultaneously, what is the need for language? In terms of figure 22.2, what is the need for the dotted line connecting the two consciousnesses by means of language if those two consciousnesses are already receiving input from the same nonlinguistic source? There are several possible answers to this question, but in general we can say that speakers sometimes wish to call attention to certain aspects of their environment, to evaluate what is being shared, to communicate their own actions with respect to the environment, or simply to offer their language as a way of clarifying or highlighting a shared experience.

As one example of a context in which the immediate mode is especially at home, we can consider the simultaneous reporting of a sports event for a television audience. The following language was produced for the benefit of listeners who had visual access to the same events on their television screens:

(1) a ... And Clárk goes áfter the fírst pítch,
    b .. híts it to the gáp,
    c in léft cénter,
    d but Dàve Hénderson,
    e móves òver to máke the cátch,
    f ... Thómpson is láte in tágging,
    g and hàs to hó = ld at sécond.

What was gained from the commentator transferring what was in his consciousness to the consciousnesses of his many listeners when the latter were confronted with the same nonlinguistic input? For one thing, of course, the inputs were not identical; the viewers had access only to those limited parts of the scene on which the cameras were focused and which the station chose to broadcast. Still, they were usually just those parts of the scene that the commentator chose to verbalize, his own attention being for the most part directed at the events that appeared on the screen. It is instructive to compare a silent videotape of those events. The experience is significantly impoverished. It would, in fact, be hard to find a better example of the difference between verbalized and nonverbalized experience, of the enrichment that language provides by organizing experience in terms of familiar categories and schemas. In sports commentaries the listeners' experiences are enriched by the commentator's superior knowledge, his familiarity with the players, and his ability to categorize events in meaningful ways. In other cases the verbalization of immediately shared experiences may simply confirm that two consciousnesses are in harmony, an important human value in itself. For someone to say

(2) It's réally hót.

when both the speaker and the listener are obviously suffering from the heat uses language as a way of bonding two consciousnesses in a situation where the explicit sharing of an experience may be comforting.

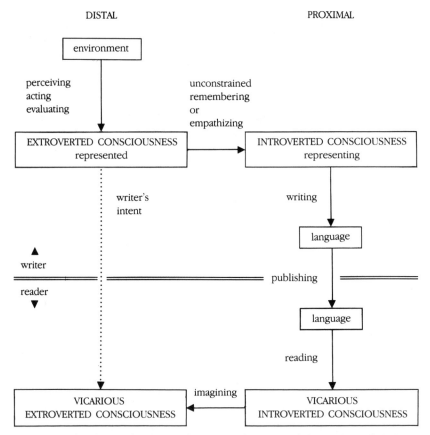

Figure 22.3 The Displaced Immediate Mode of Writing with the Reader Included

Addition of the Reader to the Displaced Immediate Mode

Figure 22.3 shifts to written language, adding the *reader* to the structure of displaced immediacy that was diagramed only for the *writer* in figure 17.1 of chapter 17 and figure 19.1 of chapter 19. The most significant difference here is the separation of language production from language reception. Instead of providing the situated bridge that was present in figures 22.1 and 22.2, the desituated language has become, through publication,[1] portable in space and time, no longer tied to the environment in which it was produced. The reader, at quite a different place and time, replicates the writer's representing consciousness and from that experience is led to imagine something that resembles (again imperfectly) what was in the introverted consciousness of the writer at the time of writing,

---

1. Within "publishing" I include the entire range of activities that intervene between the writer's production of a manuscript and the reader's viewing of a printed page.

or at least that is the writer's intent. The represented consciousness may be either remembered by a fictional first-person narrator, as in chapters 17 and 18, or accessed through unconstrained empathy with another, fictional self, as in chapter 19.

It is especially interesting to examine the flow of consciousness and language in writing that shows displaced immediacy—a topic that will occupy us for most of the rest of this chapter. We can begin with identifiability, which highlights especially well a writer's options in this mode. We can then turn to activation cost, and after that we can examine both the light subject constraint and the one new idea constraint in writing of this kind. I will take examples again from Hemingway's "Big Two-Hearted River," whose displacement of self is especially revealing.

Identifiability

In the ordinary displaced and immediate modes of *speaking* diagramed in figures 22.1 and 22.2, the identifiability of a referent depends on the speaker's assessment of the mind of the listener in three respects (chap. 8). The speaker assumes that the referent is shared, that the language used to verbalize it will serve the listener as sufficiently identifying, and that it is a contextually salient instance of the category used to verbalize it. The question now is whether and how these or similar criteria can apply in the situation of displaced immediacy pictured in figure 22.3.

It would seem that two properties of displaced immediacy preclude a direct transfer of the criterion of shared knowledge. One is the fact that the represented consciousness is distinct from the consciousness doing the representing, a fact that raises the question of which consciousness would make judgments with regard to sharing. Would it be Nick's? Would it be Hemingway's? The other is the fact that the reception of the language is separated from its production. Can there be sharing with an unknown mind that will perceive the language at an unknown place and time? In the largest perspective such language involves three consciousnesses—the represented consciousness of a fictional self and the unacknowledged consciousnesses of the writer and the reader. With respect to which of these consciousnesses is identifiability determined?

What we find is that identifiability is often determined with reference to the represented consciousness of a fictional self alone, but also that that is not consistently the case. Whereas for a referent to be shared in conversation means that it is assumed by the speaker to be already known to the listener, here it may mean simply that the referent is already known to a protagonist. At the very beginning of the Hemingway story, for example, we read:

(3) The train went on up the track out of sight (1987, p. 163)

There is evidently no point in asking with whom the knowledge of the train or track was judged to be shared, or who would judge the sharing. What determined their identifiability was the fact that these ideas were already part of Nick's knowledge. Here we have what can be called a *protagonist-oriented* identifiability, as contrasted with the *listener-oriented* identifiability that is operative in conversational language. It is easy to see that protagonist-oriented identifiability strengthens the effect of displaced immediacy, depending as it does on the nature of the distal extroverted consciousness. It can thus be added to the list of resources available for this purpose that were discussed in chapters 17–19.

With identifiability established in this protagonist-oriented way, it is interesting to observe the circumstances under which referents are treated as *nonidentifiable*. Presumably they are referents *not* already known to the protagonist: ideas encountered de novo as the protagonist's experience flows through time in synchrony with changes in his environment. Two good examples appear in the fourth paragraph of the story:

(4) A kingfisher flew up the stream . . . a big trout shot upstream (P. 163)

Neither the kingfisher nor this particular trout was previously known to Nick, and the use of the indefinite article expresses that fact. It would have been inappropriate here to have written of *the kingfisher* or *the big trout*.

Somewhat later in the story there is fine-grained detail as Nick makes camp, setting up his tent and preparing his supper. Some of the items in the camping gear are treated as identifiable on first mention, while some are not:

Identifiable	Nonidentifiable
the ax	a long nail
the blankets	a paper sack of nails
the frying pan	a can of pork and beans
the tin plate	a can of spaghetti
	a wire grill
	a bottle of tomato catchup

There is evidently a pattern here. The identifiable referents are necessary elements of the camping gear schema, items a camper would be expected to have with him (the blankets now updateable to a sleeping bag). The nonidentifiable referents are incidental to this schema; a camper might or might not have them. Thus, when

(5) He took the ax out of the pack (P. 166)

Nick already knew about this ax (he must have put it in the pack), and when he became actively conscious of it, it was identifiable to him. When, on the other hand,

> (6) Nick went over to the pack and found, with his fingers, a long nail in a paper sack of nails, in the bottom of the pack. (P. 167)

both the long nail and the paper sack of nails were treated as nonidentifiable. The long nail is like the kingfisher and the trout; there is no reason to think that Nick had focused on this particular nail before this moment. The sack of nails, however, is different. Like the ax, Nick must have packed it earlier and must therefore have known about it. Could its incidental nature with respect to the camping gear schema be responsible for its nonidentifiability? If that interpretation is correct, it suggests the need to modify our understanding of identifiability in the context of displaced immediacy. The relevance of the camping gear schema in establishing identifiability must involve the mind of someone other than Nick, who himself has no need to consult a schema to identify a paper sack about which he already knows. If Nick's mind alone had been involved, Hemingway could have written:

> (7) ~Nick went over to the pack and found, with his fingers, a long nail in *the* paper sack of nails, in the bottom of the pack.

The definite article would have been dictated by Nick's point of view and would in fact have strengthened the effect of displaced immediacy. Hemingway *could* have written (7), but he would have created a minor problem for the reader, who might well have wondered, "What paper sack of nails?" Whereas Hemingway could assume the identifiability of the ax, the blankets, the frying pan, and the tin plate on the basis of the reader's presumed knowledge of the camping gear schema, the identifiability of the paper sack of nails had no such justification. Nor did that of the wire grill:

> (8) Over the fire he stuck a wire grill, pushing the four legs down into the ground with his boot. (P. 167)

This object too was already known to Nick—it was another thing he had packed—and the fact that it was treated as nonidentifiable must again be attributable to its assumed absence from the *reader's* camping gear schema.

It appears, then, that in the context of displaced immediacy an author does not, or need not, consistently follow a purely protagonist-oriented strategy. *A paper sack of nails* and *a wire grill* are examples of an alternative strategy in which the unacknowledged writer is concerned with identifiability for the unacknowledged reader—a *reader-oriented* strategy. Even though the writer's and readers' consciousnesses are unacknowledged, they make themselves felt not only in the use of past tense and third person, but also in the identifiability or nonidentifiability of certain referents that are associated or not associated with schemas with which the reader can be assumed to be familiar. Their presence is also felt in passages like the second sentence of the story:

(9) Nick sat down on the bundle of canvas and bedding the baggage man had pitched out of the door of the baggage car. (P. 163)

If Nick's consciousness alone were involved, there would have been no need to identify the bundle as one that *the baggage man had pitched out of the door of the baggage car*. Nick had no need for this information. Thus, the reader-oriented strategy is also recognizable in the provision of sufficiently identifying language, such as this relative clause.

In the style of displaced immediacy, then, a writer may often express identifiability on the basis of the protagonist-oriented strategy, thereby adding to the effect of displaced immediacy, but the alternative reader-oriented strategy provides an option that is available when the protagonist orientation would fail to serve the reader's needs. Writers have creative license in the manner in which they choose to balance these two alternatives.

Activation Cost

Analyzing a sample of *conversational* language in terms of activation cost involves discovering the distribution within it of given, accessible, and new information, and tracing the effect of this distribution on its language. The principal techniques applied to conversations include:

(a) observing which ideas are represented with pronouns and which are spelled out in full noun phrases;

(b) observing the location of primary, secondary, and weak accents; and

(c) observing the status of ideas within both the linguistic and the extralinguistic context: whether they were activated immediately before or sometime earlier within the same discourse, or are inferrable from something activated earlier, or were not activated at all.

These same techniques are applicable to written language, with two reservations. First, although written language has a prosody, evidence for it, including evidence for the location of accents, is for the most part indirect and often ambiguous. Second, the extralinguistic environment usually plays no role in determining the activation state of ideas, since little can be assumed to be held in common between the environment in which the writer writes and that in which the reader reads. This second difference does not hamper an activation cost analysis of written language, since it is easy to ignore the environment, but the absence of overt indications of prosody can make such an analysis more difficult and, in many cases, indeterminate. Let us first, however, examine the relatively straightforward kind of evidence provided by (a): the choice between pronouns and full noun phrases.

Pronouns versus Full Noun Phrases
In both speaking and writing the use or nonuse of pronouns depends in a fundamental way on taking account of the consciousness of the language receiver, whether that person is a listener or a reader. A pronoun is minimally informative, and whereas it might be all that a protagonist-oriented consciousness would require (since the referent is already known to the protagonist), very often a pronoun would not satisfy the needs of a reader. We can return here to the beginning of the Hemingway story:

(10) The train went on up the track out of sight, around one of the hills of
        burnt timber. Nick sat down on the bundle of canvas and bedding the bag-
        gage man had pitched out of the door of the baggage car. (P. 163)

What was happening in Nick's consciousness with respect to activation cost? Very likely the idea of the train was still active in his mind, and thus given. The track and the hills of burnt timber must have been at least in his semiactive consciousness, so that, as he turned his attention to each of them in turn, they constituted at least accessible information. What is new in the first sentence is the idea of *going on out of sight,* an event newly perceived by Nick. At the beginning of the second sentence, the idea of Nick himself was obviously given. The *sitting down* occurred for the first time in the flow of Nick's experience and was thus new information. The bundle of canvas and bedding was at least accessible, as were the baggage man, the door, the baggage car, and the act of pitching. If the use of pronouns and full noun phrases had expressed Nick's own activation costs, therefore, at the very least two of the referents would have appeared as pronouns:

(11) ˜*It* went on up the track out of sight, around one of the hills of burnt tim-
        ber. *He* sat down on the bundle of canvas and bedding the baggage man
        had pitched out of the door of the baggage car.

This language would have taken the in medias res strategy farther than Hemingway chose to take it, leaving the reader uninformed with regard to the referents of *it* and *he.* Hemingway's decision to use the full nouns *the train* and *Nick* reflects a reader orientation warranted by a need to make the language intelligible. To say that is not to commit ourselves to an interpretation of these two referents as either given or new in any absolute sense. In Nick's consciousness they were given, in the reader's they are new. Later we will see one respect in which the language in (10) includes a bias in favor of Nick's consciousness, in spite of the fact that the use of full nouns is a concession to the reader.

Prosody

Activation cost is reflected not only in the use of pronouns or full noun phrases, but also in prosody. In another study (Chafe 1988b) I explored in some depth the question of whether written language *has* a prosody, elaborating on observations by Dwight Bolinger and others that "we monitor our writing sub-vocally, reading in an intonation, and the fact that the intonation is not actually shown and our reader is going to have to guess at it is as likely as not to escape our attention" (Bolinger 1975, p. 602). The fact is that "writers when they write, and readers when they read, experience auditory imagery of specific intonations, accents, pauses, rhythms, and voice qualities, even though the writing itself may show these features poorly if at all. This 'covert prosody' of written language is evidently something that is quite apparent to a reflective writer or reader" (Chafe 1988b, p. 397). It may, nevertheless, be degraded by fast reading or skimming, and probably comes closest to spoken prosody when the reader maintains a tempo close to that of speech.

If we want to study the distribution of accents in a written text, even though there is a valid sense in which those accents are experienced by the writer or reader, we are hampered by the fact that they are seldom overtly indicated as such (outside of the occasional use of italics or capitals). Is there any way to make these covert accents overt? One possible way is to ask people to read a text aloud. Since oral reading produces sound, one can then observe its accents just as one can observe them in any spoken language. Unfortunately the results are problematic in several ways. Reading aloud is a peculiar and unnatural activity which almost always produces language that is prosodically deviant. Furthermore, different oral readers assign different prosodies to the same piece of language, so that it is difficult to establish any unique prosodic interpretation in this way. Beyond that, there is no assurance that the prosody assigned in oral reading mirrors what would be assigned in silent reading. It may be that the very process of converting visual symbols to sound distorts whatever prosody a silent reader would experience. In spite of these reservations, reading aloud can at least be suggestive. The variability of its results reflects what is surely a fact—that there really *are* different prosodic interpretations which can be assigned quite validly to the same piece of writing. From different oral readings we can gain some idea of the range and consistency of those alternative interpretations. It is not without interest that five individuals who were asked to read the Hemingway story aloud unanimously assigned a primary accent to both *the train* and *Nick,* a fact which suggests that for those readers those referents were understood as new. And of course for the readers they were. It was only in Nick's consciousness that they were given, and it would only have been an oral reader's unconstrained empathy with Nick's consciousness that would have led to weak accents.

In summary, with respect to activation cost we can say that Hemingway's language, in its use of full noun phrases rather than pronouns, reflects a reader-oriented rather than a protagonist-oriented strategy. The prosody, since it is not shown on the printed page, is open to alternative interpretations. While Nick's interpretation would have reflected his own consciousness, oral readers' interpretations reflect theirs. But more will be said below regarding the ambiguity of activation cost in written language.

The Light Subject Constraint

One reason for concerning ourselves with the distribution of activation cost in written language is to be able to examine the effect on such language of the light subject and one new idea constraints, both of which significantly influence the shape of spoken language. Chafe (1991) discussed the light subject constraint as it applied to several samples of writing, including the Hemingway story, on which we can focus here.

In chapter 7 we found that by far the greatest proportion of subjects in a sample of conversational language expressed given information. A smaller proportion expressed accessible information, while only a very small proportion expressed information that was new. All of those new subjects were of trivial importance and identifiable. These characteristics of subjects, all of which involve the expenditure of a minimum amount of mental effort in the activation of subject referents, were combined in the light subject constraint. Because the desituatedness of writing may free it from some of the requirements imposed on the situated flow of consciousness in conversation, we might expect that some writing, at least, would relax a constraint of this kind. What we find is that the light subject constraint is indeed relaxed, but to varying degrees in different kinds of writing and usually with some influence retained. Let us see what can be said about the Hemingway story in this regard.

In the first thousand words of this story there are eight new subjects, if newness is interpreted as protagonist-oriented—that is, if new subjects are identified as those newly activated in Nick's consciousness as he interacted with his changing environment. They constitute 11 percent of the subjects in this sample, a proportion somewhat higher than the 3 percent found in conversational language. The eight new subjects are:

(12) a the thirteen saloons that had lined the one street of Seney
     b the foundations of the Mansion House hotel
     c the stone
     d the surface
     e a kingfisher
     f the shadow of the kingfisher
     g islands of dark pine trees
     h Nick's heart

The first general observation we can make is that all of these subjects are of trivial importance; all are incidental participants in the development of the story. In that respect they conform perfectly to one of the constraints on new subjects observed in conversational language. All but two of them, (12)e and (12)g, also conform to the conversational requirement that new subjects be identifiable. One of these nonidentifiable referents provides a clear instance of language that is deviant with respect to the light subject constraint:

(13) *A kingfisher* flew up the stream.

The kingfisher enters the story through the ongoing new experiences of the protagonist. What is the effect of introducing it in the subject role, in conflict with spoken norms? Apparently this very conflict is used as a literary device. The unexpected appearance of *a kingfisher* as a starting point in (13)a dramatizes the startling effect on Nick of its appearance on the scene. Linguistic unexpectedness, in other words, can be used by a writer as a way of conveying iconically the unexpectedness of an experience.[2]

In brief, in the displaced immediacy of this story the distribution of subjects in terms of activation cost is not greatly different from that found in conversations. The somewhat more numerous *new* subjects all express referents of trivial importance, and most are identifiable. The occasional nonidentifiability of a new subject may be used as a way of expressing iconically the suddenness with which a referent appears in the flow of the protagonist's experience.

The One New Idea Constraint

In order to investigate the extent to which a sample of written language mirrors the constraint that limits spoken intonation units to one new idea,

---

2. Compare the use of *this van* as a subject in example (25) of chapter 7.

it is obviously necessary not only to analyze written language in terms of activation cost—being able to locate given, accessible, and new ideas—but also to establish the boundaries of intonation units. As we found with the location of accents, there is no reason to believe that a particular piece of writing dictates a unique segmentation into intonation units. The writer may have a particular segmentation in mind and will usually make some use of punctuation to show what that segmentation is. In fact, the presence of punctuation can make the evidence for intonation unit boundaries less ambiguous than the evidence for accents. But because writers vary in their ability to use punctuation effectively, because some punctuation is dictated by nonprosodic considerations, and because styles of punctuating change with different eras and different writers, it is impossible consistently to equate punctuation units (segments of language bounded by punctuation marks) with a writer's intended intonation units. (Chafe 1988b discusses the relation of punctuation to the covert intonation units of writing.)

In spite of these difficulties, it can be rewarding to examine punctuation units as if they did reflect intonation units, since there is a strong if variable tendency to punctuate in that way, and to examine the distribution of activation cost within such units. As an illustration of this approach we can look once more at the first two sentences of the Hemingway story, divided this time into three punctuation units:

(14) a The train went on up the track out of sight,
    b around one of the hills of burnt timber.
    c Nick sat down on the bundle of canvas and bedding the baggage man had pitched out of the door of the baggage car.

A reader-oriented interpretation would find here many violations of the one new idea constraint. If (14)a contains three ideas—the event expressed by *went on out of sight* along with the referents expressed by *the train* and *the track*—all three are new to the reader. For Nick, on the other hand, it was only the event that was new; the train and the track were either given or accessible. It follows that (14)a does adhere to the one new idea constraint to the extent that it expresses the consciousness of the protagonist. To read it as if it adhered to a consistent, if subconsciously appreciated constraint on conversational speech provides an unusually subtle yet significant kind of additional evidence for displaced immediacy. The same can be said of (14)b, where all that was new to Nick was the train's trajectory, whereas for the reader the hills and the burnt timber were also new. In (14)c it was only the act of sitting down that was new in Nick's consciousness, whereas the reader would have to interpret all the other ideas as new: Nick, the bundle of canvas and bedding, the baggage man, the door, the baggage car, and the act of pitching.

Throughout this story, in fact, there is continuing evidence that the one new idea constraint is maintained if it is based on the distribution of activation cost within Nick's mind, whereas from the reader's point of view it has no validity whatsoever. This fact, combined with observations regarding the light subject constraint, suggests that there is a level of understanding the story at which it expresses the flow of ideas through Nick's consciousness with respect to activation cost, even though the author's use of full noun phrases may suggest a reader-oriented admixture that reflects the author's wish to have the reader understand.

Expository Writing That Lacks a Represented Consciousness

What happens to the flow of consciousness and language when there is no acknowledged consciousness at all, but only, in addition to the unacknowledged reading consciousness, an unacknowledged writing consciousness whose knowledge comes from omnipresence rather than from either the environment or remembering? This configuration is typified by expository nonfiction, where factors like activation cost, identifiability, the light subject constraint, and the one new idea constraint can be related *only* to the unacknowledged consciousnesses of the writer and reader. If the writer produces language that takes account of his or her own consciousness alone, comprehensibility is thereby diminished for the reader, whose consciousness the writer intends to influence. Expository writing is therefore more congenial to the reader—more readable, as is usually said—to the extent that the writer gives consideration to both the light subject constraint and the one new idea constraint with reference to the unacknowledged reader's consciousness.

As an example we can look at the beginning of an academic article in the field of anthropology, more specifically the subfield of paleodemography (Buikstra and Konigsberg 1985):

(15)   Broadly conceived, paleodemography is the study of vital rates, population distribution, and density in extinct human groups, especially those for which there are no written records. This charting of differential reproduction and survival in humankind's unwritten past is as elusive as it is crucial in defining the course of human evolution. Persons familiar with the problems inherent in the estimation of demographic parameters for living human groups characterized by small size and a lack of census records should scarcely be surprised to find that paleodemography is controversial. (P. 316)

It is especially interesting to focus on the last sentence in this excerpt, since it might seem to violate flagrantly both the light subject and one new idea constraints. Within its lengthy subject, some ideas (that expressed by *demographic parameters,* for example) are accessible from what preceded, but others (*living human groups, small size, a lack of census records*) can only be interpreted as new, thus clearly violating the light subject constraint. Furthermore, the entire sentence is presented without punctuation breaks, and obviously if it were to be regarded as a single intonation unit there would be an egregious violation of the one new idea constraint as well.

This excerpt was read aloud by eight individuals, all of whom broke it into a number of intonation units. The following is a segmentation based on intonation unit boundaries inserted by at least six (75 percent) of those readers:

(16) a Persons familiar with the problems inherent in the estimation of demographic parameters for living human groups,
   b characterized by small size,
   c and a lack of census records,
   d should scarcely be surprised to find,
   e that paleodemography is controversial.

Interestingly, these intonation units approximate conformity to the one new idea constraint. Although (16)a is rather long, it could be argued that it contains only one new referent, that expressed as *living human groups.* The other intonation units adhere quite satisfactorily to the constraint. It thus appears that even though the writer used no punctuation at all to segment (16), readers are able to process language of this kind in a manner not unlike the manner in which they process speech. That, at least, is the evidence from reading aloud. Whether silent readers follow a similar pattern as they assimilate such language into their consciousness without overt sound is a major question. One might hope that a study of eye movements would be a profitable way of investigating the hypothesis that reading takes place in terms of one new idea per major period of visual attention, each such unit embracing a segment of language which, like an intonation unit, reflects a single focus of consciousness. So far as I know, eye movement research has never addressed such a question.

Summary

There is a need to integrate the understandings of immediacy and displacement discussed in part 3 with the understandings of flow developed in part 2. An initial finding is that, from the perspective of immediacy and displacement, part 2 described a special case that was based on the conversational modes of speaking discussed in chapters 15 and 16. The present chapter was a preliminary attempt to deal with flow in other modes.

Aspects of flow such as activation cost, identifiability, the light subject constraint, and the one new idea constraint all involve assessments by the language producer of what is happening in the mind of the language receiver. For that reason it is necessary to add the consciousness of the listener or reader to the structures of immediacy and displacement discussed in earlier chapters, as was attempted in figures 22.1, 22.2, and 22.3. The chapter devoted most of its attention to the flow of consciousness in written fiction in the style of displaced immediacy, with displacement of self. Here, as in other writing, the production of the language is separated from its reception, and that separation affects the flow of consciousness in interesting ways.

So far as *identifiability* in this style of writing is concerned, it may be defined, not with relation to the unacknowledged writer and reader, but with relation to the consciousness of the protagonist. We can speak of a protagonist-oriented strategy that serves to reinforce the effect of displaced immediacy. That strategy, however, may alternate with a different, reader-oriented strategy in which the unacknowledged consciousness of the writer takes account of the unacknowledged consciousness of the reader, thereby increasing comprehensibility for the latter. So far as *activation cost* is concerned, it too may show concessions to the reader's consciousness, while continuing in other ways to reflect the protagonist's. For example, the choice of full nouns rather than pronouns may take the reader into account. Prosody can be interpreted with either a protagonist or a reader orientation, but understandably enough it reflects a reader orientation when the language is read aloud. So far as *the light subject constraint* is concerned, we found in one sample that the proportion of new subjects was somewhat larger than in conversational language but that, as in conversations, all were of trivial importance and almost all were identifiable. The deviant appearance of a nonidentifiable referent in the subject role conveyed iconically its unexpectedness in the protagonist's consciousness. To study *the one new idea constraint* it is necessary to find a way of segmenting written language into units that are comparable to spoken intonation units. Punctuation units, despite their variability, provide some approximation to such units. Hemingway's punctuation units in this story are largely compatible with the one new idea constraint so long as that constraint is interpreted on a protagonist-oriented, not a reader-oriented basis—a subtle kind of evidence for displaced immediacy.

We turned briefly at the end to an example of information flow in academic writing: a sentence in which the writer provided no punctuation at all to guide the reader's segmentation. Oral readers, however, segmented this sentence into intonation units that conformed to the one new idea constraint, suggesting that even without punctuation, oral readers interpret writing in terms of well-behaved foci of consciousness. The ultimate question is what silent readers do. Perhaps eye movements will help.

There is a sense in which this chapter is the culmination of this book, finally bringing together the concerns of part 2 with those of part 3, uniting flow with displacement. It provides, however, only a very preliminary taste of what can be done—nothing more than a first introduction to a very large topic that requires attention to diverse styles of writing. Still another book is called for, but before we are finished with this one the concerns of chapters 10 and 11 of part 2 need to be related to the concerns of part 3.

23

Written Paragraphs and Discourse Topics

Chapter 11 discussed manifestations of topic, supertopic, and subtopic boundaries in speaking: prosodic evidence for reorientations in semiactive consciousness, usually related to changes in space, time, character configurations, and event structures. The more significant the reorientations, the stronger the prosodic boundaries. In writing, a somewhat analogous function is performed by paragraph boundaries: beginning a new line, adding an extra space, and/or indenting. To what extent do paragraph boundaries reflect the same kind of reorientations of semiactive consciousness?

Written paragraphs have received much attention, but most of it has been prescriptive rather than descriptive. It has aimed at telling writers how they *should* segment their writing into paragraphs, not at observing how writers actually do it. Paul Rodgers (1965, p. 405), for example, speaks of "the present-day nomenclature of the three canons of paragraph structure, which Baldwin (1898) summarized and passed on to the twentieth century: Unity, Coherence, Emphasis." Probably the single most influential tenet of paragraph prescriptivism has been the notion of the topic sentence:

> Most paragraphs focus on a central idea or unifying device expressed in topical material. Occasionally this topical material is complex, involving more than one sentence and some subtopics; sometimes it carries over from a previous paragraph and is assumed to be understood or is referred to briefly; but usually it simply takes the form of a sentence, sometimes amplified or made more specific in a sentence or two following it. This topic sentence may appear at the end of the paragraph as a kind of summary or somewhere within the paragraph, but most frequently it opens the paragraph or follows an opening introduction or transition. (Gorrell and Laird 1967, p. 25, quoted in Braddock 1974, p. 291)

Richard Braddock examined paragraphs in twenty-five expository essays which had appeared in such American magazines as *The Atlantic, Harper's, The New Yorker, The Reporter,* and *The Saturday Review.* He found problems in deciding what constituted a topic sentence, but doing the best he could, he estimated that "only 13% of the expository paragraphs of contemporary professional writers begin with a topic sentence, that only 3% end with a topic sentence" (Braddock 1974, p. 301; see also Stern 1976). All things considered, one can say that the prescriptions that have been offered for paragraphs do not have a great deal to do with how paragraphs are really written, but only with how some people wish they were written.

Rodgers (1966) studied paragraphs written by Walter Pater in his essay "Style" (Pater 1910). The literary historian George Saintsbury said of Pater that "no one . . . has ever surpassed, and scarcely any one has ever equalled Mr. Pater in deliberate and successful architecture of the prose-paragraph—in which may, for the sake of a necessary difference, be called the scriptorial in opposition to the oratorical manner" (Saintsbury 1896, p. 400). Rodgers showed that Pater's reasons for establishing paragraph boundaries were diverse and complex. Logic and coherence played some role, but were by no means the only determining factors: "the logical partitioning of complex discourse into paragraphs can occur at so many junctures that additional non-logical criteria often have to be invoked to account for a given decision to indent." He identified such other criteria as reader expectation, paragraph size, readability, rhythm, parallelisms, juxtapositions, and "tonal fluctuations." Rodgers's study is perhaps unique in showing how diverse the grounds for paragraphing may be, in this case by a writer who prided himself on how well he did it.

There is a style of writing in which paragraphs are coterminous with sentences, each paragraph consisting of a single sentence. Examples are easy to find on the front page of a newspaper:

(1)   In the calm following seven hours of hectic worry, Santa Barbara police Friday reflected on how they handled the case of the misplaced 5-year-old girl on Thursday.

And they smiled.

Not because it turned out to be a case of simple misunderstanding and not kidnapping, but because they were able to galvanize their forces in record time.

Police searched the homes of relatives and friends, where the child might possibly have been taken, and within hours were able to locate and arrest the person they felt most likely to have taken the girl. (*Santa Barbara News-Press,* January 25, 1992)

These sentence-paragraphs are deliberate. William Zinsser (1980, pp. 111–12) advises: "Keep your paragraphs short, especially if you are writing for a newspaper or a magazine that sets its type in a narrow width. This is purely visual and psychological advice. Short paragraphs put air around what you write and make it look inviting, whereas one long chunk of type can discourage the reader from even starting to read. A newspaper paragraph generally shouldn't have more than two or three sentences." In fact, most paragraphs in front-page news reports contain no more than one sentence. Zinsser associated this practice with narrow-width columns, but that cannot be the only determining factor. *Time,* for example, which also uses narrow columns, prefers a style with a mean of about five sentences per paragraph, and *The New Yorker,* also with narrow columns, was not in the past averse to paragraphs several pages long. The following excerpt from John McPhee's *La Place de la Concorde Suisse* (1984; first published in *The New Yorker*) consists of one unusually long paragraph followed by a much shorter one:

(2)   Airspace is so limited that some training is now done in Sweden, but there is only one place to practice flying in the Alps. The jet pilots fly low in the valleys and close to the rock. Nearly all Swissair pilots are in the Swiss Army's air force—and some doctors and dentists as well. They choose their own training time, and they need a good deal more than three weeks a year to learn to do what they can do. The air force is an example of contemporary technology demanding more time than a militia is set up to provide. Like specialists in electronic warfare, the pilots give extra time. When conditions are what they want for practicing, they take their Mirages, their Tigers, their Hunters and go. They develop incredible skill. They don't seem to use maps—having so little glancing time, having every contour in their heads. During the Second World War, after a Swiss pilot shot down a German bomber over the Canton de Neuchatel the Germans sent fighters along on a mission that deliberately traversed Swiss air. Swiss pilots engaged the Luftwaffe in a dogfight and shot four Germans down. Victors and vanquished were using German airplanes. Swiss pilots now have infrared equipment and fly the mountain valleys at night. They can hide in the Alps. They know where they are and where to go. An enemy foolish enough to follow them will end up farming rock. At Gornergrat one day, at the top of a cog railway five thousand feet above Zermatt, I was sitting in an almost windless stillness, slowly moving my gaze in full circumference from the Breithorn to the Matterhorn to the Dent Blanche to the Zinalrothorn to the Weisshorn to the Dom—all well above four thousand metres—and on to the Dufourspitze, the highest mountain in Switzerland. Up out of the Mattertal came a Swiss Mirage. It skimmed over Gornergrat and dived toward the glaciers below. Its inclination appeared almost vertical, and it continued its dive until there seemed no chance that the plane could miss the ice and the pilot survive, but then it was climbing the glaciers close to the crevasses until it was deep in the cirques on the shoulders of the Dufourspitze, over which it rolled to plunge out of sight toward the Mattmarksee. The pilot was probably taking pictures. Mirages work for Renseignements. The jets sometimes fire on targets and then, like high jumpers, flip over ridges upside down. It

is a way to stay close to the rock. Their armament depends on their mission. Variously, they carry cannons, missiles, bombs. Even when cloud cover is extremely low during exercise engagements with the enemy, if someone calls for air support he will almost surely get it if there is any kind of airspace between the cloud and the ground. The Mirage drops out of the cloud, fires on the target, disappears upward in the cloud. It happens again a minute later. The target is destroyed twice. The cloud is packed like a snowfield among the Pennine Alps.

At Axalp, over the Brienzer See, the military attachés of at least twenty-five nations—including the United States, China, and the Soviet Union—sat down one day for a show. As the program began, a Mirage appeared from nowhere, rattled the reviewing stand, did a back flip over the Schwarzhorn, and was gone. Before the program ended, each attaché was handed a photograph of himself looking up with startled expression.

The spatiotemporal shift responsible for the single paragraph boundary near the end is clear, but it is not so clear why the same rationale did not dictate a boundary before the story that began with *During the Second World War,* or before the episode beginning *At Gornergrat one day,* or before the generic passage that started with *The jets sometimes fire on targets.*

What can we make of this extreme variety in paragraph length? In chapter 11 we saw that there can be varying degrees of change in semiactive consciousness, from minor changes of scene to major changes in mode of consciousness. We saw also that such changes tend to be reflected in briefer or longer periods of hesitating as speakers modify their semiactive consciousness to a greater or lesser degree. If one is editing transcripts of spoken language, one has a legitimate choice of whether to insert paragraph boundaries at points of minor change, at points of maximum change, or somewhere in between. There is, in other words, a continuum from fine- to coarse-grained topic boundaries that can be reflected in fine- to coarse-grained paragraph marking. News reporters set their thresholds very low, more or less equating paragraphs with sentences. The effect is that of a writer who assumes the reader's semiactive consciousness has an extremely limited capacity, with a need for a fresh start at every step. *Time* writers achieve a happy medium. *New Yorker* writers have sometimes set their thresholds maximally high, evidently assuming readers with a semiactive consciousness of enormous capacity.

It is helpful to think in terms of a distinction between those linguistic units that are naturally determined by cognitive constraints and those that result from conscious decisions—between boundaries that appear because of natural properties of the mind and those that appear because writers manipulate those properties. So far as speaking is concerned, we have seen that intonation units result from changes in focal consciousness, and topics from changes in semiactive consciousness. Spoken sentences, on the other hand, are not directly determined by such natural constraints but result from on-line, variable decisions regarding the boundaries of coherent intonation unit clusters. When we turn to writing, we find that writers' punctuation units and sentences tend very roughly to imitate spoken intonation units and sentences respectively, although they often expand and elaborate them. It would now appear that written paragraphs constitute attempts to go beyond what is possible for a written sentence. In that respect they can be regarded as *supersentences,* just as spoken sentences can be regarded as super–intonation units. But paragraphs are also attempts at imitating the topics of speaking. Writers must have a tacit awareness that spoken topic boundaries exist, reflecting changes in semiactive consciousness. In the end, paragraphs turn out to be neither fish nor fowl. They constitute a variable resource whose form and content is not fully dictated by either cognitive or conventional constraints. Less limited in their purpose and possibilities, they are available to be used by writers as another creative resource.

Summary

Reflecting a correspondence to topic boundaries in speaking, writing makes use of paragraph boundaries, associated at diverse levels with changes in semiactive consciousness: changes in space, time, character configurations, event structure, and/or modes of consciousness. Most discussions of paragraphs have been prescriptive rather than descriptive, dictating qualities such as unity, coherence, and emphasis, and especially recommending the use of topic sentences. Observations of actual writing cast doubt on the frequency with which writers follow such prescriptions in any consistent way. Paragraphs differ greatly in size, depending on the conventions of different genres and styles. This variation mirrors the degrees of hesitating that are observable in speaking, which in turn are correlated with varying degrees of change in the orientation of semiactive consciousness. It was suggested that paragraphs constitute a variable rather than a cognitively determined resource, one that can be manipulated by writers for diverse effects.

24

Epilogue

I have tried in this work above all to show that observations of naturally produced speech and writing, combined with relatively unproblematic introspections, can help us understand certain important ways in which consciousness and language interact. Ideas of events and states and their participants flow in and out of fully conscious activation in a manner that is reflected in the intonation units of speech. When they leave this fully active state, ideas remain for some time semiactive. Speakers monitor the activation states of ideas in the minds of their listeners, treating ideas accordingly as given, accessible, or new. In speaking they attach each newly activated idea to a starting point that is usually given or at least accessible, and judged identifiable to the listener; in English and some other languages this starting point role has become grammaticized in the role of subject. It has proved fruitful to hypothesize that people are able to activate no more than one new idea at a time, especially since the question of what constitutes "one idea" has important implications for an understanding of how ideas become lexicalized.

Beyond this process of successively activating ideas of events, states, and their participants, people also operate in terms of larger discourse topics that are held for a longer time in the semiactive state, scanning each topic with the focus of fully active consciousness before moving on to the next. This process, too, is both reflected in and illuminated by the flow of language. While events, states, referents, and discourse topics appear to be more or less stable units of memory, the boundaries of sentences, often intermediate in coverage between active foci and semiactive topics, appear to reflect passing judgments with regard to less stable "centers of interest" as language is produced on the run.

Human consciousness has the remarkable ability to focus much of the time on ideas that are displaced from the immediate time and location of the conscious being, a fact well demonstrated by the content of most conversations. Taking this ability into account, I distinguished between an extroverted and an introverted consciousness, discussing their qualitative differences with respect to continuity and detail. In certain kinds of written fiction, the desituated nature of writing has made it possible for the consciousness that is represented by the language to be separated from the consciousness that does the representing. Language of this kind exhibits the qualities of an extroverted consciousness, extended even to its use of spatiotemporal adverbs, while at the same time it preserves displacement in its use of tense and person. It is hospitable to devices I have called verbatim indirect speech, verbatim indirect thought, and verbally uncommitted thought, the three often lumped together as free indirect style. Fiction writers may enhance their insights into the human condition by interspersing displaced immediacy with language that lacks a represented consciousness altogether. Nonfiction writing presents an even more mixed bag so far as the representation of consciousness is concerned, but even the most "autonomous" writing usually implies an author and reader with limited knowledge and opinions.

The book culminated in an attempt to integrate the flow and displacement of consciousness by looking at the handling of activation cost, starting points, identifiability, and the one new idea constraint in the context of displaced immediacy. It was found that an author may exploit a protagonist-oriented strategy as a means of reinforcing the effect of an extroverted consciousness, while resorting to a reader-oriented strategy when necessary to accommodate the reader's needs. In the final chapter I noted how the varying lengths of written paragraphs can reflect the varying strengths of topic boundaries, just as analogous variations are often manifested in speech by varying degrees of hesitating.

Finally, for those in my linguistic audience who have had the patience to follow me this far, I would like to point out that various phenomena generally placed at the heart of linguistic studies may ultimately depend for their fullest understanding on the kinds of considerations introduced here. Among such phenomena belong anaphora, prosody, subjecthood, definiteness, sentences, paragraphs, spatiotemporal adverbs, tense, and person. If I am right, linguistics will never be able to deal adequately with these and doubtless other matters without taking the flow and displacement of consciousness into account.

That is the story for now. It is, I think, a reasonably consistent and coherent story, but one that is certainly incomplete in many ways. Further observations can be expected to expand, strengthen, and modify it. Some of it will surely have to be replaced or discarded, but I am optimistic that a significant portion will stand. I hope at the very least that this exploration will have clarified not just the desirability but the necessity of opening up investigations of both language and the mind by observing language as it really is, by taking introspection seriously without fear of being labeled unscientific, and by allowing one's imagination to roam free over more encompassing visions of the ways in which human minds relate to their environments and other minds. These closing years of the twentieth century could find us at the threshold of important new understandings, but whether we cross it will depend on our success in integrating the literary scholar's appreciation of what language does, the ethnologist's respect for what actually happens, the philosopher's perspective on the larger picture, the psychologist's concern for experimental manipulations, the computer scientist's and neuroscientist's fascination with how things work, and the artist's capacity for productive dreams.

References

Akinnaso, F. Niyi. 1982. On the Differences between Spoken and Written Language. *Language and Speech* 25:97–125.

Andree, Herb, and Noel Young. 1980. *Santa Barbara Architecture.* Santa Barbara, Calif.: Capra Press.

Ariel, Mira. 1988. Referring and Accessibility. *Journal of Linguistics* 24:65–87.

———. 1990. *Accessing Noun-Phrase Antecedents.* London: Routledge.

———. 1991. The Function of Accessibility in a Theory of Grammar. *Journal of Pragmatics* 16:443–63.

Baars, Bernard J. 1986. *The Cognitive Revolution in Psychology.* New York: Guilford Press.

———. 1988. *A Cognitive Theory of Consciousness.* Cambridge: Cambridge University Press.

———. 1991. Consciousness and Modularity. *Behavioral and Brain Sciences* 14:440.

———. 1993. Putting the Focus on the Fringe: Three Empirical Cases. *Consciousness and Cognition* 2:126–36.

Backus, Joseph M. 1965. "He Came into Her Line of Vision Walking Backward": Nonsequential Sequence-Signals in Short Story Openings. *Language Learning* 15:67–83.

Baddeley, Alan D. 1976. *The Psychology of Memory.* New York: Basic Books.

Baldwin, Charles Sears. 1898. *The Expository Paragraph and Sentence: An Elementary Manual of Composition.* New York: Longmans, Green.

Banaji, Mahzarin R., and Robert G. Crowder. 1989. The Bankruptcy of Everyday Memory. *American Psychologist* 44:1185–93.

Banfield, Ann. 1982. *Unspeakable Sentences: Narration and Representation in the Language of Fiction.* Boston: Routledge and Kegan Paul.

Barbeau, Marius. 1915. *Classification of Iroquoian Radicals with Subjective Pronominal Prefixes.* Canada Department of Mines, Geological Survey, Memoir 46, Anthropological Series 7. Ottawa: Government Printing Bureau.

Barthes, Roland. 1966. Introduction à l'analyse structurale des récits. *Communications* 8:1–27.

———. 1982. The Reality Effect. In Tzvetan Todorov, ed., *French Literary Theory Today: A Reader.* Cambridge: Cambridge University Press.

Bartlett, Frederic C. 1932. *Remembering: A Study in Experimental and Social Psychology.* Cambridge: Cambridge University Press.

Benson, Morton, Evelyn Benson, and Robert Ilson. 1986a. *The BBI Combinatory Dictionary of English.* Amsterdam and Philadelphia: John Benjamins.

———. 1986b. *Lexicographic Description of English.* Amsterdam and Philadelphia: John Benjamins.

Benveniste, Emile. 1971. *Problems in General Linguistics.* Trans. Mary Elizabeth Meek. Coral Gables, Fla.: University of Miami Press.

Berlin, Brent, Dennis E. Breedlove, and Peter H. Raven. 1973. General Principles of Classification and Nomenclature in Folk Biology. *American Anthropologist* 75:214–42.

Bevan, William. 1991. Contemporary Psychology: A Tour inside the Onion. *American Psychologist* 46:475–83.

Biber, Douglas. 1988. *Variation across Speech and Writing.* Cambridge: Cambridge University Press.

Bing, Janet Mueller. 1985. *Aspects of English Prosody.* New York: Garland.

Bloomfield, Leonard. 1933. *Language.* New York: Henry Holt.

Bolinger, Dwight. 1952. Linear Modification. *Publications of the Modern Language Association* 67:1117–44. Reprinted in Bolinger 1965.

———. 1965. *Forms of English: Accent, Morpheme, Order.* Ed. Isamu Abe and Tetsuya Kanekiyo. Cambridge: Harvard University Press.

———. 1975. *Aspects of Language.* 2d ed. New York: Harcourt Brace Jovanovich.

Booth, Wayne C. 1961. *The Rhetoric of Fiction.* Chicago: The University of Chicago Press.

Braddock, Richard. 1974. The Frequency and Placement of Topic Sentences in Expository Prose. *Research in the Teaching of English* 8:287–304.

Brett, George Sidney. 1965. *Brett's History of Psychology.* Ed. and abridged by R. S. Peters. 2d rev. ed. Cambridge: MIT Press.

Bronzwaer, W. J. M. 1970. *Tense in the Novel: An Investigation of Some Potentialities of Linguistic Criticism.* Groningen: Wolters-Noordhoff.

Brown, Gillian, and George Yule. 1983. *Discourse Analysis.* Cambridge: Cambridge University Press.

Buikstra, Jane E., and Lyle W. Konigsberg. 1985. Paleodemography: Critiques and Controversies. *American Anthropologist* 87:316–33.

Buswell, Guy T. 1935. *How People Look at Pictures: A Study of the Psychology of Perception in Art.* Chicago: University of Chicago Press.

Chafe, Wallace. 1961. *Seneca Thanksgiving Rituals.* Bureau of American Ethnology, Bulletin 183. Washington, D.C.: Government Printing Office.

———. 1967. *Seneca Morphology and Dictionary.* Smithsonian Contributions to Anthropology, vol. 4. Washington, D.C.: Smithsonian Press.

———. 1968. Idiomaticity as an Anomaly in the Chomskyan Paradigm. *Foundations of Language* 4:109–27.

———. 1970. *Meaning and the Structure of Language.* Chicago: University of Chicago Press.

———. 1972. Discourse Structure and Human Knowledge. In Roy O. Freedle and John B. Carroll, eds., *Language Comprehension and the Acquisition of Knowledge.* Washington, D.C.: V. H. Winston.

———. 1973. Language and Memory. *Language* 49:261–81.

———. 1974. Language and Consciousness. *Language* 50:111–33.

———. 1976. Givenness, Contrastiveness, Definiteness, Subjects, Topics, and Point of View. In Charles N. Li, ed., *Subject and Topic.* New York: Academic Press.

———. 1977a. Creativity in Verbalization and Its Implications for the Nature of Stored Knowledge. In Roy O. Freedle, ed., *Discourse Production and Comprehension,* pp. 41–55. Norwood, N.J.: Ablex.

———. 1977b. The Recall and Verbalization of Past Experience. In Roger W. Cole, ed., *Current Issues in Linguistic Theory.* Bloomington: Indiana University Press.

———. 1979. The Flow of Thought and the Flow of Language. In Talmy Givón, ed., *Discourse and Syntax.* New York: Academic Press.

———. 1980. The Deployment of Consciousness in the Production of a Narrative.

In Wallace Chafe, ed., *The Pear Stories: Cognitive, Cultural, and Linguistic Aspects of Narrative Production*. Norwood, N.J.: Ablex.

———. 1982. Integration and Involvement in Speaking, Writing, and Oral Literature. In Deborah Tannen, ed., *Spoken and Written Language: Exploring Orality and Literacy*. Norwood, N.J.: Ablex.

———. 1986. Beyond Bartlett: Narratives and Remembering. In Elisabeth Gülich and Uta M. Quasthoff, eds., *Narrative Analysis: An Interdisciplinary Dialogue*. Special issue of *Poetics*, vol. 15.

———. 1987a. Cognitive Constraints on Information Flow. In Russell Tomlin, ed., *Coherence and Grounding in Discourse*. Amsterdam and Philadelphia: John Benjamins.

———. 1987b. Humor as a Disabling Mechanism. *American Behavioral Scientist* 30:16–25.

———. 1988a. Linking Intonation Units in Spoken English. In John Haiman and Sandra A. Thompson, eds., *Clause Combining in Grammar and Discourse*. Amsterdam and Philadelphia: John Benjamins.

———. 1988b. Punctuation and the Prosody of Written Language. *Written Communication* 5:396–426.

———. 1990a. Repeated Verbalizations as Evidence for the Organization of Knowledge. In Werner Bahner, ed., *Proceedings of the XIVth International Congress of Linguists, Berlin 1987*.

———. 1990b. Some Things That Narratives Tell Us about the Mind. In Bruce K. Britton and Anthony D. Pellegrini, eds., *Narrative Thought and Narrative Language*. Hillsdale, N.J.: Lawrence Erlbaum.

———. 1991. Grammatical Subjects in Speaking and Writing. *Text* 11:45–72.

———. 1992a. The Flow of Ideas in a Sample of Written Language. In Sandra A. Thompson and William C. Mann, eds., *Discourse Description: Diverse Analyses of a Fund Raising Text*. Amsterdam and Philadelphia: John Benjamins.

———. 1992b. The Importance of Corpus Linguistics to Understanding the Nature of Language. In Jan Svartvik, ed., *Directions in Corpus Linguistics*. Berlin: Mouton de Gruyter.

———. 1992c. Intonation Units and Prominences in English Natural Discourse. In *Proceedings of the IRCS Workshop on Prosody in Natural Speech*. Institute for Research in Cognitive Science, Report No. 92-37. Philadelphia: University of Pennsylvania.

———. 1993. Types of Inference Involved in Identifiability and Accessibility. Paper presented at the 4th International Pragmatics Conference, Kobe, Japan.

———. In press. The Realis-Irrealis Distinction in Caddo, the Northern Iroquoian Languages, and English. In Joan Bybee and Suzanne Fleischman, eds., *Modality in Grammar and Discourse*. Amsterdam and Philadelphia: John Benjamins.

Chafe, Wallace, and Jane Danielewicz. 1987. Properties of Spoken and Written Language. In Rosalind Horowitz and S. J. Samuels, eds., *Comprehending Oral and Written Language*. New York: Academic Press.

Chafe, Wallace, and Deborah Tannen. 1987. The Relation between Written and Spoken Language. *Annual Review of Anthropology* 16:383–407.

Chatman, Seymour. 1975. The Structure of Narrative Transmission. In Roger Fowler, ed., *Style and Structure in Literature: Essays in the New Stylistics*. Ithaca, N.Y.: Cornell University Press.

Chesterman, Andrew. 1991. *On Definiteness: A Study with Special Reference to English and Finnish*. Cambridge: Cambridge University Press.

Chomsky, Noam. 1957. *Syntactic Structures*. The Hague: Mouton.

————. 1965. *Aspects of the Theory of Syntax.* Cambridge: MIT Press.

Christophersen, Paul. 1939. *The Articles: A Study of Their Theory and Use in English.* Copenhagen: Einar Munksgaard.

Clark, Herbert H. 1977. Bridging. In Philip N. Johnson-Laird and Peter C. Wason, eds., *Thinking: Readings in Cognitive Science.* Cambridge: Cambridge University Press.

————. 1992. *Arenas of Language Use.* Chicago: University of Chicago Press and Center for the Study of Language and Information.

Clark, Herbert H., and Eve V. Clark. 1977. *Psychology and Language: An Introduction to Psycholinguistics.* New York: Harcourt Brace Jovanovich.

Clark, Herbert H., and Susan E. Haviland. 1977. Comprehension and the Given-New Contract. In Roy O. Freedle, ed., *Discourse Production and Comprehension.* Norwood, N.J.: Ablex.

Clark, Herbert H., and Catherine R. Marshall. 1981. Definite Reference and Mutual Knowledge. In Aravind K. Joshi, Bonnie L. Webber, and Ivan A. Sag, eds., *Elements of Discourse Understanding.* Cambridge: Cambridge University Press.

Clark, Herbert H., Robert Schreuder, and Samuel Buttrick. 1983. Common Ground and the Understanding of Demonstrative Reference. *Journal of Verbal Learning and Verbal Behavior* 22:245–58.

Clark, Herbert H., and Deanna Wilkes-Gibbs. 1986. Referring as a Collaborative Process. *Cognition* 22:1–39.

Clark, Walter Van Tilburg. 1940. *The Ox-Bow Incident.* New York: New American Library.

Cohen, Gillian. 1989. *Memory in the Real World.* Hillsdale, N.J.: Lawrence Erlbaum.

Cohn, Dorrit. 1968. K. Enters *The Castle*: On the Change of Person in Kafka's Manuscript. *Euphorion* 62:28–45.

————. 1978. *Transparent Minds: Narrative Modes for Presenting Consciousness in Fiction.* Princeton: Princeton University Press.

————. 1981. The Encirclement of Narrative: On Franz Stanzel's *Theorie des Erzählens. Poetics Today* 2:157–82.

Cole, Peter, Wayne Harbert, Gabriella Hermon, and S. N. Sridhar. 1980. The Acquisition of Subjecthood. *Language* 56:719–43.

Comrie, Bernard. 1989. *Language Universals and Linguistic Typology.* Chicago: University of Chicago Press.

Crane, Stephen. 1895. *The Red Badge of Courage: An Episode of the American Civil War.* New York: Modern Library.

Cruttenden, Alan. 1986. *Intonation.* Cambridge: Cambridge University Press.

Csikszentmihalyi, Mihaly. 1975. *Beyond Boredom and Anxiety.* San Francisco: Jossey-Bass.

————. 1990. *Flow: The Psychology of Optimal Experience.* New York: Harper and Row.

DeLancey, Scott. 1981. An Interpretation of Split Ergativity and Related Patterns. *Language* 57:626–57.

Dillon, George L., and Frederick Kirchhoff. 1976. On the Form and Function of Free Indirect Style. *PTL: A Journal for Descriptive Poetics and Theory of Literature* 1:431–40.

Dixon, Robert M. W. 1982. *Where Have All the Adjectives Gone? And Other Essays in Semantics and Syntax.* Berlin: Mouton.

Du Bois, John W. 1980. Beyond Definiteness: The Trace of Identity in Discourse. In Wallace Chafe, ed., *The Pear Stories: Cognitive, Cultural and Linguistic Aspects of Narrative Production.* Norwood, N.J.: Ablex.

————. 1987. The Discourse Basis of Ergativity. *Language* 63:805–55.

Du Bois, John W., Stephan Schuetze-Coburn, Susanna Cumming, and Danae Paolino. 1993. Outline of Discourse Transcription. In Jane A. Edwards and Martin D. Lampert, eds., *Talking Data: Transcription and Coding in Discourse Research.* Hillsdale, N.J.: Lawrence Erlbaum.

Du Bois, John W., Stephan Schuetze-Coburn, Danae Paolino, and Susanna Cumming. 1992. Discourse Transcription. In *Santa Barbara Papers in Linguistics,* vol. 4. Santa Barbara: University of California, Department of Linguistics.

Ehlich, Konrad. 1983. Writing Ancillary to Telling. *Journal of Pragmatics* 7: 495–506.

————. 1989. Zur Genese von Textformen: Prolegomena zu einer pragmatischen Texttypologie. In Gerd Antos and Hans P. Krings, eds., *Textproduktion: Ein interdisziplinärer Forschungsüberblick.* Tübingen: Max Niemeyer.

Ehrlich, Susan. 1990. *Point of View: A Linguistic Analysis of Literary Style.* London: Routledge.

Fillmore, Charles J. 1974. Pragmatics and the Description of Discourse. In *Berkeley Studies in Syntax and Semantics,* 1:V1–V21. Berkeley: University of California, Department of Linguistics.

Firbas, Jan. 1986. On the Dynamics of Written Communication in the Light of the Theory of Functional Sentence Perspective. In Charles R. Cooper and Sidney Greenbaum, eds., *Studying Writing: Linguistic Approaches.* Beverly Hills, Calif.: Sage.

————. 1992. *Functional Sentence Perspective in Written and Spoken Communication.* Cambridge: Cambridge University Press.

Fleischman, Suzanne. 1990. *Tense and Narrativity: From Medieval Performance to Modern Fiction.* Austin: University of Texas Press.

————. In press. Imperfective and Irrealis. In Joan Bybee and Suzanne Fleischman, eds., *Modality in Grammar and Discourse.* Amsterdam and Philadelphia: John Benjamins.

Fludernik, Monika. 1993. *The Fictions of Language and the Languages of Fiction.* London: Routledge.

Ford, Cecilia E., and Sandra A. Thompson. In press. Interactional Units in Conversation: Syntactic, Intonational, and Pragmatic Resources for the Projection of Turn Completion. In Elinor Ochs, Emmanuel Schegloff, and Sandra A. Thompson, eds., *Grammar and Interaction.* Cambridge: Cambridge University Press.

Fox, Barbara A. 1987. *Discourse Structure and Anaphora.* Cambridge: Cambridge University Press.

Francis, W. Nelson, and Henry Kučera. 1982. *Frequency Analysis of English Usage: Lexicon and Grammar.* Boston: Houghton Mifflin.

Fraurud, Kari. 1990. Definiteness and the Processing of Noun Phrases in Natural Discourse. *Journal of Semantics* 7:395–433.

Frost, Robert. 1969. *The Poetry of Robert Frost.* Ed. Edward Connery Lathem. New York: Holt, Rinehart and Winston.

Genette, Gérard. 1980. *Narrative Discourse: An Essay in Method.* Trans. Jane E. Lewin. Ithaca, N.Y.: Cornell University Press.

————. 1988. *Narrative Discourse Revisited.* Trans. Jane E. Lewin. Ithaca, N.Y.: Cornell University Press.

Gernsbacher, Morton Ann. 1990. *Language Comprehension as Structure Building.* Hillsdale, N.J.: Lawrence Erlbaum.

Givón, Talmy. 1975. Focus and the Scope of Assertion: Some Bantu Evidence. *Studies in African Linguistics* 6:185–205.

———, ed. 1983. *Topic Continuity in Discourse: Quantified Cross-Language Studies*. Amsterdam and Philadelphia: John Benjamins.

———. 1984. *Syntax: A Functional-Typological Introduction*. Vol. 1. Amsterdam and Philadelphia: John Benjamins.

———. 1990. *Syntax: A Functional-Typological Introduction*. Vol. 2. Amsterdam and Philadelphia: John Benjamins.

Glucksberg, Sam, and George N. Cowan, Jr. 1970. Memory for Non-Attended Auditory Material. *Cognitive Psychology* 1:149–56.

Goldman Eisler, Frieda. 1968. *Psycholinguistics: Experiments in Spontaneous Speech*. New York: Academic Press.

Goodwin, Charles, and John Heritage. 1990. Conversation Analysis. *Annual Review of Anthropology* 19:283–307.

Gorrell, Robert M., and Charlton Laird. 1967. *Modern English Handbook*. 4th ed. Englewood Cliffs, N.J.: Prentice-Hall.

Grice, H. Paul. 1975. Logic and Conversation. In Peter Cole and Jerry L. Morgan, eds., *Studies in Syntax*, vol. 3. New York: Seminar Press.

Gumperz, John. 1982. *Discourse Strategies*. Cambridge: Cambridge University Press.

Gundel, Jeanette K. 1988. *The Role of Topic and Comment in Linguistic Theory*. New York: Garland.

Gundel, Jeanette K., Nancy Hedberg, and Ron Zacharski. 1993. Cognitive Status and the Form of Referring Expressions in Discourse. *Language* 69:274–307.

Haiman, John, and Pamela Munro, eds. 1983. *Switch Reference and Universal Grammar*. Amsterdam and Philadelphia: John Benjamins.

Halliday, M. A. K. 1985a. Dimensions of Discourse Analysis: Grammar. In Teun A. Van Dijk, ed., *Handbook of Discourse Analysis*, vol. 2. New York: Academic Press.

———. 1985b. *An Introduction to Functional Grammar*. London: Edward Arnold.

———. 1987. Spoken and Written Modes of Meaning. In Rosalind Horowitz and S. Jay Samuels, eds., *Comprehending Oral and Written Language*. New York: Academic Press.

Hamburger, Käte. 1973. *The Logic of Literature*. Trans. Marilynn J. Rose. Bloomington: Indiana University Press.

Harris, Zellig. 1951. *Methods in Structural Linguistics*. Chicago: University of Chicago Press.

Hatcher, Anna Granville. 1956. *Theme and Underlying Question, Two Studies in Spanish Word Order*. Supplement to *Word* 12.

Haviland, Susan E., and Herbert H. Clark. 1974. What's New? Acquiring New Information as a Process in Comprehension. *Journal of Verbal Learning and Verbal Behavior* 13:512–21.

Hawkins, John A. 1978. *Definiteness and Indefiniteness: A Study in Reference and Grammaticality Prediction*. London: Croom Helm.

Hawthorne, Nathaniel. 1961. *The House of the Seven Gables: A Romance*. New York: New American Library. First published 1851.

Heim, Irene R. 1982. The Semantics of Definite and Indefinite NPs. Ph.D. diss., University of Massachusetts, Amherst.

Hemingway, Ernest. 1940. *For Whom the Bell Tolls*. New York: Charles Scribner's.

————. 1987. *The Complete Short Stories of Ernest Hemingway: The Finca Vigía Edition*. New York: Charles Scribner's.

Hernadi, Paul. 1972. *Beyond Genre: New Directions in Literary Classification*. Ithaca, N.Y.: Cornell University Press.

————. 1976. Literary Theory: A Compass for Critics. *Critical Inquiry* 3:369–86.

Hjelmquist, Erland, and Ake Gidlund. 1985. Free Recall of Conversations. *Text* 5:169–85.

Hockett, Charles F. 1960. The Origin of Speech. *Scientific American* 203(3): 89–96.

Hopper, Paul. 1979. Aspect and Foregrounding in Discourse. In Talmy Givón, ed., *Discourse and Syntax*. New York: Academic Press.

————. 1986. Some Discourse Functions of Classifiers in Malay. In Colette Craig, ed., *Noun Classes and Categorization*. Amsterdam and Philadelphia: John Benjamins.

Humphrey, George. 1951. *Thinking*. New York: Wiley.

Hymes, Dell H. 1981. *"In Vain I Tried to Tell You": Essays in Native American Ethnopoetics*. Philadelphia: University of Pennsylvania Press.

Iwasaki, Shoichi. In press. The Structure of the Intonation Unit in Japanese. *Japanese/Korean Linguistics 3*. Stanford: Center for the Study of Language and Information.

Jackendoff, Ray. 1987. *Consciousness and the Computational Mind*. Cambridge: MIT Press.

James, William. 1890. *The Principles of Psychology*. 2 vols. New York: Henry Holt. Reprinted 1950 by Dover Publications, New York.

Jarvella, Robert J. 1971. Syntactic Processing of Connected Speech. *Journal of Verbal Learning and Verbal Behavior* 10:409–16.

Jelinek, Eloise. 1984. Empty Categories, Case, and Configurationality. *Natural Language and Linguistic Theory* 2:39–76.

Jesperson, Otto. 1924. *The Philosophy of Grammar*. London: George Allen and Unwin.

————. 1931/1961. *A Modern English Grammar on Historical Principles*. Part 4. London: George Allen and Unwin.

Johnstone, Barbara. 1990. *Stories, Community, and Place: Narratives from Middle America*. Bloomington: Indiana University Press.

Karttunen, Lauri. 1968. What Makes Definite Noun Phrases Definite? RAND Corporation Report P3854. Santa Monica, Calif.

Katz, Joseph, ed. 1969. *The Portable Stephen Crane*. New York: Viking Press.

Kay, Paul. 1977. Language Evolution and Speech Style. In Ben G. Blount and Mary Sanches, eds., *Sociocultural Dimensions of Language Change*. New York: Academic Press.

Keenan, Edward L. 1976. Towards a Universal Definition of "Subject." In Charles N. Li, ed., *Subject and Topic*. New York: Academic Press.

Keenan, Elinor Ochs, and Bambi Schieffelin. 1976. Topic as a Discourse Notion: A Study of Topic in the Conversations of Children and Adults. In Charles N. Li, ed., *Subject and Topic*, pp. 335–84. New York: Academic Press.

Klatzky, Roberta L. 1991. Let's Be Friends. *American Psychologist* 46:43–45.

Kühn, Ingrid. 1988. Beziehungen zwischen der Struktur der "Erlebten Rede" und ihrer kommunikativen Funktionalität. *Zeitschrift für Germanistik* 9:182–89.

Kuhn, Thomas S. 1970. *The Structure of Scientific Revolutions*. 2d ed. Chicago: University of Chicago Press.

Kuno, Susumu. 1987. *Functional Syntax: Anaphora, Discourse, and Empathy*. Chicago: University of Chicago Press.

Labov, William. 1972. *Sociolinguistic Patterns*. Philadelphia: University of Pennsylvania Press.

Labov, William, and Joshua Waletzky. 1967. Narrative Analysis: Oral Versions of Personal Experience. In June Helm, ed., *Essays on the Verbal and Visual Arts: Proceedings of the 1966 Annual Spring Meeting of the American Ethnological Society*. Seattle: University of Washington Press.

Ladd, D. Robert. 1986. Intonational Phrasing: The Case for Recursive Prosodic Structure. *Phonology Yearbook* 3:311–40.

Lakoff, George. 1987. *Women, Fire, and Dangerous Things: What Categories Reveal about the Mind*. Chicago: University of Chicago Press.

Lee, Hyo Sang. 1987. Discourse Presupposition and the Discourse Function of the Topic Marker nin in Korean. Bloomington: Indiana University Linguistics Club.

Leech, Geoffrey N., and Michael H. Short. 1981. *Style in Fiction: A Linguistic Introduction to English Fictional Prose*. London: Longman.

Lenneberg, Eric. 1967. *Biological Foundations of Language*. New York: John Wiley and Sons.

Lerdahl, Fred, and Ray Jackendoff. 1983. *A Generative Theory of Tonal Music*. Cambridge: MIT Press.

Lethcoe, Ronald James. 1969. Narrated Speech and Consciousness. Ph.D. diss., University of Wisconsin.

Li, Charles N. 1986. Direct Speech and Indirect Speech: A Functional Study. In Florian Coulmas, ed., *Direct and Indirect Speech*. Berlin: Mouton de Gruyter.

Li, Charles N., and Sandra A. Thompson. 1976. Subject and Topic: A New Typology of Language. In Charles N. Li, ed., *Subject and Topic*. New York: Academic Press.

Libet, Benjamin. 1981. Timing of Cerebral Processes Relative to Concomitant Conscious Experiences in Man. In G. Adam, I. Meszaros, and E. I. Banyai, eds., *Advances in Physiological Science* 17:313–17. Elmsford, N.Y.: Pergamon.

Linell, Per. 1982. *The Written Language Bias in Linguistics*. Linköping, Sweden: University of Linköping Press.

Loftus, Elizabeth F. 1979. *Eyewitness Testimony*. Cambridge: Harvard University Press.

Longacre, Robert E. 1983. *The Grammar of Discourse*. New York: Plenum.

Lounsbury, Floyd G. 1953. *Oneida Verb Morphology*. Yale University Publications in Anthropology 48. New Haven: Yale University Press.

Lyons, John. 1968. *Introduction to Theoretical Linguistics*. Cambridge: Cambridge University Press.

———. 1977. *Semantics*. Cambridge: Cambridge University Press.

Lyons, William. 1986. *The Disappearance of Introspection*. Cambridge: MIT Press.

McHale, Brian. 1978. Free Indirect Discourse: A Survey of Recent Accounts. *PTL: A Journal for Descriptive Poetics and Theory of Literature* 3:249–87.

McPhee, John. 1984. *La Place de la Concorde Suisse*. New York: Farrar Straus and Giroux.

MacWhinney, Brian. 1977. Starting Points. *Language* 53:152–68.

Mangan, Bruce. 1993. Taking Phenomenology Seriously: The "Fringe" and Its Implications for Cognitive Research. *Consciousness and Cognition* 2:89–108.

Mathesius, Vilém. 1929. Zur Satzperspektive im modernen Englisch. *Archiv für das Studium der neueren Sprachen und Literaturen* 155:202–10.

Mayes, Patricia. 1990. Quotation in Spoken English. *Studies in Language* 14:325–63.

Mel'čuk, Igor A. 1982. Lexical Functions in Lexicographic Description. In *Proceedings of the Eighth Annual Meeting of the Berkeley Linguistics Society,* pp. 427–44. Berkeley.

Mel'čuk, Igor A., with Nadia Arbatchewsky-Jumarie and others. 1984/1988. *Dictionnaire explicatif et combinatoire du français contemporain.* Montreal: Presses de l'Université de Montréal.

Mel'čuk, Igor A., and Alexander K. Zholkovsky. 1984. *Explanatory Combinatorial Dictionary of Modern Russian.* Vienna: Wiener Slawistischer Almanach.

Meyer, Leonard B. 1956. *Emotion and Meaning in Music.* Chicago: University of Chicago Press.

Miller, George A. 1956. The Magical Number Seven, Plus or Minus Two: Some Limits on Our Capacity for Processing Information. *Psychological Review* 63: 81–97.

———. 1990. The Place of Language in a Scientific Psychology. *Psychological Science* 1:7–14.

Mithun, Marianne. 1984. The Evolution of Noun Incorporation. *Language* 60: 847–94.

———. 1985. Disagreement: The Case of Pronominal Affixes and Nouns. In *Georgetown University Round Table on Languages and Linguistics 1985.* Washington, D.C.: Georgetown University Press.

———. 1989. Historical Linguistics and Linguistic Theory: Reducing the Arbitrary and Constraining Explanation. In *Proceedings of the 15th Annual Meeting of the Berkeley Linguistics Society,* pp. 391–408. Berkeley.

———. 1991. Active/Agentive Case Marking and Its Motivations. *Language* 67: 510–46.

———. 1992. Is Basic Word Order Universal? In Doris L. Payne, ed., *Pragmatics of Word Order Flexibility.* Amsterdam and Philadelphia: John Benjamins.

———. 1993. "Switch Reference": Clause Combining in Central Pomo. *International Journal of American Linguistics* 59:119–36.

———. In press. Morphological and Prosodic Forces Shaping Word Order. In Pamela Downing and Michael Noonan, eds., *Word Order in Discourse.* Amsterdam and Philadelphia: John Benjamins.

Murdoch, Iris. 1967. *The Italian Girl.* New York: Viking Penguin. First published 1964.

Natsoulas, Thomas. 1983. Concepts of Consciousness. *Journal of Mind and Behavior* 4:13–59.

———. 1988. Is Any State of Consciousness Self-Intimating? *Journal of Mind and Behavior* 9:167–204.

———. 1989. An Examination of Four Objections to Self-Intimating States of Consciousness. *Journal of Mind and Behavior* 10:63–116.

Neisser, Ulric. 1967. *Cognitive Psychology.* New York: Appleton-Century-Crofts.

———. 1978. Memory: What Are the Important Questions? In Michael M. Gruneberg, Peter E. Morris, and Robert N. Sykes, eds., *Practical Aspects of Memory.* London: Academic Press.

———. 1982. *Memory Observed: Remembering in Natural Contexts.* San Francisco: W. H. Freeman.

———. 1991. A Case of Misplaced Nostalgia. *American Psychologist* 46:34–36.

Ohala, John J. 1987. *Linguistics as an Experimental Discipline. Linguistics in the Undergraduate Curriculum.* Washington, D.C.: Linguistic Society of America.

Olson, David. 1977. From Utterance to Text: The Bias of Language in Speech and Writing. *Harvard Educational Review* 47:257–81.

Ong, Walter. 1982. *Orality and Literacy: The Technologizing of the Word.* London: Methuen.

Pascal, Roy. 1977. *The Dual Voice: Free Indirect Speech and Its Functioning in the Nineteenth Century European Novel.* Manchester: Manchester University Press.

Pater, Walter. 1910. *Appreciations: With an Essay on Style.* New York: Macmillan.

Pawley, Andrew. 1985. Lexicalization. In *Georgetown University Round Table on Languages and Linguistics 1985,* pp. 98–120. Washington, D.C.: Georgetown University Press.

Pawley, Andrew, and Frances Syder. 1983a. Natural Selection in Syntax: Notes on Adaptive Variation and Change in Vernacular and Literary Grammar. *Journal of Pragmatics* 7:551–79.

———. 1983b. Two Puzzles for Linguistic Theory: Nativelike Selection and Nativelike Fluency. In Jack C. Richards and Richard W. Schmidt, eds., *Language and Communication.* London: Longman.

Pierrehumbert, Janet B. 1980. The Phonology and Phonetics of English Intonation. Ph.D. diss., Massachusetts Institute of Technology.

Pierrehumbert, Janet B., and Mary E. Beckman. 1988. Japanese Tone Structure. Cambridge: MIT Press.

Pierrehumbert, Janet B., and Julia Hirschberg. 1990. The Meaning of Intonational Contours in the Interpretation of Discourse. In Philip R. Cohen, Jerry Morgan, and Martha E. Pollack, eds., *Intentions in Communication.* Cambridge: MIT Press.

Polanyi, Livia. 1989. *Telling the American Story: A Structural and Cultural Analysis of Conversational Storytelling.* Cambridge: MIT Press.

Prince, Ellen. 1981a. On the Inferencing of Indefinite *this* NPs. In Aravind K. Joshi, Bonnie L. Webber, and Ivan A. Sag, eds., *Elements of Discourse Understanding.* Cambridge: Cambridge University Press.

———. 1981b. Toward a Taxonomy of Given-New Information. In Peter Cole, ed., *Radical Pragmatics.* New York: Academic Press.

Quirk, Randolph, Sidney Greenbaum, Geoffrey Leech, and Jan Svartvik. 1985. *A Comprehensive Grammar of the English Language.* London: Longman.

Rauh, Gisa, ed. 1983. *Essays on Deixis.* Tübingen: Gunter Narr.

Reinhart, Tanya. 1982. Pragmatics and Linguistics: An Analysis of Sentence Topics. Bloomington: Indiana University Linguistics Club.

Rodgers, Paul C., Jr. 1965. Alexander Bain and the Rise of the Organic Paragraph. *Quarterly Journal of Speech* 51:399–408.

———. 1966. A Discourse-Centered Rhetoric of the Paragraph. *College Composition and Communication* 16:2–11.

Rosch, Eleanor, Carolyn B. Mervis, Wayne D. Gray, David M. Johnson, and Penny Boyes-Braem. 1976. Basic Objects in Natural Categories. *Cognitive Psychology* 8:382–439.

Russell, Bertrand. 1967. *The Autobiography of Bertrand Russell.* Vol. 1. Boston: Little, Brown.

Sachs, Jacqueline Strunk. 1967. Recognition Memory for Syntactic and Semantic Aspects of Connected Discourse. *Perception and Psychophysics* 2:437–42.

Saintsbury, George. 1896. *A History of Nineteenth Century Literature (1780–1895).* New York: Macmillan.

Sapir, Edward. 1921. *Language: An Introduction to the Study of Speech.* New York: Harcourt, Brace.

Saussure, Ferdinand de. 1916. *Cours de linguistique générale.* Paris: Payot. Trans. Wade Baskin. 1959. *Course in General Linguistics.* New York: McGraw-Hill.

Schank, Roger C., and Robert P. Abelson. 1977. *Scripts, Plans, Goals, and Understanding: An Inquiry into Human Knowledge Structures.* Hillsdale, N.J.: Lawrence Erlbaum.

Schiffrin, Deborah. 1981. Tense Variation in Narrative. *Language* 57:45–62.

———. 1987. *Discourse Markers.* Cambridge: Cambridge University Press.

Schlicher, John J. 1931. Historical Tenses and Their Functions in Latin. *Classical Philology* 26:46–59.

Schober, Michael F., and Herbert H. Clark. 1989. Understanding by Addressees and Overhearers. *Cognitive Psychology* 21:211–32.

Schuetze-Coburn, Stephan, Marian Shapley, and Elizabeth G. Weber. 1991. Units of Intonation in Discourse: A Comparison of Acoustic and Auditory Analyses. *Language and Speech* 34:207–34.

Searle, John R. 1990. Consciousness, Explanatory Inversion, and Cognitive Science. *Behavioral and Brain Sciences* 13:585–642.

———. 1992. *The Rediscovery of the Mind.* Cambridge: MIT Press.

Singer, Jerome L. 1975. *The Inner World of Daydreaming.* New York: Harper and Row.

Spencer, Andrew. 1988. Bracketing Paradoxes and the English Lexicon. *Language* 64:663–82.

Sperling, George. 1960. The Information Available in Brief Visual Presentations. *Psychological Monographs* 74 (whole no. 11).

Stanzel, Franz Karl. 1984. *A Theory of Narrative.* Trans. Charlotte Goedsche. Cambridge: Cambridge University Press.

Stern, Arthur. 1976. When Is a Paragraph? *College Composition and Communication* 27:253–57.

Tannen, Deborah. 1982. Oral and Literate Strategies in Spoken and Written Narratives. *Language* 58:1–21.

———. 1989. *Talking Voices: Repetition, Dialogue, and Imagery in Conversational Discourse.* Cambridge: Cambridge University Press.

Taylor, Wilson L. 1953. Cloze Procedure: A New Tool for Measuring Readability. *Journalism Quarterly* 30:414–38.

Thompson, Sandra A. 1988. A Discourse Approach to the Cross-Linguistic Category 'Adjective.' In John Hawkins, ed., *Explanations for Language Universals.* Oxford: Basil Blackwell.

Todorov, Tzvetan. 1966. Les catégories du récit littéraire. *Communications* 8: 125–51.

Vande Kopple, William J. 1991. Themes, Thematic Progressions, and Some Implications for Understanding Discourse. *Written Communication* 8:311–47.

Wald, Benji. 1983. Referents and Topics within and across Discourse Units: Observations from Contemporary English. In Flora Klein-Andreu, ed., *Discourse Perspectives on Syntax.* New York: Academic Press.

Ward, Gregory L. 1988. *The Semantics and Pragmatics of Preposing.* New York: Garland.

Weinrich, Harald. 1964. *Tempus: Besprochene und Erzählte Welt.* Stuttgart: W. Kohlhammer Verlag.

Welty, Eudora. 1983. *The Collected Stories of Eudora Welty.* San Diego, Calif.: Harcourt Brace Jovanovich.

Wilensky, Robert. 1982. Points: A Theory of the Structure of Stories in Memory. In Wendy G. Lehnert and Martin H. Ringle, eds., *Strategies for Natural Language Processing.* Hillsdale, N.J.: Lawrence Erlbaum.

Wolfson, Nessa. 1982. *CHP: The Conversational Historical Present in American English Narrative.* Dordrecht: Foris.

Wolter, Allan B., trans. 1986. *Duns Scotus on the Will and Morality.* Washington, D.C.: Catholic University of America Press.

Wright, Suzanne, and Talmy Givón. 1987. The Pragmatics of Indefinite Reference: Quantified Text-Based Studies. *Studies in Language* 11:1–33.

Zinsser, William. 1980. *On Writing Well: An Informal Guide to Writing Nonfiction.* 2d ed. New York: Harper & Row.

Index

Frequently used terms such as "given (information)" or "intonation unit" are indexed only for passages that define, subcategorize, or significantly elaborate on them.